Explorer
Thailand

Tim Locke
Martin Clutterbuck
Dick Wilson

AA Publishing

Front cover (a): a floating market
Front cover (b): young girl at Mae Sai
Front cover (c): Buddhist monks
Page 2: detail from Wat Phra That Phanom
Page 3: Ko Phi Phi Le
Page 4: street vendor in Sukhothai
Page 5(a): Buddhas at Wat Suthat, Bangkok
Page 5(b): painted fishing boat, Songkhla
Page 5(c): temple bells, Wat Phra Doi Suthep, Chiang Mai
Pages 6/7 (a): sunset over Chiang Rai
Page 6(b): getting around in Chiang Mai
Page 7(c): temple shrine, Betong, Southern Thailand
Page 8: floating market, Bangkok
Page 9: Wat Mahathat, Sukhothai
Spine: detail in Wat Phra Keo in Bangkok
Back cover: the unusual construction of Wat Manee Pasi Son in Mae Sot

Written by Tim Locke, Martin Clutterbuck and Dick Wilson
Original photography by Rick Strange
Edited, designed and produced by AA Publishing
Maps © Automobile Association Developments Ltd 1998, 2001
Reprinted 2002
Revised fourth edition 2001
Reprinted 2000
Reprinted with new cover 1999
New edition 1998
First published 1995

Distributed in the United Kingdom by AA Publishing

A CIP catalogue record for this book is available from the British Library.

ISBN 0 7495 3037 5

Published by AA Publishing (a trading name of Automobile Association Developments Limited, whose registered office is Millstream, Maidenhead Road, Windsor, SL4 5GD. Registered number 1878835).

Colour separation by L C Repro & Sons Ltd, Aldermaston
Printed and bound in Italy by Printer Trento srl

Titles in the Explorer series...
Australia • Boston & New England • Britain • Brittany
California • Canada • Caribbean • China • Costa Rica
Crete • Cuba • Cyprus • Egypt • Florence & Tuscany
Florida • France • Germany • Greek Islands • Hawaii •India
Ireland • Israel • Italy • Japan • London • Mallorca • Mexico
New York • New Zealand • Paris • Portugal • Provence
Rome • San Francisco • Scotland • South Africa • Spain
Tenerife • Thailand • Tunisia • Turkey • Turkish Coast
Venice • Vietnam

AA World Travel Guides publish over 300 guidebooks to a full range of cities, countries and regions across the world. Find out more about AA Publishing and the wide range of services the AA provides by visiting our website at www.theAA.com

How to use this book

ORGANISATION

Thailand Is, Thailand Was
Discusses aspects of life and culture in contemporary Thailand and explores significant periods in its history.

A–Z
Breaks down the country into regional chapters, and covers places to visit, including walks and drives. Within this section fall the Focus On articles, which consider a variety of topics in greater detail.

Travel Facts
Contains the strictly practical information vital for a successful trip.

Hotels and Restaurants
Lists recommended establishments throughout Thailand, giving a brief summary of their attractiions.

ABOUT THE RATINGS
Most places described in this book have been given a separate rating. These are as follows:

▶▶▶   Do not miss

▶▶   Highly recommended

▶   Worth seeing

MAPS
To make each particular location easier to find, every main entry in this book has a map reference to the right of its name. This comprises a number, followed by a letter, followed by another number, such as 72B2. The first number (72) refer to the page on which the map can be found, the letter (B) and the second number (2) pinpoint the square in which the main entry is located. The maps on the inside front cover and inside back cover are referred to as IFC and IBC respectively.

Some of the maps in this book use internationally agreed symbols to denote nation states:
    BUR   Burma
    K   Cambodia
    LAO   Laos
    VN   Vietnam
    MAL   Malaysia

KEY TO ADMISSION CHARGES
Standard admission charges are categorised in this book as follows:
    Inexpensive   under 50 baht
    Moderate   50–150 baht
    Expensive   over 150 baht

Contents

Tim Locke (above) is the author of several walking and touring guides published by the Consumer's Association. He is also a contributor to *AA Essential and Explorer Guides* to Britain, Germany and Boston & New England; he has travelled widely in the Far East.

Martin Clutterbuck has lived and worked in Thailand for several years. He speaks fluent Thai and has written two editions of the *Travellers' Guide to Thailand*.

Dick Wilson has been editor of the *China Quarterly*, editorial advisor to *The Straits Times*, and has also written a book about Thailand for St Martin's Press/Macmillan.

My Thailand

Whenever I revisit Thailand, I savour my first impressions. The taxi ride from Bangkok Airport into the city feels like half of Asia is on the move, but away from the major din it's a different world. A temple compound provides an oasis of peace, but the glinting gold dazzles; I take off my shoes and enter the cool, dark *wiharn*, where the Buddha image smiles inscrutably.

From Bangkok's Noi station a third-class only train rattles through the jungly fringes of the city. Kanchana Buri, at the end of the trip, seems incredibly sleepy after Bangkok. Outside the station a bicycle rickshaw "driver" conveys me to my "room" – a bamboo cabin perched above the Kwai, looking across to a dreamy, serpentine chain of hazy limestone peaks.

On the east coast I hitch a lift from a fishing boat to the island of Ko Si Chang. I scramble among the ruins of the summer palace, now running riot with cacti and frangipani. By a ruined temple a pair of turtles idle in a lily pond. At the centre of the island I scale some 500 steps to a dizzily sited hilltop temple.

In a remote town in western Thailand, I alight from a *songthaew*. I have no idea where to head for, but I am immediately taken into hand by the local headmaster. We head on to a rockface where a Buddhist monk has set up his own hermitage in a cave entrance. He lights a lantern and silently leads us through a labyrinth of chambers, the floors soft with bat droppings.

The great temples of Bangkok, the ruins of Sukothai and the dreamlike beaches of the south are among the most celebrated tourist attractions of Thailand. But for me, the pleasure is just being there, riding a bus or giving impromptu English lessons to a gang of Thai student monks, or watching a game of *takraw* in a sidestreet. More perhaps than most countries, Thailand repays the effort to get off the beaten track, and to try to learn a few words of the language; Thai is not easy, but a little goes a long way. Above all, try to keep *jai yen* – a cool heart. Be open to the country and her people, be patient and allow events take their course.

Tim Locke

Thailand
Is & Was

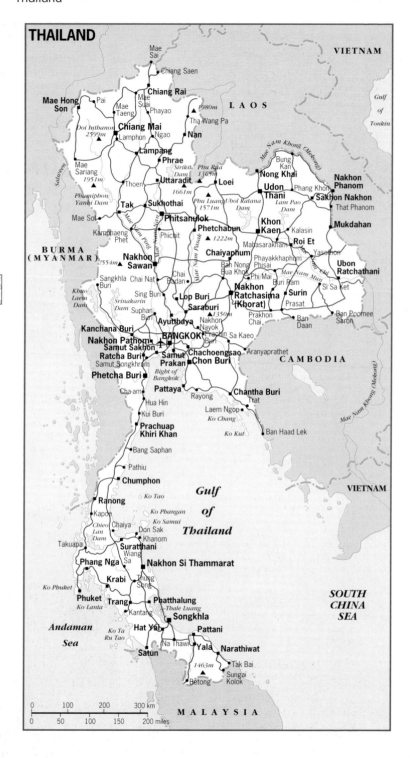

Thailand is a country of tropical abundance, inhabited by gentle and courteous people mostly professing Buddhism. "Land of the free" is the literal meaning of Thailand and most Thais consider themselves, with justification, to be one of the freer societies in Asia. They have borrowed from both Chinese and Indian civilisations, and the result is distinctive and interesting.

SOMETHING FOR EVERYONE To the Western visitor, Thailand is not just another land; it's another way of life. Tradition and development rub shoulders here as nowhere else. In Bangkok, wooden houses built on stilts over the water stand in the shadows of gleaming condominium blocks. The air is filled with different smells: stir-fry cookery, diesel fumes, dried coconuts, incense, canal water…Exotic *wats* (Buddist temple compounds) glimmer in the sunlight, their cool interiors a welcome refuge from the city din.

A bus-ride into the country brings a vivid glimpse of Thai variety. Buses equipped with hi-fi and videos also have their mirrors draped with garlands of everlasting flowers for good luck. Instead of pin-ups there are photos of venerable monks above the driving seat. The driver tears along the road, blaring his horn, passing the occasional ox-drawn cart. Women mount the buses to sell Coca Cola from plastic bags and sticky rice concoctions wrapped in banana leaves to the passengers – who include immaculate schoolchildren, saffron-robed monks and hill-tribe women in dazzling home-embroidered clothes and grubby, Western-style trainers.

VISITING THE COUNTRY Thailand has a huge amount to offer, endowed with resorts well-attuned to the needs of Western tourists as well as many places that are still remote, either in character or in location. Visitors can get a good idea of the range of experiences by staying in Bangkok for a few days and then taking some excursions into the surrounding areas. Many stay on for months. The Thais' gentle and laid-back nature, coupled with the ease of getting around and making one's own discoveries, contribute to Thailand's popularity.

This country has dazzling temples and some extraordinary historic sights. Beyond the great rice plains, where farmers bend over in their lampshade hats to tend the crops, rise mountains harbouring hill-tribe cultures. In the south are some of the loveliest beaches anywhere, with squeaky white sands backed by lofty limestone cliffs and fringed with palm trees.

Most importantly, Thailand is its people: in spite of spiralling economic change they have kept their traditions, their festivals and their essential national identity. It would take a great deal to change all that.

A Thai classical dancer

Thailand has a distinctive shape on the map, tailing away in the south into a long, narrow strip of land. Some people have likened the outline of the country to an elephant's head, with the trunk curling down towards Malaysia. With a land area of about 513,000sq km, Thailand is no small state – it is, in fact, roughly the same size as France or Texas, and it has a population of over 60 million.

HOW THE LAND LIES Thailand has Malaysia as its neighbour in the south, Myanmar (Burma) in the west and Laos and Cambodia in the north-east and east.

> ❑ In the 19th century, French and British cartographers decided to map a narrow stretch of Burmese and Laotian territory in order to cordon off Thailand from China. ❑

The **north** of the country is hilly and mountainous, with outriders of the Himalayas separated by narrow valleys, notably formed by the Nan, Yom, Wang and Ping rivers. The high ground gradually rises towards the west and north, where Doi Inthanon (2,595m), Thailand's highest mountain, is to be found. The rivers flowing down these north–south valleys come together to form the Chao Phraya, Thailand's principal river, the floodplain of which constitutes the central plateau of the country.

The **central plain** is Thailand's rice bowl, and as a consequence, the area where population is most dense. Most of the political, economic and intellectual life of Thailand goes on in this central area.

The Khorat plateau dominates the **east** of the country, and is shut off from the central plain by the Phetchabun range. The plateau is drained by the Mun and Chi rivers, and by the Mekong into which they ultimately flow, and which forms Thailand's border with Laos. A large shallow basin, the Khorat plateau is 200m above the sea, encircled by hills; its rolling terrain gives way to swampland at the approach to the Mekong River.

A long cordillera, the Tennasserim range, runs from northern Thailand down the **western border** to connect with peninsular ranges that continue down the centre of the Thai isthmus into Malaysia. This **southern peninsula** is rich in tropical vegetation and has the resources of rubber and tin.

The **main coastline** is round the Gulf of Thailand, which merges into the South China Sea and thus gives Thailand a window on to the Pacific Ocean. There is also a shorter coastline on the Andaman Sea, on the other side of the peninsula, which makes Thailand an Indian-Ocean state as well.

WEATHER AND NATURAL RESOURCES Tropical forest used to cover much of Thailand, supporting a variety of animals and plant life, but over the past 50 years forests have disappeared at an alarming rate, with a consequential decline in the natural resources to be found in those areas. In 1945, over 90 per cent of Thailand was forested; now estimates are nearer 25 per cent.

Until recently, farmers made use of the natural nutrients brought down by annual floods of streams and rivers in order to grow rice. On the hill farms of **northern Thailand** elaborate systems of irrigation – ditches, dikes and terraces – can still be seen.

POPULATION The rapid increase in population, especially between 1950 and 1970, unnaturally swelled the size of the capital city of Bangkok, which is now 5.7 million. The second largest city is Nakhon Ratchasima, with a population of 2.5 million.

Population growth has now been brought down to about 0.3 per cent a year, largely as a result of a successful campaign by the government to popularise family planning, especially through the use of condoms. But today the population faces a bigger threat from AIDS, which some Thai experts believe may reach disastrous proportions.

Three-quarters of the inhabitants are ethnic Thais, with the Chinese community making up to 15 per cent of the population. The remaining 10 per cent includes Malays, Khmers, Laotians, Mons, Shans and a number of hill-tribes.

❑ Thailand is in the tropical belt, and stands in the path of the monsoon storms which boil up from the South China Sea. There is heavy rainfall from July to October, cool dry weather from November to February and dry heat from March to June. ❑

❑ The Chinese population in Thailand is said to be the largest outside China, although Chinese Thais are usually considered to be Thai by Thai people. ❑

The image presented to the world: two girls in formal Thai dress

The Thai wat, the name of a Buddhist temple compound, encompasses a range of buildings serving a variety of functions. As you travel through the country you will see a variety of architectural styles. To a newcomer it can all be somewhat confusing, but with practice you will learn to identify the component parts of a site.

14

THE COMPOUND Although virtually no two *wats* are precisely the same, there are certain types of building common to all of them.

The monks live in a dormitory compound known as the *sanghawat* and attend lectures on Buddhist scriptures in a meeting hall known as a *sala kanparien*.

Not generally open to the public, the *bot* (or *ubosot*) is the central chapel or ordination hall for new monks. It is oriented eastwards and often contains the *wat's* principal Buddha image. On the roof may be a horn-like finial or *chofa* symbolising the head of the legendary beast, the *garuda*. There may also be a bodhi tree close by – held in high esteem because Buddha attained enlightenment beneath

Golden beasts on the roof guard Wat Phra That Haripunjaya in Lamphun

one. Sacred boundary stones (*sima*) delineate the consecrated ground around the *bot*.

Provided you cover your shoulders and legs, and take off your shoes, you can usually enter the *wiharn* (or *viharn*), the assembly hall, which is often similar in style to the *bot* but is generally larger and is not surrounded by *sima* stones. Some larger compounds have more than one *wiharn*. Sculpted *nagas* (dragon-headed snakes) may line the steps at the approach. Some *wats* will house their sacred scriptures in a library known as a *ho trai*, which are generally compact buildings, sometimes raised from the ground to avoid attack by insects. As with the *bot* there is no public admittance. The unmistakable *ho rakang* (bell tower) is also raised.

The *chedi* is a solid, bell-shaped chamber, topped with a tapering spire. It will usually contain the relic of Buddha or another highly esteemed person. An ornate square-based reliquary tower is termed a *mondop*, and contains sacred texts or some other object of worship. The corn-cob shaped tower in a Khmer temple is known as a *prang*.

HISTORIC STYLES Dvaravati (6th–11th century) Buddha images of this period are strikingly naturalistic, with flattened noses and thick lips. The only Dvaravati surviving building is the *chedi* at Wat Ku Kut in Lamphun.

❑ Buddha images present him in one of four postures. The seated Buddha, the most commonly seen in Thailand, shows him in meditation. The reclining pose is a representation of Buddha entering Nirvana at his death. Standing and walking postures indicate his descent from heaven. Housed within a *mondop*, Buddha stucco-moulded "footprints", gigantic in scale, symbolise the 108 "auspicious signs" (among them the 16 Buddhist heavens). ❑

The elaborate reliefs seen at Phi Mai are impressive examples of the Khmer style

upwards; his body is rounded, his abdomen prominent, the flap of his robe ends above the nipple and one shoulder is bare. Chiang Mai has many fine examples of Lanna *wats*.

Ayutthaya (mid-14th–late-18th century) This delicate, dignified and elaborate style features ornate *cho fas* and door and window pediments, as well as ringed, tapering *chedis*. The architects of the former capital of Ayutthaya drew from Khmer and Sri Lankan elements, notably in the *prangs* which they modified in shape.

Rattanakosin (late-18th century– present) With the fall of Ayutthaya, *wats* sprang up in the new capital of Bangkok, continuing more or less where the Ayutthaya style had left off but grander still. Wat Benchamabophit, a dazzling creation in Carrara marble and sporting Western-style stained glass, and the sumptuous Wat Phra Keo in the Grand Palace, are two examples of this new architectural grandeur.

15

Above and right: the attention to detail and the use of gilding make Thai temples a dramatic sight

Khmer and Lopburi (9th–14th century) Khmer temples (*prasats*) feature elaborate *prangs* within central sanctuaries (see panel on page 206). They are found in Northeast Thailand, notably at Phi Mai and Prasat Phanom Rung. The smaller Lopburi temples adhered to the Khmer style but with local modifications.

Sukhothai (13th–15th century) Slender lotus-bud *chedis* and oval-faced Buddhas with blissful expressions are typical features of this era. The historic cities of Sukhothai and Si Satchanalai are the best-known sites.

Lanna (mid-13th–19th century) Also known as Chiang Saen, this style from the far north of Thailand was inspired in turn by Dvaravati, Sukhothai, Indian and Sri Lankan architecture. The cross-legged seated Buddha has his soles pointing

King Bhumiphol Adulyadej was born on 5 December 1927 in Cambridge, Massachusetts, where his father was a hospital doctor. He came to the throne unexpectedly in 1946 when he was only 18, after his elder brother, King Ananda Mahidol, was found dead with a bullet in his head. The mystery of that death has never been explained.

KING BHUMIPHOL has now become the longest-reigning king in Thai history, and one of the most respected and beloved of the Chakri monarchs. Pictures of the king and the royal family hang in almost every house. The 50th anniversary of his accession was celebrated in 1996 with great splendour. The Thai royal family is one of the very few remaining in Asia.

In his earlier years on the throne he cultivated a dilettante image, gaining fame as the king who played the saxophone well enough to accompany Benny Goodman and Louis Armstrong in Dixieland numbers.

In his youth, the king was an enthusiastic sailor, building his own boats and winning many trophies. He painted in oils, published translations from English and exhibited much-admired photographs. His queen, Sirikit, was one of the great Thai beauties of her day.

> ❏ King Bhumiphol won a gold medal in sailing for Thailand in the Southeast Asian Peninsular Games in 1967. His musical compositions include *Blue Day* (a revue song of the 1950s), the Thai royal anthem and the ballet *Manohra*. ❏

Gradually the king's interests shifted to the country's more serious concerns of rural, social and political reform. In a country where the pace of economic growth swamped the interests of farmers and tribespeople who found it hard to adapt, Bhumiphol had much personal involvement in helping to reconcile different interests.

PRACTICAL INVOLVEMENT The king took the lead in putting rural development programmes firmly on the Thai agenda, jogging the government into giving them higher priority. He regularly tours rural areas to see the problems for himself, and has become something of an expert on small irrigation projects and introducing better farming practices as well as reafforestation.

In the political arena, the king found a place as a focus for national unity, mediator and source of stability. While generals, prime ministers and dictators rose and fell from power, he supplied the balancing role. No *coup d'état* has sought to overthrow him: on the contrary, the prospective *coup* leaders have always sought to gain his approval, if necessary moderating their programme.

The immense popularity and adoration which he has built up during over 50 years on the throne enable him to play this role to the utmost, sometimes tipping the balance in a power struggle or even preventing a *coup* in the making.

Celebrating the king's birthday

The king lives with his family in the Chitladda Palace close to central Bangkok. Queen Sirikit also carries out a wide range of social duties

> ❏ Insane General Taksin (see page 55) issued a curse to the effect that the monarchy would end after nine kings had sat on the throne – the present king is the ninth. ❏

including the leadership of the Girl Guides and the very successful promotion of peasant handicrafts.

THE SUCCESSION Bhumiphol's health is not good, and there is likely be a controversy over the succession. His eldest daughter, Ubol Rattana, has returned to Thailand permanently after many years in the United States where she lived with her now ex-husband, an American engineer. However, the only son and heir to the throne, Crown Prince Vajiralongkorn, does not share in his father's popularity. Trained as an air force pilot, he has a reputation for having a bad temper and has not shown any interest in politics.

Some Thais would like to see Princess Sirindhorn, the king's second daughter, succeed instead, but a woman has never taken the throne in Thailand, and the prevalent male chauvinism, as well as such a radical break with tradition, would probably stand in the way despite her great popularity and capability.

Bhumiphol is very wealthy, with properties including a controlling share of the Siam Cement Corporation as well as many banks and other companies. These are managed by the Crown Property Bureau, a major asset holder and investor in Thailand. Dividends from these assets supplement the king's government budget allocation and help him play a larger part in the political arena.

The king has a strong scientific bent, having studied science in Lausanne in Switzerland. His quick reaction to the arrival of artificial rain-making in Western science has led to a regular scheme and programme within the Ministry of Agriculture.

Undoubtedly, King Bhumiphol has built up goodwill for the monarchy which should last for some time. Without a monarch acting as a lynch-pin, Thai politics would be much more unstable.

17

The ceremonial Royal Barges on the Chao Phraya river

Thai society is built on the family, though there is also scope for individualism; group discipline is not one of the country's strong points. Nowadays modern middle-class children usually choose their own marriage partners but rural fathers expect deference to their wishes, and most rural societies teach loyalty is due to parents. Even in the towns family solidarity is the norm.

18

HOUSING In Bangkok the relatively affluent middle class lives increasingly in a style similar to its counterparts worldwide. Some of the wealthier élite prefer to live in traditional spacious wooden houses, with high roofs and large gardens, including a fish-pond. Such houses are cool and breezy and can also be moved to another place if necessary. Now, however, new estates of Western-style white-walled houses with stone balconies and red tiles can be seen across the city.

A modern Thai wedding

❏ Until recently it was acceptable for Thai men to have "minor" wives (*mia noi*) in addition to their first "major" wife (*punraya*). However, this is increasingly frowned upon due to the emergence of women's rights groups and AIDS. ❏

The fashion for rich Thais is to buy, say, two traditional houses-on-stilts (the stilts protect from wildlife and floods) from the countryside, dismantle them, take them by lorry to a quiet suburb of Bangkok and reassemble them as old-fashioned bedroom wings on a modern concrete house – thus gaining the advantages of both styles.

Life is considerably more basic and simple in the countryside, but a TV, refrigerator and other modern appliances are commonplace.

MARRIAGE, CUSTOMS, EQUALITY
A wedding is usually celebrated in stages, the couple being ceremonially blessed in the morning at the bride's house, and having holy water poured into their hands (a Brahmin ritual in origin) in the afternoon. That is usually followed by an informal party. In rural areas ceremonies can last for two or three days, and during this time the groom is not supposed to touch the bride.

Women rank below men in the traditional order of things, though changes in the legal system have meant that women now share the same marriage and divorce rights as men. Many Thai women pursue

successful careers in such realms as business, medicine and politics.

Thailand was the first Asian country to give women the vote (in 1933), and several big corporations have women at their head.

EDUCATION Formal education begins at an early age for most children, and many can read and write quite well before starting school: there is an increasing take-up of pre-school education to enable children to compete in a highly competitive system. By law all Thai children must complete six years of primary and three years of secondary education. After that stage about half of all students continue their studies for a further three years, and many continue into tertiary education. In schools there is a morning ritual of flying the national flag and singing the national anthem.

Buddhist groups are opposing the new government curriculum, which cuts down the hours devoted to Buddhism in favour of the sciences.

The two best-known universities are Chulalongkorn, the oldest, and Thammasat, which is traditionally the more radical. Both are in Bangkok. There are many others in the capital as well as in the provinces.

HEALTH AND FAMILY PLANNING
Health facilities in Bangkok are generally good, but those in the more distant provinces are very poor. However, one area of public health where Thailand excels is that of family planning.

The population has increased at a rate of only about 0.3 per cent, lower than most developing countries. The

❑ When the first consignments of American condoms to arrive in Thailand proved to be too big, Mechai Viravaidya hired five "massage-parlour girls" to measure more than 500 of their customers to produce a Thai national size for manufacturers to meet. ❑

man chiefly responsible for this low population growth is Mechai Viravaidya, a tough, imaginative, bold and determined publicist who has championed the controversial issues of population growth and the fight against AIDS with great enthusiasm and some considerable success.

Mechai's plain speaking about the need for condoms, vasectomies and sterilisation has made him so much a part of the health education scene that condoms in Thailand are often referred to as "Mechais".

In publicising their use he has employed unorthodox but effective methods such as making them into balloons, filling them with water and introducing them at festivals. He also invented catchy slogans to put on T-shirts.

❑ Meatball vendor Tek Kop lives in a house with seven wives and 22 children. Mechai offered to pay for the children's education if Tek had a vasectomy. He refused, and Mechai acknowledged his worst failure. ❑

Thailand has now joined the second wave of emergent Asian economies, or NICs (Newly Industrialising Countries). The "dragons" (Thailand, Malaysia, Indonesia and the Philippines) are racing to catch up with the richer "tigers" (Hong Kong, Singapore, Taiwan and South Korea). Despite rapid recent growth, Thailand's standard of living remains low.

AGRICULTURE Thailand has always been a rich agricultural producer, especially of rice. More than 20 million tonnes are normally harvested every year – and of better quality than that of other countries. Not only rice, but also rubber (about a million tonnes a year), maize, cassava, sugar, soyabean, coconut, fish and shrimps are also produced in large quantities.

Spectacular increases in crop yields have been won over the last few years through the use of chemical fertilisers and pesticides, and irrigation canals. Unfortunately some of the new strains of high-yielding rice which were introduced into farming have proved vulnerable to insects and other pests.

This has resulted in a new trend towards what some Thais call "Buddhist farming", where natural organic fertiliser and herbal sprays are used to deter rather than kill pests. On some farms the natural balance has been restored under this regime, so that birds have returned to prey on the insects which eat the crops. This is praised as being consistent with Buddhism and with Thai tradition, although it is still only a minority system.

Some Thai exports are restricted. The European Union made Thailand cut its exports of tapioca although it gave funds for the development of alternative crops. Thai textiles and garments are restricted in most Western markets, and British manufacturers once demanded restrictions on Thai TV sets.

One in every two cans of pineapple opened in America comes from Thailand, while a Thai company now stands as Asia's largest exporter of

> ❏ Textiles are currently the biggest export, followed by rice, rubber, precious stones and jewellery, tapioca, sugar, integrated circuits and canned fish. ❏

tuna fish, commanding one fifth of the world market, which has enabled them to absorb one of the largest American companies.

Traditional farming is beginning to give way to agribusiness, in particular the production of broiler chickens and shrimps. This is symbolised by Charoen Pokphand, the Chinese-founded agribusiness conglomerate, which employs 80,000 staff around the world and has a turnover of more than US$9 billion a year.

MANUFACTURING INDUSTRY A more recent development, this now accounts for over a third of the gross domestic product, while service industries account for almost half. Tourism alone supplies a tenth of this figure.

The manufacturing industry has benefited from the pool of cheap unskilled labour (newly landless farmers) which comes from Thai rural areas. Two out of three Thai workers are in agriculture, yet they account for only one-sixth of the national production. Many multinationals and manufacturers from Japan, Northeast Asia, Europe and America are attracted by this, and electronics and textiles in particular are flourishing as a result.

These developments are pursued by private enterprise, mostly due to the government taking a back seat in the economy. This has caused particular problems for industry, such as the inadequacy of infrastructure (especially transport and communications) and the inferiority of higher education, technology and technical training. This in turn has lead to a severe shortage of engineers.

STEEL AND PETROCHEMICAL INDUSTRIES
are in evidence, and exports to markets as far afield as Africa have been established. Most large automobile companies have manufacturing and assembling plants in Thailand, including Toyota, Isuzu, Mitsubishi, Ford and Honda. Pickup trucks account for a quarter of the national sales. Some cars are exported with almost 60 per cent made of locally produced parts.

The country is blessed with mineral deposits, notably tin, lead, zinc and lignite. The relatively recent discovery and exploitation of natural gas offshore has rendered Thailand less dependent on oil imports.

THAI SILK
is one of the best dollar-earners from the traditional textiles, a business developed initially by Jim Thompson, an American who stayed in Thailand after World War II. He built a major industry of Thai silk by introducing modern dyes and designs to the hand-loom workers.

WORKING CONDITIONS
Things are improving slowly as the authorities expose companies with sub-standard conditions, poor safety records and illegal use of child workers.

> ❏ Jim Thompson started by selling silk in the foyer of the Oriental Hotel, and later introduced it to Hollywood costume designers with great success. Jim Thompson silk is still considered the best in this billion-dollar export industry. ❏

Only one worker in ten is organised in a trade union, although that is mainly because Thais prefer to retain their individual freedom. However, the unions are relatively strong in public enterprises. There is a minimum wage, which is reviewed and raised on a regular basis. It is now 140 baht (about £2.50) per day.

FINANCE During the early and mid 1980s Thailand enjoyed good growth and a strong currency, assisted by a loosely regulated finance industry which included more than 30 commerical and foreign banks in the Bangkok market and over 100 finance and security firms. Since the collapse of the Asian economy in 1997 the number of financial institutions has shrunk dramatically. Thailand is still struggling with huge debts despite assistance from the International Monetary Fund (IMF), a move seen by some patriotic Thais as a sellout of the economy to foreign interests. Others see this as less of a problem because the economy was originally built on borrowing foreign money.

21

Buddhism, due to its central beliefs, might be considered as an opponent of business. However, it does not favour the collapse of bankrupt companies since that causes hardship for employees and shareholders.

Thai currency is now worth less than two-thirds of the pre-economic crisis levels on the international exchange markets.

Banking used to be a common ambition for young graduates, although nowadays the trend is towards a career in computers. The biggest local bank is the Bangkok Bank, still controlled and largely owned by the Sophonpanich family, now second-generation Chinese immigrants. Thousands of young men and women in almost identical navy blue and white outfits flock into the headquarters in Silom Road and the myriad branches around the country every morning – and at lunchtime you will see them tumbling out into the streets, heading for their favourite cafés and street stalls.

Individuals are taxed on a sliding scale from 5 to 55 per cent, while

corporations pay 35 per cent on profits (less for those publicly traded on the Securities Exchange).

Significant tax holidays and tax reductions are available for approved new investments. A 7 per cent value-added tax was implemented in 1992.

LOOKING TO THE FUTURE Financial liberalisation is progressing, with exchange control already at an end. The government intends to loosen regulations and controls on many more aspects of financial activity.

THE ECONOMY In the 1990s the Thai economy slowed down dramatically in response to the world recession, Gulf War, oil price increases and domestic overheating. It was once predicted to be one of the world's leading eight economies by 2020, but many Thais believe the price to achieve this is too high. Growth at that pace widens the gap between rich and poor, leading to social unrest. However, the proportion of the population in extreme poverty has fallen in recent years (see page 201).

Among many worries for the future are the decline in rice exports, and

Pepsi plant at Bangkok

A ruby mine in the southeast: gems were once a major export

the likelihood of Vietnam taking away some of Thailand's old markets at the cheaper end.

Some Western managers in Thai factories have been heard to carp about their workforce. But the degree of hard graft put in by Thais is evident: for proof of this, look at the many building sites in and around Bangkok, which are mostly manned by relatively new labour from the northeast.

Neither does the lazy image square with the US$1 billion which some 300,000 Thais have sent home while under long-term contract in construction projects in the Middle East and other Asian locations. None of the recent economic achievements of Thailand could have been attained if every Thai was shirking work.

THE TOURIST INDUSTRY is thriving. It now brings more than 8.6 million foreigners to Thailand every year. They arrive at the rate of 900 an hour, and the average tourist spends over

US$1,000, which adds up to over US$9 billion a year, a figure that is about half of total Thai exports. The average length of stay of a tourist is eight days.

Half of Thailand's tourists come from Western countries, the remainder come from Asia – especially Japan, Taiwan, Korea, Malaysia and Singapore.

The natural attractions of Thailand, in terms of climate and scenery, as well as its historical sites, colourful festivals and exotic experiences add up to a powerful draw.

❏ The Oriental Hotel, beloved of Somerset Maugham, has been consistently voted "best in the world" in international travellers' polls every year for over a decade. ❏

The Thai mentality is shaped partly by the country itself, with its tropical climate and heavy rain; it is a land of plenty, where food is bountiful. Thai people believe strongly in Buddhist philosophy which teaches them to put self-cultivation above social works. It does not offer a universal ethic, but accepts the inequalities among men in their spiritual progress.

SOCIAL ATTITUDES Thailand is a society of vertical hierarchy, where people respect the authority of those above them (fathers, schoolteachers, prime ministers, the king) but this is not quite the same system as is found in Japan. Even family ties tend to be looser in Thailand than those found in Northeast Asia.

This also means that Thais are generally more receptive to foreign influences, something reinforced by their history of resisting colonialism in the 19th century. The inferiority complex which can be noted amongst some people in former colonised states (such as India and Indonesia) is missing with the Thais, whose authority structure has been unbroken for centuries.

It can be almost a taboo to contradict someone directly. National politics is an exception, where slanging matches during election time are acceptable and enjoyed.

The self-respect of other people is normally considered so important that it is rarely infringed. One story tells of the Thai hired to teach the Thai language to a foreigner, but who never corrected the foreigner because he would not embarrass a person by drawing attention to his mistakes.

Thais often make a big effort not to inconvenience or upset another person, and on that basis they expect to get the same treatment in return. There is heavy reliance on the smile and on the phrase *mai pen rai* (never mind), but if that suggests an underlying gentleness of character it has to be reconciled with the extraordinary violence which does occasionally break out.

A servant may endure the rude treatment of an employer for many years without complaint, but then his or her patience might suddenly break, and he or she might even kill the persecutor. There are many *crimes passionnels*, and Thailand is said to have one of the highest murder rates in the world.

Becoming absorbed in self-cultivation, and dealing with the intricate problems of social relationships in such variety has another consequence. Thais usually avoid

People at prayer

> ❏ The ideal man would have "...the moral principles of a *farang*, the diligence of a Chinese and the heart of a Thai". Heart is: "Love of peace, contentment with little, concern for others and a sense of moderation". – From Botan's novel *Letters From Thailand*. ❏

Bangkok's Brahmin Erawan shrine

❑ During World War II villagers in Thailand brought food to British POWs in a Japanese camp. When the Japanese surrendered in 1945, they brought food for the Japanese prisoners with the same solicitude. ❑

❑ "The Thai way of life is an elegant sort of life, surrounded by benevolent and exuberantly plentiful nature, with adaptable morals and a serene detachment to the more difficult problems of life…To a Thai, life itself is one long relaxation." – Kukrit Pramoj, Thailand's ex-prime minister and most famous novelist. ❑

becoming involved in other people's problems. They normally avoid conflict, and keep contact with other people down to a minimum.

There is a legitimate outlet for relaxation in *sanuk* (fun). *Sanuk* is a very old feature in Thai life. It means getting pleasure from carefree amusement with congenial friends or companions. No one is criticised for doing this, indeed it is considered a positive trait in the code of behaviour.

Spontaneity is valued. Thais dislike planning, and meetings are often much better without an appointment because the impromptu encounter is considered more enjoyable.

The concept of *sanuk* sounds idyllic, but for Westerners the Thai mentality can be difficult to work with.

Objectivity is an elusive quality in Thai life, even at university level. If a professor gives an opinion on a matter under discussion, junior lecturers or students will rarely argue with him or put forward a different point of view. If they think it important enough they might approach him privately afterwards. It is not timidity, or fear, but a concern for the professor's self-respect that prevents what Westerners would regard as a normal productive discussion opening up.

Many Thais have a strong sense of hierarchy, and take immense care in their behaviour towards other people. Different gradations of respect or treatment need to be given and this is reflected in the language. Learning Thai involves a system of "honorifics", where different pronouns are used according to social status. Speaking to a bus conductor, a teacher, a student or to royalty all call for different words. To a Thai, these distinctions in social status can be very important indeed.

PUTTING ONE'S FOOT IN IT Never touch a Thai, even a child, on the head. Thais consider the head to be the most important part of the body, deserving the most honour – the foot is the least honoured. The head is the seat of the *khwan*, or vital spirit, which lives in the body. Students who have to pass in front of a seated teacher will instinctively lower their heads as they pass. A servant will do the same in a house.

❏ It is still said that men are comparable to the front legs of an elephant, and women to the hind legs. Male chauvinists in Thailand like to say that the elephant seems to be walking backwards these days. ❏

FORMS OF GREETING The Thai form of traditional greeting is the *wai*, in which both hands are raised slowly and gracefully, palm to palm and close to the body. It is considered to be more than a greeting; it is a way of paying one's respects. The higher the hands are raised the greater the respect signalled.

The *wai* is the normal form of greeting between Thais but some more Westernised Thais are just as likely to shake hands with foreigners.

❏ Traditionally, Thais should not stand higher than their royal family. A prince was unable to inspect the first printing press because there were residences over it whose occupants might walk over his head. When President Lyndon B Johnson visited in 1966, police cleared the second and higher storeys of buildings lining the route. ❏

The wai: *both a form of greeting and paying one's respect*

WOMEN'S RIGHTS AND WRONGS

Women have traditionally deferred to men in society, and are thought to have adverse *khwan*. Thai men will still refuse to walk underneath a clothesline where female clothing is hanging, in case their head is touched by them. For this reason women's clothes are usually hung out to dry on a very low clothesline which has to be walked around.

DOS AND DON'TS No one would ever enter a house or a temple without taking off the shoes first. Nowadays, although it is impractical to have everybody leaving shoes at the door of a very large building (for instance at a bank or department store) in temples, or private houses belonging to Thais, foreigners would be expected to take off their shoes and walk about inside in socks or in slippers provided by the host. Never give a Thai friend or colleague a red pen with which to write a signature. Names are written in red at the side of coffins awaiting cremation.

Thais will generally touch each other less than Westerners, though physical contact such as holding hands is becoming more acceptable. However, in the northeast such

> ❏ "Never sleep with your head facing to the west. That is where the sun sets, and the setting sun symbolises death." – Thai superstition. ❏

behaviour can even result in a fine. The traditional dance, the *Ramwong*, demonstrates how this avoidance of bodily contact does not inhibit a graceful dance movement in which neither partner touches the other.

YOU BET! Many Thais are inveterate gamblers, who bet on horses, with cards, and on all kinds of contests – Thai boxing, cockfights, fish fights, bullfights…if there is scent of a competition they will be there with a wager. Poker, mahjong, checkers and chess are all played with rising excitement for sums of money.

The national lottery is a huge business; the generals who used to manage it became rich men. The government now run the lottery, but it faces strong competition from an illegally run operation. Thais may devote enormous time and energy to accumulating enough merit by their actions to get a lucky lottery number.

> ❏ "If you want to be somebody in this country you have to dress like a European", complained Sulak Sivaraksa, the well-known critic and writer, after an incident when, wearing his usual traditional Thai dress, he was refused admittance to the Oriental Hotel in Bangkok to see the then German Foreign Minister Herr Genscher. ❏

Thailand is predominantly Buddhist. More than 90 per cent of the population believe in some form of Buddhism, even though they may not perform the ceremonies or visit the temples frequently. The picturesque temples in every village and dotted about in each city are tranquil oases to which almost all Thais are drawn to some time in their lives.

BUDDHIST TRADITIONS Thai Buddhism follows the Theravada tradition, which is based on the oldest Buddhist writings recorded in Pali, the ancient Indian language. **Theravada Buddhism** aims to preserve the way of life described in those early writings. The other important Buddhist tradition is the **Mahayana**, which spread to China, Korea, Japan and Vietnam, and developed Buddhist philosophy while also trying to make the early teachings more accessible to lay followers. Buddhism was founded in the 6th century BC by Siddhartha Gautama, an Indian prince who turned ascetic. After years of fasting and meditation he arrived at a unique vision of the world, centred around the Four Noble Truths. The Thais became converted in the 7th century, and can now boast the largest unbroken ordination chain in any of the Theravada countries.

The millions of Buddha images which can be seen in Thailand in every house and temple are deeply respected by ordinary men and women, though not always approved of by Thai intellectuals. Visitors must be very careful not to give offence by behaving disrespectfully towards Buddha statues, which are felt to represent the Buddha in person. Some tourists who were photographed sitting on the head of a Buddha statue aroused a furore of criticism. It is forbidden to take Buddha statues out of Thailand without special permission from the Fine Arts Department. Shops will advise you and can sometimes get an export licence.

BUDDHIST BELIEFS Buddhism does not involve a belief in any god or gods. The central feature of Buddhism is the concept of *karma*, which literally means action. Every action, word or thought has a consequence which becomes manifest sometime in the future. Evil acts produce evil consequences or suffering. Inequalities between people in the present world are rationalised by the idea that *karma* can be carried over from previous lives, though meritorious acts (*tam boon*), such as giving alms or releasing fish and birds in religious ceremonies, can redeem bad *karma* from both present and past lives.

The effort to achieve a high degree of spirituality is left on the whole to the monks in their monasteries or *wats* (temples). The central building of the *wat* is the most sacred and is known as the *bot*. It is here that the ceremonies of ordination, the daily morning and evening chanting of monks and services on days of fasting (on the first, eighth, 15th and 23rd days of the lunar month) take

---

❏ The Four Noble Truths:
- *dukkha* or suffering is life's central problem
- the cause of suffering is desire
- the way to eliminate suffering is to eliminate its cause, desire
- the way to achieve this is to follow the Eightfold Way which describes standards of morality and qualities to be encouraged in meditation to this end. ❏

28

place. Lesser buildings called *wiharn* are often used for religious services for lay people as well as living accommodation for the monks.

Lay Buddhists gain merit by giving alms to the monks, and by following basic moral guidelines – not to kill or tell lies, and to be moderate in physical indulgence. Every morning at dawn the saffron-robed monks go out with their begging bowls to ask for alms in the form of food, and traditionally every house will spare a little for them.

RELIGIOUS HIERARCHY All monks are members of the *sangha* or the Buddhist order of monks. The *sangha* is supervised by an executive council headed by a supreme patriarch appointed by the king. There are two main sects in the Thai *sangha*: the **Thammayut**, which was formed in the last century and follows strict rules, for example, taking only one meal a day, and the larger **Mahanikai**.

The central mosque in Pattani, where Muslims have a strong presence (see page 31)

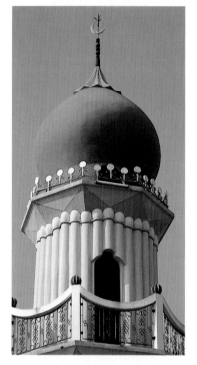

❏ The Buddhist teachings (*dharma*) are taught to every child in primary school: that is how Buddhist morality is diffused. ❏

The tradition survives of laymen spending a week or so as monks in a monastery subject to the same discipline and routine as the monks. Even King Bhumiphol took alms from the people on the streets of Bangkok when he performed this traditional act early in his reign.

Monks are greatly respected by the public. They get free food in the morning, and travel free or half-price on the buses and trains. Some are involved in local development projects, helping to plan and build bridges, dams and schools, and to modernise farming methods.

BUDDHIST TEMPLES Bangkok has the greatest concentration of important temples. The most renowned is the **Wat Phra Keo**, which is also called the Temple of the Emerald Buddha, containing the mysterious Emerald Buddha statue, a Thai national symbol. Established in 1782, adjoining the Grand Palace, it is the ceremonial temple of the Thai kings. **Wat Mahathat** is the chief temple of Thailand's largest monastic sect, the Mahanikai. The national headquarters of the Thammayut sect is **Wat Bowonniwet** (Bowornives) which is where King Bhumiphol was ordained as a monk. **Wat Po** (Wat Phra Chetuphon) is the oldest and largest *wat* in Bangkok, with Thailand's largest collection of Buddha images.

BUDDHIST SECTS There is a general consensus that the *sangha* is becoming remote from everyday problems, and for this reason new sects have been

❏ Thai intellectuals were furious when a 13th-century carved stone lintel from the Khmer sanctuary of Phanom Rung turned up in a museum in Chicago. The lintel has now been returned. ❏

29

Muslim people in Narathiwat

founded. These frown on more old-fashioned fortune-telling, and the traffic in amulets and charms which are supposed to carry good luck. They try to teach a combination of Buddhist philosophy and meditation techniques suitable for the urban lifestyle. The best known of these is **Santi Asoke** (Peace and No Sorrow), founded by Phra Bodhirak. He is half Chinese and was a TV producer and singer before his ordination. His followers, strict vegetarians who wear white robes, were excommunicated from the *sangha* in 1989. A major theme of theirs is that monks have to be involved with the people and so cannot remain distant from politics.

DHAMMAKAYA (Body of Truth) is another controversial sect, in which monks are said to have bribed their way into higher positions, and allegations of embezzlement have led to the arrest of the abbot and other followers.

This highly materialistic sect was founded by a Thai Chinese, Phra Dhammachayo, who graduated in economics. This sect holds many industrial investments, and its leaders will drive out in a Rolls Royce or Mercedes to collect their morning alms. In a neat dovetailing of *karma* and property management, Dhammachayo persuades his lay supporters to donate land to his monks with the promise that the merit acquired will ensure that they enjoy more land in their next life. There is also a sect called **Suan Mokh** (Garden of Liberation), which preaches "dharmic socialism", a

> ❏ Phra Bodhirak once claimed that he had personally attained the same level of enlightenment as the Buddha himself, something which no Thai had ever dared to claim before. Although it led to his excommunication he still has a popular following. ❏

decentralised and non-competitive form of social co-operation among farmers which is free from greed.

OTHER RELIGIONS There is an undertow of Indian Brahminism that the Thais acquired from the Indian-influenced societies which they conquered and absorbed as they settled into the present territory of Thailand. Indeed, some of the shrines with figures of deities which are to be seen in Bangkok are Brahmin rather than Buddhist. One of these is the *naga*, a semi-divine god and fertility symbol

recently been some concern about the growth of fundamentalist Shiite adherents. The three provinces of Yala, Pattani and Narathiwat are dominated by Muslims, especially in the countryside. There is a smaller minority of **Christians**. The Roman Catholic cemetery in Silom Road and

which often takes the form of a dragon-headed serpent.

BUDDHISM is a tolerant religion, and there are (small) minorities of other faiths, notably two million **Muslims** in the southern provinces, adjoining Malaysia. They are mostly Sunni Muslims although there has

Buddhist monks receive their alms

the Protestant one on the river bank are two of the historical sites of Bangkok. A few Thais have become Catholic or Protestant, and some of the refugees from Vietnam are Catholic, but all co-exist in Thai society without difficulty.

> ❏ Women are not allowed to attend Buddhist schools, but they enter *bots* in large numbers. They can take eight or 10 precepts and wear the white robes of a nun, or *mae chi*. ❏

> ❏ Buddhism injects an element of fatalism into the Thai mentality. This accounts for the passiveness, acceptance and social calm which the outsider observes in Thai society. ❏

It is believed that the Thais first migrated into their country from China many centuries ago. That ancient connection has been reinforced by further large-scale immigration of Chinese into Thailand; an estimated nine million or so Chinese may have crossed during the past hundred years, making the Chinese the largest minority group in Thailand.

32

ROOTS Archaeological evidence in the past 35 years has raised the interesting possibility that prehistoric sites such as Ban Chiang, Mae Hong Son and Kanchana Buri could have predated the Chinese by several thousand years. If these theories are verified, it will call into question the ideas of who came from where originally.

The Chinese coming into Thailand in the early days of commerce were merchants, who travelled widely in Asia. The Thais were tolerant towards the Chinese immigrants, allowing them to settle and gradually to become Thai. There was a time in the 1930s when Thai nationalism made things difficult for the Chinese. Further immigration was stopped – and halted completely in 1950, but in the period following World War II the Chinese completed their assimilation into Thai society. They could be said to be responsible for much of Thailand's economic success.

THE BORDERS ARE BLURRED Most of those coming into Thailand were single males who married Thai women, starting a process of inter-marriage which has gone on over many generations. It is almost impossible now to disentangle the ethnic origins of the mainly Chinese, the mainly Thai and the full Thai.

Almost everyone in the ruling élite, from the royal family to the politicians, civil servants and army officers – and especially business leaders – have some degree of Chinese ancestry.

Many Chinese in Thailand no longer speak or read Chinese, but still perform some occasional Chinese rituals. Thailand is their home, and inspires their loyalty and patriotism, but many feel curious about China, which is similar to the interest that many Australians show in Britain.

TRADING PLACES On arrival, Chinese immigrants had to slot into whatever niche was available in order to make a living. Many turned towards trade and industry and other forms of business. From fairly humble merchants and shopkeepers to major bankers and industrialists the Chinese are well represented. Indeed, some very big names on the present scene are Chinese.

Virtually all of the country's industrialists and entrepreneurs are either recent Chinese immigrants or "Sino-Thais", as the mixed lineage people are sometimes called. Dhanin Chearavanont is the most successful Chinese businessman, running the Charoen Pokphand agribusiness

> ❏ The best way to understand the motivation and early experiences of the migrant Chinese is to read the heart-warming novel *Letters From Thailand* by Botan (a pseudonym). ❏

group. Other famous Chinese business families are Sarasin, Sophonpanich (who own the Bangkok Bank) and Techapaibul.

Patpong Road, which is visited because of its red-light notoriety, was originally built by a typical Chinese immigrant, Poon Pat. He came to Bangkok from Hainan (a large island off the south China coast) at the age of 12 and became a skilful buyer of

A glimpse of life in Bangkok's Chinatown

rice and who made his fortune supplying limestone for the king's new cement factory.

INTEGRATION The Chinese resemble the Thais physically in many respects – although there are no distinctly typical Thai features – and the two can easily be confused. By now most of them have taken Thai names, and the fact that they were not made to adopt an alien religion, as the Chinese immigrants did in Malaysia and Indonesia, was a great help.

Nevertheless, there are differences, some of which are cherished by the Chinese. With typical Thai tolerance, however, these are generally accepted and respected.

One of the few traits which does mark out the Chinese from the Thai people is the Chinese respect for the family tree. Another trait is the practice of burying their dead, whereas Thais have traditionally practised cremation. There also tends to be a greater prevalence of Christianity among the Chinese which is not the case with the Thais, who mostly believe in reincarnation.

DUAL IDENTITY Some of the Sino-Thais lead, in effect, a double life. They are Thai in public but then choose to be Chinese among their family. There are still some Chinese-language newspapers published, and there are several Chinese Christian churches.

Most Thais will accept anyone born in Thailand as being Thai. Additionally such celebrities as the king and Tiger Woods, who were born outside the kingdom, have almost universal acceptance by the Thai people.

33

❑ All children, whether they be Thai, Chinese or from another race, are expected to learn the Thai language from an early age in school. Until relatively recently, Chinese languages were not available for study at university level. ❑

A Chinese Taoist shrine in Bangkok

Thai society may appear permissive in some respects, but can be somewhat reserved in public; nudity on beaches and even bare shoulders in public may offend sensibilities. Increasingly, authorities are cracking down on sex with under-age prostitutes.

Dictator Field Marshall Sarit's 100 or so mistresses did not shock the Thais. Older men hark back to the days of their youth when a man could have as many wives and/or mistresses as he could afford.

The public health ministry in Thailand estimates there are around 600 brothels in Bangkok but until recently their existence was officially denied. Countless women and boys earn their living from sex – some younger than 13 are pressurised into prostitution. Recent moves to decriminalise prostitution have had the support of Mechai Viravaidya, who has campaigned hard for AIDS awareness. There is currently anxious debate about the economic consequences of sexual permissiveness and who will pay the medical expenses of employees who contract AIDS. Mechai proposals involve making prostitutes carry health cards and legalising brothels to enforce health standards. However, as yet, these are only proposals.

> ❏ The Thai government prosecutes hundreds of foreigners each year in a move to counter the prostitution industry. In 1995 Swedish authorities successfully prosecuted a Swedish man who hired an under-age boy for sex in Thailand. ❏

THE WOMAN'S POINT OF VIEW

Within a marriage a woman overtly takes second place, but in practice she is often the keeper of the purse.

Attitudes are changing slowly. Women are becoming more assertive and vocal. Scores of women are now far up the coporate ladder.

THE GAY SCENE Although the Thais might be considered conservative in many ways, they generally do not frown on homosexuality of either sex. There are many gay bars and clubs which can be found, in particular, in Bangkok, Chiang Mai, Phuket and Pattaya.

> ❏ A Thai doctor describes AIDS as "...worse than any war. It will destroy every fibre of our social and economic life. We need a movement so intense that it can uproot men's sexual habits..." ❏

An AIDS awareness poster

The army has been an extremely important group in Thai society and politics, ever since the 1932 revolution when it forced King Prajadhipok to abandon his absolute powers. Periods of civilian rule have often been interrupted by military coup attempts – 17 in all since 1932.

THE MILITARY PROFILE was kept high from the 1950s by the perception that Thailand was the "next domino" likely to fall to Communism in Southeast Asia, and by the threat of Communist insurgency.

The army runs its own bank, radio and television stations, and regional economic development programmes. It is firmly part of the Thai establishment. However Chuan Leek Pai bought a civilian influence into the

❏ Thai military leaders commonly control private business concerns, sometimes through their wives, children or friends, a trend which reached its peak in the early 1970s when the military dictators Thanom and Praphas held 150 company directorships. ❏

military forces when in 1997 he used his position as Prime Minister to take the position of Minister of Defence.

THE 1973 STUDENT REVOLUTION produced a sea change in Thai politics which permanently weakened the legitimacy of military rule in Thailand. The military, however, retained enormous influence and have made comebacks – first in the late 1970s as part of a rightist reaction to the weak and unstable civilian coalition governments of the mid-1970s, and most recently in 1991 as a result of corruption and personality clashes with members of Chatichai Choonhavan's administration.

IN RECENT YEARS With the ending of the Vietnam war, the subsiding of domestic Communist insurgency,

❏ The Thai armed forces are well equipped. A few years ago they purchased cheap Chinese arms, but on finding the reliability and quality poor they placed orders again with the Americans for tanks, anti-submarine helicopters and torpedoes. Some of these new arms are to be installed on the four Chinese frigates bought earlier by Thailand. ❏

35

Armed guard at Bangkok's National Assembly

and the withdrawal of Vietnamese troops from Cambodia, the Thai army has sensed a loss of purpose and direction.

Possibly as a reaction to this, the air force wants to purchase more F16 fighters and the navy is lobbying for more powerful vessels. So far the civilian bureaucrats have resisted their demands as these do not appear justifiable purchases, and are hardly necessary for Thailand's current defence needs.

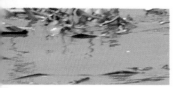

With very fast economic growth in recent years and a culturally permissive attitude to life, Thailand now presents a very bad case indeed of pollution of the natural environment.

DISAPPEARING FORESTS AND WILDLIFE In the face of increasing exploitative pressures, Thailand is attempting to conserve its rich natural resources. Legislative measures have included a total ban on logging activities, the establishment of protected areas and heavy fines for those caught poaching or trading in wild animals. These measures have had some success, though there is a long way to go.

As in so many other parts of the world, the main threat to the survival of wildlife is habitat destruction by mankind. Thailand is a country that has been denuded of its trees to a spectacular extent. The nation's forest cover has declined remarkably from about 53 per cent in 1961 to only about 20 per cent today. Slash-and-burn agriculture and illegal logging have contributed significantly to this deterioration, as the richly varied forest canopy gives way to eerie skeletal wastelands of burnt tree stumps.

A coconut-picking monkey, trained to work for men in the forests which men are destroying

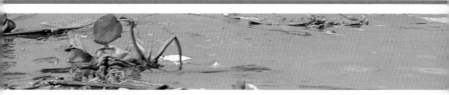

Road construction, mineral exploitation, hydroelectric projects and resettlement programmes, together with the boom in the tourist industry, have also greatly increased the pressure on forest, wildlife and other resources.

Illegal hunting and poaching of wildlife is another serious problem. Commercial exploitation for international trade has severely reduced certain populations of wild animals, some to the point of extinction.

Since the introduction of the first national park at Khao Yai in 1962, the Royal Thai Forestry Department have made tremendous efforts to conserve these protected areas. Wildlife sanctuaries differ from national parks in that they are closed to the public. However many of these areas are still been encroached upon. Loggers claimed hill-tribes widely practised slash-and-burn techniques, which is now illegal, whereas advocates for the tribes say the amount of land they used was negligible compared to big business. Some claim the barring of slash-and-burn was merely a tool used to oust the hill-tribes.

After the disastrous 1987–8 floods commercial logging was banned. The loss of trees from watershed areas in upland districts shifted the pattern of rainfall and actually reduced the water supply to farmers below.

In that flood, hundreds of people were drowned in the south and whole villages washed away. The removal of the trees resulted in disastrous soil erosion; whole communities were buried in mudslides.

LEGISLATION Unfortunately any legislation passed by the government is hard to implement. Many logging companies, including army enterprises, negotiated alternative contracts across the border moving into the forests of Myanmar, Laos

❏ Bangkok was an idyllic "village of wild plum trees" when the Chakri kings founded their capital there 200 years ago. There were only 12,750 registered motor vehicles in the city when King Bhumiphol was born (1927). ❏

and Cambodia, which just exports Thailand's environmental problem.

The logging companies themselves are powerful politically and do not find it hard to continue logging in remote areas of Thailand by bribing officials. In Laos, Thai logging companies are building hotels in return for access to the local forest stands.

POSITIVE PROGRESS Some constructive measures were started in the 1980s. One interesting conservation project is at Ban Sup Tai village on the edge of one of Thailand's last virgin forests. This forms a national park, sheltering 180 elephants and 50 tigers.

The villagers had been poaching and encroaching on the national park. In response to this, voluntary groups from Bangkok organised German finance and set up a number of measures including a credit co-operative, a co-operative store, animal husbandry activities, tree planting and conservation awareness sessions.

The villagers have stopped farming inside the park boundary and the deer and elephants have returned to the fringes of the village for the first time in over a decade. In fact, wild pigs are now feeding freely on the villagers' rich corn and soybean crops and are not being killed as they were in the past – because villagers have caught the new conservation bug.

AIR POLLUTION By the 1980s the number of cars on Thailand's roads was increasing by their original total figure every month. Today there are 2.4 million registered cars in Bangkok alone. More than ten tonnes of lead, not to mention quantities of other toxic matter, are released into Bangkok's air every day. The problem has been aggravated by the proliferation of factories in Bangkok since the 1960s. The number has increased more than a hundredfold.

BOOM! In the 1960s and '70s the urban area in the capital doubled and then doubled again during the first half of the 1980s. This rapid sprawling development swamped any ideas of planning for transport or other infrastructure. More than half of the country's manufacturing takes place in Bangkok. Together with Bangkok's governmental and administrative functions this has created a nightmarish problem of traffic congestion. The average speed of traffic in the central area is only 8kph. During the school term time, or in the rainy season floods, it is even worse. Some 70 per cent of Thailand's energy consumption is used in transportation.

A traffic policeman equipped with respirator in Bangkok

> ❏ "The purpose of development is to create a liveable environment."– King Bhumiphol. ❏

THAT SINKING FEELING Bangkok is slowly sinking, at the rate of about 25mm a year. It has been suggested by a city official that it might just finally collapse under its own weight one day. Little can be done about it as the city grew up over a riverine delta with what used to be a network of *khlongs* or canals, reminiscent of Venice. However, these are now mostly built over. Bangkokians await their doom with customary fatalism, and will no doubt go and build a new city somewhere else when the collaspe does actually happens.

WATERY ISSUES Thailand's big dam era started in 1957 with the Bhumiphol Dam in Tak province. Since then throughout the dictatorial regime of Thailand a dozen other dams have been constructed, mostly without input or agreement from environmental groups or local villagers. The consequences of this have been disastrous, both socially and environmentally. In particular, the building of dams without proper consultation have lead to protests.

In 1987 the Nam Choan Dam project was successfully halted by protesters. Thirteen years later in 2000, villagers from Pak Moon in the northeast carried out a prolonged protest in front of the Government House in Bangkok against the Pak Moon Dam. This scheme has wrought devastation upon a large area and has resulted in the loss of many livelihoods. What makes this issue all the more frustrating is that the Pak Moon Dam is remarkably inefficient: it can only produce small amounts of energy during the wet season, when the country's other dams are producing power at their full capacity.

Bangkok uses so much water that there is now talk of diverting a major northeastern river into the Chao Phraya. The booming tiger prawn fishery business is one of the culprits,

Choking the city to death? Bangkok's traffic

as it has led to the destruction of many of Thailand's ancient mangrove swamps. Things are no better in the countryside, where farmers have for decades been applying too much chemical fertilizer and insecticide. The malignant residue remains in canals, rivers and reservoirs. Once in the soil it gets into the food chain and builds up to fatally toxic levels in animals. This will inevitably affect humans too. Only when the enormity of the situation has sunk in will effective action for change take place which has been the case in other parts of the world.

ALTERNATIVES There are some signs that the process has begun. An Eastern form of "green" response has been "Buddhist farming", a form of organic farming influenced by the Japanese pioneer Masanobu Fukuoka (author of *The One Straw Revolution*). Its main features include the abandonment of chemical pesticides and herbicides in favour of natural herbal sprays and the encouragement of natural predators such as birds. Soil fertility is maintained by natural leaf-based fertilisers and intercropping, which is the practice of growing a variety of crops in the same field. The growth of interest in organic farming in the West is also giving Thai pioneers in this field, such as Prawase Wasi and Wibul Khemchalerm, renewed confidence.

FUTURE DEVELOPMENT There is a debate in Thailand over the pace of economic growth, and whether Thailand should aspire to compete with Asia's other "tiger economies". Some argue that Thailand's future does not lie in industrialisation and all its associated environmental problems, but rather in an agricultural, food processing, tourist and service economy.

Eating is a great social event and Thai food is one of the major Asian cuisines, quite distinct from Chinese, Indian or Indonesian cookery. And now Thai food, with its low meat and fat content and profusion of skilfully prepared vegetable dishes, has become increasingly popular in the West (see also pages 102–103).

Fifty years ago the dictator, Field Marshal Phibul, made the use of spoons and forks compulsory in his naïve attempt to Westernise the country. Before this the Thais used to eat with their hands.

As Buddhists, Thais avoid eating too much red meat, so main dishes are likely to be either shellfish, game or fish, perhaps cooked with a sauce of galingale (mild ginger), tamarind, lemon grass and chilli. The dishes are often washed down with a chilled beer: Singha is a favourite local brand.

The introduction of spices into Thai cooking dates roughly from the time of King Mongkut, whose encouragement of openness to Western ideas and technology also extended to the import of spices from China, India and Java. Once introduced, they became subjected to the distinctive application, mixtures and measures of Thai taste.

QUINTESSENTIALLY THAI That taste begins with the five flavours which also lie at the root of Chinese cookery, namely bitter, salt, sour, hot and sweet; but the Thais use them in quite a different way from the Chinese.

❑ The staple food is rice, usually eaten with a spoon. One type, a fine long grain called *khao hom mali*, is so delicious that some Thais see it as a meal in itself. Thais grow many varieties of rice, and its pearly white rice grain is in particular demand for export. ❑

❑ At least six different types of *phrik* (chilli pepper) are used. The smaller the chilli, the stronger it is. The smallest variety, known as "mouse droppings" (*phrik kee noo*), should be handled with particular care. ❑

Some ingredients used in Thai cuisine are not found in either Chinese or Indian cooking. Lemon grass is a tall grass (totally unrelated to the lemon), the leaf and root of which are used to flavour soups and salads, as well as curries and stews. The *makrud* leaf comes from a large type of lime tree native to Thailand. Its juice and rough green skin add a strong, tart flavour to soups, sauces and curries.

There is almost a national obsession with sauces. *Nam phrik* is an extremely spicy sauce which can prove too fiery for the Western palate, but Thais adore it. *Nam plaa* (literally "fish water") is a pungent fish sauce made from fermenting anchovies. It is as common a condiment on the Thai dining table as salt is in the West. *Tom yam*, a spicy soup containing shrimp flavoured with lemon grass, kaffir lime leaves, fish sauce and lemon juice, is extremely popular. *Khao tom* is a clear rice soup flavoured with vinegar or chillies with scraps of meat or poultry. It is regarded as a cure-all for fevers, colds and especially hangovers.

A TYPICAL DINNER in Thailand might include boiled rice; two soups; a bland Chinese-style stir-fry vegetable; a pungent Indian-style curry;

and boned chicken wings, stuffed with minced pork and spices and then steamed and subsequently fried, served with a sweet-sour plum sauce.

Thai curries (*gaeng*) are cooked with coconut milk or cream to thicken the stock at the end, thus softening the fierceness common in Indian curries. Red curries (*gaeng dang*) are made with Indian chilli, garlic, and onion laced with Thai lemon grass, *makrud* leaf and galanga root. Green curries are made with green chilli, usually with chicken and beef. Sour curry is made with shrimp paste, used with seafood.

Coconut cream ranges beyond the curry pot to find uses in soups and desserts as well, for example spicy coconut cream and chicken soup (*tom kha gai*) or bananas in coconut cream with mango and sticky rice.

An evening meal, Thai style

CHINESE INFLUENCE Thai chefs use the wok to stir-fry crispy green vegetables, sauté seasoned slivers of pork, beef and chicken, and to prepare fried rice and fried noodles. Steaming fish (*plaa neung*) is another technique which the Thais have adopted from China. Thai cooking also mirrors in some ways the regional division of staple grains found in China. Rice predominates in the south, while dumplings and

41

❏ The harvest of many fruits is marked by annual pageants featuring beauty competitions to find "Miss Pineapple" or "Miss Mango". ❏

Chiang Mai noodles are a speciality of the north.

The Thais are extremely fond of fresh vegetables and salads (known as *yum* in Thai). Freshly cut cabbage and lettuce leaves, scallion stalks, coriander sprigs, chilli pods and mint leaves are served with lightly poached seafoods, eggplants, roast chicken or duck.

FRUIT is one of the great Thai culinary experiences. Thailand's tropical climate is ideal for the growing of a wide variety of fruits such as mangos, durians, pineapples, guavas, longans, rambutans, custard apples, pomelos and jackfruits. Thailand produces about seven million tonnes of fruit each year, although only about one per cent of it is exported.

For the Thais the "king of fruits" is the durian. Oval in shape, it is about

20–25cm long and almost as wide. Its olive-green yellowish skin is covered with a fearsome armour of thick sharp-pointed spines up to 2cm long. Inside, the flesh is "custard-like" – creamy and yellow – and *extremely* pungent. Don't be put off by the smell, it really does taste good. There are at least five varieties of *mamuang* (mango), which are often eaten with glutinous rice, and topped with coconut cream, as a dessert. *Lamyai* is a marble-sized fruit with a hard brown skin which peels away to reveal a firm translucent flesh surrounding a black seed.

The lychee is similar to the *lamyai* but slightly larger with a pinkish flesh. The *mangkhut* (mangosteen) season lasts from May until July. It is a small dark purple fruit with a white flesh which is sweet but slightly tart. Thais are fond of trying

Mae Hong Son's early morning market, Northern Thailand

42

to guess the number of seeds they will find inside.

Thais will eat bananas when they are fully grown, but not yet ripe, fried and seasoned with sugar and salt, as a snack called *kluai chap*. If they are ripe, they can be made into all kinds of sweetmeats, including *kluai ping* (grilled banana soaked in syrup), *kluai buat chi* (pieces of banana boiled in coconut milk and seasoned with sugar and a pinch of salt) or *kluai khaek*, which Westerners will recognise as banana fritters.

However, this does not end the banana's role in the Thai kitchen. They are also turned into wrappings, cooking utensils or plates. The flowers will be put into a soup or a salad, and the leaves and trunk used for flower arrangements.

THE PRESENTATION OF FOOD is extremely important. Meals are sometimes served with vegetables carved into the shape of blossoms and leaves. Puddings and salads may be garnished with flowers such as roses or orchids.

> ❏ In May the Songkhla festival has an annual fruit-carving competition. ❏

REGIONAL DISHES The **northeast** speciality, *som tam*, is a salad made from grated unripe papaya, mixed with sliced tomatoes, chopped garlic and chillies, with pounded dried shrimps, fish sauce and lemon juice. Northeasterners usually like to take it with sticky rice and salted beef (the beef seasoned with pepper, marinated in garlic and soy sauce and dried in the sun).

The north is the best place to savour vegetables, taken raw or very slightly cooked, with *nam phrik ong* which is a thick dipping sauce of tomatoes, ground pork, garlic and chilli, seasoned with soy sauce and sugar and served with streaky pork.

Many of the **central** Thailand dishes have already been described. Chicken green curry would be very typical, served with salted egg and *yum*, the Thai salad which does not use oil.

In the **southern** provinces there is an even wider range of curries, using all kinds of green, yellow or red curry paste. These curries range in "heat", and some of them are very hot indeed. Southerners also enjoy fried fish, often coated with turmeric and other herbs and spices, then deep fried and served with an aromatic sauce.

Western food is served in Thailand, along with many other cuisines, in restaurants and hotels, and there is a huge variety of Chinese restaurants to patronise. But don't leave Thailand without at least trying Thai food. Even if you find your first Thai meal a little too hot, too spicy or too strong, don't give up. There are so many kinds of dish that it is worth persevering – and there is usually something on the menu to suit even the most conservative western palate.

A mouth-watering market display

43

The Thai language is one of the oldest in the Orient, but the Thai script is more recent. Thailand has epic folk tales drawn from mythology and modern award-winning writers. Classical works of art are often based on Buddhist religious texts, but modern works are more experimental. Thai music is different from the West's, using different instruments and tones. A classical orchestra accompanies the traditional khon, *or masked dramas.*

44

LANGUAGE The spoken word is tonal: the same sound can have different meanings according to the tone with which it is pronounced. There are five tones – low, high, midpitch and rising and falling. Westerners find it difficult to learn when one word – *ma* – can mean "horse", "dog" or the verb "to come" depending on pronunciation.

EPIC TALES Thai folk tales draw on Indian mythology, using themes of romance or the feats of divine heroes. They were usually written in verse form. *Khun Chang Khun*

Painted fishing boat, Songkhla

Phan is a Thai epic about a love triangle of a woman with two lovers and is often recited with a rhythmic percussion accompaniment.

Another classic is the *Ramakian*, the Thai version of the famous Indian epic *Ramayana*. The version current in Thailand today was written by the first two kings of the Chakri dynasty. It records the state ceremonies and traditions of the Thai royalty and is the theme of the large murals which adorn the walls of Wat Phra Keo, the Royal Chapel of the Emerald Buddha in Bangkok.

The *Jataka* are popular folk tales relating to the previous lives of the Buddha, mixing traditional folklore and pre-Buddhist legend with down-to-earth wisdom and high spirituality. One of the most popular, which teaches the virtue of generosity, is the tale of Prince Vessandan (a previous incarnation of the Buddha) who gives away everything, including his wife and children. Its thousand verses are usually chanted at temples over a three-day period in October, at the end of *Phansa*, the Buddhist Lent.

MODERN LITERATURE A journalistic heritage is reflected in modern social realism novels which deal with problems such as poverty, prostitution and corruption, as well as the formulaic themes of cops and robbers, romance and ghost stories.

One of Thailand's most famous novelist is the late Kukrit Pramoj, whose career as writer, critic and left-of-centre politician eventually led him to become prime minister in

> ❏ King Ramkhamhaeng is said to have been responsible for developing Thai script and the first Thai literary work, a famous stone inscription, supposedly of the late 13th century, extolling the glories of the Sukhothai kingdom. Thai script reads from left to right, although vowel sounds may be written after, before, above or below the consonant they follow. ❏

1975. One of his best known works is *Red Bamboo*, the conflict between two boyhood friends in a remote village: one becomes a Buddhist monk, the other a Communist cell organiser. Both have a zeal for improving the village but disagree totally on how to do it. They finally unite to drive out a rapacious landowner.

One of the most celebrated of the new-wave writers is Pira Sudham, a Thai who writes in English about life in poverty-stricken Isan, in the northeast of Thailand. His *Monsoon Country* portrays the odyssey of Prem, an outcast in his own village. He is taunted by the other village children who call him Tadpole.

Prem manages to escape his village to attend university in Bangkok, and wins a scholarship to study in England. His quest for knowledge leads him to become thoroughly Westernised, leading a life of luxury in Germany and even winning poetry prizes in Western languages.

But Prem never forgets his roots in Isan. Eventually he rejects Western materialism, burns his Western clothes and goes back to his village to become a Buddhist monk.

FILMS Recent films showing the darker side of modern teenage society have revealed to the older generations attitudes and behaviour of their children. *Fun Bar Karaoke* portrays how misguided ambition leads to compromise of morals and self-respect: a teenager desires to be a model and ruins herself with drugs, giving sexual favours for contracts.

Hard-hitting *Dek Saeplae* focuses on the theme of how uncaring or ignorant parents force their children out of the home and onto the Bangkok streets, where gangs are formed as a substitute for comfort and protection.

Kon Jorn reintroduces Buddhist virtues to society: a young boy from a broken family comes to live on the streets, but his positive frame of mind elevates him above members of a society who are struggling with materialism and are unhappy with their lives.

PAINTING The theme of much Thai painting is the *Tosachat*, the name given to the last 10 of the Buddhistic *Jataka* tales. These can be seen on wall murals, temple banners, canvas paintings, manuscripts and carvings on bookcases. Some of the best examples are at Wat Suwannaram

> ❏ Recent research has shown that the Thais may have been the originators of many Oriental styles of ceramic which later developed in China, not the other way around. Some pottery kilns date back to AD 900. ❏

in Thonburi where formal gestures and religious symbols are skilfully blended with naturalistic observations of people working, relaxing, gossiping and even flirting.

Modern art made its appearance with the heroic realism of the Italian sculptor Corrado Feroci. He was invited to the court of King Vajiravudh and commissioned in Thailand's first flush of "democracy" to sculpt the

Democracy Monument (1939) and the Victory Monument (1941).

During the 1960s and 1970s many Thai artists experimented with abstract forms. King Bhumiphol himself is an accomplished artist. The style of his more abstract works has been compared to that of Expressionist artists Edvard Munch and Oskar Kokoschka.

Lop Buri is famed as the birthplace of a distinctive and highly developed school of sculpture specialising in both Mahayana and Theravada figures of the Buddha in bronze and, later, sandstone. The best Lop Buri Buddhas are marvellously authoritative with diadems enclosing a conical *ushnisha* – this is protuberance on the crown of the head which symbolises enlightenment.

MUSIC Traditional Thai music, pentatonic in origin, is sometimes difficult for Westerners to appreciate. It is a rich polyphony of subtle variations in tone, texture and

pipe instruments are common in the north and northeast. In some of them several bamboo pipes are bound together to form a sort of mouth

> ❑ "... [in Thai music] not a single note between a starting note and its octave agrees with any of the notes of the European scale."– Sir Hubert Parry (19th-century British composer). ❑

organ called a *khaen*.

The Thais have developed their own version of a classical orchestra called a *piphat*, which can include as many as 20 players. The *piphat* was the traditional accompaniment to classical shadow theatre (*nang*) and dance-dramas, *khon*.

Khon or "masked" drama is on of several traditional forms which were revived by the early Chakri kings. It is believed to be about 400 years old and is almost always an

Thai musicians

mood, tuneful and often played at a fearsome pace. Behind the strange melodies lies an eight-note scale, but unlike Western music the stress is on full note intervals without semitones.

One common instrument is the *pi*, a woodwind instrument with a reed mouthpiece. One place you can hear it being played at Thai boxing contests. The *pin* is similar to the Indian banjo (*vina*), while the *ranad ek* is like a wood-block xylophone. Bamboo

enactment of the *Ramakian*. It was developed from the ancient Thai arts of *nang yai* ("shadow play") and *krabee-krabong*, which is a form of theatrical fencing. Originally all the actors would wear masks and mimed one of the 138 *Ramakian* episodes to the music of a *piphat* orchestra. Over the centuries the costumes and head-dresses have become more and more stylised. There are also established musical idioms for moods such as anger and grief and actions such as weeping.

46

The ancient art of Thai massage – nuat phaen boran – is quite an experience. Like other Eastern forms of massage, it balances the body's energies by working on the acupressure points and meridians – sen – in a similar way to acupuncture. It can be quite vigorous, but it feels wonderful and it's certainly a great cure for sitting in any one place too long.

The beach is a good place to find a massage. Pattaya and Phuket in particular are home to the bands of blue-shirted women who have cards of accreditation; most hire out their services individually. Hotels and guesthouses will also provide facilities and the larger ones, such as The Pearl in Phuket, will have specialised staff. (traditional massage for 200 baht per hour, with a minimum of two hours. The Rajdamri Spa also offers spa facilities, which are available for 350 baht per person). In Chiang Mai is Massage Salon Loi Kroh found at 63/3 Loi Kroh Road, tel or fax: 053 274 681 (150 baht per hour and teaching courses are also available).

❏ *Caveat emptor!*
Watch out for the distinction between the ancient and "modern" massages.
The latter is a quaint euphemism for sexual services and some establisments offer both! ❏

Take time out at one of the establishments offering traditional massage for a thoroughly relaxing experience

WHERE TO GO In Bangkok, massage is available at many large hotels. The "jet-lag massage" in the Oriental's Health Spa will soothe fatigue. **The Two Doctors** apothecary shop is on Ha Prachan Road near Wat Mahathat. Here are preserved some traditions of the Thai masseur such as the prayer to Jivaka Kumarabaccha, the Buddha's personal physician and early disciple. The scriptures mention practices which bear a striking resemblance to those of today.

   Places offering massage in Bangkok include Emiri Massage, which employs practitioners from Wat Po, 212/38 Sukhumvit Plaza Soi 12, tel: 02 253 0566 (500 baht for 2 hours; open 11 AM-1 AM); and Rajdamri Spa, 35/2-8 Rajdamri Road, Lumpini, Pathumwan, tel: 02 6550557-8

Thailand is well served with internal flights to all important cities and major tourist resorts and a railway network extends into most regions of the country. Buses run in and between most towns and cities, but in city centres the traffic can be chaotic. River boats are the favourite means of travel from Bangkok up river – to Ayutthaya, for example.

IN THE EARLY DAYS The first rickshaw was introduced to Bangkok about 1871, and within a generation it became so popular that the government had to regulate its control and safety. Horse-drawn trams arrived in 1888, later converted into electric trams. Just after the beginning of the new century Prince Rabi, one of King Chulalongkorn's sons, could be seen driving the first motor car.

RAILWAYS The first railway was completed in 1900, between Bangkok and Nakhon Ratchasima. Major railway lines now connect the cities of

On the road, Southern Thailand

Chiang Mai, Nong Khai and Ratchathani with Bangkok. Trains also run directly into Malaysia and Singapore. Before the French Indo-China War (1945–54) there were trains to Cambodia too, and these are

being resumed. Trains are often more comfortable than buses over long distances – but tickets must be booked several days (at least) in advance.

CANALS AND RIVERS Bangkok was full of *khlongs* (canals) up until the 1950s, with many small boats plying up and down. Although that network has collapsed, the mayor of Bangkok has organised limited service of river and canal taxis along those waterways that remain. The Chao Phraya express service is great fun and often faster than bus or taxi. It can be picked up from many points on either side of the river. There are also long-tail boat taxis which are shared with other passengers. In northern Thailand, the boat trip from Tha Ton to Chiang Rai is strongly recommended for its views, while Nong Khai offers scenic cruises on the Mekong River.

BUSES running regular routes in the city are reliable and cheap, once you get the hang of how to use them. The conductor keeps tickets and loose change in a metal tube about 40cm long. The hinged metal lid of the tube is used to clip off tickets from the roll. Although buses are frequent, the signs are seldom in English and can be confusing. Local passengers will often help if you get lost or confused.

There are three kinds of bus in

❏ People often complain, with regard to transportation, that when Thai civil servants take out their scissors to cut red tape, "they cut it lengthwise". ❏

48

Bangkok: the regular public buses follow a more or less standard timetable along fixed routes; air-conditioned buses connect the main bus stations and centres and private air-conditioned bus services are available at many hotels and offices with a de luxe service. Buses are extremely inexpensive, but are also nearly always packed to capacity.

OVERHEAD TRANSIT In 1999 Bangkok celebrated the opening of the Skytrain, its overhead transit system, which has proved popular for those who can afford the fairly high price of a ticket.

The system runs two interconnecting lines which cover the commercial areas of Silom, Sukhumvit and the central shopping districts, and extends out to the Chao Phraya river and both Northern and Eastern bus terminals.

Construction has also begun on an underground system which must rely heavily on high-tech engineering to overcome the difficulties of the swampy terrain and problems of flooding that occur almost every year.

ALTERNATIVES IN TOWN Many *tuk tuks* (motorised trishaws or *samlors*), are cheaper than taxis over short distances – provided you bargain a little. *Tuk tuk* drivers mostly rent their vehicles and operate on a very tight budget, working long hours to ensure that they at least break even. The original non-motorised *samlors* still survive in the provinces, but were banned in Bangkok some years ago. In Chiang Mai and other regional centres there are *songthaews* – small pickup trucks with two rows of seats – which pursue a more or less fixed route. Taxis, where all the windows can be tightly closed and some air-conditioning turned on, afford a little more comfort but can be expensive.

❏ Until the 1930s trains and canal boats were the only means of communication between Bangkok and the provinces. ❏

The Skytrain has helped to reduce traffic

The king is the most famous person in Thailand. His portrait appears everywhere, including in nearly all Thai homes, his name is endlessly invoked and his appearances attract huge crowds. Besides the king, there is a host of cultural figures who have high profiles, ranging from sportsmen, actors, authors and singers to Buddhist monks and beauty queens.

ROYALTY AND POLITICS On one of his regular walks through remote villages the king discovered that people knew in advance that he was coming and would "get things ready" for him. He decided not to tell anybody where he wanted to go, so that his fairly large retinue would set out with no idea of their destination. However, this proved too chaotic in terms of logistics, so now the king compromises. Half of his visits are a surprise, half are planned in advance – a very Thai solution!

In politics, General Chamlong Srimuang, the Mayor of Bangkok and a Buddhist ascetic, has endeared himself to the Bangkok population. He has foresworn sex, meat and alcohol, sleeps on the floor and is regular in his Buddhist prayers.

RELIGIOUS FIGURES Some Buddhist monks have become celebrities in Thailand, such as the popular Phra Bodhirak, the former TV producer and singer, who is now the flamboyant and controversial leader of the radical Santi Asoke (Peace and No Sorrow) sect. Buddhadasa, the founder of the Suan Mokh movement, is well known throughout the country for preaching "dharmic socialism" (see page 30).

In the world of industry and commerce Dhanin Chearavanont and Chatri Sophonpanich, heading the Charoen Pokphand group and the Bangkok Bank respectively, are the leaders. In each case their father emigrated from China, and they represent the first generation of their family to be Thai-born. Both are famous for having key friends in the leadership of the political parties and the army.

WRITERS Thailand's most famous writers are the late Kukrit Pramoj, author of *Red Bamboo*, and the new-wave writer Kampoon Boontawee. Kukrit also wrote *Four Reigns*, a fictionalised story of the royal family, of which he was a minor son. He founded the newspaper *Siam Rath*, one of the few successful radical publications, and as a result became highly regarded among journalists. He also portrayed the prime minister of Sarkis in the film *The Ugly American*, in which Marlon Brando was the star.

> ❑ Phornthip Narkhirunkanok was Thailand's most successful beauty queen of the late 1980s, and became a national heroine after winning the Miss Universe competition in 1988. Many Thais did not seem to care that she had spent almost her entire life abroad in California. ❑

POPULAR CULTURE Thongchai McIntyre (known as Bird), born to a Scottish-Thai father and a Malaysian mother in Bangkok, was the ninth of ten children: he has always held his parents in very high esteem. He joined the Grammy Company where he met Rewat Budhinan, the man behind his success. P'Teur, as he is called, wrote many songs for Bird, including those on the *Boomerang* album which catapulted him to fame. Bird went on to release many successful albums, most notably *Bird Chilli*, and became a movie actor, winning widespread acclaim in *Sunset at Chaophraya*.

The king visits his people

Former Miss Thailand winner (1994), Pop Areeya Sirisopa, was born in 1971. She grew up in Thailand and eventually went to the US where she graduated from Michigan State University. She wrote an autobiographical book about her life as a soldier and military instructor, and co-starred in the film *Niramit* ("Creation") with Bird Thongchai.

Christina Aguilar, born in the Philippines of Filipino, French and Spanish blood, is one of a new generation of "non-Thais" to make it big in the Thai entertainment industry. Her song *Pik lok* ("Turned Upside Down") launched her career, for which she won the MTV Asian viewer choice award for best music video in 1992. Since then she has achieved remarkable success with the Grammy recording studios of popular and dance music.

GOLF Eldrick "Tiger" Woods, born in 1975 in Cypress, California, now resides in Orlando, Florida. Hugely popular in Thailand, he was awarded honorary Thai citizenship in 1998, as he is one quarter Thai by birth; in fact his father is half black, one-quarter American Indian and one-quarter Chinese, while his mother is half Thai, one-quarter Chinese and one-quarter white. He dropped out of university to become a professional golfer in his junior year. His first tournament as a pro was at the Greater Milwaukee Open on 29 August, 1996, in which he tied for 60th place: he is now regarded as the world's greatest player, holding several golfing world records. He was granted an honorary Doctorate of Philosophy by Kasetsart University in 2000 in recognition of his talent.

Tiger Woods has become one of the most successful golfers of all time

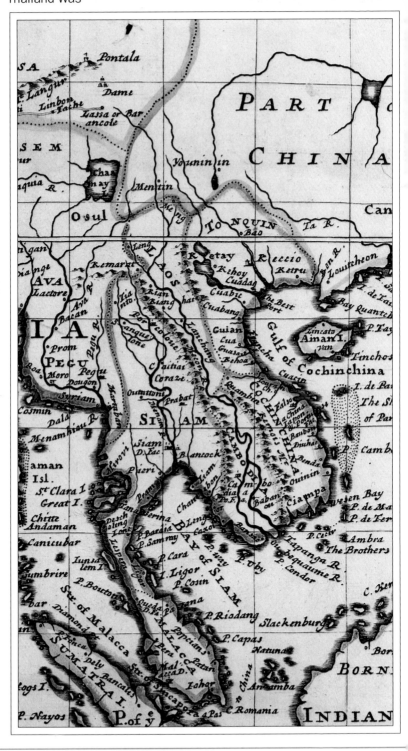

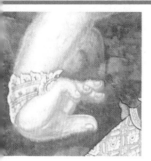

The origins of the Thai people themselves are obscure. It is generally accepted that the ancestors of the Thais were, by the 7th century AD, living in the kingdom of Nanchao, in what is today China's Yunnan province. The slow migration southwards began in about AD 900 and was probably speeded up by the Mongol invasions of China in the mid-13th century.

BEGINNINGS Before the Thais reached Thailand there had already been sophisticated Mon and Khmer civilisations, influenced by India, in the region. Some artefacts remain from these early cultures, in the form of Indian Gupta-style Buddhas, terracotta heads and some stucco reliefs on the walls of the few remaining buildings of antiquity. Theravada Buddhism may have been introduced to these agrarian city state cultures by Indian missionaries as early as the 2nd or 3rd century BC.

> ❏ Rama Tibodi I is noted for the promulgation of the first recorded Thai legal system. ❏

The early Thais practised a rice agronomy, and their religion was a mixture of Buddhism and animism. This was a country ruled by a monarchy with periodic corvée (forced) labour; as yet there were no instances of peasant revolt or class warfare. In the 12th and 13th centuries the Thai migrants from China, by now converted to Theravada Buddhism, set up little fiefdom states in the upper reaches of the Chao Phraya valley. These began to impinge on the Khmer empire to the south and the Mons to the west in Burma.

THE SUKHOTHAI PERIOD Many histories mark the beginning of the Thais as a distinct people with King Phra Ruang's capture of Sukhothai in 1253 from the Khmers; and the

Detail from temple mural, Wat Phra Kaeo

Sukhothai period is often seen as the golden age in Thai history.

The Thais were strongly influenced by the Indianised culture of the Mons, especially their art, sculpture and literature. From the Khmers the Thais borrowed Brahminical doctrines of political organisation, a written script and improved agricultural technology. Sukhothai reached its peak with the late 13th-century reign of Ramkhamhaeng (the first Thai king to be called "the Great"), who extended his kingdom to the Bay of Bengal, Luang Prabang and the Malay peninsula.

The second Thai capital was founded at Ayutthaya in 1350 by Rama Tibodi I, who captured Khmer and Sukhothai territories until his realm extended from Laos in the north and as far as the Malacca straits in the south.

> ❏ Paul Benedict (in *Austro-Thai Language and Culture*) has speculated on linguistic evidence that the Thais came from Indonesia and Southeast Asia before migrating northwards into China. ❏

It was during the Ayutthaya period that elaborate royal rituals and the Khmer ideas of the king being a god were introduced. However, in spite of all the pomp and tribute the Thai kings' power was actually quite limited until the great centralising reforms of King Trailok (1448–88), who set up the Thai civil service and stipulated carefully the amount of land to which each rank of official

53

was entitled. He also codified the bemusing complexity of royal household etiquette and introduced the idea of having a second or vice-king to simplify succession problems.

FROM OUTSIDE THAILAND

Thailand's first Western contact was with the Portuguese at the beginning of the 16th century; a century later, French, English, Japanese, Dutch and Spanish mercenaries, missionaries and traders were visiting Ayutthaya in considerable numbers. They were stunned by the wealth of the city.

Thai tolerance of Westerners became strained after a charismatic Greek adventurer, Constantin Phaulkon, achieved such a high

status in the Thai court that he began to take over Thailand's foreign policy, favouring the French at the expense of the Dutch. He was executed in 1688 – perhaps the only Westerner ever to have been executed in Thailand.

Throughout this period, Thailand was fighting wars against both Burma (now Myanmar) and Cambodia. After several defeats in the mid-16th century, Thailand became for a time little more than a vassal state of Burma. The Burmese invaded again in 1765. After a two-year siege the Burmese razed the great Thai metropolis of Ayutthaya to the ground and carried off an immense amount of booty and 30,000 prisoners. The sack of Ayutthaya and the loss of all her cultural treasures was a terrible blow to the Thais, who have never completely forgiven the Burmese.

A temple mural from the 18th-century Wat Phra Keo, where the Emerald Buddha is contained

Chao Phya Chakri became King Rama I of the new Chakri dynasty (reigned 1782–1809). His many achievements included the founding of a new royal palace and temple and the construction of Bangkok, originally designed to be an exact replica of Ayutthaya. He also reformed the Buddhist sangha. *He repelled a full-scale invasion by Burma in 1785 – and fought four more wars with Burma before his death in 1809.*

BEFORE RAMA I Phya Tak, or Taksin, was a general of mixed Thai–Chinese parentage, who showed great courage in fighting the Burmese. As King Taksin he established a new capital further down the Chao Phraya River at Thonburi (on the opposite bank from Bangkok), and eventually brought the provinces and large areas of Laos under Thai control.

Taksin's descent into madness and increasing cruelty eventually led to a rebellion in Thonburi in 1782. The king's most trusted general, Tongduang (Chao Phya Chakri), was summoned back from military campaigning in Cambodia to take a lead.

A Wat Phra Keo mural (below); and (above) King Rama I

❏ The first printing press was set up in Bangkok in 1835. The future King Mongkut (Rama IV) was the first Thai to set up his own press, which he used to print Buddhist books. ❏

It was decided that both the king and the rebels should be put to death. Taksin was put into a sack and beaten to death with sandalwood clubs. So Chao Phya Chakri became King Rama I and founder of the Chakri dynasty.

THE 19TH CENTURY By the time Rama III was crowned, the Burmese were engrossed in fighting the British colonialists on their western frontier, leaving Thailand free to build up an empire to the east in Indo-China.

The early 19th century was also a time when European nations began to make a real impact on Thai life: trade treaties were signed with Britain (1826) and the USA (1833) – the first such American treaty with an Asian country.

By the late 1840s there was increasing diplomatic and military pressure to revise earlier trade agreements, but Thailand scented the threat of Western imperialism, to which its neighbours were fast succumbing.

❏ During King Taksin's 1778 invasion of Laos the 2,000-year-old sacred Emerald Buddha was recaptured and installed at Thonburi. ❏

In 1851 King Mongkut ascended the throne of Thailand for a reign of 17 years, during which the foundations of the kingdom's modernisation were firmly laid. He was succeeded by his 16-year-old son, Chulalongkorn, who instituted many reforms and managed to keep the European colonial threat at bay.

KING MONGKUT At the age of 20 Mongkut had been ordained as a Buddhist monk, and before becoming king he spent 27 years in the monkhood. This gave him the opportunity to tour the country, discovering the people's needs and complaints, and learning much from the foreigners who had begun to reside in Thailand. In particular, he learned English from American missionaries, which he later used to advantage to correspond personally with Queen Victoria and President Lincoln.

MONGKUT'S ACHIEVEMENTS
Mongkut had to agree to new treaties with Britain and the US, giving foreigners extraterritorial immunity from the Thai courts. These treaties allowed Thai trade with the West to

> ❏ A *Bangkok Post* editorial called the musical *The King and I* "patronising, ignorant, stupidly comic and an affront to the Thai people". It is still officially banned, although videos circulate clandestinely in Bangkok. ❏

expand. He entirely reformed the taxation system, modernised the armed forces and police, and built roads and canals.

Mongkut was the king who hired Mrs Anna Leonowens, an English widow from Singapore, to teach his 82 children in the palace in the 1860s. It was her books, *An English Governess at the Siamese Court* and *The Romance of the Harem*, which formed the basis of the musical *The King and I*, in which Yul Brynner caricatured the part of King Mongkut.

Having studied astronomy, Mongkut astonished foreigners by correctly predicting the eclipse of the sun in 1868 – but while making the calculation in a remote part of southern Thailand, he caught malaria, and died soon afterwards. His 16-year-old son, Chulalongkorn, succeeded him.

KING CHULALONGKORN Once Anna Leonowens' star pupil, Chulalongkorn's long reign (1868–1910) allowed him to fulfil his father's plans and bring Thailand to the point of modernity. He travelled to Singapore, Java (in Indonesia) and India, and twice to western Europe, intensifying his desire to continue the Westernisation of his kingdom.

CHULALONGKORN'S ACHIEVEMENTS
Chulalongkorn abolished the practice of perpetual prostration in the royal presence, and simplified the court dress and hairstyle. He abolished slavery, reformed the Buddhist *sangha*, formed a council of state and privy council to regularise the government, and set up 12 ministries to carry out government functions. The king himself wrote more than 200 books of history, archaeology, literature and public affairs. Modern schools were started, one of them destined to become Chulalongkorn University. Until then boys – but not girls – used to study informally under the monks in the Buddhist temples.

The first railway was opened, and currency was improved with modern minting. Everything in this absolute monarchy depended on a royal lead, so Chulalongkorn's reforming zeal was indispensable. The affection which Thais still feel towards this

great king may be observed every 23 October when people pay homage to his statue at the Royal Plaza.

Apart from the continuous and systematic modernisation of the country along mainly French, British and German lines, the most important achievement during these two crucial reigns from 1851 to 1910 was the preservation of Thai independence. In the second half of his reign the king was under constant pressure from the British and French colonial advance in neighbouring territories. He had to cede Laos, parts of Cambodia and control of the four Malay states of Kedah, Perlis, Kelantan and Trengganu to those two European powers. This was agreed to reluctantly, and only because it fended off the threat of one or both of these taking over the whole of Thailand.

This was the high tide of European colonialism. The British slowly nibbled away at the Malay states and had started to overrun Burma (now

Opposite page: King Mongkut (Rama IV); and (above) King Chulalongkorn (Rama V)

Myanmar) in 1824, while the French established a foothold in Vietnam. Thailand thus faced European imperialism on three sides: to the east, west and south.

The "open door" treaties of the 1850s postponed the threat to the kingdom's independence by satisfying the short-term commercial ambitions of the French, British and others. Luckily, the appetite for further conquest began to wane in the 1890s, and there was an agreement between Britain and France not to annex Thailand.

❏ "Never having been colonised, we can only blame ourselves for our problems." – Former Prime Minister Kukrit Pramoj. ❏

Chulalongkorn's immediate successors were neither as able nor as wise. The relative unpopularity of Prajadhipok led to discontent, which strengthened conspirators during the depression of the 1930s. When fighting broke out between democrats and loyalists in 1935, King Prajadhipok abdicated in disgust, leaving his 10-year-old nephew as next in line.

KING VAJIRAVUDH (reigned 1910–25) succeeded his father, Chulalongkorn. He tried to continue the reforms of his father and grandfather, although he lacked their charisma and strength of character. The new king tried to promote nationalism by creating the Wild Tigers' Corp and the Village Scouts organisations. But this "praetorian guard" made Vajiravudh unpopular with the army and navy.

MORE CHANGES Government ministries continued to be reformed and Vajiravudh introduced surnames for Thai people – who had not hitherto felt the need of them. After his stay in Britain he introduced soccer, Western-style dancing and Western hairstyles for women. He made Siam (as Thailand was then known) the first Asian country to bring in compulsory education, and opened the country's first boarding public school. He wrote copiously, under various pen names, translating many of Shakespeare's plays, and giving his views on the Chinese in Thailand in a book called *The Jews in the Far East*. He was so generous and extravagant that the national budget was gravely overspent.

Sympathetic with the Allied cause in World War I, Vajiravudh declared war on Germany in 1917. In 1921 the Americans agreed to a new treaty foregoing their former extraterritorial demands, thus setting an example for other Western powers to follow in respecting Thailand's independence. This was King Vajiravudh's greatest achievement.

Whereas Mongkut had 39 wives and 82 children, and Chulalongkorn had 36 wives and 77 children, Vajiravudh preferred male company. Marrying late, his only child was a daughter; he was therefore succeeded by his younger brother, Prajadhipok (reigned 1925–35).

KING PRAJADHIPOK The new king, who had studied at Eton College in England, also lacked the strong will of his earlier predecessors, though he proved conscientious and thrifty, and retrenched government officials by hundreds in order to balance the books. When visiting the United States in 1931, King Prajadhipok shook hands with several Siamese students. This was the first time that any Siamese had ever touched his monarch without being punished.

The world depression of 1929–30 meant that the king had to reduce official salaries again, as well as raise taxes, and this emboldened a group of ambitious army and navy officers and civil servants to change the regime.

THE BLOODLESS REVOLUTION On 24 June 1932 the People's Party, whose leaders were almost all European-educated, led a *coup d'état* to remove the absolute powers of the king and introduce democracy. The king agreed to become a constitutional monarch and the revolution succeeded without bloodshed. A new constitution set up a national assembly, with power to name the prime minister. But the conspirators soon fell out. Their economic spokesman, Pridi Panomyong, a French-trained left-winger, was unable to persuade them to back his utopian plans to nationalise land and enterprises and put everyone on a state payroll.

58

When King Prajadhipok abdicated in 1935, retiring to exile in England, he left no son. The succession thus passed to his nephew, who was then a boy of 10, and in no position to withstand the plots and ploys of the revolutionary democrats.

One of the early acts of the revolutionaries was to celebrate the arrival of democracy by changing the name of the country from Siam to Thailand. Nationalists among the "democratic" group argued that Siam was not a Thai word but one used by foreigners to describe Thailand and therefore unsuitable for a free and independent country.

Offerings lie at the feet of the statue of reformer King Vajiravudh (Rama VI) in Bangkok

They also reasoned that the 23 million Thai-speaking people beyond the frontiers, in southern China, French Indo-China and Burma (Myanmar), needed to be reflected in the kingdom's name. It was one of the *coup* leaders, Phibul, who decided on Thailand – "Thai" meaning "free" – as the new name of the country, although many criticised it as being a bastardised conjunction for using the English word "land".

❏ The name *Prathet Thai* is now used offically, or more casually the term *Muang Thai* is heard. Both names translate as "country of the free". ❏

Two men dominated Thai public life for 25 years following the 1932 revolution – Pridi Panomyong and Phibul Songkram. Pridi was a brilliant Doctor of Law from the University of Paris, who served as Regent while King Ananda Mahidol was a minor, and then later as prime minister. Phibul became prime minister and the Army's Commander-in-Chief, surviving difficult times to stay in power.

PRIDI PANOMYONG Part Chinese, Pridi had extremely egalitarian views – bordering on Marxist – although he was acquitted of being a Communist by a high-powered committee including a royal prince, the Chief Justice and a British legal adviser. He became Foreign Minister and tackled the further revision of treaties with foreign countries, something high on the agenda of the revolutionaries.

After Thailand declared war on Britain and the US in 1942, Pridi organised an underground resistance movement against the Japanese. When the Japanese surrendered, Pridi, in his capacity as Regent, officially repudiated the earlier declaration of war on the US and Britain, an action which saved Thailand immense trouble in the post-war period. In the following year Pridi became prime minister.

At this point Pridi seemed to be in the ascendant, triumphing over his conservative opponents. But an unexpected tragedy snatched the prize from his grasp. The young king, who had returned from Switzerland, where he had been studying, was found dead in bed in the Grand Palace on 9 June 1946, a revolver by his side and a bullet wound in his head. The story behind his death has remained a puzzle, in spite of public investigations.

Meanwhile the economy had suddenly plunged, with high prices and scarcity of food, and this encouraged the right-wingers to act. There was another bloodless *coup d'état* in November 1947, as a result of which Pridi had to flee from the country, leaving his rival Phibul as the new Army Commander-in-Chief, poised for a prolonged domination of the country's politics.

Pridi Panomyong poses with his family during his years of exile

PHIBUL SONGKRAM was one of the leaders of the 1932 revolution. He then led the army again in the *coup d'état* of 1933. In 1938 he was made prime minister on a platform of national reconstruction along progressive lines. In the immediate

> ❏ Phibul decreed that men and women should wear Western clothes, kiss each other in public, give up chewing betel-nuts and learn Western dancing. ❏

aftermath of World War II, Phibul was in semi-disgrace, having backed the Japanese side. But he was soon to make a comeback, being confirmed as Army Commander-in-Chief in 1947 and resuming the premiership in 1948.

During this time, Phibul excluded the Chinese from many occupations (including farming, taxi-driving and hairdressing), and made Chinese schools teach the Thai language and culture. However, following visits to many Western countries, his hitherto autocratic regime became more liberal; he had come back deeply impressed by the way in which Western democratic governments were organised.

He encouraged public debate, passed many labour laws and recognised the Trades Union Congress. The result was that the government's manipulation of the general elections of 1957 was exposed and denounced, where before the scandal would have been endured in silence.

Phibul himself was no money-grabber, but others in his cabinet were hugely corrupt, especially his Minister of Defence, Sarit Thanarat. In July 1957 disaffected army officers led by Sarit deposed Phibul, and he fled to exile in Japan.

Yet Phibul's physical resilience was legendary. He was once shot in the neck and shoulder at a football match, but recovered. A couple of years later his family dinner was poisoned, but again he recovered. He escaped from a ship where he was being held by rebels in the middle of the Chao Phraya River. His side strafed the vessel and everyone jumped overboard but he swam to the bank held by rebel soldiers. Later, a prince who had witnessed the scene asked why he hadn't made for his own side. Phibul replied that no one would have recognised him in

> ❏ Pridi's great memorial is the Thammasat University, which he founded, and which remains a centre of radical thinking in Thailand. ❏

the dark and anyway his side were better shots!

Both Pridi and Phibul remained in exile. Pridi spent many years in Canton, in the People's Republic of China, and later lived just outside Paris. He made several soundings to successive Thai governments for a return, but none of them felt the risk was worthwhile, given the former prime minister's radical views and powerful personality.

The great international wars of the 20th century have been crucial in the formation of Thai policy and the alignment of the kingdom in its regional and global setting. Thailand entered World War I on the side of the British and French; the position in World War II was more complicated; while the Vietnam War was far closer to home and much more dangerous.

WORLD WAR I In spite of the trouble experienced at their hands in the colonial period, Thailand backed the British and French in the Great War. This was largely because King Vajiravudh had become an Anglophile, with many English friends from his years at the Sandhurst military college and at Christ Church, Oxford. The decision enabled Thailand to participate in the conference of Versailles in 1919 and to lobby effectively for the abolition of the unequal treaties with Western countries.

WORLD WAR II saw fierce fighting going on in neighbouring countries and a seemingly unstoppable Japanese advance. There was no reason for Thailand to become involved in the European war, but Thailand

Thai soldiers help a released prisoner of war in Vietnam

and Japan had the distinction of being the only Asian countries to be independently represented at Versailles, and they had naturally formed some ties. When Japan sent armies into China and Southeast Asia, attacking European colonies, the Thais had mixed feelings. The Japanese could hardly restrain themselves from occupying Thailand, after their success in Vietnam, and there was no effective British or French force available to protect Thailand. Temptingly, the Japanese offered to restore some of the territory which Thailand had given up to France earlier. The Thais actually had a short war with France in early 1941 and lost a naval engagement.

One of Phibul's advisers warned that Japan's intention was "to chase away the white men from Asia and put itself in their shoes". But Phibul's government declared war on the

Allies, though it allowed a degree of ambiguity as to whether the declaration had been effectively delivered to them. Thailand continued technically independent and sovereign throughout the war period.

The presence of more than 50,000 Japanese troops made it impossible for Phibul to act against Japan. All the same, he was no puppet: he would not enter the Japanese Co-Prosperity Sphere, or attend the Greater East Asia Conference, or send his children for schooling in

government was able to take over in Bangkok. This was the moment for Pridi, who was able to persuade the Allies not to treat Thailand as an enemy, but almost as a friend. As a result, there was no formal occupation by the British army, as might otherwise have been expected.

THE VIETNAM WAR In 1954 the Thais had already joined Pakistan and the Philippines with the Western powers in the South East Asia Treaty Organisation, under which Thailand

A US pilot makes contact

Japan. A measure of real independence was maintained. Meanwhile, Thais who disagreed with the Axis alignment started a Free Thai Movement in the USA which linked with pro-Allied agents within Thailand, so that when Japan was defeated in 1945 a new pro-Allied

❏ "…like a fox arbitrating a dispute between two rabbits in a cabbage patch, preparing to fatten them before eating both of them." – An American critic of the Japanese offer.
"What would you do if you were a rabbit?" – A future Thai prime minister. ❏

provided bases from which American bombers wreaked havoc on Vietnam in the 1960s and early 1970s. Thailand had little option but to join the United States in contesting Vietnamese Communism, which was loudly hostile to Thailand. The Queen's Cobra Regiment of Thailand actually served in South Vietnam, fighting against the Communists. However Thailand's other neighbours were mostly neutral in the conflict.

When the Vietnam War ended in 1975 it was followed by the Vietnamese invasion of Cambodia. This was also a threat to Thailand, and so the Thais collaborated in helping those resisting Vietnamese occupation, including the Khmer Rouge, whose brutal treatment of their own population was later revealed to a shocked world.

After the two dominating personalities of Pridi and Phibul came three more generals who tried to play the same role, though they were less successful. Field Marshal Sarit Thanarat was succeeded by the weaker Field Marshal Thanom Kittikachorn and his portly, pugnacious deputy, Field Marshal Praphas Charusathien.

FIELD MARSHAL SARIT THANARAT

Sarit was half Laotian. He had the temerity to bundle Phibul out of the country, largely because the former dictator had interfered with Sarit's improper profits from the state lottery.

In spite of his corruption, however, he proved to be rather popular. He reversed many of Phibul's unpopular reforms, including those dictating the style of dress; he even tried to bring down the prices of electricity, sugar, charcoal and other items. The Chinese were encouraged, during his dictatorship, to feel that they were an accepted part of Thai society. He brought the young King Bhumiphol forward and gave him a bigger role in public affairs – something which the king fully exploited – as a symbol of Thai nationalism and traditional culture. Sarit could also be tough: he closed down the weekly dance at the Lumphini Garden; arrested men with long hair, tight trousers or flashy clothes; made rock-and-roll and the Twist illegal; and ordered summary executions of arsonists.

Sarit often expounded the idea that democracy needed to be adapted to the Thai genius in order to succeed. Political parties were abolished. Sarit governed without a parliament and managed to postpone indefinitely the writing of a new constitution. He set a new precedent in Thailand for open army rule. He never studied abroad and did not share the ideals of those who promoted Western-style parliamentary democracy. His direction of the economy proved invaluable, since he turned away from the state-enterprise ideas of both Pridi and Phibul to encourage investment of private capital, both domestic and foreign. Sarit's First Six-Year Plan (1961) provided the basis for the economic development that was to astonish observers later.

Everyone knew that Sarit had a strong appetite for sex, and that he had many mistresses. Only after his death in 1963, however, did it come out that he maintained 100 mistresses in great style, using illegal income from various official funds and using government influence for private financial gain. Sarit left an estate of US$140 million on his death, and everyone knew that it could not have come from his salary.

FIELD MARSHAL THANOM KITTIKACHORN

Sarit's successor was reticent by comparison. Under Thanom's rule (1963–73) the army had to come to terms with the idea of a constitution. After many years of drafting, a new constitution was proclaimed by the king in 1968. This made the prime minister responsible

> ❑ Thanom's son, Narong, married Praphas's daughter and became particularly hated as a crude implementer of the dictator's commands. The three were nicknamed "father, son and wholly gross". ❑

to parliament, and a general election was held in 1969: Thanom's party won a majority. But the various parliamentarians were so demanding and so unwilling to collaborate with the government in administering the country, and there was such insurgency in the border areas, that Thanom abrogated the constitution and proclaimed martial law in 1971.

Thanom and his deputy, Field Marshal Praphas Charusathien, were then faced with renewed demands for democracy and a constitution, and this came to a head in a bloody confrontation in 1973.

THE STUDENT RISING IN 1973

(see also pages 66–67) The students' revolt was sparked by the refusal of Premier Thanom's government to speed up the drafting of a new constitution. When 25 democrats protested about this near to the Thammasat University, half of them were arrested. This brought 100,000 students onto the streets into a rally and a protest march to the police headquarters took place.

The explosion finally came on 14 October 1973, when the soldiers and students clashed in a bloody battle, leaving 69 dead and more than 800 wounded, while the police headquarters was burnt down. Thanom and Praphas resigned, and were advised by the king to leave the country in order to prevent further violence.

With hindsight, the era of Thanom and Praphas was beneficial for Thailand in economic affairs and in many other respects. Sarit's policies were broadly followed especially within the economy. However, a harmful precedent was created in asserting the army's right to rule, and it did nothing for the concept of clean government.

Field Marshal Sarit Thanarat (centre), one of the Thai Generals

65

The students who had been so successful in 1973 sought to consolidate and extend their new-found power. They formed an alliance with workers and peasant groups, and also to some extent with the Communist Party of Thailand. The army leaders were demoralised by the exposure of corruption, and the new senior general showed no desire to enter government. The proliferation of political parties made democratic government ineffective. The king therefore filled the power vacuum.

The king came into his own after Thanom and Praphas had fled, appointing as new prime minister a British-trained judge, Sanya Dharmasakdi. The first civilian head of government for more than two decades, he and the king between them organised a large National Convention to elect a new Legislative Assembly.

The students and workers were forming groups and unions without police registration, contrary to the law, but Sanya persevered and a general election was held at the beginning of 1975. The first prime minister to be elected under the new

An anti-Generals statement

constitution was Kukrit Pramoj, a minor royal who was also a brilliant editor and novelist. Kukrit's chief success was in diplomacy. He was the first Thai premier to visit the People's Republic of China, where he secured the opening of diplomatic relations between the two countries. But his parliamentary support was unstable, and another election was held in 1976, which led to his elder brother, Seni Pramoj, becoming prime minister.

A rash of strikes broke out in factories and these were often supported by the students. In the rural areas, the new phenomenon of landless tenant farmers threw up peasant organisations which also lobbied for improvement. The Farmers' Federation of Thailand was set up with student help, to become a large and powerful body. In November 1974 about 50,000 students and farm-workers, led by young Buddhist monks, demonstrated in Bangkok.

While the army had been willing to take a back seat in the political arena after the scandals of previous military dictators, it was greatly concerned by the growth of radical and sometimes Communist-influenced pressure groups in the country. The students, however, seemed oblivious of the backlash which their actions were inviting.

RIGHT-WING BACKLASH Just as the students had sponsored new radical groups, so now right-wing military officers countered by sponsoring or supporting right-wing movements.

Some of them had wide popular support in the middle classes and lower-middle classes. The most famous of these was the Red Gaurs, organised by the controversial Major-General Sudsai Hasdin, who commanded the Army's Internal Security Operations Command. The Red Gaurs became, in effect, a paramilitary group, recruiting former mercenaries who had fought against the Communists in Laos. Among supporters of the Red Gaurs were vocational students in Bangkok, who had distanced

> ❏ A charismatic monk supported Navapol, preaching that it was not a sin to kill Communists. ❏

themselves from the more radical university students, being more concerned about future jobs than political ideals.

Another group was Navapol, which was also established by right-wing army officers. It stood for a commitment to the Thai monarchy, nation and Buddhism.

In 1974–75 the leadership of the farmers' movement was systematically assassinated, and in 1976 some 30 leading personalities of left-wing parties were killed. The 1976 elections produced a weak civilian coalition government which was not able to prevent the army from arranging for the former dictators, Thanom and Praphas, to return to

Thailand. Two students distributing posters which were promoting the expulsion of Thanom were arrested in September 1976, and later found hanged. This sparked large-scale student protest, and on 5 October a group of students staged a mock hanging to publicise the murder of their two comrades. On the next day large numbers of Navapol, Red Gaurs and other right-wing organisations launched an assault on the Thammasat University.

MASSACRE Many students were brutally murdered. Indeed, some were lynched, burnt alive, beheaded or had their eyes gouged out. This horrific episode prompted yet another *coup d'état* by armed forces leaders. The king then installed a strongly anti-Communist judge, Thanin Kraivixien, as the new prime minister of the country.

The right-wing reaction to student radicalism, fuelled by the army, had now set in.

The 1973 uprising

Judge Thanin turned out to be the most repressive prime minister in Thai history and was soon ousted by the army leaders, who put one of their own men, the pipe-smoking moderate General Kriangsak Chomanan, into the premiership. He could not retain the support of the army and stepped down in 1980. Another general, Prem Tinsulanonda, took over, and he was to transform the face of Thai politics entirely.

JUDGE THANIN was an ideological rightist who banned political parties and student groups, made strikes illegal, imposed strict censorship and made thousands of arbitrary arrests. He even ordered Thomas More's *Utopia* and George Orwell's books to be burnt. Many of the student leaders involved in the 1973 uprising now left Bangkok in fear of their lives. They went "to the forest" (the jungle) to join Communist Party guerrillas (see page 185). There they were disillusioned to

> ❏ General Kriangsak Chomanan invited the returned leftist students to his house and cooked breakfast for them. ❏

find that the Communist leaders in Thailand were mostly Chinese, and ardent Maoists, many of whom could not even speak Thai. Eventually, when the fury of the right-wing backlash had subsided, most came home to Bangkok.

The 1982 bicentenary of the Chakri dynasty – one of Prem's public relations successes

During this period of right-wing backlash in the late 1970s, Thailand had to cope with the withdrawal of the Americans from Vietnam and the fall of South Vietnam, formerly capitalist, to Communist control. It was a time of nervousness and danger, because the Vietnamese Communists, free from engagement with US forces, were able to turn their attention to Laos and Cambodia on the Thai frontier.

When Thanin was ousted, **General Kriangsak Chomanan** came to power, and he returned to a more open style of government and removed many of the restrictions, even holding elections in 1979. But in spite of his efforts, General Kriangsak could not command the support of the army. He eventually gave way to General Prem Tinsulanonda.

GENERAL PREM was not a great intellectual, and had no strong power base of his own apart from the support of some other generals. Instead, he offered a style of leadership which was calm and consensual. He began as a serving officer heading the government, and ended eight years later as a prime minister nominated by the elected National Assembly.

In the 1980s the Thai economy first began to sprint, especially from 1987, when Thais sensed that they could become the next Newly Industrialised Economy in Asia – and double-digit growth was maintained for four years running.

Perhaps the vital thing for Thailand was that General Prem listened to the technocrats in the civil service and

followed their advice, particularly about the economy. Prem brought his senior planners and Finance Ministry officials into regular consultation with private businessmen, under his own chairmanship, to resolve disputes between the private and public sectors which were harming the economy. He agreed to a substantial devaluation of the baht, something that certain sections within the country found difficult to accept.

He did not lack rivals and enemies within the armed forces. Two *coups d'état* were attempted during his

General Prem sings for Thai TV

premiership, and many physical attacks were made on him. When General Arthit Kamlang-ek opposed the baht devaluation and called Prem a liar, Prem dismissed the army commander.

Prem's genial manner endeared him to almost everyone, from the king to ordinary citizens. He ensured the success of the double celebration in 1982 of the bicentenary of the Chakri dynasty and of the foundation of the new capital at Bangkok. Both events brought the king a great deal of publicity. The royal gratitude for this was expressed when King Bhumiphol gave his personal protection to General Prem during one of the unsuccessful coup attempts. However, the king was gravely ill in 1982, and out of public life for three months.

By allowing the constitutional political process to resume, providing him with an elected cabinet, Prem satisfied the liberals, while his stern attitude to crime and corruption pleased the right wing. This winning formula might have gone on for longer, but after almost a decade in power, one of the MPs threatened to reveal secrets of the bachelor Prem's private life. At that point he decided to stand down, leaving the political parties in the National Assembly to find their own candidates.

Prem will take his place in history as the man who served as leader of a civilian administration longer than anyone else, and who gave technocrats their lead, which in turn helped the economy.

The man who stepped into Prem's shoes as prime minister in 1988 was a former cavalry general turned diplomat and businessman, Chatichai Choonhavan, leader of the Chart Thai party, which was the largest in the elected Assembly. For three years Chatichai set a rather different style of government from the passive Prem's.

UNDER CHATICHAI the economy began to develop rapidly, with 10 per cent annual growth and the private sector leading. It was no coincidence that businessmen occupied many of the party leadership and cabinet positions during the Chatichai era. Many new development projects were started, and there was fierce controversy about alleged corruption.

Chatichai (above), and his deputy, General Chaovalit Yongchaiyudh (below), elected Prime Minister in November 1996

By this time the amounts of money involved in election-time vote-buying and bribery had multiplied. The political parties needed more and more funds to be sure of doing well in elections, and ministerial corruption – a bribe in return for official approval of a big project – was the easiest way to get them. The army in particular urged changes in the constitution to make elected MPs resign their seats if they joined the cabinet.

COUP Despite accusations of corruption, Chatchai became a respected prime minister, gaining popularity and strengthening ties with neighbouring countries. The region prospered, and the Thai economy began to develop.

However, two army generals Suchinda Kraprayoon and Sunthorn Kongsompong called for a democratic election, claiming that Chatchai had not been officially elected. In 1991 the two generals used their power to take over the government in a bloodless coup, and Suchinda positioned himself as prime minister. Public dissatisfaction led to a mass uprising that reached a head in May 1991 when demonstrating students were mercilessly shot down on Ratchadamnoen Road near the parliament buildings, and "truckloads of bodies" were reported to have been carried out of the city for burial. Suchinda shamefacedly resigned and the army installed a caretaker government.

The Democrat party won the ensuing elections, and Chuan Leek Pai became the prime minister; soon after, he resigned and government was dissolved when a land ownership scandal came to light.

Those MPs remaining in the House of Representatives then elected Barnharn Silapa-Archa, instigator of the land ownership scandal and leader of the Chart Thai party as prime minister; he later refused to step down when he lost a motion of no confidence, but instead dissolved the coalition government.

CRISIS The following election was plagued with vote buying, especially in rural areas. General Chaovalit came to power in 1996 with his New

70

Aspiration Party and yet another volatile coalition government; Chuan Leek Pai's reformed Democrat Party was in opposition. Chaovalit floated the baht in an effort to free up an ailing economy; the baht devalued by 50 per cent and the economy, built mostly upon foreign loans and investment, promptly collapsed: unemployment soared. Protests against Chaovalit led to his forced resignation in November 1997, and with the king's consent Chuan Leek Pai returned to power.

since it was written and proposed entirely by the people.

Chuan Leek Pai was seen as a stabilising prime minister and his cautious dealings with the International Monetary Fund (IMF) to ease the country's financial burden showed signs of slowly reviving Thailand's economy. However he was often criticised as being too slow and indecisive.

After elections in 2001, in which, according to *The Economist*, at least 20 million baht in bribes was estimated to have been given out and 43 Thai

General Suchinda Kraprayoon

PEOPLE'S REFORM Meanwhile a petitionary referendum was circulating throughout the country, calling for constitutional reforms – including a greater voice for citizens, a more open style of government and more regulation against corruption in the public service. The draft constitution became legalised in 1997, marking a new era in democracy for Thailand,

politicians and canvassers were murdered, Thaksin Shinawatra of the newly formed Thai Rak Thai (TRT) party became prime minister. Thaksin is seen as an unknown quantity: he made a fortune from telecommunications but has little political experience. It remains to be seen whether his risky campaign promises will lift Thailand from the economic doldrums, or whether anti-corruption laws will bar him from parliament.

Bangkok

0   1/2   1   1 1/2 km
0   1/2   1 mile

BANG PHAT

Krung Thon Bridge

Khlong Sam Sen

NAKHON CHAISI

National Library

Wimanmek Palace

Dusit Zoo

Chitlada Palace

DU

National Assembly

King Chulalongkorn Statue

Bank of Thailand

Wat Indrawihan

Wat Suwannaram

Royal Barges

Govt House

Wat Benchamabophit

Bangkok Noi/Thonburi Station

National Gallery

BANG LAMPHU

Royal Turf Club

National Theatre

BANGKOK NOI

KHAO SAN ROAD

Ratchadamnoen Boxing Stadium

PHRAN NOK ROAD

Sanam Luang

RATCHADAMNOEN KLANG RD

Tourist Office

LANLUANG ROAD

Thammasat University

National Musenni

Democracy Monument

Wat Rajanada

Wat Mahathat

Giant Swing

Golden Mount (Wat Saket)

Silapakorn University

Lak Muang Shrine

Wat Phra Keo

Grand Palace

Wat Suthat

Tourist Office

Wat Rajabophit

CHAROEN

Wat Po

Wat Arun (Temple of Dawn)

Nakorn Kasem

CHINATOWN (YAOWARAT)

PHRA BUDDHA YOTFA (MEMORIAL BRIDGE)

YAOWARAT ROAD

Hualampho Main Station

Wat Kalayanimit

PHRA POKKLAO BRIDGE

Mae Nam Chao Praya

Wat Traimit

Bangkok Centre

THONBURI

SOMDET CHAO PHRAYA RD

INTRAPHITHAK ROAD

LATYA ROAD

PHET-CHAKASEM 7 ROAD

GPO

SURAWON

Wongwian Yai Station

SIPHAYA

SILO

WONGWIAN YAI

KRUNG THONBURI ROAD

Bangrak Market

TALAT PHLU

KHLONG SAN

TAKSIN BRIDGE

Wat Yannawa

A   B   C

72

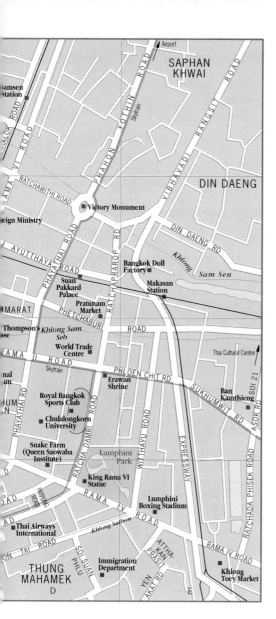

Lumphini Park, one of Bangkok's open spaces

▶▶▶ BANGKOK

Sometimes it is hard to find a good word to say about Bangkok. The air is thick and the roads clog up with traffic. The oppressive heat is unrelieved by trees or greenery and after walking for half an hour you can become seriously dehydrated. Visitors ask themselves how it is possible to live like this.

Yet amazingly a great many people come to love the place – or at least come to develop a love–hate relationship with it. The basic rule to beat the heat is to remain calm. Bangkok does have its cool oases, and it is the focal point for the rest of Thailand, with which most people get on famously.

Contrasts Unlike old-established Western capitals, Bangkok has the exhilarating feeling of growth at a breakneck pace. Official figures indicate 5.7 million live in Bangkok, though millions more pour in from the Northeast at the end of the harvest season, so they can seek work. Meanwhile foreign capital is allowed to

move freely, which helps to create employment. It is a modern city showing extremes of wealth and poverty, and at the same time it has a strong sense of history and an unmistakable identity.

The dark side to this is evident in the acres of leaky timber shacks that form a vista from the expressway as it flies over Khlong Toey port. Most people are cheerfully resilient; out of the tourist areas many will smile and say hello. The phrase *ot thon*, "to endure" finds an equivalent in the Buddhist lexicon, *ubekha*, "equanimity".

At just over two centuries, Bangkok may be considered relatively young, but it is firmly founded on the heritage of the 14th-century city of Ayutthaya (Bangkok's official designation of Manakhorn [Metropolis] once prefixed Ayutthaya). The Grand Palace, with its sumptuous spires and roof, is for outsiders the best-known symbol of Thailand; the Palace and all the major monuments are described in this section one by one.

But Bangkok is not just about buildings, it is vibrant, alive and full of hope. It gives a strange feeling that anything might be possible – and it usually is.

Bangkok is still growing fast, and its traffic grows at the same pace – making life in the city dirty and dangerous

**PLACATING
THE SPIRITS**
Persistent misfortune dogged the construction of the first Erawan Hotel during the 1950s. In the end, experts diagnosed the problem. Tree spirits were angry at being disturbed when the hotel's foundation beams were cut from their dwellings. When the Erawan Shrine was built to provide them with a new home, the bad luck stopped. Since then, Bangkok citizens have taken care to respect and appease the local spirits with jasmine garlands and incense.

Wat Arun, decorated with mosaics of broken porcelain

Temples and shrines

▶▶▶ Arun, Wat 72B2
Arun Amarin Road
Open: daily 8:30–5:30. Admission: inexpensive

The "Temple of Dawn" is built on the site of Wat Chang, the focus of King Taksin's Thonburi, the former capital. Taksin was paranoid about his status as an outsider king and alienated the court, who had him executed. King Rama II and King Rama III raised the main *prang* (tower) to its present height of 74m.

As you come up the river, the glittering tower is an impressive sight. Nowadays dwarfed by skyscrapers, there is still one of the city's finest views from halfway up the main *prang*, reached by a very steep and narrow staircase. A representation of Mt Meru, the centre of traditional Indian cosmologies, it depicts the first 33 heavens immediately above it. The four small accompanying *prangs* are dedicated to Phra Phai, the god of the wind. Bizarre mosaics made of broken Chinese porcelain cover the *prangs*.

A pavilion in the compound has images of important stages in Buddha's life: birth, enlightenment, the first five disciples and his death or *Parinirvana*.

The locals frighten their children with a tale of the guardian *yaksha* of *wats* Arun and Po slugging it out in the Chao Phraya.

Wat Arun is best reached by river ferry from Tha Tien (the pier for Wat Po).

▶ Benchamabophit, Wat 72C3
Si Ayutthaya Road
Open: daily 9–5. Admission: inexpensive

Built of Carrara marble, this is also known as the "Marble Temple", and is the last *wat* of comparable size with Arun to go up in the modern era (1901). As at Wat Niwet Thamprawat, King Rama V commissioned stained glass representations of Thai and Buddhist themes. The main image is a copy of the reputedly flawless *Phra Phuttha Chinnarat*, the original of which is to be found in Phitsanulok.

The most interesting aspect of the temple is its bronze Buddha images – 53 of them line an inner courtyard, the epitome of harmony and symmetry.

The temple is easily found on Si Ayutthaya Road near Chitladda Palace, and could usefully fit in a day tour to Wimanmek Palace and/or Dusit Zoo.

▶ Erawan Shrine 73D2
Ploen Chit Road
Open: daily 7 AM–11 PM. Admission free

The Erawan Shrine, at a busy crossroads on Ploen Chit Road, is always milling with people. They come here to seek favour of the Brahmin god, Phra Pom; such favours may be as simple, or as secular, as help with winning a lottery. There is a resident dance troupe which starts performing at 7 AM and many of the supplicants commission the dancers to give a performance by way of an offering.

Spirits were said to inhabit the site of the shrine, which was built in 1956 at the same time as the Erawan Hotel –

which has now been demolished and replaced with a much larger, modern structure.

▶▶▶ Grand Palace   72B2
See pages 78–81.

▶ Indrawihan, Wat
Wisut Kasat Road
Open: daily 9–5. Admission free
Wat Indrawihan (full name Wat Indra Mawasihara) on Wisut Kasat Road, a short way north of Banglamphu, has a huge (32m) statue of a standing Buddha dating from the mid-19th century. There is also a lifelike image of Luang Phor To, a venerated former abbot, cradling his alms bowl and housed in an air-conditioned, hollowed-out *stupa*.

▶ Mahathat, Wat   72B3
Sanam Luang
Open: daily 9–5. Admission free
This extensive *wat* of the mid-19th century is centrally located on the west side of Sanam Luang near the National Museum and stretches back to Maharaj Road and the river. The home of Mahachulalongkorn Buddhist University, it is also a place where lay people can go to get instruction in meditation. The higgledy-piggledy *kuti* or monks' quarters make up most of the floor area.

It is especially worth visiting for the market which is held here on *wan phra*, the Buddhist holy days (full, new and half moons). Stalls offering herbal medicines, old Buddhas, precious stones, amulets and symbolic figures jostle with strange foods and fortune-tellers.

MEDITATION CLASSES
The International Buddhist Meditation Centre at Wat Mahathat offers classes in English every second Saturday. It specialises in the type of meditation known as *Vipassana*, in which enlightenment is taught by "mindfulness", involving a concentrated examination of internal physical sensations. Novices and experienced practitioners are welcome. For more information, contact the monks in Section Five of the temple compound. The other main type of meditation practised in Thai monasteries is called *Samantha*.

People gather round the Lucky Sara Tree (Buddha's Birth Tree) at Wat Mahathat, one of the most important centres of Buddhist teaching in Thailand

► **Lak Muang Shrine (City Pillar)**   72B3
Sanam Luang

Lak Muang dates from the time of the city's foundation and was erected in 1782 by Rama I (rebuilt under Rama VI). This pillar, containing the city's horoscope and protected by a little shrine, is over the road from the east wall of Wat Phra Keo.

The phallic pillar, or *lingam*, symbolises the fertility and energy of the Hindu god Siva, and is accredited with the power to grant wishes. Originally made of wood, it is covered in gilt, as well as flowers and other offerings. All distances in Thailand are measured from here.

Likay performers – classical Thai dancers – are available to be commissioned to perform by Thai worshippers. As part of the ceremony the people read their fortunes with the *siem sii* and light the obligatory joss sticks and candles to put themselves in the right mood.

There is a public park near the shrine, as well as several ministries, the Defence Ministry easily spotted by the cannon outside at Sanam Luang's southeastern corner.

Inside and out, Wat Phra Keo glitters with ornamental gilded figures, including the strange, mythical, birdlike creatures known as garudas *and* kinnarees

78

The **Sanam Luang** (Royal Field) is a huge open space adjacent to Lak Muang. It is a popular rendezvous for Bangkokites and a fascinating place to watch kite-fighting contests (see page 111) between March and May. It is also a haunt of fortune-tellers and amulet vendors.

►►► **The Grand Palace and Wat Phra Keo**   72B2
Sanam Chai Road. Open: daily 8:30-12, 1-3:30. Admission: expensive, tickets also cover entry to Wimanmek Palace.

The immense Grand Palace is one of the most dazzling sights in all Asia. It was once a city within a city, residence and last bastion of the Chakri dynasty. It covers 218,400sq m and the perimeter walls are 1.9km long.

This statue on a plinth by the rear wall of the bot at Wat Phra Keo represents the Hindu hermit credited with the invention of yoga and herbal medicine

The harem Guarded by eunuchs, no men apart from the king had any right to enter, on pain of severe punishment. Anna Leonowens' books (see page 56), give a rare inside picture of the harem, which played an important role in feudal politics. Unlike the characters in the fanciful musical *The King and I*, Leonowens' books present an intellectual woman, with a dry sense of humour. Although the harem was disbanded and the king moved out to Wimanmek, the buildings still stand, and some still have important ceremonial functions. (Closed to the public.)

Wat Phra Keo (The Chapel Royal) This is the building containing the image of the **Emerald Buddha** (see over), the holiest shrine in Thailand. The chapel was completed in 1784 and is unique among Thai temples in having no resident monks; it also functions as the monarch's private chapel. To that end there is a partition to either side of the image that serves as a retiring room. Murals inside the chapel depict Buddha's life, besides medieval cosmology and stories of the Buddha's former lives.

The Emerald Buddha was supposedly discovered in the 15th century when a lightning bolt struck an old *chedi* in Chiang Rai, revealing the image. It remained in the possession of the northern Lanna kingdom until a Lao king was offered the vacant Lanna throne – from there it went to Wiang Jan (Vientiane) in Laos. When Chao Phya Chakri, later to become King Rama I, made an expedition to Vientiane in 1779, the small, green jade image was the prize among the spoils. It may not be photographed.

A curiosity that is near to the Royal Pantheon is a model of Cambodia's famous Angkor Wat, built by King Rama IV. Next to it stand the Repository of Scripture and the large golden *chedi* (a pagoda where holy relics are kept) modelled on Phra Si Sanphet, Ayutthaya, in Ceylonese style.

The Palace Compound is an eclectic and dazzling jumble that some have called the "Siamese Disneyland." Statues of white elephants vie with the reliquary *chedis* and mythological giants (*yuk*) and the half-bird, half-woman *kinnaree*. The entire epic story of the *Ramakian* is depicted in mural form along the galleries which enclose the chapel compound.

In the palace itself, the audience hall of Amarindra is open to viewing by the public. It is part of the "Mahamonthien" where kings are crowned in the room that is home to the country's guardian spirit, *Phra Siam Deva Dhi Raj*. Behind that is the Chakrabardiman, where kings traditionally stay the night after their coronation.

The audience hall of the Dusit Maha Prasa was the first brick building in the compound, completed in 1789. It is a cruciform plan of pure Siamese design, where kings lie in state.

The **Chakri palace** (1882) is of architectural interest for its efforts to combine Western and traditional Siamese styles (a trend taken to greater extremes at Bang Pa-In, Ayutthaya). King Chulalongkorn, the creator of all this whimsy, conceived the Italian colonnades. A conservative faction at court insisted on the Thai roofs. The spires hold royal ashes; kings in the middle, princes to the left.

Galleries depict diplomatic endeavours of the past, such as missions exchanged between King Narai and King Louis XIV of France, and King Rama IV's delegation to Queen Victoria. Today, foreign ambassadors present their credentials here to the king.

The **Grand Palace Museum**, a stone building to the northeast of the palace complex, provides invaluable explanations of the methods used in the construction and restoration of the various monuments. Upstairs an array of artefacts can be contemplated in air-conditioned silence. These include two detailed models which give a startling picture of how the palace has been changed and added to in the course of its 200-year history.

Visiting heads of state might attend banquets at the Sala Sahathai and stay in the Boromabiman building, which was richly decorated by King Rama VI with a square dome and the written listing of the "ten kingly virtues."

Numismatists may be interested in the **Coins and Royal Decorations Museum** (*Open* daily to 3:30. *Admission: moderate*) near the ticket office. Exhibits date from the 11th century onwards.

THE EMERALD BUDDHA
The Emerald Buddha's robes are changed three times a year by the king to symbolise the passing of the seasons – cool, hot and rainy. Many of the yearly rites such as the ploughing ceremony (see page 94) start with his blessing.

The Temple of the Emerald Buddha bristles with a dazzling array of stupas, prangs, mondops and chedis (monumental towers), many smothered in gold

▶▶▶ Po, Wat (Wat Phra Chetuphon)   72B2
South of the Grand Palace (entrance on Chetupon Road)
Open: daily 8–5. Admission: inexpensive
This large *wat* of 16th-century foundation took about 12 years for King Rama I to restore in the 1780s. Many come from far and wide to see the massive reclining Buddha, 46m long. The mother-of-pearl inlay on the feet represents the 108 "auspicious signs" whereby a Buddha is recognised. It is the oldest temple in Bangkok.

More mother-of-pearl is used on the chapel doors to depict scenes from the Thai epic *Ramakian*, also shown on Ayutthaya-period tapestries that were literally snatched from the flames when the city was destroyed by the Burmese in 1767. Rubbings are sold of the bas-reliefs around the chapel's base.

CODE OF DRESS
Dress respectably to visit the Grand Palace of Wimanmek. Shorts, sleeveless shirts, skimpy lowcut dresses and open sandals are frowned on and you may be refused admission. If they are feeling good-humoured, the guards may provide suitable clothing for you to borrow, but they may just direct you to a nearby clothes stall to purchase your own. Remember to remove your shoes before entering the main chapels.

A temple guard (above) and a young Buddhist (below) at Wat Phra Keo

THE 10 KINGLY VIRTUES
Giving, ethics, self-sacrifice, honesty, humility, concentration, patience, avoidance of wrong-doing, non-anger and non-violence.

These comic-looking statues are Chinese caricatures of Europeans. Some of these statues reached Thailand in rice cargoes, where they were used as convenient ballast

Inscriptions and treatises on medicine, botany and massage are left over from a host of other subjects formerly on public view, which earned this *wat* the epithet "great storehouse of knowledge", and made it a forerunner of the modern university.

Herbal medicine is still practised and taught here and Wat Po counts as the country's foremost institution in the training of Thai massage (courses, available to foreigners, last 10 or 15 days). By the east wall is a massage area where anyone feeling aches and pains can try the Wat Po version, which costs around 250–500 baht per hour (see page 47).

▶▶ Rajabophit, Wat 72B2
Off Atsadang Road
Open: 8–5. Admission: inexpensive
A kilometre south of the Lak Muang, this attractive *wat* of radical circular architecture was built around 1870 by King Rama V or Chulalongkorn. The tall, gilded *chedi* is in a concentric cloister, and both are decorated with porcelain and chandeliers. Inside, the Buddha image is seated on a *naga* or dragon-headed serpent, originating in Lop Buri.

The *bot* (chapel) has both mother-of-pearl doors and windows bearing the insignia of the five royal ranks conferred by the king. The interior is vaulted and four chapels lead off from the central gallery. All in all this is an unusual and interesting *wat*.

▶ Rajanada, Wat 72B3
Off Mahachai Road
Open: daily 9–5. Admission free
A 19th-century *wat* graced with a curiously tiered roof, this temple is distinguished for its amulet market in an adjoining compound. The amulets or *phra phim* depict images of the Buddha and Thai deities and the more prominent or famous monks.

The amulets reputedly have magic powers and are said to protect the wearer – the more expensive ones are worn by soldiers and these can cost thousands of baht, although not all come so dear. There are various classes of amulet, each with its own special purpose: some are love amulets; some have many eyes to protect the wearer from all directions. Amulets are often made of terracotta and are usually worn around the neck on a gold or a silver chain. The amulet market is not the cheapest place to buy amulets of any kind.

▶▶ Saket, Wat (Golden Mount) 72C3
Off Worachak Road
Open: daily 9–5. Admission free (inexpensive charge for the summit of the Golden Mount)
Once a charnel house, after a disastrous plague in the reign of King Rama II, this *wat* is distinguished by the 80m-tall Phu Khao Thong (Golden Mount), which was started by King Rama III. Rama IV had 1,000 teak logs piled into the foundations to strengthen it because the underlying ground was in fact too soft to support the original structure.

The *chedi* was added in 1863 by Rama V and relics were

brought from Nepal in 1897, a gift of the British viceroy. The spire is worth the climb – the view from the top affords a surprisingly panoramic vista over the Bangkok rooftops and beyond, but first you must negotiate the 318 steps.

Every November there is a large festival in the grounds of this *chedi*, during which there is a candle-lit procession up the Golden Mount. Food stalls and stage shows appear by the dozen and the mount is lit up with different coloured lights.

▶▶ Suthat, Wat and the Giant Swing   72B2
Bamrung Muang Road

Look closely at the doors here: they are said to have been personally carved by King Rama II.

There are some Jataka murals of an informal style, showing Buddha at various stages in his life. However the most notable item is the 8m-tall main meditating Buddha image, which comes from ruined Wat Mahathat in Sukhothai and was brought down the river by King Rama I. The peculiar statues of generals, scholars and sailors were brought in as ballast for Chinese rice hulks.

The Buddha image is housed in the tallest *wiharn* (Open 9–5, weekends and public holidays only) in Bangkok, and the *bot* (chapel) is impressively large.

THE GOLDEN MOUNT
The Golden Mount is an artificial slag-heap composed of the earth dug out when the canal system was constructed. The only "hill" in pancake-flat Bangkok gives one of the best views over the city. Directly below lie the roofs of Wat Rajanada, with the multiple spires of the Grand Palace further afield and the ceramic towers of Wat Arun glinting across the Chao Phraya River.

The metallic Burmese-style spires jutting from the elegant roofline of Wat Rajanada give it its alternative name – "Iron Monastery"

83

Giant Swing (*72B3*) Wat Suthat's most famous asset is the Sao Ching Cha or Giant Swing (see panel). This was originally used for a Brahmin ceremony held once a year in which Siva and Vishnu were reputed to visit the temple. Every January, up until the 1940s, men would take turns to try to grab bags of gold attached to a 15m pole by swinging in great arcs. This Sivaic rite was often a fatal one, as the arc of the swing was so vast that many men fell and died.

The place where people used to fall to the ground is now the "land of pigeons", with a Brahmin temple (Wat Suthat) opposite. This houses a gilded bronze Buddha, and murals illustrating moments from his life.

Reclining at the feet of Wat Suthat's Golden Buddhas

THE GIANT SWING RITUAL
The Giant Swing ritual re-enacted a Brahmin ceremony commemorating the Hindu god Siva's annual return to earth. The swinging action symbolised the rising and setting of the sun, tempered the force of the monsoon, and promoted good harvests. It also cost the lives of many brave, or foolhardy, young men who risked their necks in a terrifying attempt to wrench a bag of gold from a bamboo pole with their teeth.

▶▶ **Traimit, Wat**   *72C2*
East of junction between Yaowarat and Charoen Krung roads
Open: 9–5. Admission: inexpensive
This *wat*, said to date from the 13th century, is definitely worth a visit. If, by coincidence, you have to wait for a train from the nearby Hualamphong Station bags can be checked in at left luggage, and the Wat Traimit is a short stroll away down the road of the same name.

The *wat's* name translates to the "temple of the golden Buddha" and indeed vendors and schoolchildren usually crowd the entrance where the star exhibit, the Golden Buddha, is marked with signposts and a small entry fee is collected.

From the outside, this *wat* may not appear to be the most impressive, but inside this Sukhothai-style Buddha is the largest solid gold image in the country; if it were melted down its five and a half tonnes would be worth over US$46 million at today's prices.

However, the Buddha was very nearly not on display, as it had been lost to the world for a long time: its discovery is said to have been an accident. Like many valuable images in times of warfare and civil strife, it had been camouflaged in stucco. Only some 40 years ago the image was rediscovered when the stucco casing cracked while the image was being moved by crane after the East Asiatic Company took over the building. This crack hinted at what was underneath and the plaster removed to reveal a 3.5m Buddha cast of solid gold.

The Chinese quarter in Bangkok is of huge size and influence, tracing its beginnings to a river-station – Bangkok – used for the building of Krung Thep. The identity of the Chinese Thais is blurred by intermarriage and assimilation, but most are only a few generations removed from the original immigrant Tia (Father). The predominant group speak tae-jiw, a branch of Cantonese, although Hokkien is also important. Around the turn of the century, the Chinese quarter gained a reputation for vice.

Yaowarat Road, with its forest of Chinese signs, could easily be taken for Hong Kong or Singapore. Off the busy thoroughfare are timeless alleys and elaborate temples. Gold shops abound and others sell gaudy paraphernalia such as paper houses and the Benzes burnt in the Kong Teck ceremony. Old men hang around the tea-houses.

85

Catching up with the news in Chinatown

The area is best explored on foot as the one-way system is a nightmare. Soi Wanit 1 to the south – better known as Sampheng Lane – runs parallel to Yaowarat. Wat Patuma, at its eastern end, was once the execution ground for royal criminals. Continue east to *talat gao*, one of the oldest and most pungent Chinese markets. To capture a real sense of what the market is like, make it an early morning experience. Ancient Wat Chakrawat, with its pond of crocodiles, is about halfway along Sampheng.

North from the old market is a new version, set up along Soi Issaraphap, which also leads to Wat Mangkon Kamalawat (Neng Noi Yee) on Charoen Krung (New) Road. This is the largest Mahayana temple in Bangkok, where laity are allowed to consult oracles and can worship the Buddha Matreiya. A glimpse of the classically proportioned and decorated monks' quarters is permitted. Mayanist monks are vegetarian and do not collect alms.

Turn right down Plapachai Road behind this temple to reach Li Thi Miew. This is a Taoist shrine decorated in ancient style. Yaowarat is also home to the "Thieves' Market", so-called as stolen goods used to be sold here, up Boriphat Road near the canal. Soi Wanit leads across the canal to Pahurat, Bangkok's Indiatown, which is famous for its textile markets.

Other sights

▶ Ban Khamthieng (Siam Society)　　73E2
131 Soi Asoke (Soi 21), off Sukhumvit Road, tel: 02 258 3491
Open: Tue–Sat 9–12, 1–5. Admission: inexpensive
Originally constructed in Chiang Mai some 120 years ago, this fine old teak residence was moved to Bangkok in the 1960s and rebuilt on its present site in attractive grounds. There is also a museum of folk art, covering areas not represented in the national museum; exhibits tend to concentrate on the more humble aspects of daily life, such as fishing and cooking, as experienced 150 years ago.

The house is the headquarters of the Siam Society, a scholarly organisation devoted to researching obscure aspects of Thai culture. Their journal is a widely respected source material for academic writing of all disciplines. An invaluable venue for any serious study of Thailand, there is a reference library and books are on sale.

▶ Bangkok Doll Factory　　73E3
85/2 Soi Rachada Phan
Open: Mon–Sat 8–5. Admission free
Bangkok Doll Factory is situated on Soi Rachada Phan, winding down the *soi* 800m from Ratchaprarop Road. It is entirely the creation of Khunying Thongkorn Chanvimol, who set up the current factory and showroom in 1961.

The attached international dolls' museum has over 700 exhibits which demonstrate the doll-maker's craft. Khunying Thongkorn has specialised in miniature representations of Thai life, from the colourful hill-tribes to tableaux from the classics of Thai literature.

The delicate figurines are handmade from cloth and painstakingly detailed. They have received royal favour as gifts for foreign dignitaries. The most famous subjects for the dolls are the *Khon* dancers, whose distinctive painted masks in small scale have become popular in their own right.

Commissions and special occasions have, on the other hand, produced representations of figures as diverse as Miss Universe and the pope. Other interesting themes covered include rural life, the history of Thai dress, the national dress of neighbouring countries, and various regional dances. Check for details of special exhibitions on 02 245 3008.

▶ Chitladda Palace　　72C4
Sri Ayutthaya Road
This is the official residence of His Majesty the King: casual visitors are not welcome, and soldiers will not hesitate to shoot on sight. The wooden palace, built by Rama VI, is sited in the middle of spacious grounds and is therefore virtually invisible from the road. However, the imposing moat around the compound cannot be missed. The grounds are used for some of the king's agricultural research projects.

▶ Dusit　　72C4
This area around the National Assembly contains Thailand's "corridors of power", being headquarters to the powerful defence establishment. It is, unlike the rest

JIM THOMPSON'S HOUSE
In Jim Thompson's House (see opposite) every room contains a treasure. Look out for a 6th-century Buddha image in the study and a cute Chinese "mouse house" in the bedroom. The shop is highly recommended for its authentic souvenirs: paintings of Siamese cats, the rice goddess and even the whole Thai zodiac.

ROYAL WHITE ELEPHANTS
About a dozen rare white elephants enjoy a pampered existence in the Royal Stables at Dusit. These exotic albinos are sacred creatures in Thailand, and all found legally belong to the king. A white elephant is distinguised not so much by its colour (a pale brown) as by its fastidious behaviour. It is, of course, far too rare to work for its living, and the phenomenal cost of its upkeep thus gives rise to the phrase "white elephant" to describe an obsolete or burdensome possession.

of the city, spread out and leafy. The imposing Ananta Samakhom throne hall, the former National Assembly, has a big dome.

Behind it is the current parliament building, while next door are the **Amphorn Gardens** (*Open daily 8–6. Admission free*), frequently the site of exhibitions, and the city's main zoo – **Dusit Zoo**. It is more of a park than a zoo.

▶▶▶ Jim Thompson's House   73D2

Soi Kasem San 2, off Rama I Road, opposite the National Stadium, tel: 02 612 3742-3

Open: Mon–Sat 9–5. Guided tours in English. Admission: moderate, all admission fees are donated to a number of good causes

This is well hidden at the end of Soi Kasem San 2, but a delightful surprise awaits. This remarkable haven, over-looking a characterful if odour-laden canal, is one of the most appealing places in Bangkok.

The former owner, Jim Thompson, is something of a local legend (see page 101). Arriving with the US Army in 1945, he soon adopted Thailand as his permanent home. He made both name and riches promoting Thai silk, but his interest was in the Thai fine arts, as these buildings, his monument, attest.

The ingenious structure, which was cobbled together out of six old red teak structures, is a series of small rooms, with a surprise in each. The place has bags of charm and the personality of its former owner still pervades. The collection is an outstanding one and a lesson in good taste.

THOMPSON'S DISAPPEARANCE
The strange disappearance of Jim Thompson is one of the most intriguing mysteries of 20th-century Thailand. He vanished in 1967 on a jungle trek in the Cameron Highlands of Malaysia, but his body was never recovered. Rumours circulated that he was a spy and had been abducted or murdered by Communists or the CIA. It is more probable that he met his fate under the wheels of a truck, and was quickly buried to hide the evidence.

The contents of Jim Thompson's House constitute a world-class collection of Southeast Asian art. Many artefacts were acquired from local markets in Chinatown or from rural temples

87

THE NATIONAL MUSEUM
The National Museum's main collections of Thai and pre-Thai sculpture can be found in the two large modern wings (North and South) which surround the older buildings. In the South Wing you will find art of the following periods: Dvaravati (6th–11th century), Srivichaya (8th–13th century), Khmer and Lopburi (7th–14th century). The North Wing houses the Chiang Saen (12th–20th century), Sukhothai (13th–15th century), Ayutthaya (15th–18th century), and Bangkok periods (18th–20th century).

*Lumphini Park:
a pleasure by day,
a danger by night*

▶ **Lumphini Park** 73D1
Between Rama IV and Sarasin roads
Bangkok's largest park is named after the Buddha's birthplace. Distinguishing features include a large artificial lake (where paddle boats may be hired), a Thai boxing stadium, and a standing statue of King Rama VI at its southwest corner. By day it is pleasant enough, with a fitness and recreation park used for *tai-chi*, jogging and *tagraw* (see page 112). It is one of the places that comes to a halt when the national anthem is played at 8 AM and 6 PM.

Beware of the park at night, however, when the story is different – the dark acres are irresistible to the violent and seedy element from Patpong to the south and Sarasin to the north.

▶ **National Gallery** 72B3
*4 Chao fa Road (north of National Museum), tel: 02 281 2224
Open: Wed–Sat 9–4. Admission: inexpensive*
This collection of 20th-century Thai art gives some insights into the Thai ways of seeing, although many of the exhibits are of rather minor artistic significance.

▶▶▶ **National Museum (Pipitaphan)** 72B3
Off the Na Phra That Road to the north of Sanam Luang, by Thammasat University, tel: 02 224 9912. Admission: inexpensive
A few baht will get you into this treasure trove of art and culture. Excellent guided tours (free of charge) are available in several languages, lasting about two hours. Those in English take place on Wednesday and Thursday at 9:30. Topics covered include Thai and pre-Thai art and culture, and Buddhism. The nucleus of the collection was first put on show in 1874 and was organised seriously as a national collection in 1933. The museum is housed in several different buildings, which are themselves fine examples of Thai architecture.

The oldest buildings in the compound date from the 1780s and were built as a palace for the second or deputy king. When the office of second king was abolished by King Rama V, the buildings were handed over to become a museum.

The Pavilions The main acreage is spread out in pavilions behind the **Buddhaisawan Chapel** (1795–97). Built by the second king for his personal use, the chapel contains formal murals depicting 28 scenes from the Buddha's life. The main image, **Phra Buddha Sihing**, is anointed in the official celebrations of Songkran in April.

Halls behind the chapel are devoted to various themes; the large **Atsaraavinitchai Pavilion** is used for travelling and other temporary exhibitions. The emphasis is on artefacts and arts from Siamese history. Gold, palanquins, shadow puppets, ceramics, mother-of-pearl, ivory, weapons, royal regalia, stone inscriptions, wood-carving, textiles, Buddhist utensils and musical instruments each have their own room among the sprawling whitewashed cloisters. Of the ceramics, there are Chinese (Ming Dynasty) examples and native Thai Benjarong (five-coloured) ware.

The rear porch of this hall has models of ships and a large doll's house. One prize exhibit is a model train presented to King Rama IV by Queen Victoria. The Textile Hall has examples of classical Thai patterns, including those picked out with gold thread. A portico at the end of this hall has some delicate silk embroidery – pictures of In-Jan, the original Siamese twins.

The **Mahasurasinghanat Building**, to the left of the main structure, is devoted to pre-Thai art and work of non-Thai civilisations. The Mon-Indic culture of Lop Buri is to the fore, along with art from Dvaravati sites. The Mon are presumed heirs of Dvaravati culture, which appears to have been a peace-loving society occupying the Chao Praya basin some 900 years ago.

Meanwhile in the south, the Javanese influence, as yet untamed by Islam, was very strong. Sumatra, next door, was centre of the Srivijayan empire which overran the

THAI SCRIPT ORIGIN
"The ruler does not collect *jagthorp* (a Khmer tax)" – Part of the inscription of King Ramkhamhaeng of Sukhothai from which, it is said, the Thai script is derived.

89

Malay peninsula, leaving a wake of cultural objects across southern Thailand.

The **Prapas Pipitaphan**, to the right, tells the story from the 13th- to 14th-century kingdoms of Lanna (Chiang Mai) and Sukhothai onwards. The introduction of writing had meant that Thai history could at last begin to be recorded. Various alliances and royal houses contested the supremacy of Siam. This hall also has coins and Buddha images.

Sivamokkhaphiman Pavilion, the original audience hall, is the main building within the pavilion and houses the

Bangkok's National Museum is one of the largest in Southeast Asia. A visit here gives an excellent introduction to Thai art and culture

Suan Pakkard Palace contains a superb collection of antiquities and works of art, but the peaceful gardens are just as enjoyable

SUAN PAKKARD PALACE
The lovely old teak houses of Suan Pakkard Palace are some of the best examples of traditional Thai architecture in Bangkok. Rather than daunting royal residences, they are on an agreeably domestic scale. The Lacquer Pavilion, originally a temple, was dismantled from its original site and brought to Bangkok as a 50th birthday present for the Princess Chumbot by her husband.

proudest exhibit – the 1283 inscription of King Ramkhamhaeng of Sukhothai setting forth the prospectus of the Thai nation. It is referred to by some as the first Thai Constitution.

A smaller gallery of Thai prehistory is located here at the back of the same building. The most interesting exhibits here are the Bronze-Age whorl-patterned pots which were produced by the Ban Chiang civilisation (see pages 194–195), and also some unusually shaped Stone Age vessels.

Other small buildings are scattered across the compound. A fine collection of cremation chariots has its own pavilion on the right, and a Chinese house of the court service is tucked away behind exhibits of Thai art.

Also of interest is the **Red House**, or **Tamnak Daeng** (*Open* Wed–Sun 9–4), a splendid wooden structure which was once the residence of the older sister of King Rama I. Once situated in the grounds of the Grand Palace, nowadays it is home to a collection of furniture which was once used by royalty.

A small bookshop in the foyer of the main gallery, selling books on Thai history, has a range of titles in English explaining the exhibits.

▶▶ **Suan Pakkard Palace**   73D3

352 Si Ayutthaya Road
Open: 9–4. Closed Sun. Admission: expensive

Translating as "the lettuce farm" this little palace is Bangkok's most serious rival, in sightseeing terms, to Jim Thompson's House, from where it is a short *tuk tuk* ride. Five traditional wooden houses were brought here in the 1920s for Princess Chumbot Nagara Svarga and set in a landscaped garden.

The main reason to visit the palace must be the splendid **Lacquer Pavilion**, which was discovered in Ayutthaya, its inner walls portraying the life of the Buddha, among other themes.

Other noteworthy exhibits are the gold and lacquer manuscript cabinets and a good collection of elegant Ban Chiang pottery (see pages 194–195) and Khmer statuary.

▶▶▶ **Thonburi**   72A2

West bank of Chao Phraya River

Thonburi, Thailand's former capital city between the fall of Ayutthaya and the establishing of Bangkok in its place, occupies the west bank of the Chao Phraya River, just a ferry ride away from the Grand Palace and Wat Po. The great draws for the visitor are **Wat Arun▶▶** (see page 76), the **canals▶▶▶** and the famous **floating market▶▶**.

The floating market in Wat Sai, to be found in the Bang Khun Thien district, was the first to attract tourists and has now become commercialised.

The left bank at Thonburi is gradually assuming the character of the modern day Bangkok. Wongwien Yai (Big Roundabout) boasts an impressive statue of King Taksin, who was Thonburi's founder. The immediate environs, the narrow streets, canal bridges and *wats* preserve much of the atmosphere from King Taksin's temporary capital.

FLOATING MARKET
Although run primarily as a contrived tourist attraction, the floating market is nevertheless worth a look if you can't get to see the more authentic one at Damnoen Saduak (see page 124). Long-tail boat tours begin at 7am from Tha Chany and the Oriental Hotel Pier.

91

Commercialised, but undeniably photogenic: Thonburi Floating Market

TEAK

Once one of Thailand's greatest natural resources, teak made particularly good house-building material. A hardwood, its naturally occurring teak-oil made it durable and weather resistant. The teak forests have been felled drastically, but new propagation techniques are being tried (see pages 244–245).

The collection of state coaches at Wimanmek Palace reveals Rama V's interest in European culture. Many artefacts on display were imported after the king's foreign travels

▶▶▶ Wimanmek Palace (Phra Thi Nang Wimanmek) 72C4

Off Ratchawithi Road near to the National Assembly, tel: 02 280 1565.

Open: daily 9:30–4. Last tour 3. Admission: inexpensive, or free if you use a ticket already purchased for the Grand Palace

"The palace in the clouds" is claimed to be the world's largest structure made entirely of golden teak and contains over 80 rooms. On the orders of King Chulalongkorn (Rama V), the palace was dismantled and moved in sections in 1900 from Si Chang island in Chonburi province. The work was finished in seven months, and set a trend that brought more royalty to the area to build their homes.

Wimanmek was designed by Prince Naritsaranuwattiwong; two wings, each measuring 60m long, each contain three floors. There are 31 rooms, not including balconies. His Majesty would come here with his queens, favoured concubines and daughters. The Amporn Sathan extension was added in 1907 to accommodate these influxes. The queen gave orders for it to be made into a museum, and it now contains some of the king's personal effects and *objets d'art*.

After the reign of Rama VI the palace was used merely to store things and its condition deteriorated. It was opened to the public to mark the 200th anniversary of Bangkok's foundation in 1982 .

It has the appearance of an island, being partly flanked by pools of water. A jade pool, green with vegetation, lies to the south, and beyond is a Thai house built for the use of visiting guests. The silver room has much detailed original work, such as a silver tree with woven leaves. On the wall are photos of various royals and aristocrats. There is a metal room with bronzes, models of warships and steamships belonging to King Rama VII. Two trophy rooms contain swords and guns and the traditional colonial elephants' feet.

The ceremonial barges are brought out only on very special occasions. Intricately carved, they were formerly used every year in a traditional journey when the king made his way to Wat Arun to present the krathin robes and gifts from the Grand Palace to the monks as a symbol of the end of the rainy season and the Buddhist "Lent" in October.

A colourful spectacle Over 2,000 men straining at the oars, chanting ancient hymns and all dressed in brilliant costumes used to make quite a sight as the royal barges were brought out to mark important events such as the celebration of the 200th anniversary of the Chakri Dynasty and the 12-year birthday cycles of the king. The barges were last presented for the king's Golden Jubilee in 1996. However, due to their frailty, they had to be fixed to stationary piles in the river bed – signifying that perhaps the royal barges had reached the end of an era.

93

The principal barges The king's barge, named *Sri Suphannahong*, is the biggest (about 44m long, with over 50 oarsmen) and is also the oldest and most ornately carved. It takes the form of a golden swan-like bird called a *hongsa,* with a great bauble dangling from its beak, which is a national symbol used on coinage. His Majesty sits under a golden central canopy, tiered umbrellas of state set along the mid-line. Ceremonially dressed crews pull the angular swan's head forward and there is a special crew member whose job it is to chant the rhythm of the oars.

The next biggest barge is *Anantanagaraj*. This has a seven-headed serpent prow and, like the others, elegant carvings along the sides. The full-blown ceremony uses 50 barges in all.

WHERE TO SEE THEM
Visitors can visit the Royal Barge Museum (*Open* 8:30–4:30. *Admission: inexpensive*) on the bank of Bangkok Noi Canal. It is best reached by boat (the regular long-tail from Tha Chang), but vehicles can also gain access at 80/1 Rim Khlong, Arun Amarin Road.

Royal barges at night

Festivals and fairs are celebrated with gusto in Bangkok. Thais seem to celebrate at the drop of a firecracker, at almost any time of year, although dates will vary according to the lunar calendar. See also pages 228–229 and 268. Below are some significant occasions.

THE MOON GODDESS
In September the Chinese community makes offerings of food to the moon goddess. Special altars are crammed with goodies, including "moon cakes", which passers-by are invited to try. There are also dragon dances and fireworks.

94

THE KING'S BIRTHDAY
On 5 December the Sanam Luang area becomes a feast of neon, and outdoor movies play all along Ratchadamnoen Klang Road. It is also "Father's Day" (The Queen's birthday on 12 August is "Mother's Day"). Every fifth year in the 12-year animal cycle is considered to be particularly auspicious; 1999 saw a fine spectacle.

Buddhist festivals Maga Puja, in mid-February, celebrates the spontaneous gathering of 1,250 disciples to hear Buddha's sermon. There is mass merit-making and a candlelit procession. Wat Benchamabophit is a major venue.

Visaka Puja, in May, commemorates Buddha's birth, enlightenment and death. This is the most fervently celebrated Buddhist festival; structures are erected in Sanam Luang for the faithful to listen to sermons. It immediately precedes the ploughing ceremony. Takes place at Wat Benchamabophic.

The **ploughing ceremony** – the royal ceremony known in full as *jarot hangkhai raek na Khwan* – has its roots in the Sukhothai period. The exact day is chosen by astrologers, usually in May, the start of the rains. After the procession, the king and queen appear and the "lord of the first field" comes out to greet them. A white bullock is then yoked to a plough and the lord makes three furrows in each direction.

Astrologers can then predict the next year's harvest. Before leaving, the king asks the lord for some rice seeds to sow in a special patch at Chitladda Palace, to provide the new seed for the next year's ceremony.

Asalha Puja, in July, commemorates Buddha's first sermon to his five original disciples. A few days later, the Buddhist Lent, **Khao Pansa**, marks the start of the rains, traditionally a time when wandering monks take shelter.

Kathin is held during the rainy season, when banknotes attached to "money trees" are presented to *wats*; and **Ok Pansa**, in October, marks the end of the rains.

Wat Saket
The "Golden Mount" hosts a lively fair in November. Typical of *wat* fairs that are held across Thailand, it has amusements, performers and side-stalls, loud music and lots of people milling about, even all the way upstairs to the top of the *chedi*.

Right: making a splash at the Songkran Water Festival (Thai New Year, April)

Trips along the Chao Phraya River or its connecting canals (khlongs) give the visitor a glimpse of how the city must have appeared to the Europeans, who dubbed Bangkok "the Venice of the Orient." The picturesque khlong-*side life with its glittering* wats *and cool palms is being replaced by the concrete mayhem that is Bangkok today.*

No visitor should miss a tour of what remain of the city's *khlongs*. Either take an organised tour; some of these begin from the Oriental Hotel pier, and feature trips on a narrow speed boat, known as a long-tail, followed by a gentle cruise on a converted rice-barge. Or go to Tha Tien, Tha Chang or Maharaj piers, from where inexpensive long-tails leave regularly. It is possible to charter your own long-tail, but beware of being charged an extortionate rate. Long-tail boat rates are about 300–500 baht per hour, depending on size of party; avoid the touts and order a boat from ticket booths located by a wharf.

Chao Phraya express boat service: central stops

Boats can get crowded, but it is great for both views and local colour. North of Krung Thon Bridge the service heads under Rama VI Bridge and eventually reaches Nonthaburi (last boat returns at 5:45). The boat mainly stops along the east bank, but there are ferries crossing to the other side at certain points. There are three fare zones; prices are extremely low.

The great water-trips around Bangkok include those to Bang Pa-In and Ayutthaya, leaving from Maharaj pier at 8 AM, and the floating markets at Thonburi (see page 91) and Damnoen Saduak (see page 124).

Travelling by river

Pier (*tha*)	
Thewes	Just south of Krung Thon Bridge
Wisut Kasat	Samsen Road guest houses
Wat Samphraya	—
Phra Arthit	For Khao San Road guest houses
Maharaj	Just south of Phra Pin Klao Bridge; opposite Noi railway station; canal bus; ferry for Royal Barges
Chang	Grand Palace; canal bus
Tien	Wat Po; river ferry for Wat Arun; canal bus
Rajinee	—
Memorial Bridge	Just north of Memorial Bridge
Rajawongse	For Chinatown
Harbour Department	—
River City	—
Si Phraya	—
Wat Muangkae	For GPO
Oriental	Oriental Hotel
Taksin	For Sathorn Road

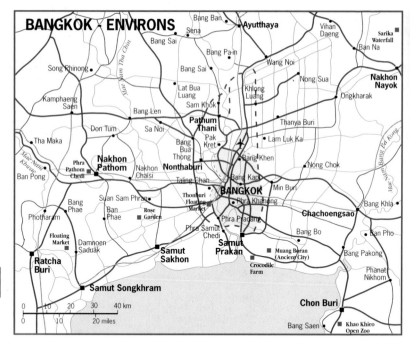

BANGKOK · ENVIRONS

KANCHANA BURI

Start early if you want to visit Kanchana Buri on a day trip. The buses are faster, but less atmospheric than the trains. Special rail tours leave Bangkok soon after 6 AM (weekends and holidays) and take you right to the end of the Death Railway line at Nam Tok, returning (with a stop) via Kanchana Buri in the evening. For a more leisurely visit, stay overnight in one of the raft houses on the River Kwae.

Outside Bangkok

In addition to the places described below, many places mentioned in the chapter on Central Thailand can be visited on a day trip. Early risers should try to make it to the floating market at **Damnoen Saduak**▶▶▶ (see page 124). **Kanchana Buri**▶▶ (see pages 128–131) can be reached by bus or train; allow time to travel the Death Railway section to Nam Tok at the end of the line. The ancient remains of the former capital at **Ayutthaya**▶▶ (see pages 119–122) can be visited by boat, train or bus; stop off on the way at **Bang Pa-In summer palace**▶▶ (see page 121). A less hectic visit is by train to **Lop Buri**▶▶ (see pages 138–139), which has impressive ruins.

If help is needed, there is no shortage of travel agents in Bangkok offering organised tours outside the capital.

▶▶ Muang Boran (Ancient City)

Sukhumvit Road, Bang Puu, Samut Prakan Province
Open: daily 8–5. Admission: moderate
What did Thailand's ruins look like when the buildings were new? This question may be answered at Muang Boran, a collection of reproduction buildings, most of them scaled down to one-third size.

Muang Boran is the brainchild of one man with a great love for the architectural fabric of his country. It is situated near the Crocodile Farm, which is 33km east of Bangkok; the drive takes about two hours. However, be careful when asking for Muang Boran as it means "ancient city" and could be interpreted to mean a real ancient city like Ayutthaya. Numerous tour operators run trips here from Bangkok.

This fascinating attraction presents over 100 of Thailand's major monuments modelled in over 130ha of attractive gardens, laid out in the same shape as Thailand itself. Vehicles are available to explore the site so this could be a short-cut to appreciating the country's cultural diversity.

Hop from province to province in Muang Boran, from the distinctive That Phanom in Nakhon Phanom to Wat Mahathat in Sukhothai. Ayutthaya's Royal Palace, long ruined, has been re-created from old chronicles. The Muslim minority has not been forgotten: there is also a model of the famous Pattani mosque. More humble scenes abound, such as a floating market, and the overall attention to detail is remarkable. There are a variety of refreshments in a pleasing *khlong*-side ambience.

The Ancient City Company can give more details about the Ancient City; its office is at 78 Democracy Monument Circle, Ratchadamnoen Klang Road (tel: 224 1057/226 1936), in the shadow of the *Democracy Monument*, a reproduction of another famous structure. Weekend and holiday tours can be booked here.

▶ Samut Prakan Crocodile Farm and Zoo

30km south of Bangkok on Highway 3
Open: daily 7–6. Admission: expensive

This is the world's largest crocodile farm, boasting over 30,000 beasts. Hundreds of individuals from a variety of both saltwater and freshwater species can be inspected or even fed from a raised walkway. There is a croc-catching show daily and a shop selling crocodile-skin products. "Crocodile Wrestling" and "Acrobatic Elephant" stage shows are given – with audience participation! The place is emphatically *not* to everyone's taste.

▶▶ Suan Sam Phran (Rose Garden)

Off Highway 4, one hour west of Bangkok, tel: 034 322590
Open: daily 8–6. Admission: inexpensive

The banks of the Thachin river in Nahkon Pathom provide the setting for the Rose Garden resort. Visitors pay a small fee to get into the landscaped gardens, lakes and bridges. Choose to picnic, dine in the riverside restaurant, swim, play bowls, boat, waterski or look at the model village. A longish afternoon show at extra charge depicts some costumed aspects of Thai culture, rites of passage, dancing, with shows of Thai boxing and *krabee krabong*, sword and stave fighting. This is a contrivance for tourists, but is very nicely done.

CAPTIVE CROCS
The wild crocodiles that once infested the swamps of the central plains are now confined to zoos or farms like the one at Samut Prakan, but an occasional specimen has been known to escape into Bangkok's sewerage system during the rainy season. The captive crocodiles are not farmed solely for their skins; crocodile meat is a popular delicacy on local restaurant menus. If you're feeling adventurous, it tastes rather like salty chicken.

97

THE SAVAGE CROCODILE
The endangered crocodile was among the most dangerous jungle predators during the "bad old days". Thai respect for this savage old monster can be found in the folk tale of Kraithong, the eponymous hero being the only "crocodile doctor" skilful enough to catch the diamond-toothed Chalawan.

A keeper entangled with a Siamese estuarine crocodile at the Crocodile Farm

A Bangkok street vendor carries her wares in traditional woven baskets, perfectly balanced from a pole on her shoulder

Shopping

CITY FOR SHOPPERS Whether you are shopping in the colourful, lively but swelteringly hot markets or the glitzy space-age department stores, one thing is clear: a cornucopia beckons that can empty your purse more quickly than you can say *thii-raleuk*, the Thai word for souvenir.

There are two tiers of prices in Thailand: "basic" and "luxury". The "basic" items cost approximately 30–40 per cent of their equivalents in Western homes. Prices of luxury, imported goods are roughly comparable with those in the West.

CLOTHES These are obviously popular with visitors. Indeed, the resourceful traveller could take just one change of clothes and purchase a holiday wardrobe going along. The holiday wear is of the casual, brightly patterned "Hawaiian" variety, but bargains do not stop at casual wear; Thailand is justly famous for its bespoke tailors. They might offer some standard styles to choose from, but it is possible to get any style run up from a sketch or photograph. A man's formal suit should cost upwards of 4,000 baht and at least 48 hours should be allowed for fitting and adjustments. A word of caution: there are some tales of people being fobbed off with shoddy workmanship, so be sure of your purchase.

The fabrics available for shirts and dresses are legion. **Cottons** come in brilliant hues and prints. Batik, in particular, is enjoying something of a boom. Some shops sell only cloth, huge bolts of it waiting to be cut. The famous Thai **silk** is still cheap, and you will notice that it is, for many women in Bangkok, just regular office wear (see page 203). Top-quality silk products are offered at Jim Thompson's Thai Silk Company, 9 Suriwong Road.

SOUVENIR SHOPS Most people understandably want some souvenir proof of their visit. Although the charity Oxfam has done sterling work promoting village handicrafts, major credit for the currently booming Thai handicraft scene should go to Queen Sirikit, whose "Support" foundation saved many of the traditional Thai crafts from extinction.

Common everywhere are baskets and furniture made of **bamboo** and **rattan**. These wicker goods are surprisingly cheap, and the *yan lipao* vine from the south can be woven into elegant accessories. The north is famous for intricate **wood-carving** – either figurines or scenes in bas-relief. It is unlikely that you will have space in your luggage for furniture, but it can be shipped anywhere in the world. Whether ornamental or functional, it is all very reasonable. However, it is important to remember that certain types of wood, especially hard woods which have an excess of moisture from the tropical climate, may shrink and crack once shipped back to a drier climate.

MARKETS These are everywhere. The streets of the city are in themselves one huge market, selling anything from silk artificial flowers to a job-lot of barbers' scissors. The grand-daddy of them all is Chatuchak, up by the Northern Bus Terminal on Phahon Yothin Road, accessible by overhead rail or No. 3 bus from Banglamphu. Open only on Saturday and Sunday, it has become known as the "Weekend Market". China, wood, pets, books (including cheap second-hand paperbacks), fabulous food displays and, of course, clothes are sold at stalls cheek by jowl over a huge area. It can get hot, but the experience is worth it.

Other popular markets include **Sampheng** in Chinatown, **Nakorn Kasem Road** by the canal, **Pahurat** and **Penang Market** in Khlong Toey, near the port. In Pratunam, a large covered area on Ratchprarop Road is a good place to find down-market clothes and covers the scene fairly comprehensively.

DEPARTMENT STORES Popular department stores in the central commercial district include Mahboonkrong, Zen and the Siam Centre, which are all within easy reach of each other and surrounded by smaller boutique stores. Other names to look out for are the department store giants of Central and Robinson which also provide Western-style shopping in branches throughout the country.

JEWELLERY AND HANDICRAFTS Jewellery is another of the luxury goods which Thailand exports in large amounts, and which is correspondingly cheap locally. Thais love gold and still buy it by the baht, showing the origin of their money (a baht of weight is 15 grammes of gold). Local production alone provides pearls (from farms in Koh Samui and Phuket), rubies and blue sapphires to be set into gold and made into jewellery.

The factories are concentrated around **Soi Mahesak** to the west of Silom Road. Look for TAT accreditation to make sure the stones are what they say they are; there are a lot of fakes about and "amazing bargains" will probably turn out to be cons. To be on the safe side, the

Lard Phrao department store

BEWARE RIP-OFFS!
Tourists are often approached on the street by smartly dressed people posing as government officials, university professors or similar professionals who strike up a conversation which leads to the tourist being encouraged to buy something valuable, usually gems. To save heartache and disappointment, say no.

THAI SILK
Every colour of the spectrum is available in Thai silk including some fabulous shot-silk which could be called the "Thai hologram", warp and weft shimmering in alternate colours. Enough to make a skirt will set you back anything from a few hundred baht upwards. The *mut mee* pattern is made by tie-dying the threads before they are woven. Not all of it is the real thing, so beware. With a little effort, you can learn to distinguish between the real and the fake by feel.

Shopping

SECOND-HAND GOODS

In the back of Phanthip Plaza, a shopping mall in Phetburi Road, is a second-hand mart, bursting at the seams with odd rubbish. This is a "must" for fans of flea markets in general, as are Wat Mahathat, the canalside and Chatuachak. Wat Mahathat is host on holy days to a market of herbal medicine and Buddha amulets.

FAKE DESIGNER GOODS

Tourist areas have encouraged the growth of several peculiar retail phenomena. Fake goods, whether a designer garment, a watch or a video or music tape, are serious breach of copyright. Pirated tapes are cheap, but pressure from the music industry may well stop the trade.

nearest Tourism Authority of Thailand office or Tourist Police office to recommend a government-accredited gems dealer.

More down-market, but still very attractive, is silver jewellery set with turquoise. Like woodcarving, it is considered to be a northern craft. Many hill-tribes people trek down to Bangkok so they can sell their distinctive tribal designs.

Another fine handicraft is lacquerware. After a block of teak has been transformed with the shiny black lacquer, patterns are either appliquéd in gold leaf or just painted.

OTHER CRAFTS Alternative options of Thai handicrafts include hand-painted blue celadon ware, a craft taught them by the Chinese. Cushions, whether the triangular *morn khwan* or the square *morn kit* are ornately embroidered. Also from the north come hand-painted paper umbrellas and hill-tribe crafts (see page 162). Khao San Road and Patpong Road have numerous craft shops and market stalls.

Narai Phand, on Ratcha Damri Road, is a government-sponsored store with the widest selection of handicrafts from all over the country. Here the stallholders, selling paintings of rural scenes and mounted and framed dead insects, are profoundly deaf. It is a good place to buy as money that is spent here goes directly to the producers rather than to middlemen.

UNUSUAL SHOPS The tourist emporia in Khao San Road has a large selection of music tapes, many of which are pirated. There is a Buddhist bookshop opposite Wat Boworn, with a selection of English titles. Just around the corner from Khao San Road (on the corner of Chakraphong and Ratchadamnoen Klang Roads) is a shop selling papier-mache face masks. Of more practical use to the traveller may be the Camping and Army surplus stores along Krung Gasem Road in the BoBae market area, where good but inexpensive quality camping equipment may be purchased.

A traditional musical instrument workshop can be found on the corner of Tanao and Ratchadamnoen Klang Roads and a huge government school supplies shop on Ratchadamnoen Klang, by the bus stop, is fascinating.

Traditional crafts from all over Thailand can be found in Bangkok. This stall offers models and dolls. Shop around for quality, and don't forget to bargain

Thailand is a hospitable country and this is reflected in its attitude to foreigners (farangs). Almost every nationality can be found here, especially in Bangkok's business community. Some businessmen, such as Englishman David Tarrant of the Inchcape Group, can become very influential in the country's economy.

Westerners The archetypal foreigner was Jim Thompson, the American who set up the Thai silk industry in a big way after the war. He mysteriously disappeared in the Cameron Highlands of Malaysia in 1967, but his company is still active. His famous Thai house, full of the most beautiful Thai paintings and *objets d'art*, is open to the public.

Some Westerners are attracted by Buddhism, and some become Buddhist monks. There is one *wat* in the remote forests of Ubon Ratchatahani which has 20 permanent monks and branches in England, Australia, Switzerland, Italy and New Zealand. A few foreigners teach at the universities and colleges.

Silk was Jim Thompson's fortune. His Thai Silk company shop still offers silk of the highest quality

South Asians Most of the foreigners living in Thailand are from other Asian countries. In addition to the Chinese, there is a big Indian community, many of whom used to work as tailors, producing work commonly regarded as being of the highest quality available in Thailand.

Many Indians have become extremely successful in business, like Sura Chansrichawla, a second-generation Punjabi Sikh, whose hugely valuable real estate makes him one of the biggest landowners in Bangkok.

Far Easterners There were some 40,000 Japanese troops were based in Thailand during the Pacific War. Today there are probably around 25,000 Japanese living in Thailand, most of whom are factory managers and technical advisors in joint enterprises. Although there is little resentment against Japan's wartime activities, there are many left-wing critics of Japanese investment and management methods. More negative segments of Japanese society also appear, notably the *yakuza* or gangsters, who are quite active in Thailand.

The large refugee population of Vietnamese and Cambodians that still live in the border areas of Thailand is a legacy from the IndoChina War.

THAI FOOD
Western foods such as Wiener schnitzel or burgers will make serious holes in your cash, whereas the local Thai food, which may be pricey at home, is very cheap – and genuine.

Food

Bangkok is a great gastronomic experience. The Bangkok posting is a major prize for master chefs of the big hotel chains. Like any large city which opens its doors to all nationalities, it is host to a plethora of international cuisines. See also pages 40–43.

Thai food can be a real assault on the Western palate. To them, Western food is *jeuut* – tasteless. To Westerners, Thai food may be divided into varying "degrees of difficulty."

Isan (northeastern) food is a good example of these variations. The *som tam*, or papaya salad, a speciality of the region, can be made sweet with sugar and peanuts and one chilli. *Tam thai* is made with tiny prawns, and cooked this way most Westerners would find it delicious. The average Bangkok Thai would move up to *tam puu*, with the diminutive freshwater crab and two or three extra chillies, whereas a northeasterner might add the vile-smelling fermented fish they call *plaa raa*, and employ a "scorched mouth" policy with regard to the chillies! With this in mind, it might be a good idea to memorise the phrase *phrik neung met* – "one chilli".

The most international Thai dish must be *khao phat* or fried rice. With either beef, chicken, pork or squid and an egg, you can get it almost anywhere.

SHOPHOUSE RESTAURANTS These also do fried noodles with *phat sii iw* (soy sauce) and the *phat thai* of increasing international fame. The *phat gaprao* (sweet basil fry) on rice has a unique pungence, but probably is best avoided by those with a sensitive stomach.

Much more healthy and more traditional are the 1,001 varieties of *gup* – "with". With boiled rice, that is: the main food of the central plains. *Gup* restaurants are distinguished by rows of pots or aluminium trays. Pointing at the dish of your choice alleviates the language barrier; the order *raat khaao* will get your choices "on the rice" as one dish.

UP-MARKET EATING PLACES Those with a bit of money to spend can go to a "restaurant" as we understand the term. It can be interesting to order one of the exotic dishes and see what appears.

Western sensibilities may be offended by *khai yio maa*, – literally "horse-piss eggs" – which have been steeped in goodness-knows-what for so long that they are quite black when they hit the table!

This sort of restaurant charges upwards of 80 baht for a dish, and is mainly frequented by the professional classes. Note the Thai tradition for picking up the tab: one person pays all. If a boss is dining with his underlings, "face" requires that he is the one who must oblige.

STREET FOOD In recent years the profusion of street food stalls, night markets, charcoal burners, noodle shops and kitchenettes in Bangkok has turned the city into one huge open-air restaurant, and it is here that you will find some of the best regional and local food. The Thais themselves enjoy wandering around to find out what is cooking in the next stall or street.

Bangkok's produce markets are a cornucopia of amazing sights, smells and colours. Catch them early in the morning, and remember to take your camera

Certain distinctly Chinese items have found their special niche on the street. Boiled noodles, whether *nam* (soup) or *haeng* (dry) sell from carts which are often open all night. *Ba'mee*, the yellow wheat-flour noodles, are especially recommended.

From the many rich dishes, try *khao muu daeng* (red pork in a special sauce with hard-boiled egg) or *khao man kai*, white chicken in a fatty rice with dark soy.

The bone-shaped golden crispy *Paa thong go* is a Thai version of hot buttered toast, often eaten after being dipped in sweet Thai coffee.

SWEETMEATS The sweet-toothed have a bewildering choice of *khanom* or sweetmeats. There are the cheap street kind, from the sticky Islamic *roti* to the delicate *khanom beuang*, a coconut cream crisp.

The restaurant diner may opt for the coconut milk/sticky rice concoction; this is easily the best way to appreciate the notorious durian, while mangoes are better known. Try the *pheuak* – an Asian tuber called taro, with a vanilla-like flavour – or the honeydew melon, diced and covered with shredded ice.

The other way to round off a great meal is with fresh fruit. Most kinds are seasonal, like *ngo*, the red hairy rambutans and *malagor*, the fleshy orange gourd papaya, but familiar pineapple and bananas appear all year round.

SPOTTED ON MENUS
Spicy bowel salad
Fried ash with ginge
Ear lice and Thai pepper on pork
Spicex semi biled fish
Fried fish bowel with combination
Boiled crap
Farce [stuffed] with omelette
Fried mice pork

Freshwater crab is a great Bangkok delicacy. But beware of it in remote areas, where it may be contaminated with parasites

103

THE MORNING AFTER
"The world seems tarnished the next morning." – observation after drinking Mekhong whisky.

Food arrives on oiled wheels at Tum Nak Thai, the biggest restaurant in the world, seating around 3,000 guests at a time

Nightlife

Fortunately visitors can easily avoid the sleazy side of Bangkok. By simply walking around and taking in evening street markets, the visitor can enjoy vibrant, Asian life at night, while Khao San Road becomes a meeting place for world travellers, sitting in open-fronted bars and cafés.

They say it was American soldiers looking for some recreation who got the petite farmers' daughters dancing to loud rock music, wearing bikinis and holding on to firemens' poles. That was over 30 years ago. Tourists may have more than made up for the departing GIs, but the fear of AIDS has changed the scene somewhat.

The area around Patpong Road and Soi Cowboy, off Sukhumvit Road, is full of murky dives, mainly catering for men. On the whole this is a concentrated area of spectacular sleaze. The road is named after Phat Phong, a Chinese millionaire who owns nearly everything thereabouts.

The other side of the coin can be seen in the victims of poverty, bad education, pimps, deserting husbands and illegal documents among a host of other woes. Patpong *et al* represent the visible tip of an iceberg of suffering. While the women there enter into voluntary arrangements with the bars, in other establishments their rights are not nearly so well respected.

PUBS AND CLUBS Middle-class Thais thinking along similar lines opened the first "pub", the very popular **Brown Sugar**, on Sarasin Road, north of Lumphini Park. This proved to be a wild success and pretty soon Lang Suan, the area behind Lumphini Park, was a festival of music and drink. Professional bands pump out jazz, rock, reggae and Latin rhythms. The drinks tend to be overpriced, however. Most places are open until around 2–3 AM.

Particularly recommended are **Round Midnight** (mostly Latin), and **The Old West** (South American rock). Sukhumvit Road, and Soi 55 (Thonglor) especially, have more than a few. One which helped popularise jazz in Bangkok is **The Saxophone** by the Victory Monument. Other popular venues with consistently good music are internationally known **Planet Hollywood** (Ploenchit Road) and **Hard Rock Cafe** (behind Siam Square).

Not to be outdone, there are "ladies' clubs" such as **Chippendales** in (fairly remote) Huay Khwang. Women looking for a fun night out can usually find it here.

LATE-NIGHT DINING
If the restaurant you are in looks like it is closing, there are several late openers to choose from. The Isan places are the best, their *som tam* and *nam tok* are renowned drinkers' appetisers.

The neon signs that advertise Bangkok's steamy nightlife leave little to the imagination, especially in the red-light district of Patpong

105

DISCOS Another Western-inspired fixture on the night scene is the discothèque. While small and intimate dance-halls thud in the basements of large hotels like the **Shangri-la** (Talk of the Town), the **Dusit Thani** (Bubbles) and the **Ambassador** (Flamingo), there are a few mega-palaces, whose clientele is mostly students. The most impressive of these is **NASA Spacedrome** on Ramkhamhaeng Road (turn left at the end of Phetburi New Road).

Spasso, at the Grand Hyatt Erawan, offers live music most evenings. Straights and gays are welcome at the trendy **Rome Club**, off Thanom Silom, with its hipper-than-hip music and decadent décor.

A Pattaya-style transvestite revue, **Calypso**, operates in its own large theatre on Sukhumvit Road near the Washington cinema. There are two performances given each night.

DRINKING Licensing laws are loosely enforced and almost any little restaurant can oblige with either beer or Mekhong whisky (foreign spirits being mainly confined to the pubs and discos).

Check out the rum-like Saeng Thip, which is drunk with cola, for a smoother drink than Mekhong, which can have some lethal after-effects. Of the beers, Kloster is a good choice as it lacks the formaldehyde tang of the more popular Singha.

Finally, you may be tempted to try out one of the many cafés, a very Thai institution. Off the tourist track, entertainment is provided by a roster of male and female singers in elaborate evening dress. They sing requests and are rewarded by garlands of jasmine – altogether very civilised!

The traditional khon *performances survive mainly thanks to the Fine Arts Department. Each takes the form of a masked dance-drama and can last for up to eight hours when the fuller versions are staged. Designed originally for performance at court for the pleasure of the king,* khon *drama, like all classical performances, can be a bit heavy going, even for the Thais. However, the programme is leavened with music, from classical (both Thai and* farang*) to folk and popular and the costumes are very extravagant. Actors will happily pose for photographs after a performance.*

OTHER CULTURAL ACTIVITIES

In Bangkok a diverse programme of events centres on the British Council, the American University Alumni, the Alliance Française and Germany's Goethe Institut. The Alliance puts on some excellent films, while the others encourage modern Thai artists of all disciplines.

Bangkok's National Theatre

National Theatre *(tel: 02 224 1342)* This is a large building where plays and *khon* drama in Thai are staged. As befits the theatre's status, the performances are most often adapted from such literary classics as *Phra Lor* or the *Ramakian* epic. This is the Thai version of an Indian legend (the *Ramayana*). There are tales of battles and even comedy where various colourful characters act out the parts.

One of the all-time favourites is the monkey-god *Hanuman*, who is easily distinguished by his white face. The troupe regularly participates in the joint Asian Ramayana festival.

The dancers move with slow, deliberate formality and it is an interesting spectacle, but hard – even for those who understand a little Thai – to follow. The theatre itself is large, its lush decorations and facilities mainly patronised by schoolchildren being dragged through their set texts, although the material of *Phra Lor* is very salty.

Entry to the National Theatre is around 100 baht and English-language programmes can be obtained from the Thailand Cultural Centre. These also contain a wealth of other "arty" activities, current details of which can mostly be found in the *Bangkok Post* and the *Nation*.

The Cultural Centre *(tel: 02 247 0028)* is situated east of town on Ratchadaphisek Road. It offers much more accessible attractions such as recitals, mime, ballet and singing contests. Here they also stage performances of *Likay*, a lively folk theatre. This is much more in the popular vein of entertainment and relies on pratfalls and bawdy lyrics rather than on long or complicated dialogue. The comedy of the early evening gives way to more *risqué* material and the air is thick with *double entendres* until the small hours of the morning. It is easy to see *Likay* in its spontaneous environment all over the country at provincial temple fairs.

Khon Sot (fresh) is halfway between *Likay* and court *khon*. Charity concerts, featuring music from the current Thai hit parade and old crooning standards, are sometimes televised.

Thai classical music performances are put on at the beginning of every month. These ensembles, somewhat cacaphonic to the untrained ear, are tuned on a seven-note scale and are much improved by vocals.

More accessible may be a *Luuk Thung* performance. This folk-with-modern-instruments gives concerts of old favourites sung by some of the country's top commercial stars.

PLASTIC ARTS
The Visual Dhamma Gallery (Soi Asoke 44/28 Sukhumvit) is the place to catch the best of the plastic arts. Universities and hotels likewise plug the high-culture gap; the Imperial and the Monthien in particular stage regular concerts and plays, while the Auditorium of Chulalongkorn University presents a programme similar to that of the National Theatre.

107

Traditional Thai dance

A communal toilet – including a pot and water to use instead of toilet paper

Accommodation

Bangkok offers a full range of accommodation, from the inexpensive guest houses to high-rise, high-comfort luxury hotels. Since the river affords the easiest way of getting around, and many of the major sights are situated close by, it makes obvious sense to base oneself near to it.

Despite the quantity of accommodation, these places fill up alarmingly quickly in high season and advance booking (easier for hotels than for guest houses) is advised. There are disappointingly few places to stay which have real Thai character although some of the hotel towers have breathtaking views from the upper floors.

GUESTHOUSES The popularity of the guesthouse is explained by a combination of low tariffs and informal atmosphere. Budgeteers now have a huge variety to choose from and newer developments have raised the general standard.

Twenty years ago Khao San Road was an ordinary thoroughfare in the heart of Bangkok's historical district. The first guesthouses were basic but welcoming affairs. Khao San Road itself became saturated and the guesthouses have spread out into adjoining streets, mainly around Wat Chana Songkhram up to the river. They are moving north up Samsen Road and east along Ratchadamnoen Road. These are a lot quieter but within easy reach of Khao San Road and a number of guesthouses in an enclave behind the National Library on Samsen Road have sprung up. Look for Little Home Guest House, Tavee Guest House, or on the other side of the library in Soi Wot Racha is the remarkably decorated Racha House. These guesthouses around Khao San Road are convenient for the Express Boat pier at Tha Phra Athit.

New guesthouses, eateries, internet cafés, shops and moneychangers open each year and souvenir stalls line the pavements.

OTHER BUDGET AREAS In Bangkok these include the Thonburi district (around Pata Pin Klao) and Rama IV Road. While the former area is a Khao San offshoot,

accommodation in the latter dates mainly from the days of the Vietnam War.

As a base for provincial travel, the guesthouse scene has one major advantage over conventional hotels. Up-country relatives of the proprietors often advertise in them with enticing notices and business cards, so providing a ready-made basis for somewhere to stay further down the line.

This way, too, there is more chance of finding an English-speaking place that understands how Westerners like to relax, and more chance of meeting other travellers.

MOVING UP-MARKET Above all Thais are keen hoteliers and so the choice for the traveller is great. Hotels in the moderate to expensive bracket are scattered about the city in a bewilderingly random fashion. If you wish to stay in Banglamphu, the **Viangtai** is one of the most comfortable choices, if rather pricey. Moving "downtown", many moderate hotels have the advantage of being open 24 hours a day. One such is the **Reno** in Soi Kasemsan, Rama I, which also has a pleasant swimming pool.

The **Honey Hotel** (Sukhumvit Soi 11) and the **Rex**, prominent on the south side of that road, are two recommended establishments of very similar calibre.

AT THE TOP END Of up-market hotels, the **Oriental**, Bangkok's best-known riverside hotel, is a tourist attraction in itself. The former building has been carefully preserved with details of the famous writers who have stayed there, such as Conrad and Somerset Maugham.

COMMUNICATING
The atmosphere on the streets may be like a mini-United Nations, but curiously enough houses often become favoured by a specific nationality. Nevertheless, English remains the universal contact language.

DISCOUNTS
Hotel construction boomed during the rapid economic expansion of the 1980s, with the result that the number of rooms available in Bangkok usually exceeds demand. In low season, and as a result of recent recessions, hotels often offer very substantial discounts both to tour operators and to individual clients. At certain times of the year, however (festivals, major events, conferences and so on), beds are in short supply and prices soar. Watch out for high service charges and extra tax in luxury hotels.

109

The tradition is kept alive with an award ceremony every year for writers in Southeast Asian languages. Even if you are not staying here, do try to sample the ambience, maybe by stopping by for cocktails at sunset (respectable dress is required).

Gargantuan riverside neighbours such as the **Shangri-La** offer similarly luxurious standards. Luxury hotels further from the river include the **Siam Intercontinental**, which has splendid grounds and traditional-style architecture, the **Regent**, the **Imperial**, the **Dusit Thani**, the **Montien**, the **Ambassador** and international chains such as the **Hilton** for five-star diners or guests. The Regent has a light and airy lobby and the Hilton has refreshingly green gardens.

The cool, spacious lobby of the Imperial Hotel is typical of many of Bangkok's top international hotels. No expense is spared on décor, furnishings and facilities

EARLY DAYS

Thai boxing is supposed to have developed from hand-to-hand combat with the Burmese. King Naresuan the Great was himself a skilled fighter and made it compulsory training for his troops in the 16th century.

MUAY THAI

"Vicious and little controlled" was how one visitor described Thai boxing and certainly it is not hard to believe that only 60 years ago *Muay Thai* – as it is known to its adherents – was illegal. Until the 1930s horsehair strappings were used instead of gloves and rules were non-existent.

The apparent savagery of Thai kick-boxing may alarm Westerners, but there are some rules. Elbow-stabs and drop-kicks are far more common (and effective) than punches

Sports

THAI BOXING Ratchadamnoen and Lumphini are the main stadiums for this part-sport, part-martial art. The audience will bet furiously but won't take a *farang* wager.

There is a lot of bleeding and lost consciousness, with legal blows including such charming moves as the elbow thrust and drop-kick. Looking at the fanatical level of interest in this national sport today, it comes as no surprise to discover that when it was outlawed prior to the 1930s an unregulated underground scene flourished. Eventually a set of rules was adopted: a fighter can use his feet, elbows, legs, knees and shoulders, in fact almost any part of his body. However, butting, biting, spitting and kicking an opponent when he is down are all forbidden. Kick-boxers fight in bare feet and are drenched with buckets of water in between rounds, when they are also pummelled by their masseurs almost as hard as by their opponents.

The kick-boxing ring has proved a successful training ground for regular boxing, Thai fighters consistently taking world honours in the lighter-weight divisions. Junior Bantamweight champion Khaosai Galaxy stayed the course longer than most. The Isan lads produce *Muay Thai* champions like Rambo. Size is not a decisive factor and is not necessarily a measure of potential. Skill and dexterity are more important and a well-delivered kick can floor an opponent.

Tension is heightened by a band which plays drums and the oboe-like *pii chawa*. Before a fight commences, fighters pay homage to their teachers and then start with an elaborate dance. When the fists start flying, the band crashes with the action. There are usually five three-minute rounds, and the referee has the power to stop the fight if one of the contestants is seriously injured.

If you want to sample the frenzied atmosphere of a bout, Lumphini on Rama IV Road is open Tuesdays, Fridays and Saturdays, while the stadium on Ratchadamnoen Nok is open on the other days. However, be warned that tickets for home defences are hard to come by! Ticket prices vary from 1,000 baht or more for a ringside seat to 150 baht for the outer ring.

Kite-flying is now entirely recreational, but when Sukhothai was the capital of the first Thai kingdom (13th–15th century), kites played a more deadly role in warfare. The heads were packed with gun-powder, and the long tails were set alight to act as fuses. Other kites were used to ward off evil spirits, or as festive elements in great state occasions. Nowadays, kites are still sometimes used in rural areas as bird-scarers.

Colourful kites brighten the skies above Sanam Luang when the south winds blow in spring. Traditionally this is a time of leisure for rural workers after the rice harvest is over

111

KITES Kite-fighting as a sport survives today from its origins in the Sukhothai period. Nowadays it tends to be an after-work activity that starts at around 4:30, when the larger offices close for the day.

The large star-shaped "male" *julaa* kite is pitted against several smaller square "female" *pakpao*. Sometimes the *julaa* can be up to 2m long and take up to 10 men to fly; the *pakpao* are smaller and faster and can usually be flown by an individual. For the purposes of a match the "male" and "female" teams will face each other from opposite ends of the field. The object is to force the opponent out of the sky. The *julaa* tries to cross the boundary and capture the *pakpao*, bringing it to the ground back in its own territory. This is achieved by flying a series of skilful loops and sometimes by putting powdered glass on the strings.

Although the days of grand tournaments sponsored by kings are now over, the Mecca for Bangkok fliers is Sanam Luang, the Royal Field. This is a large open expanse between the Grand Palace and Ratchadamnoen Avenue. Ornamental and specialist models are hung up across the paths for sale.

Prime season for kite flying is between March and May when the southerly winds are blowing regularly. Watching this colourful spectacle is really a very pleasant way to pass the time.

The best vantage point for watching the kites in action is probably the benches which can be found under leafy shade to the north of Sanam Luang. The ubiquitous mobile snack-sellers are usually on hand as well to ply the visitor with snacks such as hard-boiled eggs and chilli fish broth noodles.

The children also have kites of their own which are usually in the form of dragons and bats, which they fly for the sheer fun of it, leaving the serious fighting to the grown-ups.

First records of kite-flying as a recreational activity traditionally come from the Sukhothai period. Ramkhamhaeng's father, Sri Intharadit was a major enthusiast. Legends tell how he met the daughter of Phaya Eua retrieving a kite from her roof in the dead of night.

Sports

SWORD FIGHTING

Three levels of the sport of sword fighting are practised: with real weapons, with toy weapons for a striking game, or with decorated toy weapons for a dancing game.

TAGRAW PLAYERS

Tagraw is a national sport and men of all ages spend their time playing in their off-duty moments. Skilled players make the movements look effortless and dance-like as they use different parts of their bodies to keep the ball in the air.

There is no shortage of participants for Thai boxing matches. Despite the jasmine goodluck charms, the prize will go to the most skilful and determined fighter

SWORD FIGHTING Hand-to-hand combat with swords has been successfully turned into a very popular spectator sport by the exponents of fencing and a little-known variant with the traditional Thai battle sword called *krabee krabong*. Also involved in this are the long, spear-like *ngaao* and the stave, *phlorng*, which does give it a resemblance to *Tai-kwondo*.

The sword (the straight-handled *daap*) is used double-handed, or with a shield. The *krabee* with its proper hand-guard is used alone. The *mai san* are short shields for the forearms, which link the sport with Thai boxing. Another similarity is the band which accompanies the fighting, as are the ceremonies paying respect to the masters which start a "bout".

In the sport version, players are arranged in suitable pairs, often matching one weapon against another of a different type: so the stave may be pitted against the arm-shield, for example. There is no firm deciding test of victory – the players attempt set pieces in the roles of "attack" and "defence".

Many children still learn the art while at school and demonstrations are included in cultural shows put on for tourists at such places as the Rose Garden.

TAGRAW or *takraw* is played with a special touch-sensitive rattan ball volleyed between two teams who face each other over a badminton-like net. The object of the game is to keep the ball aloft and any part of the body, such as elbows, shoulders and the back of the head, can be used, except the hands. It is a moot point whether the game originated in Thailand or Malaysia. Malays take it very seriously; their word for it, *sepak* (kick), is added in the combined name *sepak-tagraw* in the Southeast Asian games.

Formal matches can be watched at Hua Mark or the National Stadium on Rama I, although it is very much a participatory sport, with matches going on everywhere. Another version, *Takraw Buang*, resembles basketball. Those without equipment stand around in a circle and anyone who wants to develop their skills can have a go at trying to put the ball through a suspended hoop.

Other sports

BOAT RACING Numbered among the many popular minor sports in Thailand, boat racing involves crews of 20 to 100 paddling brightly bedecked hardwood canoes. The occasional Thai versus Lao contest on the Mekong river is a far cry from Oxford and Cambridge universities' crews battling it out in the annual boat race on the River Thames! Inside Thailand, the Phichit Regatta at the beginning of September is well known, but there are races in provinces as far afield as Nan, Buri Ram and Ratchburi.

FIGHTING FISH Buddhist fish-lovers may be appalled at the bizarre practice of putting fighting fish together in a jam jar to tear each other to pieces to satisfy a wager. On their own they are quite attractive and show no signs of their aggressive potential, but it is a different story if they are allowed to see one another. Two fish in separate jars must be shielded from each other's view.

GOLF Many Thais are great fans of Western sport. While their soccer pitches struggle with floods and droughts, golf courses are well looked after. Courses spring up everywhere as the focus for suburban development and golf is tremendously popular with the leadership élite. Recommended courses in the Bangkok area include the **Navatanee** at Bang Kapi (par 72), **The Rose Garden** at Nakhon Pathom (par 72), the **Royal Thai Air Force** at Don Muang (par 68) and the **Krungthep Kritha** at Hua Mark (par 72).

Of provincial courses, the **Royal Hua Hin** (par 72) is the oldest, having opened in 1924. The **Thaai Muang** (par 72), north of Phuket in Phangnga province, features an 18th hole which is parallel to the beach.

Back in the city, a golf driving-range has been built on Rama IV Road at Soi 26, where it is possible to practise your swing without the tedious long walk afterwards.

SNOOKER This went through a boom after the success of James Wattana and as a legacy of that period there still remain a reasonable number of snooker halls throughout the country.

THAI CHESS The board-game fanatic may enjoy a game of Thai Chess (*Mark Rook*) which is often played on the pavement. The moves are more restricted than in the Western version of the game and it is played faster.

THAI BULL FIGHTING
Bull fighting takes place in the south, but the Thai version is bull versus bull, rather than man versus bull.

SNOOKER STAR
James Wattana, or "Tong", as he is known at home, was Thailand's first snooker player to have major success in world tournaments. In 1986 at the age of 18 he beat three former world champions, Steve Davis, Denis Taylor and Terry Griffiths, to win the Camus Masters' Trophy. In the 2000 British Open he made it into the finals where he was defeated by the world number one Mark Williams.

113

Whatever the weather, golfers in Bangkok pursue their sport with every bit as much enthusiasm as their counterparts in the West

THAI TERMINOLOGY

Thailand is divided into 76 provinces – *jangwat* – which in turn are subdivided into districts – *amphur* – then communes – *tambon* – and then groups – *moo*. A group of houses –*moo-ban* – is the Thai for village. Each province has a hospital, hotels, banks and specialist shops. Districts (*amphur*) may have a hospital or bank, *tambon* and *moo-ban* will have at least petrol and food.

TAXIS AND *TUK TUKS*

If you are travelling by taxi or *tuk tuk*, it is useful to have a good map with you, as some drivers are woefully or wilfully ignorant of the city's geography. Ask your hotel to write the name of your destination in Thai for you to show to the driver. Always negotiate and agree the rate before you set off in a *tuk tuk*. Many taxis now have meters; check it is set at zero when you start your journey.

Practical points

GETTING ABOUT in Bangkok can be a nightmare. Pollution is high on the list of Bangkok's troubles, and masks are now a common sight on the streets. As cars increase, the roads can't cope, and road budgets are a political football.

Trying to drive in Bangkok itself is usually a particularly unpleasant experience – slow, dangerous, smelly, confusing and best avoided. Getting out of Bangkok is a blessed relief. Up-country driving has its drawbacks but jams are not often among them, although there is a shortage of dual carriageway.

Driving at night, especially for motorcycles, is also best avoided. Cars must put up with heavily insect-smeared windscreens, particularly around dusk, and motorcyclists must put the visor on the helmet down or endure an unexpected diet of flies.

The river bus (see page 95) is the quickest way of getting between places within easy reach of the river. For travel from the airport, see pages 256–257.

MOTORCYCLE TAXIS, whose drivers will know the backstreets and can squeeze down alleys, are cheaper than personal vehicle hire, and although their bikes are not all that powerful, they are usually quicker than taxis. They are, however, an extremely risky form of transport.

TUK TUKS, or motorised trishaws, as a practical form of transport do not rate too highly, being uncomfortable, dangerous (unless you are firmly wedged in), and noisy. They are good, though, for loads such as backpacks and giant baskets of fruit and can nip in and out of traffic jams with more agility than buses or car taxis.

TAXIS are clean and air-conditioned and have drivers who will often complain in English about the traffic. They can get expensive and often you may need to insist on the use of the meter to avoid being overcharged.

CITY BUSES are the cheapest form of public transport. Fares range from about 3 to 30 baht. There are several types: non-air-conditioned, air-conditioned, microbuses and express buses. The more comfortable and faster services are a little more expensive, but all buses get very crowded, and pickpockets are not unheard of. Bangkok's chronic heat and traffic congestion make non-air-conditioned buses an unappealing option.

Crews personalise their vehicles with Buddhas and amulets, and Buddhist monks have a right to the back seats, so leave these alone. Women must avoid sitting next to monks. Many frown on the backpacker habit of blocking the gangway with their backpacks.

An indispensable aid for the visitor is the latest edition of the Bangkok Bus Map, which shows all the bus routes in the city.

PROVINCIAL BUSES (see also pages 271–272). Operated by a sprawling state enterprise calling itself the Transport Company, the Thai system is cheap and extensive. If you are trying to get out of Bangkok, the three main terminals are sensibly sited on the major routes out of the city.

North/Northeast terminal
Morchit, Phahon Yothin Road
Destinations served include: Ayutthaya, Bang Pa-In, Khao Yai, Lop Buri, Nakhon Nayok, Nakhon Sawan, Petchaburn, Saraburi, Suphan Buri, Chiang Mai, Chiang Rai, Mae Hong Son, Mae Sai, Phitsanulok, Sukhothai.

From a separate northeastern terminal: Khon Kaen, Nakhon Ratchasima, Ubon Rachathani.

South terminal
Sai Tai, Nakhon Chaisri Road
Destinations served include: Damnoen Saduak, Hua Hin, Kanchana Buri, Hat Yai, Krabi, Phuket, Songkhla, Sungai Kolok, Suratthani.

East terminal
Ekamai, Sukhumvit Road
Destinations served: Ko Samet, Pattaya, Si Racha, Trat. Additionally, numerous travel agents in and around Khao San Road offer bus services; these include frequent minibuses to the airport.

SKYTRAIN The Skytrain (BMTS) officially opened to the public in 1999 and has gone a long way to relieving the hassles of getting around the inner city. The fast and comfortable trains run on two interconnecting lines covering a total of 25 stations. One of these lines runs from Chatuchak Park near the Northern Bus Terminal through the middle of the commercial district and finishes just past the Western Bus Terminal; the other line begins at Taksin Bridge and ends at the National Stadium just east of the Mah Boon Krong Centre. The two lines intersect at busy Siam Square station where passengers can switch between the two lines. The minimum fare is 10 baht and the maximum is 40 baht.

SUBWAY Construction is underway for a subway system, due for completion in 2003.

MICROBUSES
A useful addition to Bangkok's complex hierarchy of bus services is a smart, zippy little red vehicle known as an executive microbus. These are more expensive than the ordinary buses, but with air-conditioning, on-board telephones, newspapers, fax machines and a guaranteed seat, they are understandably popular with Bangkok's hapless commuters, who frequently spend hours in choking traffic jams. A flat fare is charged which you place in a box near the driver.

115

TRAFFIC LIGHTS
Everybody wants to get somewhere quickly. The traffic light sequence in Thailand is red – stop (or when it's clear of other cars and police – go); amber – go; green – go. The normal response to a changing green-to-red signal is to speed up. Only the traffic jams are effective in bringing vehicles to a halt.

Nang Khruan Waterfall

Phop Phra

Kamphaeng Phet Hist Park

Kamphaeng Phet

Bang Krathum

Sai Ngam

Wang Sai Phun

Wan Pon

Phichit

2194m

Khlong Lan

Khlong Khlung Res

Mae Nam Ping

Pho Thale

Taphan Hin

5

Khlong Lan N P

Ban Bang Khao Saan

Khlong Khlung

Khanu Woralaksaburi

Banphot Phisai

Thap Khlo

Bang Mun Nak

Mae Wong Res

Lat Yao

Kao Lieo

Chumsaeng

Cho Dae

Nakhon Sawan

Bung Boraphet

Nong Bua

Khlong Pho Res

Lan Sak

Krok Phra

Tha Tako

Phaisali

Thap Salao Dam

1554m

Thap Than

Uthai Thani

Phayuha Khiri

Tak Fa

Esa Waterfall

Sai Poe Waterfall

Huai Kot

Chai Nat

Takhli

Khoi Charoe

4

Pra Chedi Sam Ong

1810m

Three Pagodas Pass

Sangkhla Buri

Srinakarin Dam

Ban Samo Thong Hot Spring

Ban Rai

Sanphaya

Ban Mi

Khok Samron

Hankha

Sing Buri

Lop Buri

Khao Laem Dam

Dan Chang

Doembang Nangbuat

Chaiyo

Phra Phutthabat

Thong Pha Phum

Chaloem Rattanakosin N P

Si Siwat

Lao Khwan

Don Chedi

Ang Thong

Wat Visu Chi Chan

Tha Rua

Saraburi

Hin Dat Hot Spring

Tham Than Lot

Bo Phloi Sapphire Mines

U Thong

Pratham

Suphan Buri

Ayutthaya

Sai Yok N P

Erawan Waterfall

Bo Phloi

Song Phinong

Sena

Bang Pa-in

Noi Su

Khao Pang Waterfall

Ban Nam Tok

Mae Nam Khwae Noi

Mae Nam Khwae Yai

Phanom Thuan

Kamphaeng Saen

Sa Noi

Pathum Thani

3

BUR

Hellfire Pass

Prasat Muang Singh Hist Park

Ban Kao

Kanchana Buri

Tha Muang

Nakhon Pathom

Nonthaburi

Bang Khen

BANGKOK

Photharam

Floating Market

Rose Garden

Pra Khanong

Samut Prakan

Ratcha Buri

Damnoen Saduak

Samut Sakhon

Crocodile Farm

Andaman Sea

Suan Phung

Pak Tho

Samut Songkhram

Bang Saer

Ban Hin See

Khao Yoi

Ban Laem

Bight of Bangkok

Si Racha

Khao Luang

Nong Ya Plong

Phetcha Buri

Ko Sichang

Kaeng Kra Chan Dam

Tha Yang

Cha-am

Ban Lamung

Ko Phai

Pattaya

Ko Lan

2

Kaeng Kra Chan N P

Marukkha Thaiyawan Palace

Klai Kang-Won Palace

Ko Kbram

Sattahip

Ban Pa La-u

Hua Hin

Pran Buri Dam

Pran Buri

Ban Yang Chum

Khao Sam Roi Yot Mountain

Gulf of

Kui Buri

Khao Sam Roi Yot N P

1

Prachuap Khiri Khan

Huai Yang Waterfall

Thap Sakae

A   B   C

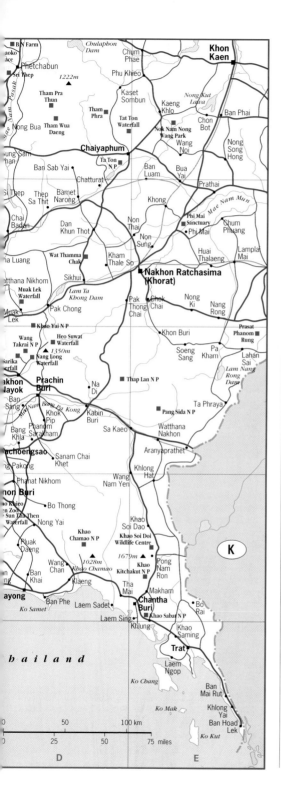

Central Thailand

K

▶▶▶ REGION HIGHLIGHTS

Ayutthaya
pages 119–121

Damnoen Saduak
page 124

Erawan Waterfalls
page 131

Kanchana Buri Province
pages 128–131

Khao Yai National Park
pages 134–136

Bangkok's hinterland, the Chao Phraya Basin, is the most densely populated and agriculturally productive of the country's main rural regions. For the purposes of this book it includes the eastern coast of the Gulf of Thailand.

The **central plain** is drained by the Chao Phraya, the Tha Chin and the Bang Pa Kong rivers, and is very fertile. When the Thai people first arrived here from the north they found civilisations that offered them useful lessons in city-building, administration and statecraft.

The 9th-century Dvaravati culture passed on the strain of Theravada Buddhism that remains Thailand's official religion. Some say Nakhon Pathom may have been the chief city of Dvaravati, although most visitors come to see the 19th-century *chedi*.

A Buddha's head encased by a tree in Ayutthaya

RICE GROWING
The central plains are the rice bowl of Thailand. During the dry season, lampshade-hatted farmers plough the land and plant the new crops to await the rains. Through the summer, the paddy fields turn from green to gold, then the whole community helps with the harvest in November. Modern technology has changed this annual cycle very little in over 700 years. Thailand is still the world's leading exporter of top-quality rice.

When the Mon withered under Khmer pressure, Thai chieftains took the lead. During this time Lop Buri was a Mon-Indic centre offering valuable tutelage. The foundation of Ayutthaya soon afterwards hastened the Thai adoption of Indic rituals and mythologies.

The name "Siam" dates from the Khmer (10th–11th century), who employed Thai mercenaries. Khmer sanctuaries are scattered far to the west. For 400 years the focus of Siam was Ayutthaya (although King Narai decamped briefly to Lop Buri). Although it weathered innumerable vicissitudes, Burma (now Myanmar) finally put paid to its dreams. Rallying quickly, the Siamese drove them out, and Bangkok replaced Ayutthaya as the regional trade hub.

Ayutthaya, Phetcha Buri and Lop Buri are the most striking of the ancient cities within this region. In the far west, Kanchana Buri stands out as a rewarding area for those interested in World War II history and has great natural beauty. It is also easily accessible from Bangkok. Meanwhile, the coast is a well-established pleasure ground, with Hua Hin and Cha-am popular among weekending Thais. Further east, Pattaya is a capital of sleaze and sex, but Ko Samet is an idyllic, though much discovered, tropical island.

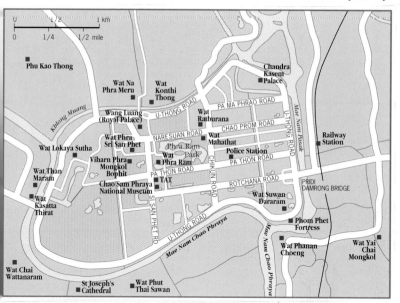

▶▶▶ **Ayutthaya** 116C3

76km north of Bangkok. Trains, boats and buses (northern terminal) from Bangkok

A pleasant day trip from Bangkok, especially by boat or train, the ancient city is littered with the remnants of its former glory. In its heyday, Ayutthaya was one of the biggest cities in the world and the centre of a civilisation that had diplomatic relations with Louis XIV of France. It was his Jesuit mission that built Siam's first observatory. This vast area, scattered over the large modern town, is really too much to attempt to see on foot, but there are fleets of *tuk tuk* drivers on hand to guide people round for half a day.

History In 1350, when it was newly founded, Ayutthaya was just another Thai city state in the Chao Phraya basin. There was Lop Buri, still a centre of Mon-Indic culture, and there was Sukhothai, the overlord. Less than 100 years later, in 1438, Ayutthaya wrested control of the lower Chao Phraya basin from Sukhothai and did not yield it for another four centuries. Whereas Sukhothai represented a rebellion from the Angkor (Khmer) yoke, Ayutthaya's kings, in particular King Boromtrailokanat, sought to consolidate their power through the reimposition of Khmer social controls such as slavery.

By the early 16th century the first voyages of exploration had led to the establishment of European trading settlements. The remains of these can be found to the southeast. Portuguese and Dutch were the most persistent settlers, although the English and French had an important presence.

It is quite easy to imagine Ayutthaya as a bustling city at the hub of an empire. Tourists come to see the ruins, but may be disappointed with the sandstone stumps – all that remained after the Burmese had finished with the capital; their destruction of the city in 1767 was total.

BOAT TRIPS

Many visitors like to visit Ayutthaya from Bangkok via a cruise on the *Oriental Queen* river boat, with a stop-off at Bang Pa-In summer palace. This is a slow but delightful trip; the train and bus provide useful alternatives for getting back (see page 95).

AYUTTHAYA'S HEYDAY

The weathered ruins at Ayutthaya give little inkling of the city's former glory. From the mid-14th century until its catastrophic destruction by the Burmese in 1767 it enjoyed enormous prestige. By the 17th century it was a cosmopolitan trading centre of world renown with a population composed of 40 different nationalities and greater in number than contemporary London. Merchants and diplomats from East and West alike marvelled at its golden temples and splendid pageantry.

Wat Yai Chai Mongkol

SURIYAT AMARIN HALL
King Narai built the
Suriyat Amarin Hall, to the
north of the city, to review
boat races. Banyong
Ratanat Hall was built by
his son, Phetracha, a few
years later in 1688.

The monuments There are altogether the ruins of some
375 monasteries, 29 fortresses and 94 city gates. At the
heart of the city is the huge compound of **Wang Luang
(Royal Palace)**►►► (*Open* daily 8:30–4:30. *Admission:
inexpensive*), attributed to King Boromatrailokanat. Here
are the spectacular remains of **Wat Phra Sri San Phet**: a
trio of *chedis* lined up together contain ashes of Ayutthaya
kings. This was the most important temple in the palace,
and although the Burmese torched the standing Buddha,
you get a good idea of its former glory. Further south is
the 12m-tall bronze Buddha image at **Viharn Phra Mongol
Bophit►**. **Wat Phra Ram,** begun 1369, retains some stucco-
work displaying *nagas, garudas* and other mythical beasts;
elephant gates can be seen in the walls.

Wat Mahathat (1384), with its tall Khmer-style tower, is picturesquely reflected in the pools of centrally located Phra Ram Park. Near by is impressive old Wat Ratburana (1424) (*Open daily 8:30–4:30. Admission: inexpensive*).

Another monument to Ayutthaya's past is Wat Lokaya Sutha, with its large reclining Buddha, recently renovated in gleaming whitewashed cement.

The oldest temple to be found here is Wat Phanan Choeng to the south of the city, which predates the city's foundation by 26 years. Near by, and also beyond the river, is Wat Yai Chai Mongkol.

On the north side of the city, Wat Na Phra Meru►► is worth a detour as it was the only temple that escaped damage. Built in 1503, the *bot* has typical Ayutthaya-period features; there is a wonderful seated Buddha image beneath a gorgeous red and gold ceiling. Some 2km northwest, on the very edge of the city, Phu Kao Thong (Golden Mount)► is a large, slightly out of perpendicular *chedi*; if you have the energy and can bear the heat, climb to the top (the upper portion is restored) for an extensive view of the pancake-flat countryside.

SAMURAI
King Narai the Great had a bodyguard of mercenary Samurai. The Japanese built their own village in the same area, which is marked with memorials.

121

Museums There are two national museums in the city, both with exhibits from Ayutthaya. The **Chandra Kasem Palace**►► (*Open Wed–Sun 9–4. Admission: inexpensive*) is a beautiful pavilion-style building. It was built by the 17th king of Ayutthaya, and reconstructed by King Mongkut as a royal residence. **Chao Sam Phraya museum**►►► (*Open – as Chandra Kasem Palace above*) has a dazzling array of treasures and features displays relating to outside influences on Thai art.

Workers make intricate models of historical figures in Ayutthaya. The city's illustrious past gives them plenty of subject matter

▶▶ Bang Pa-In 116C3

Buses from Bangkok (northern terminal); boat from Maharaj Pier at 8 AM, returning around 5–5:30 PM
Open: daily 8:30–5. Admission: moderate

The famous **summer palace**▶▶ of King Chulalongkorn was originally built by King Prasat Thong of Ayutthaya and abandoned when the city was sacked. King Chulalongkorn used the place to indulge his love of eclectic style. The formal Siamese element jostles with Greek, Italian and Chinese influence.

Most bizarre of all is perhaps **Wat Niwet Thamprawat**▶, reached by a cable car, which proves that the beauties of Gothic cathedral architecture can just as well be used to praise Buddha. The place is none the less sombre and unsettling – Westerners may expect to see a black-clad minister in this setting, but all around are monks in their orange robes. The grounds themselves are pretty and have some curious topiary.

▶ Cha-am 113B2

Buses from Bangkok (southern terminal), Hua Hin and Phetcha Buri. Off Highway 4

Like Hua Hin (see page 125), Cha-am is a seaside resort with a history – though its future is perhaps looking even more high-rise. A mere 20km north of its royal neighbour, Cha-am's beach lies 1km off Highway 4.

The long sandy beach here is the closest west of Bangkok, and the last decade has seen plenty of new guest houses, hotels and resorts spring up. Cha-am is best visited during the week to avoid the weekend crowds from Bangkok.

QUEEN SUNANDA
An obelisk at Bang Pa-In commemorates Sunanda, the favourite queen of King Chulalongkorn, who drowned in a boating accident in 1881. Her boat capsized in full view of many horrified onlookers who could easily have rescued her, but in those times it was strictly forbidden for a commoner to touch any member of the royal family, on pain of instant execution. After this tragedy, the laws of *lèse-majesté* were swiftly reformed in Thailand.

Creative topiary at Bang Pa-In

▶ Chantha Buri 117E2

Buses from Bangkok (eastern terminal) and Pattaya

This ancient port is about 330km from Bangkok, south along Highway 3 and the eastern coast. Popularly known as Muang Chan, it is replete with natural resources. The rainy season feeds the waterfalls and the lush forest; the dry season is the time to take to the province's beaches; and the best time of all is the fruit season.

The town itself is particularly attractive, with many traditional houses and shop fronts. It is home to Thailand's largest Catholic cathedral, built by an emigré Vietnamese community.

Somdet Phra Chao Taksin Maharaj Public Park▶ This is a 60ha public park in the centre of Chantha Buri town (opposite the provincial court). Boats can be hired for

punting. In the middle of the park is an island with a statue of King Taksin, who rallied Siamese troops here in their darkest hour against the Burmese.

The gem industry "Chan" (as Chantha Buri is locally known) is more famous for its position as a centre of Thailand's booming gem industry. The most convenient gem mining region for the casual visitor is **Tha Mai▶▶**. It is reached along Highway 3 and day tours are organised from Pattaya. Twelve kilometres along the route is the small peak of **Phloi Waen**, with **Wat Khao Phloi** at the top. Thai miners have more or less worked out the reserves; jewellers say the last big area for rubies is Phailin, in Cambodia. Beware of the rip-offs and false guarantees that plague the gem trade; see pages 99 and 260.

Laem Sadet Khung Kraben has long, clean beaches. It is off Sukhumvit Road (Highway 3) at km 301, a right turn along a laterite road. Many of the restaurants have bathing rooms for swimmers.

Laem Sing▶, too, is worth a visit, on the left of the river mouth. It can be reached in 10 minutes by boat from one of the fishing villages. A walkway passes one of several ancient forts, **Phai-rii Phinat**, and there are fine views to be had from this hill. To the west of Laem Sing is a clean yellow beach with great views of the islands **Ko Chula**, **Ko Nom Sao** and **Ko Pehrit**, a pair of old cannon remain by a sentry post. In town there are several budget hotels awaiting independent travellers.

Along the road to Laem Sadet Khung Kraben, a right fork leads to the smaller beach of **Khung Wiman**; just before the beach is a large standing Buddha, "subduing the ocean".

National parks Khao Khitchakut National Park lies about 28km northeast of Chantha Buri off Route 3249. It is mostly forest and spots well worth visiting include the nine-level Krathing Falls. Great care should be exercised when climbing the levels.

There are two national park dormitories, capable of sleeping 10 to 15 people each; a large camp here takes 100 people. A fee is collected on the way in.

Wat Khao Sukrim, a further road 16km from Krathing Falls and about 16km from Chantha Buri, is a "reformist" *wat* with a 24-hour supply of free food and a library for overnight stays: this is a *wat* for the devotee rather than the tourist.

Phliw is a particularly charming, three-stage waterfall at the end of a metalled road 16km from Chantha Buri. There are some chedis 200m up, dating from the reign of King Rama V, and a pyramid contains the remains of one of his queens who drowned tragically at Bang Pa-In.

About 4km further on are **Trork Nong Falls**. The "twin peaks" of **Khao Soi Dao** are thickly forested with beautiful mountain views, and a vast wildlife reserve is home to Soi Dao Falls, a 16-level waterfall said to be the biggest and most beautiful in Eastern Thailand (65km north on the Prachin Buri road).

FLOATING MARKETS

Apart from Damnoen Saduak (see below), other floating markets of interest include Wat Sai in Bang Khun Thien, Thonburi, whose over-popularity has spoiled the original atmosphere. In the neighbouring province of Samut Songkhram, several good markets are held on the canals of the Mae Khlong River, especially in Amphawa District. The turn-off from Route 35 is very clearly signposted; Route 325 from Nakhon Pathom is an alternative.

Damnoen Saduak's floating market is one of the most photogenic sights in Thailand. Start early, and take plenty of film with you

▶▶▶ **Damnoen Saduak floating market**   *116C3*

104km southwest of Bangkok; bus service 78 from the southern terminal

Buses run regularly from Bangkok to Damnoen Saduak, a popular tour destination, starting at 6 AM.

Visitors go to see the floating market – most popular of the many that have grown up in the region. All over the navigable system women paddle their little boats, selling food to householders on the banks. The market is held early to avoid the midday heat. The classic Thai peasant's straw hat is much in evidence among the women who mostly trade in fruit and vegetables, visitors looking on from the bridge spanning the canal.

▶ Hua Hin   *116B2*
South on Highway 4, about 230km from Bangkok
Hua Hin is a historic resort, the site of King Rama VII's palace, Klai Kang-won or "far from worries". Of period interest are the royal golf course, the railway station and its hotel, which are now in private hands. The spacious Edwardian verandas are quite impressive.

Hua Hin is well endowed with hotels, guesthouses and golfing resorts – budgeteers can shop around for a homely atmosphere – but maybe this "endowment" has gone too far, as blocks of flats and apartments crowd out the skyline; Hua Hin can be said to be bidding to become Pattaya without the nightlife. The beach is pleasant enough, but lacking in shade.

▶ Kaeng Kra Chan National Park   *116B2*
Off Highway 4, Phetburi (Phetcha Buri) Province
Covering an area of 3,000sq km, Kaeng Kra Chan is Thailand's biggest National Park, located 60km from Phetburi (Phetcha Buri) town. The park office is a further 8km from Kaeng Kra Chan dam, built to service a smaller dam further down the River Phet. Its reservoir has 20 to 30 islands and supports waterfowl and fish. Boats can be hired for 10 to 12 people.

The Thor Thip waterfall Boasting 18 stages, this dramatic spectacle is to be found 15km from Khao Phanoen Thung, the tallest peak in the park at 1,207m; the peak is 20km from the park office.

For walks further into the forest, a guide can be hired to take you to Paa Son Khao Thammachat (a native mountain pine forest) requiring about three days of trekking with viewpoints, cliffs and rock gardens *en route*. The park is not greatly developed but has potential for the future with correct management.

Staying over There is an accommodation service at usual national park rates and it is advisable to make a reservation on 02 579 0529. As with similar places elsewhere in Thailand, the accommodation gets most heavily booked at weekends.

PA LA-U
The Karen village of Pa La-u, a 27km jaunt from Hua Hin, has two stunning waterfalls. If camping, take every precaution against malaria. Attractive features in town include a thriving night market. Walkers can have a go at the stairs up Khao Tagiap (Chopstick Mountain), which has a monastery, a band of monkeys and tremendous views of the coast.

Hua Hin – tranquillity under threat from development

Thailand has suffered huge losses of natural habitats in the second half of this century. It is still rich in wildlife ranging from the exotic insects in town gardens to the giants of the jungle. But many creatures – tigers, elephants and the Sumatran rhinoceros, which is now believed to be extinct – are the creatures most visibly under threat from the desecration of jungles and other habitats – a problem which Thailand is at last trying to counter.

Thai wildlife: fighting a losing battle? A female firetailed sunbird...

Threats Loss of habitats is not the only threat to Thailand's wildlife: in settled, heavily populated regions, it is neither safe nor convenient to have large, potentially dangerous animals wandering around. Hunters and poachers take a huge toll; the rarer some species become, the more desirable they are to unscrupulous collectors, and the prizes to be gained are therefore very high. Several species of mammal, bird, plant and even insect have been brought close to extinction by poachers and collectors. Trading in the meat of wild creatures is commonplace, and media reports on trafficking in pro-tected animal products, such as birds, bears and reptiles, are quite common, especially bound for other Asian countries, including Vietnam, China and South Korea. The Wildlife Protection Division, which has only a handful of permanent officials, faces a grave shortage of funds and manpower to carry out its job.

WILD ELEPHANTS
The numbers of wild elephants roaming the forests of Thailand have fallen dramatically in the last few years. It is estimated there may be fewer than 2,000 left, mostly in the national parks of Khao Yai and Khao Sok. Domestic elephants, too, have dwindled rapidly. Many of the few domesticated elephants have been relegated to the role of entertaining tourists rather than their traditional task of hauling timber.

Variety Thailand is at a geographical crossroads, and has "captured" species from the Indian subcontinent, north-ern Asia and Australasia, as well as southern Asia. This diversity is particularly noticeable in its birdlife; over 900 species have been recorded, making this one of the most exciting places in the world for birdwatchers.

When it comes to insects, the species are literally innumerable. It is possible that they become extinct even before they are recognised, as forests tumble under the loggers' chainsaws.

126

Optimism The Thai authorities are anxious to preserve and enhance the country's wildlife, if for no other reason than its appeal to tourists. Already there are over 80 national parks, protecting more than 40,000sq km of unspoiled areas. One of the best and most accessible is Khao Yai (see pages 134–137), which covers a huge area of tropical rainforest. The rainforests are Thailand's greatest natural treasures, with staggering diversities of plants and creatures. Also of great interest and beauty are the coastal regions, with mangrove swamps, forested islands, salt pans, marshes and beaches.

Elephants The elephant is Thailand's most revered animal and national symbol, once featured on its flag. But that doesn't deter the poachers. A chief warden at a national park recently committed suicide in desperation because his rangers were repeatedly attacked by elephant poachers, armed with M-16s and other sophisticated military weaponry. The maximum fine for poaching is so small as to be derisory.

A century ago there were about 100,000 domesticated elephants here. They were used in war, to carry logs and to open up virgin forest. Now there are just over 2,000 in the wild, and an equal number of working elephants around the country. A very small proportion of them are "white" elephants. These are not actually white all over, but have lighter patches of skin.

THAILAND'S FLAG
The former flag of Thailand was unintentionally flown upside down at the Versailles Peace Conference and people said it looked like "a small domestic animal", so King Vajiravudh changed it to stripes.

127

BEARS' PAWS
In 1991 a raid on a wildlife farm in Damut Prakan province revealed a grisly haul of 40 bears' paws. These are a particular delicacy in the Chinese and Korean cuisines and are believed to enhance sexual prowess.

...and white water buffalo, which like most of Thailand's larger mammals, hover on the verge of extinction, along with many other species

RAILWAY TRIP TO NAM TOK

Three trains daily make this two-hour trip from Kanchana Buri along the 77km that remain of the Death Railway. Advanced booking is not possible. Near the end, the train grinds slowly along a wooden viaduct with views over the river and surrounding mountains. At Tham Krasae it is possible to break the journey and lunch at the bungalow resort below. At the end of the line, *songthaews* leave Nam Tok for Sai Yok Yai, a roadside waterfall. There are frequent buses back to Kanchana Buri.

The Bridge on the River Kwai, immortalised in the film by David Lean, evokes one of the most harrowing events of World War II

▶ ▶ ▶ Kanchana Buri Province 116B3

Highway 323 west of Bangkok. Buses (southern terminal) and two trains daily from Bangkok Noi station

Kanchana Buri Province offers grand scenery, with waterfalls, caves and rugged hills accessible within an hour or two of Bangkok. The **train journey▶▶▶** from Bangkok, which takes three hours, is a real pleasure, passing lush wetlands, forests and paddies; the same train continues to Nam Tok (see panel).

Kanchana Buri Town▶▶, 130km west of Bangkok, has strong associations with World War II, but today the ghosts of the town's grim past seem exorcised, and it is a pleasure resort popular with residents of Bangkok, who at weekends frequent the food stalls by the river and party all night on fancifully designed rafts.

Beyond a bland town centre (bus station and TAT office), older streets towards the river retain characterful wooden shophouses with balconies, and the city gate still stands. A number of waterside guesthouses are relaxing and attractive, although the all-night weekend discos on the river can be irritating.

The Bridge on the River Kwai▶▶ Three kilometres from the town centre is a grotesque remnant, symbolic of the traumas of the Death Railway, built by POWs in World War II (see pages 132–133). Only the two central pairs of girders – the straight-topped ones – are original. The others are post-war replacements. Today trains make special stops at this macabre tourist attraction, and souvenir stalls sell plastic models of the bridge. It is possible to walk across between the rails, but caution is advised due to unguarded drops.

Two of the original locomotives are preserved here, and there are boat trips which leave for the Floating Nun Cave (see opposite), JEATH museum and the Chung Kai cemetery. In late November/early December, a strange weekend sound and light spectacular takes place here, culminating in a mock-up of the Allied bombardment on the Death Railway in 1945, complete with flashes and explosions.

Close by are the **Japanese War Memorial** and the **World War II Museum and Art Gallery** (*Open* daily 9–6. *Admission: inexpensive*). The latter's bizarre exterior is adorned with life-sized statues of historic warriors and figures from World War II.

Chung Kai War Cemetery This is located on the west bank and most easily reached by long-tailed boat from the bridge or from the pier near the old city gate; 1,750 prisoners are buried here.

The War Cemetery at Kanchana Buri

Kanchana Buri War Cemetery►► Opposite the railway station are the gates to these well-tended burial grounds, where 6,982 POWs are interred. An alphabetical register pinpointing locations of graves is kept in the office on the far left-hand side of the site. It is a moving place.

JEATH War Museum This museum (*Open* daily 8:30–6. *Admission: inexpensive*) was established by the venerable Phra Thep Panyasuthee, the chief abbot of the adjacent *wat*. JEATH is an acronym for the main nations involved, which were Japan, England, America and Australia, Thailand and Holland.

The museum is at the far south end of town and is reached by boat from the bridge, or by *samlor*. It consists of a reconstruction of a POW *atap* hut and houses a modest but sobering display which gives an idea of the prisoners' human suffering – objects from the camps, photographs, press cuttings and a series of paintings based on prisoners' sketches that resemble medieval depictions of hell.

Wat Tham Monkorn Thong *6km west of Kanchana Buri town on Highway 3429*. This cave temple is of minor interest – consisting of a staircase leading to a meditation cave – but is celebrated for the Floating Nun who sometimes meditates afloat in a pool and blesses the audience by blowing candle smoke over them.

Prasat Muang Singh Historical Park► *Follow Highway 323 43km westwards, turning left on to Highway 3229, then right on to 3455 as signposted*. On the way you pass the turning for Ban Kao Museum (*Open* daily 8:30–4:30. *Admission: inexpensive*), devoted to the archaeology of a neolithic site in the area.

Prasat Muang Singh (City of the Lions) was a Khmer outpost sited on a scenic loop of the Kwae Noi River.

129

HOG-NOSED BAT

Lawa Cave, in Sai Yok National Park, is one of 21 such cave sites in Kanchana Buri Province which is home to the kitti, or hog-nosed bat, *Craseonycteris thonglongyai*. This is the world's smallest mammal, no larger than a butterfly and weighing just 2g. It is one of the world's 12 most endangered species with only 2,000 animals recorded.

The River Kwai near Kanchana Buri is a hive of activity as tour boats and ferries ply past innumerable bamboo raft bungalows. Despite the peaceful scenery, it can sometimes be quite noisy

130

The major shrine dates back 800 years, its form pierced by four gateways. A shelter by the river houses 2,000-year-old skeletons discovered in 1979; clay pots, bronze, shell and bone bracelets are still *in situ*.

Highway 323 to Three Pagodas Pass A road notorious for its smuggling, this pass leads into Myanmar through scenery characterised by sugar cane fields and curiously shaped limestone hills. This is an unstable and unpredictable area – there have been border skirmishes in the past – and you would be wise to seek local advice before travelling there.

A bus from Kanchana Buri to Sangkhla Buri takes five hours; there are morning *songthaews* from there to Three Pagodas Pass. The main sights on the highway are:

The Hellfire Pass Memorial▶ *signposted at the 66km stone.* (*Admission: donation*) This is a short circular trail incorporating a section of abandoned track from the Death Railway. Begun by Australian POWs in April 1943, the pass was completed in 12 weeks and earned its nickname from their night-time campfires. Some rails have been relaid and a museum is located at the entrance to the trail.

Sai Yok National Park▶ *at the 82km stone, 4km off the highway.* The park is best known for its bat cave (see panel), which can be reached by boat from the pier here, and the Sai Yok Noi waterfall.

Hin Dat Hot Spring *a right turning at the 108km stone.* This spring is a pleasant 40°C – a little above normal body temperature – and can be combined with a cool dip in the adjacent stream.

Sangkla Buri▶▶ *beside the vast Khao Laem Reservoir.* Here the forest has been submerged, but eerie tree-stumps can still be seen above water-level. A spectacular matchstick-like wooden bridge straddles the water and leads into the adjacent Mon settlement. Above this there is a hilltop *wat*, which offers a good view of the lake.

Three Pagodas Pass▶ Along the dirt road to Phra Sam Ong, the route heads past three modest pagodas at the

border. It is often possible to walk into the village of **Payathonzu►** in Myanmar, but cameras must be left behind at the border post (immigration fee payable). Do not attempt to take photos in the village as those who do will have the film ripped out of their cameras by soldiers. Across the border it is strikingly primitive, in contrast to Thailand. Seek advice before travelling.

Tham Than Lot Cave►► *97km north of Kanchana Buri.* This is one of the province's finest caves (electrically lit) with a waterfall near by. There is no direct bus.

Erawan Waterfalls►► These are to be found on Highway 3199 and can be reached by hourly buses and additional excursion buses.

The splendid falls have seven stages; a wet, enjoyable walk to the top takes between three and four hours to do the sight justice. There are pools for swimming, limestone encrustations, tufa and petrified logs. Overnight accommodation is available near by.

Further north, **Huay Khamin Waterfall►►**, remote but majestic, is reached by boat across Sri Nakharin Dam from Takadan pier.

The waterfalls of the Erawan National Park are among the most beautiful and popular in Thailand

BORDER TENSIONS
The border region around the Three Pagodas Pass (Sam Phra Chedi Ong) has long been a scene of ethnic tension between the regime in Myanmar and the two hill-tribe peoples who dominate the area – the Mon and the Karen. During the past 50 years the three groups have struggled for control of the troubled hinterland, and the consequent gains from illegal smuggling, logging and drug-running.

The railway made famous by David Lean's film The Bridge on the River Kwai *commemorates one of the most appalling episodes of World War II. In the midst of the war in Southeast Asia, the Japanese saw the need for a rapid land route to get troops and supplies into Burma (now Myanmar); the voyage by sea, followed by a cross-country journey, was slow and hazardous. In January 1942 they decided to build a 400km railway over some of Asia's most inhospitable terrain.*

THE BRIDGE ON THE RIVER KWAI

David Lean's famous Hollywood film was a fictionalisation of these events, based on Pierre Boulle's novel. Among the cinematic inventions were the blowing up of the bridge by Allied commandos (when in fact it was bombed by the RAF), the use of British engineering skills to construct the bridge (the Japanese knew perfectly well what to do) and the efforts of the Allies in building as quickly and as well as possible (they botched it wherever they could).

Forced labour Allied Prisoners of War captured in Malaya, Borneo, Singapore and Indonesia were brought here to build the railway; 16,000 died. Asian labourers were also enlisted, some from foreign companies in Malaya that had closed because of bombing; others came from India, Thailand, Indonesia and Burma (Myanmar). Many were press-ganged into service. They were regarded by the Japanese as totally expendable and were treated worse than the POWs; the death toll among them was in the region of 100,000 which is the equivalant of roughly one dead for every sleeper laid.

The initial task for POWs was to construct camps at Kanchai and Ban Pong (near Nam Tok). Priority was given to the Japanese guards' accommodation, then workhouses and working parties' huts, and lastly the buildings for sick prisoners.

Work began at Thanbyuzayat in Burma (Myanmar) on 1 October 1942 and a little later at Ban Pong in Thailand. The two parties met at Nieke in November 1943 and the 423km line was completed in December. Allied Forces began Reconnaissance flights in 1943 and bombing followed; POWs were now working on patching up and maintenance, cutting fuel for the locomotives, handling stores and building roads. By the end of October, Japanese troops and supplies were getting through to Burma (Myanmar) and bombing intensified. Conditions for the prisoners temporarily improved in spring 1944 as the Japanese began to worry about world reaction to the heavy POW casualties, but things got worse from May until the end of the war.

Appalling conditions Malnutrition, disease and torture were the main causes of the high mortality rate. Food deliveries were erratic and what got through was often rotten or infested. Many prisoners came to regard maggots as a vital protein source, and some even went to the length of washing the contents of Japanese officers' latrines to retrieve beans that had passed through their captors' digestive systems. Red Cross parcels were often held up by the Japanese, who sometimes deliberately let new food consignments rot.

Malaria, dysentery, vitamin deficiency and cholera were rife. POW camp doctors had to make do with what few medical supplies they had brought with them. Equipment was ingeniously improvised; drips were made from bamboo. Only the sick could tend to the sick; even some of these were forced to work. Prisoners became walking skeletons. Tropical ulcers gnawed them to the bone; rotten flesh was "cleaned out" by fish, which ate away the loose material.

Hours were long and bamboo lashings frequent. Japanese and Korean guards devised sadistic tortures for those who were in breach of discipline or not working hard enough. Offenders were suspended by the thumbs from a branch with their feet only just touching the ground, or they were tied to trees with barbed wire. They were forced to hold heavy stones above their heads, or made to kneel on sharp sticks while bearing weights.

The shadow of death was always close and despair crept into many prisoners' minds. Many died in Allied bombing raids, as they were forbidden to build a white triangle on a blue base, the international recognition symbol for a POW camp.

After the war American corpses were repatriated but those of other nationalities were transferred from the camp burial ground to three war cemeteries – one in Burma (Myanmar) and two in Kanchana Buri. Mass graves are still discovered from time to time in the jungle.

FATE OF THE LINE
In 1945 the British dismantled 4km of track at the border and two years later gave the remaining 300km to Thailand. Thai authorities dismantled the line from Nam Tok westwards and upgraded the rest. The line reopened in full in 1958.

133

Memorial to the victims of the Death Railway at Kanchana Buri (top) and (bottom) the line itself

IN HONOURED REMEMBRANCE OF THE FORTITUDE AND SACRIFICE OF THAT VALIANT COMPANY WHO PERISHED WHILE BUILDING THE RAILWAY FROM THAILAND TO BURMA DURING THEIR LONG CAPTIVITY
THOSE WHO HAVE NO KNOWN GRAVE ARE COMMEMORATED BY NAME AT RANGOON SINGAPORE AND HONG KONG AND THEIR COMRADES REST IN THE THREE WAR CEMETERIES OF KANCHANABURI CHUNGKAI AND THANBYUZAYAT
I will make you a name and a praise among all people of the earth when I turn back your captivity before your eyes, saith the LORD

LEECHES AND TICKS

In the rainy season, cover yourself with insect repellent to guard against leeches. If a leach gets on you, remove it with a lit cigarette or a flame from a lighter. Inspect yourself for ticks, pinhead sized brown insects that fall from plants and burrow into the skin. If you get one, don't pull it out; cover the area with nail varnish or glue.

134

KING MONGKUT'S ECLIPSE

The talented King Mongkut (Rama IV) was a fine amateur astronomer and had a glass-domed observatory built at his palace of Khao Wang, near Phetcha Buri. Sadly, his hobby proved his undoing. On 18 August 1886 he took a party of European visitors into the marshlands of Khao Sam Roi Yot to witness a solar eclipse, which he predicted with startling accuracy to within four minutes. During his trip he contracted malaria and died soon afterwards.

▶▶ Khao Chamao National Park   117D2

Off Sukhumvit Road (Highway 3) at km 274 and a further 17km up to Ban Nong Nam Sai

Located in the Klaeng district of Rayong province, Khao Chamao's 83sq km were declared a National Park in 1975. Waterfalls are plentiful; on the list to see are Khao Chamao, Nam Pen, Khlong Paa Kan, Khlong Hin Phloeng and Khlong Phra Jao. Khao Chamao, also known as Khlong Nam Sai, has very beautiful rock formations. Look out for the big fish in the rock pools, especially the Pla Phluang at Wang Matcha.

Many of the caves at **Khao Wang** have extensive systems of caverns, some of which are very deep. Waai Ii Lo, Thong Phra Rong, Phra and Sa Song have plenty of stalactites and stalagmites, and some caves shelter pools of water (complete with fish). Khao Wang can be reached by turning off Sukhumvit Road at km 286 and continuing for 12km. It is a laterite road: tough going in the rainy season.

▶▶ Khao Sam Roi Yot National Park   116B1

Reach by private transport or by tour. South of Pran Buri off Highway 4, the turning to this national park is found near Kuiburi, by the 286km post, but it is quite difficult to spot. About 40km south of Hua Hin

This is a most impressive, desolate moonscape over flooded paddies, with the mountains clearly visible. The park office has refreshments and very helpful staff. Park beds are available for about 100 baht, and groups can rent a dormitory house for around 500 to 1,000 baht.

A canal behind the office can be explored in a long-tail boat. Between the office and Khao Daeng summit, birds and monkeys abound on all sides. The park is also home to the *serow*, an endangered goat-like animal.

Modest **Samphraya beach**, which is 6km north of the park headquarters, has tents for hire. The more remote and beautiful **Laem Sala beach** (17km) is accessible either by boat or by vehicle. Here, King Rama V built a glittering little pavilion at Phraya Nakhon Cave in order to catch the sun.

▶▶▶ Khao Yai National Park   117D4

Highway 1 to Saraburi, then Highway 2; frequent buses from Northern Bus Terminal and some trains from Bangkok to Pak Chong, where half-hourly songthaews leave for the park gate; here park officials will flag down private cars to take you to the park headquarters.

Thailand's richest national park for wildlife extends across 2,168sq km, straddling four provinces and rising to 1,351m. The road up to the top (Highway 3182) has a signposted viewpoint looking across the park.

Park wildlife The park encompasses a diversity of habitat – tropical rainforest, hill evergreen, dry evergreen, dry deciduous forest and grassland – that gives rise to over 2,000 plant, 70 mammal and 300 bird species. Bird checklists and trail maps are on sale at the park headquarters. It is easy to get lost here, and you would be well advised to hire a guide or take a tour.

Each evening at 8, trucks leave on night safari from the park headquarters and restaurant. As the trucks beam

Khao Yai National Park

HORNBILLS

Hornbills are among Thailand's most spectacular birds. Large, noisy and colourful, they are easily detected crashing about in the trees, or swooping for food. Khao Yai offers refuge to four of Thailand's 12 different species of hornbill. Most striking of all is the great hornbill, with vivid yellow and black plumage. The Indian pied hornbill is black and white. The other two are the wreathed and rhinoceros hornbills. They breed from January to May.

spotlights over the adjacent jungle there is a slight chance of spotting one of the park's 200 elephants which frequent salt-licks near the road. Samba deer are the largest deer species, and display magnificent antlers. Porcupines, palm civets (small spotted cats), gaurs (wild black cattle) and slow loris are commonly seen and a watchtower in the grassland is well placed for a rare view of Khao Yai's two dozen tigers.

Park trails Khao Yai has waymarked trails through its tropical forest. Look out for gibbons, civets and monkeys. Exotic birdsong haunts the forest; the birds themselves often remaining tantalisingly out of sight, but with patience you should get the odd sighting, maybe of the great hornbill, the park's largest bird.

Haew Suwat is the most accessible and popular of the park's many waterfalls, and has a beautiful pool where you can swim behind the curtain of water.

The **Million Bats Cave** is off the Pak Chong road (outside the park at the 21km stone, by a *wat* and a sign to Forest Hill; fork right after 2km to reach a parking area). A steep path leads up to a small cave where a dark swirl of countless wrinkled-lipped bats leaves at dusk. They hunt for eight to 10 hours and trap 6,000 mosquitoes each night. Their guano is used for fertilising fruit trees and also in gunpowder manufacture.

Conservation pressures Khao Yai missed out on gaining World Heritage Site status because of illegal encroachment and the threat of a major dam construction on a site partly covered with virgin forest and inhabited by elephants. In the interests of conservation, a hotel has been demolished and a golf course has been abandoned. The campsite has been retained. Guides should be arranged in advance through the Forestry Department. There are many resort hotels and golf courses on the road to Pak Chong, just outside the park.

Walk

10km circular walk in Khao Yai: trails 1, 3 & 4.

This is a five-hour walk through dense jungle. Tread quietly to enhance your chances of spotting wildlife. The paths are shown with paintmarks and despite the luxuriant vegetation, are mostly well trodden.

Start at Pha Kluai Mai (Orchid) Campsite. Turn right out of the campsite, along the road. After 350m take the trail on the left signed Gong Gheo Waterfall (7km) and follow Trail 3 (red and yellow paintmarks).
The jungle here is usually very quiet, although gibbons can sometimes be heard. Much of the birdlife can only be seen high above. Civets may be spotted on the ground and elephants' dung often litters the paths.
After 1.25 hours turn right at path junction (Trail 1; orange paintmarks). The left path is signed to Visitor Centre. Ignore another left turn for Visitor Centre 10 minutes later.

After another hour's walking continue on to Haew Suwat at the junction, ignoring the left turn to Haew Praton. The final section has fine waterfalls (excellent for swimming) and there is a well-sited restaurant.

Fifteen minutes later, Haew Sai waterfall can be reached by a short, steep path to the left, or alternatively, by continuing along the main path. Both routes unite near the foot of Haew Suwat waterfall, from which it is an easy 1.5 hour riverside stroll on Trail 4 to the campsite.

Wildlife spotting Accessibility from Bangkok means that on holiday weekends Khao Yai gets extremely crowded, with the result that most self-respecting wildlife makes itself scarce. Roaring round in a truck with headlights blazing is less likely to offer good sightings than a patient stake-out at the observation tower, or a guided walk through the jungle with a small, quiet group. Remember to take warm clothes and portable binoculars are worth packing.

MOSQUITOES
Take precautions against mosquitoes at Ko Samet: they are malarial. Netting, cream and spray are advisable for a stay here.

138

King Narai (1656–88), who presided over one of Ayutthaya's most glorious periods, spent more than half his time in Lop Buri, his second capital

▶▶ Ko Samet 117D2

Off the eastern coast of Rayong Province, in the Gulf of Thailand. It is easy to drive or get a direct bus to Ban Phe, the supply port, then take one of the regular boats. On being dropped at Samet harbour, the walk round to the beaches is not arduous, but a pick-up service is available. There are also tour buses

Also known as "the enchanted crystal island", or Ko Kaew Phitsadan, Ko Samet inspired some of the writings of the classical Thai poet Sunthorn Phu. Its beauty, however, has been under threat, and this is another national park (like Khao Yai) where the authorities have felt compelled to reinforce the National Park status in the wake of massive surreptitious development. Towards the end of 1990, and again in 1992, the island was officially closed in a tense stand-off between the government and bungalow operators. The bungalows were allowed to stay, but an unrepentant government refused to rescind the ban on extended development though older buildings continue to be replaced by newer ones under close scrutiny of the National Parks Division. Amenities and facilities have come a long way in the last decade and Ko Samet remains a firm favourite for Thais and overseas visitors alike due to its close proximity to Bangkok (around four hours in good traffic conditions) and idyllic beaches. The weekends in particular see hundreds of Thais coming to "hang out in the air" or *tak agat*, and as a result it gets very busy in August and from December to January.

Paying the national park fee first, it is an easy matter to walk down to the sea at Hat Sai Kaew. This first beach is popular with Thais who have built restaurants and bungalows here. Ao Phai beach also has a good range of bungalows and then beyond a charming little cove is Ao Wongdeuan and some up-market developments. Forest trails run west from the track, linking this string of beaches to another beach and coves, where there are splendid sunset views.

▶▶ Lop Buri 116C4

North of Bangkok on Highway 1. Buses and trains (Chiang Mai line) from Bangkok

The town of Lop Buri lies 155km to the north of the capital. Note that buses take you to New Lop Buri, which is of no intrinsic interest; take a *samlor* to the ruins, as it is much too far to walk. The railway station is within a few minutes' walk of all the historic sights. Lop Buri has considerable appeal for its compactness and modest demands, although it hasn't the wealth of historical remains found in Ayutthaya or Sukhothai. Sites of interest can be walked around comfortably in a half day.

During the Dvaravati period of the 6th to 11th centuries, Lop Buri was named *Lavo* and was one of the country's major centres. In the 10th century it became part of the Khmer empire, but its heyday occured during the reign of King Narai in the 17th century when it was the second capital after Ayutthaya.

King Narai's city wall fortification still encloses the old city, although it is little more than a rough bank. A town gate survives on the south side.

Narai Rajaniwet Palace►► (*Open* Wed Sun except national holidays, 8–5:30. *Admission: inexpensive*) The walled palace of Narai Rajaniwet dominates the town centre. It was built between 1665 and 1677 for King Narai, who died here in 1688. French architects assisted in its design, which shows European as well as Khmer influences. Numerous European emissaries stayed here. The palace stands partly ruined in a pleasant park setting of shady lawns.

Entering through the main gateway, the path leads past a former reservoir, on the left, which once supplied the city and which was fed by terracotta pipes from a source 20km away. The long red-brick building behind is the old treasure house. Over the path ahead, a pointed arch shows clear Islamic influences.

Beyond, a complex of three pavilions house the **Lop Buri National Museum**, a substantial collection, with objects from the Dvaravati period onwards, including fine Lop Buri-style religious artefacts found locally.

Behind this is the roofless audience hall, where Narai received the ambassador of Louis XIV, the Chevalier de Chaumont. Arch-shaped doors and windows hint at the European connection, although others are traditionally Thai tapering oblongs.

Wat Phra Sri Ratana Mahathat► Opposite the railway station, this impressive site dates from the 12th century. Its central *prang* is Khmer in style and later additions include *chedis* in the Ayutthaya and Sukhothai styles.

Phra Prang Sam Yot► By the railway line 200m north of the station, these three giant laterite and sandstone *prangs* show both Hindu and Buddhist influences and represent the quintessence of Lop Buri style. They denote Brahma, Siva and Vishnu, the Hindu trinity.

Across the railway, San Phra Kan is a modern Hindu shrine abutting an ancient laterite mound. Well-fattened monkeys and docile goats frequent the compound, feeding on temple offerings. Feeding of the monkeys, the "monkey feast", can be watched every afternoon at 4:30 and is a lively scene.

LOP BURI STYLE
Khmer (Cambodian) influences on art in central and northeastern regions from the 10th to the 14th centuries produced a distinctive style generally known as *Lop Buri*. Buddha images dating from this period can be seen in many Thai museums, though some fine examples have been smuggled out of the country. The main characteristics of the style include broad, flattish faces, a pronounced bump on the head (signifying enlightenment) and courtly robes with a diadem.

The Khmer temple of Sam Yot, restored by the Fine Arts Department, is a fine example of provincial art. The prangs (towers) are decorated with stucco friezes

VICHAYEN HOUSE
This was built for the Chevalier de Chaumont, and was later the residence of Constantin Phaulkon, Narai's chief minister from Greece; he was the only *farang* to hold such a post in the Siamese court and was killed in a *coup* by Phra Phetracha, who subsequently moved the court to Ayutthaya. Remains of a chapel and hall of residence are visible. There is an inexpensive entry fee.

Central Thailand

PRINCESS CHUMBOT'S GARDENS

The botanical gardens at Wang Takrai Park were established by Prince and Princess Chumbot (see Suan Pakkard Palace – page 91) during the 1950s. Princess Chumbot was a skilled and knowledgeable horticulturist, who imported many unusual varieties of plants and trees from her travels abroad. When her husband died in 1959, she opened the gardens to the public in his memory. A stream flows through the park, adding much to its attractions.

140

Flipflops are understandably popular in a country where it is customary to remove shoes on regular occasions, such as before entering a wat

"Newsmen, young ladies, senior citizens – why be slow? Happiness awaits in Nakhon Nayok. Cast off your sadness into Wang Takrai falls. Boost your morale at Sarika – where can compare with our house?" – Thai promotional leaflet.

▶ **Nakhon Nayok and Wang Takrai**　　　*117D3*
North from Bangkok along Highway 1, then Highway 305. Buses from Bangkok (northern/northeastern terminal)
Nakhon Nayok, about 140km from Bangkok, has a scattering of nearby attractions within a couple of hours of the capital.

Following Route 3049 northeast, crossing over the main intersection in town, will take you up the mountain to **Wang Takrai National Park▶**.

Sarika waterfall▶ is a 3km turn-off to the left on Highway 3049. This popular beauty spot is close to a number of prettily designed bungalow resorts such as Chor Mamuang Cottage, Sut Jai and Po Daeng Wang. These will serve the faint-hearted, while the energetic will find, above the headwaters of Sarika, the **Mae Plong waterfall**, which must be trekked to and camped at. Nang Long waterfall is a short drive to the east.

Takrai Resort was one of the first bungalow resorts built in Thailand. The **Sidari Resort** offers accommodation at Nang Long waterfall, towards the road's end.

The **Chumphot-Phanthip botanical gardens** Forming part of the Wang Takrai National Park, these gardens were founded in 1952 by Princess Chumbot and named after the lemon grass which grows here in abundance.

Dong Lakhorn To the south of the city are the ruins of this settlement, which dates from the Dvaravati period until the time that the Ayutthayan influence made Nakhon Nayok pre-eminent. It was abandoned to the forest 100 years ago.

Ironically, today the surrounding forest is all rice paddies and Dong Lakhorn itself is now a last refuge for many forest species. Artefacts excavated include glass beads and small earthenware pots.

▶ Nakhon Pathom 116C3

West along Highway 4 about 54km from Bangkok. Buses (southern terminal) and trains from Bangkok

Believed to be the oldest city in Thailand, Nakhon Pathom's name is derived from the Pali expression *Nagara Pathama*, "First City".

Phra Pathom Chedi▶▶ (*Open* daily 6–6) The whole city is dominated by this huge tower, which can be seen for miles around. At 127m, it is the highest Buddhist monument in the world. The original *chedi* was a much more modest affair, built during the Mon empire and the oldest Buddhist monument in the country. Nakhon Pathom was then one of a loose collection of city states that flourished between the 6th and 11th centuries. When the town was beseiged by King Anawrahta of Burma in the 11th century, the *chedi* was destroyed and the town left in ruins. Restoration was begun by King Mongkut in the mid-19th century, but eventually these attempts had to be abandoned as the fabric of the building proved to be so unstable. Instead, a new one was built over the original site. This new temple fell victim to a particularly bad period of rain and storms and was finally completed by King Chulalongkorn as the magnificent structure seen today. It commands an appropriately large park setting and is surrounded by trees. Dance drama is sometimes performed next to the outer walls and a fair is held in the temple grounds each November.

A nearby museum contains some interesting sculpture (*Open* Wed–Sun 9–4. *Admission: inexpensive*).

▶ Nakhon Sawan 116C5

North off Highway 117, 241km from Bangkok. By bus and train (Chiang Mai line) from Bangkok

Nakhon Sawan town is situated at a major river confluence, where the rivers Nan, Ping, Wang and Yom unite to form the great Chao Phraya. A meeting of Central and North Thailand adds significance to this large town, whose sights include Wat Chom Kiri Nak Phrot, which towers over the plain and offers excellent views of the surrounding countryside.

At the Chinese New Year a lively dragon procession draws the crowds from far around.

LEGEND OF THE *CHEDI*
Legend has it that the original 39m *chedi* at Nakhon Pathom was built as an act of contrition by a Mon prince who unwittingly murdered his father, thus fulfilling the prophecy which had caused him to be abandoned at birth. After dispatching both his tyrannical father and the unfortunate peasant woman who had adopted him (whom he blamed for his patricidal tendencies), he built the first *chedi* to expiate his sin.

141

The immense golden chedi at Nakhon Pathom is the most recent version of several temples on the same site built over the course of a thousand years

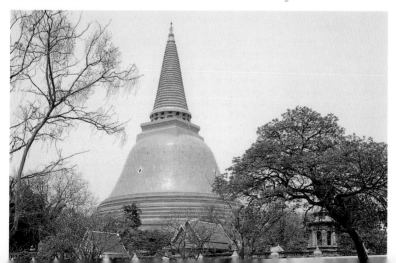

▶ Pattaya

116C2

Off Highway 3 on the eastern coast of the Gulf of Thailand. Buses from Bangkok (eastern terminal)

The legend of Pattaya is well known. From a few GIs sleeping on the beach grew a city to rival its political master, Chon Buri. Starting out with attractions aimed at the young single military man, the settlement soon added other items for family clients, as the new tourist resort turned to the Deutschmark as the main incoming foreign currency. The days of "R 'n' R" are still far from over. Make no mistake: Pattaya is no tropical idyll. Many foreign visitors arrive here on package tours, and must leave with no idea of the pleasures the rest of Thailand offers.

Garish signs and billboards herald the delights of downtown Pattaya in a rash of neon and noise. Whatever else, it's certainly lively

ISLANDS
The sleazy artificiality of modern Pattaya is inescapable. To enjoy a faint glimpse of the unspoiled tropical paradise those war-weary US troops discovered when they first landed here on leave from Vietnam, visit the coral islands just offshore. Despite some pollution and damage to reefs by dynamite fishing, the tropical sea life is still abundant. There are excellent spots for divers and snorkellers on the remoter islands of Ko Sak, Ko Lin and Ko Pai.

If it is simply sand, sun and watersports you want, then Pattaya has them in large amounts. The town itself is dominated by a relentless procession of blue-movie bars, neon signs and "massage" parlours.

Rapid growth Pattaya seems to have passed the worse of the problems it has faced previously – at one time rapid urban development left the beaches unswimmable due to the lack of waste water treatment systems and the place was strewn with building sites.

Prostitution played the major role in giving Pattaya its sleazy reputation and crime rates soared as drug trafficking and related murders and theft became rampant. Spurred on by the advent of the Amazing Thailand tourist campaign (1998–99) the local authorities and the present police commissioner banded together to clean up Pattaya's environment and image, with relative success.

Pattaya has very little to offer in the way of Thai culture, while Western restaurants, bars, clubs and discos abound. For those into nightlife and urban decadence then this is the place to come, but travellers who are seeking a quiet respite at the beach will almost certainly be disappointed.

The beaches There are two beaches here: Pattaya, named after a sea breeze, and the larger Jomtien to its south. The former area, a "ladder" of parallel *sois*, is where the night action takes place in noisy bars. Jomtien is a more pleasant venue for just enjoying the beach, though sitting in the wrong place can mean constant harassment by a stream of vendors.

Virtually every kind of water sport imaginable can be found at Pattaya – parasailing, water skiing, jet skiing, sailing, windsurfing, game fishing and (an activity most popular with young Thais) banana-boating. This is where up to six people straddle an inflatable yellow tube and get towed along behind a ski boat. All these activities make the beach a noisy place but appealing to those looking for good wet fun. Keen yachties should check out the Royal Varuna Yacht Club in nearby Jomtien, where dinghy sailing is encouraged by the king, himself a keen sailor, and where single-handed Laser dinghies can be hire.

Leaving early in the morning are tours to **Ko Lan**, which uses a glass-bottomed boat for the excursion, enabling the travller a better view of the sealife. Less than an hour away, there is a regular ferry, although most people book a tour. Further out, and for divers only, are **Ko Sak**, **Ko Lin** and **Ko Pai**, the latter having an old shipwreck.

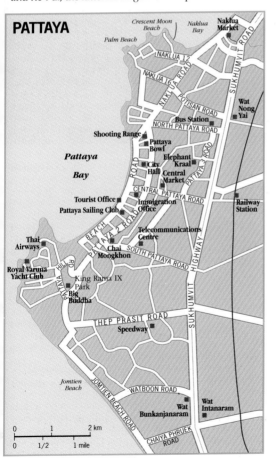

PACKAGED FUN
Water World, at the Pattaya Park Beach Resort, is the perfect water palace. A death-defying bungee jump has been installed, said to be the highest in the world. Kids may love the water scooters, or, away from the beaches, the scale-model Mini Siam and the Zoo, orchid farm, culture shows and handicraft demonstrations at Nong Nooch Orchid Wonderland are popular.

KA-TOEYS
Thailand's transvestites are transsexuals who use hormones. The *Ka-toey* is generally understood to be a passive homosexual who has long had a role in the traditional village burlesque or *Likay*. In Pattaya they make serious money by titillating coachloads of package tourists with lip-synch cabaret routines. The phenomenon has spread from there to Bangkok, and recently to Patong Beach in Phuket. The shows are genuinely entertaining, with an eclectic menu of Chinese, Thai and Western songs. Pattaya's pioneering shows, still going strong, are called Tiffany's and Alcazar.

WATER POLLUTION
Water pollution has been one of the main environmental problems caused by the unplanned escalation of Pattaya into a major resort. For years raw sewage was simply pushed into the bay, with the result that swimming close to the shore became a distinctly unsavoury prospect. Coastal bacterial counts rose to alarming levels, but eventually the government announced plans for a clean-up and invested a large sum in water treatment plants. Things are gradually improving.

MONGKUT'S PALACE
King Mongkut (Rama IV) built the palace of Khao Wang in 1858 as a holiday retreat in an eclectic style, combining Oriental and Western architecture. Views from the hill reward the steep ascent. When the king came to stay, he lodged in the summer house (now the museum), and spent many nights star-gazing from his nearby observatory (see page 134).

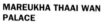

The tall white towers of Wat Mahathat at Phetcha Buri dominate the skyline for miles around. The bot *contains rich murals and fine statues*

144

MAREUKHA THAAI WAN PALACE
In 1924, the teak palace of Mareukha Thaai Wan was dismantled and moved on the orders of King Rama VI from its original location on Jao Samran beach near Phetcha Buri to the southern outskirts of Cha-am, just down the coast. Designed by an Italian, it has been under renovation for many years but is usually open to visitors.

▶▶ Phetcha Buri (Phetburi) Province   *116B2*
165km south of Bangkok, on Highway 4. Trains and buses from Bangkok (southern terminal)

The provincial capital of Phetcha Buri (or the "Town of Diamonds") is a comfortable 2–2.5-hour journey from Bangkok. Phet's proximity to the capital makes it very popular with Thai weekenders; it is worth a visit with a stopover, to take in the many worthwhile sights in and around the province's capital. The town itself is haphazardly and quaintly laid out. Rivers and canals abound and the march of the concrete shophouse is at least partially arrested.

Phetcha Buri town An ancient *wat* of Mahayanist inspiration, **Wat Mahathat▶▶** has an impressive sister temple in Nakhon Si Thammarat. The largest of its five white *prangs* (rounded spires) can be seen from some considerable distance away. Inside is a collection of Dvaravati sculpture dating from the 6th to 13th centuries. This important temple is always a hive of activity.

Wat Yai Suwannaram▶▶ has curious murals in a windowless chapel associated with Phra Jao Seua, "the tiger king".

Well worth a visit is **Wat Kamphaeng Laeng▶**, which is a complex of temples generally in good condition. Indicative of a Khmer presence a millenium ago, there are four red sandstone *prangs* which date from the reign of Woraman VII in Bayon style. In 1956 a statue of Umadevi was discovered inside a broken *prang*. On Kamphaeng Laeng Road in town, the walls remain.

On the west side of the city is the major landmark of **Khao Wang▶▶** (*Open daily 8–5:30. Admission: moderate*). It is the site of King Mongkut's palace and hilltop settlement known collectively as **Phra Nakhon Khiri** ("Holy City Hill"). A cobbled path leads up the hill or, if in need of a rest, you can take the cable car. The vista spans the city, the surrounding river and rice fields and even the border with Myanmar to the west. The area itself is dotted with various buildings of architectural interest, so its worth keeeping your eyes open. The walk up is harder than it looks, and is usually completed with the local monkeys looking on from their vantage points in the trees and surrounding walls.

The site is now a National Historical Park. There is a national museum on the site with items donated by the royal family from their own visitors (*Open* Wed–Sun 9–4. *Admission: inexpensive*).

Beaches Once a favourite haunt of 16th-century King Naresuan, **Jao Samran beach** has now been well developed with hotels and eateries. The wide choice of places to stay includes Jao Hut bungalow (in the budget range), Wong Jan bungalow (moderate to expensive) and Hat Jao Samran hotel. **Hat Beuk Tian** is another clean, wide beach, 7km to the south of Jao Samran. The broad white sands are reached by the Phetkasem highway, turning left at Thaa Yaang. Accommodation at nearby ranges from budget to expensive.

Out of town Some 5km out of town, **Khao Luang** is a famed Buddhist shrine, where a big cave has a tree-lined entrance secured by a door. In the illuminated caverns locals have installed images and a footprint. Opposite the entrance is **Wat Bun Thawee** with striking designs by its former artisan abbot.

Khao Bandai-it is about 2km west of Khao Luang. Vehicles have easy access to the mouth of this pretty Phetcha Buri cave system with its Ayutthaya-period religious accoutrements. Beyond the elephant statues by the entrance lies a labyrinth of limestone caverns crammed with hundreds of Buddha images.

Khao Yoi, another cave system, in the isolated mountain area, is 22km out of town but at least on the railway line and boasts a reclining Buddha, 10m in length. This was a favoured meditation spot of Rama IV when he was a monk.

E-Ko mountain, to the north of Khao Yoi district, has an important *chedi* and customary "merit walk".

EGG CUSTARD
If you have a sweet tooth, you will enjoy Phetcha Buri. This town is famous for its sugary egg custard, made from coconut palm juice and mung beans. Local shops, restaurant and food-stalls sell this speciality (*khanom maw kaeng*), which is still very much a cottage industry. A custard festival takes place each year, featuring a coconut-picking competition between men and monkeys (the monkeys generally win).

145

Offerings of gold leaf and rich cloth adorn the Buddha images of Wat Tham, near the caves of Khao Yai, west of Phetcha Buri

BIRDLIFE IN PRACHUAP
Prachuap Khiri Khan province is an excellent area for birdwatching. It lies on the intersection of several important migration routes between Asia and Northern Europe, and between 200 and 300 species have been recorded. The best time to watch them is between September and November, and the best place to see them is in the National Park of Khao Sam Roi Yot (The Mountain with Three Hundred Peaks – see page 134), a haven for waders and songbirds.

PRAWN FARMING
The brackish marshes north of Prachuap Khiri Khan were extensively exploited for prawn farming in recent years, and much of the environment in the national park was damaged as a result. The prawn farms did not flourish because of endemic disease and steadily the marshes are reverting to their natural state. As King Mongkut's unfortunate experience in 1868 shows, however (see page 134), malarial mosquitoes thrive in this region and precautions should be taken.

Mysterious islets loom from the waterline just offshore from Prachuap Khiri Khan. The view is taken from Khao Chong Krajok, one of the best vantage points in the area

▶ **Prachuap Khiri Khan**   *116B1*
Off Highway 4; 90km south of Hua Hin. Buses from Bangkok (southern terminal) and Hua Hin
Thailand is only 10km wide at the narrowest part of this slender lifeline linking Bangkok with the south. Attractive beaches are dotted down the coastline, although the town beach itself is unappealing. The town, with its colourfully painted houses and lively night market (where you can eat excellent fresh fish) makes a recommended stopover.

Hua Hin, known as the "Royal Resort", is a favourite Thai destination (see page 125), while **Pran Buri**, a small town just over 23km to the south, is trying to emulate its northern neighbour. The nearby beaches of **Suan Son** ("casuarina garden") and Khao Tao are good for swimming. Just off Suan Son is Ko Singto, from where boats can be hired for diving and fishing.

Prachuap Khiri Khan town has an attractive waterfront, a glittering panorama of harbour and mountain. Conveniently close is the walkway up **Khao Chong Krajok**▶▶ ("The Mountain with the Mirror") to a *chedi* and pleasant viewpoint, taking in nearby mountains in Myanmar and the town laid out below. The "mirror mountain" earns its name from a hole in its side which seems to reflect the sky. Halfway up, look out for the guardian monkeys. Apart from this, Prachuap is a typical quiet provincial centre with several bungalows in different price ranges to be found.

Twenty-two kilometres south of Prachuap Khiri Khan, **Wanakon** is a long casuarina-lined beach with clear and shallow water, fine for swimming.

Five kilometres further on lies **Huai Yang Waterfall National Park**▶, refreshing and fish-filled. South again from this is Thap Sakae. The moderately priced Chanruen Hotel (tel: 032 671 411), right on the end of Thap Sakae beach, has spotlessly clean bungalows but the overall

atmosphere is a bit bleak. The budget Chaowalit is a small hotel on a right turn off Highway 4 (tel: 032 671 010).

The last district before Chumphon is Bang Saphan Noi, where **Pa Klang Ao** is a preserved forest campsite only 2km out.

The port at Ban Pak Khlong services **Ko Thalu**, which has fine shallow beaches: a great camping spot. Near the end is **Ao Bor Thong Lang**, a pretty, crescent-shaped rocky bay.

▶ **Saraburi Province**   117D4
North of Bangkok on Highway 1
Saraburi is an unremarkable central province with three
main attractions.

Thailand's most famous Buddha footprint, **Phra
Buddhabat▶**, 27km north of Saraburi town on the road to
Lop Buri, is housed in a most impressive pagoda.

Muak Lek waterfall▶ is fine for swimming and is easy to
find in Muak Lek district on the road and railway to
Khorat (Nakhon Ratchasima).

The remarkable **Wat Tham Krabawk▶** is a Buddhist
answer to drug addiction. At the Krabawk cave monastery,
addicts undergo an intensive course of herbal medicine to
clean out their systems. The recipe was devised by the
abbot from more than 100 plants. The success rate is higher
with Thais, because of their respect for the monkhood.
Reformed addicts put on displays to warn schoolchildren
about the dangers of drugs and herbal products are on sale.

▶ **Si Racha**   116C2
*Southeast of Bangkok on Highway 3. Buses from Bangkok
(eastern terminal)*
Exactly 100km along an upgraded road from Bangkok, Si
Racha is in the middle of government efforts to develop
the Gulf of Thailand's eastern seaboard as a manufacturing base. This is not really a destination for tourists; more
a fishing port which is passed through *en route* for the
island of Ko Sichang.

South of the provincial centre of Chon Buri is **Ang Sila**
and its distinctive *wat*. Many Thai tourists head for the
beach resort at **Bang Saen**. Serious efforts have been made
to clean up this beach, which at times is clogged up with

*Si Racha is a great centre
for seafood, as its indus-
trious fishing fleet
indicates. These colour-
ful boats are searching
for squid, which is dried
on the waterfront*

BANG SAEN LEGEND
At Bang Saen, a shrine
stands on Monkey Hill in
memory of Chao Mae
Khao Sammuk, a Chinese
girl who drowned herself
during the 18th century
when her parents forbade
her to marry her chosen
suitor. It is a favourite
pilgrimage for members of
the local Chinese comm-
unity, who believe that by
paying homage to Chao
Mae Khao Sammuk their
own love lives will be
more fortunate.

JAO POR
The route to Si Racha passes the provincial centre of Chon Buri, head-quarters of the increasingly influential *Jao Por*, or Chinese mafia. It is said they arrange assassinations at bargain basement prices.

plastic bags and bits of rope. On the plus side there are deck chairs, food stalls and swimming showers.

Si Racha may not be a swimming centre, although there are two small beaches. The town has a "seaside" appeal all the same, unlike the rushed, modern Pattaya. Prime spot of the market/fishing town is pretty **Ko Loi**, a small island with a fetching Thai–Chinese temple on it. Sitting at the end of a long causeway, it cuts a pretty silhouette at sunset.

About halfway between here and Si Racha are clear signposts to **Khao Khio open zoo** (*Open* daily 8–6. *Admission: inexpensive*), an 18km detour inland. A variety of species roam over a wide area. Perhaps this is the best place to appreciate gibbons; unfortunately elsewhere in Thailand, domesticated animals are kept on chains and in the wild, mothers are shot for their babies.

Take full advantage of all the beaches have to offer

Ko Sichang►► This is one of the closest islands to Bangkok. The boat there takes 45 minutes and costs about 20 baht. It leaves from Tha Jalin, left of the intersection coming in from the main road to Si Racha.

The island has one town, where the boats arrive, and a hilltop temple overlooking it. The system of roads is toylike and not suitable for cars; however, there are motorbike taxis available. The island is small enough to walk round and a stroll to the far side will take you to several beaches.

Khao Khaat (Hin Klom) beach, on the other side of the mountains from the port area, is amazingly clean for this area, powdery grey sand and shallow waters making it ideal for swimming. It is somewhat inaccessible by road and involves a climb down the rocks. There is another beach at Hat Tham Pang, a little further south and at the end of an unmade track; it has rugged beauty but is too rocky for swimming.

Other attractions on the little island include the overgrown remains of the late 19th century **summer palace**, whose site is still atmospheric even though the best of it was moved to create Wimanmek in Bangkok (see page 92). The hilltop *wat* looks out over the developed, low-lying

side of the island and at its base is an impressive Chinese arch. The **Chakraphong caves** that are found here hold Buddha images.

Besides beaches, the hilly western coast has Tham Phang (cave), Hin Tukata (rock formations), and the garden of Kratok Rok. Pick-up services are available. The oldest established bungalows on the island are 1km from the boat jetty.

Staying at Ko Sichang Well known to travellers, but some way from the beach, is the lovely **Thiw Phai Guest House**. Prices are moderate, and facilities good, making it an excellent budget choice (see **Hotels and Restaurants**, page 279). Day trips are organised to nearby Ko Khang Khao from 10–5. The cost per group is in the region of 1,000 baht. Activities include fishing, snorkelling, swimming and sunbathing. Alternatively there are simple rooms and guesthouses in the town.

▶ Suphan Buri   *116C3*

Northwest of Bangkok and about 70km northeast of Kanchana Buri on Highway 340. Buses from Bangkok (northern terminal)
Suphan Buri town is at the apex of a triangle with Bangkok and Kanchana Buri. A moderately sized, prosperous centre, it is one of Thailand's most highly developed areas – a result of a local man, Barnham Silpa-Archa becoming Prime Minister for a brief while in the mid-1990s and channeling much public money into his home district.

There is not much tourist appeal here, though it does have its attractions, not least of which is its long history, dating back to the Dvaravati Period between the 6th and 10th centuries.

On the outskirts of town is **Wat Palalai▶**, the town's most notable and biggest attraction – biggest because of the tall whitewashed walls around the *bot*. Their height was necessary to accommodate a huge 15m seated Buddha image, which draws hundreds of believers daily to pay their respects and to worship. Many of the surrounding buildings are very old, having been built originally in the U Thong Period. To complete the scene, goats wander round outside the temple.

Nearer the Suphan Buri River and the centre of town is **Wat Phra Si Ratana Mahathat**, set a little way back off Malimaen Road. Most impressive is the Khmer *prang* which contains a chamber at the top of a staircase, which houses a replica of another *prang*.

To the west of Suphan Buri is the war memorial and famous battle site of **Don Chedi▶**. It was built to commemorate the defeat of the Prince of Burma in 1582 and the freeing of Ayutthaya by Prince Naresuan and his forces, riding on elephants.

The site fell into disrepair and was eventually lost and forgotten about. It was rediscovered in 1913, after Rama V had tried and failed to find it, but was not actually restored until the 1950s.

During fair week (see panel), buses run from Suphan Buri and, at other times, from the Northern Bus Terminal in Bangkok. Transport can also be arranged via travel agents in the capital.

U THONG NATIONAL MUSEUM
Open: Wed–Sun 9–4. Admission: inexpensive
Suphan Buri's considerable history is documented in the U Thong National Museum (7km west of town on Malaimaen Road), housing a collection of artefacts dating back to neolithic times. The Bronze Age and several eras of Buddhist sculpture are also covered, and a special section is devoted to the culture of the Lao Song people, a local ethnic minority.

CELEBRATIONS
Don Chedi Monument Fair is held annually during the week which includes Armed Forces Day, 25 January. As part of the celebrations there is a re-enactment of the battle of the princes and their elephants.

PEPPER WATER
Si Racha is famed for its seafood, and even more for the powerful spicy sauce called *nam phrik* (pepper water) that no Thai kitchen would be without. There are several different kinds, but the one manufactured in Si Racha is reckoned to be the best. Made from the ferocious crushed "mouse-shit" chillies and fermented shrimp paste, blended with pepper, garlic, onions and lemon juice, it is an acquired taste for Westerners.

THE GEM MARKET

Opium and teak finance many of the ethnic struggles on Thailand's immediate borders, but near Cambodia, another resource fuels conflict. This region is one of the world's most important sources of corundum gems – rubies and sapphires. When Burma (now Myanmar) ceased overseas trade in the 1960s, the Thai gem dealers seized their chance, and although the Thai mines are virtually worked out, still have immense influence.

▶ Trat Province 117E1

Southeast from Bangkok down Highway 3. Buses from Bangkok (eastern terminal)

Trat province is on the border of Cambodia, some 400km southeast from Bangkok. Its strange shape dates from Siam's most serious tussle with France, when Rama V gave up swaths of the north to remove French troops from this strategic shoreline in the late 19th century.

Malaria still plagues the province, so be sure to take good precautions as you go east. To prevent mosquito bites, it is as well to use several methods of protection (for example screens, net, repellent, coil) simultaneously.

Owing to Cambodia's troubles, and also because of its remoteness, some unpleasant incidents have unfortunately given rural Trat a poor reputation for safety. Travelling alone is not to be recommended. Tension in this area seems to be easing, but take local advice before venturing into remote regions.

Thailand's east coast is an intensely fertile region, full of fruit orchards, rice paddies and rubber plantations. Coconuts are another important crop

The gem markets Northern Trat, like Chanta Buri, is a famous ruby-mining area. The province's most important gem market is in Bo Rai district, found by taking one of the many roads about 50km north towards the Cambodian border. Use the afternoon market on the road to Khlong Yor for small souvenirs, bearing in mind that it is possible to be taken in by some of the wares – it takes a trained eye to tell the value of a raw stone. An added attraction at Bo Rai is the nearby **Khao Salak Dai waterfall**.

Trat town is best used as a starting point for trips to the offshore islands. Its large market is well suited for stocking up with equipment and provisions. All the boats to Ko Chang leave from Laem Ngop district, which is 19km to the southwest of the town of Trat.

Incurable sightseers will want to see the 300-year-old **Wat Bupharam** off the road to Bangkok. In the older quarter, too, are some reminders of the brief French occupation. Several beaches on the coast along from Trat town are excellent for swimming, such as Mai Rut, where purple shellfish litter the beach. On the western side of the Trat estuary is remote but beautiful Ao Tan Khuu, found by carrying on west from Laem Ngop.

Khlong Yai▶▶ Frequent *songthaews* leave from Trat to this atmospheric fishing port close to the Cambodian border. It is a memorable place, with a pier and stilt houses, and the journey to reach it passes through some magnificent mountain scenery.

The offshore islands Trat's 39 islands are becoming increasingly well known; this whole area is a Marine National Park. **Ko Chang**, Thailand's second largest island, has become another popular holiday destination for Thais and foreigners alike, and while it still remains largely unspoiled, the beaches along the west coast of the island have been taken over by bungalow and resorts operators. The development seems to have been reasonably controlled however, and a peaceful atmosphere still just pervades. With such large numbers of visitors arriving, accommodation can be awkward to find at certain times of the year. Due to the heavy monsoons people tend to stay away from Ko Chang between May and October.

Ko Chang▶▶ Here on the Khlong Mayom, whose beauty attracted kings, are some beautiful waterfalls. The park office is at the *khlong* mouth and a passable road links settlements on the northern coast. The **Thanmayom** waterfall is a rewarding sight, as is **Nonsee** waterfall, opposite Tha Dan Mai jetty.

The main beach is Hat Sai Khao, on the northwest side 2km from the ferry terminal (walk or take a *songthaew*), with a number of bungalow developments providing accommodation, from budget to upmarket. On the south side, the atmosphere at **Bang Bao** comes recommended. This place marks the end of the trail some 20km further south of the ferry landings, where a beach stretches over the mouth of a stream. Sadly the island's beaches are plagued by sand fleas.

Ko Kut This, Trat's second biggest island, has become the next victim of development. The trip takes six hours if you can talk your way onto a coconut- or fishing-boat leaving from Laem Ngop, or package tours can be arranged from Bangkok with Kut Island Resort (tel: 02 374 3004). The boats leave several times a month. A trip east down the province's thin tail (Highway 318) enables you to get a (quite expensive) long-tail boat at Ban Ta Neuk, from where the trip takes only an hour. Ko Mat is another smaller island passed on the way to Ko Kut.

THAI–CAMBODIAN BORDER
Carrying on further south from Ban Neuk, Khlong Yai is the last district before the Thai border melts into the sea, surrounded by Cambodia. A border market is conducted near here, and there are some budget and moderate hotels. Not so far away on the Khmer side is Pailin, whose underdeveloped ruby mines are some of the best left. Exports from Cambodia are mostly handicrafts exchanged for everyday Thai consumer goods. Khlong Yai is just one of many markets on the Thai–Cambodian border now thriving in a tentative post civil-war atmosphere.

151

KHAO LAN REFUGEE CAMP
Halfway to Khlong Yai at Aranyaprathet, the Khao Lan refugee camp museum documents a period of history many local people would rather forget. During the late 1970s, Cambodians fled across the border into eastern Thailand to escape the violence of Pol Pot's regime. Khao Lan was the largest of the Red Cross camps operating in Trat province. A decade later, the refugees were mostly resettled and Thai policy changed: Cambodian refugees are now classed as illegal immigrants.

Northern Thailand

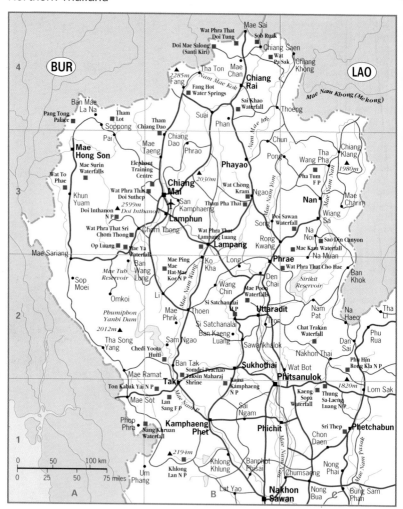

NATIONAL MUSEUMS

Thailand's Fine Arts Department operates the excellent National Museums found in Bangkok and many provincial capitals, especially in areas with important historic or archaeological sites. There are more than 35 museums all over the country. Most have similar opening times (Wed–Sun 9–4). Admission charges are generally very moderate, but signs may not always be in English.

THE GREEN, INTRICATE FOLDS of Thailand's northern mountains merge into the wilds of Myanmar and Laos. Teak forests and patchworks of slash-and-burn agriculture dominate the highlands above the pancake-flat rice plains and prosperous-looking cities. High up, hill-tribes subsist in villages of bamboo huts, roofed with palm thatch or corrugated iron. Waterfalls, hot springs and bat-inhabited caves exist in profusion.

Northern Thailand is still culturally distinct. It retains its own dialects, cuisine and architecture, and it is the temples in particular that show legacies of ancient Lanna and Burmese styles. Although much of the best of the region lies in unsignposted obscurity, fortunately the north is well endowed with tour agencies and trekking companies that get to places that an individual would never find. Tortuous dirt tracks winding up into remote jungle make exciting but demanding driving. Given the very real dangers of the notorious Golden Triangle, one of the world's foremost drug-producing regions, it is best to go with a guide.

CHIANG MAI is likely to be most visitors' first stop when visiting the north. Though smaller than a number of other large industrialised centres, Northern Thailand's main city makes a good starting point: accommodation is plentiful, including good hotels, eating out wonderfully varied and the range of Thailand's famous souvenir shopping comprehensive. It is well placed for Doi Inthanon, the mountain described as the roof of Thailand, and for organised trips to see waterfalls and elephant shows. Yet there are indications that the city has become too commercialised; many tourists find that for all its packaged convenience it has lost its innocence; the real rewards for exploratory travel lie elsewhere.

MAE HONG SON AND CHIANG RAI provinces offer fine scenery and examples of hill-tribe culture, gaining much popularity, especially among independent travellers. Seekers of the real back of beyond should also sample the Mekong River to the east of the Golden Triangle, or the highlands of Nan province.

The lower north has a trio of historic ruined cities, of which Sukhothai is the undisputed pearl. Westwards, Mae Sot is on the edge of some of the grandest mountains in the country.

Northern Thailand

Lisu women in northern Thailand

Map: Northern Thailand

Ban Huai Pung
Mae Aw
(BUR)
Pang Tong
Palace
▲ 1521m
Ban Nai Soi
Ban Tha
Prong Daeng
Mae Hong Son
Ban Balaan
Ban Huai Pang
Ban Sa Pe
Ban Mae
Ngao
Wat To Phae
Khun Yuan
Nong Haeng
Hot Spring
Ban Pa Thaw
▲ 1818m
Ban Hua Pon
Mae La Noi
Tham Mae Hu
▲ 1715m
Ban Mae
Ha Tai
▲ 1634m
**Mae
Sariang**
Ban
Kong Loy
Ban Wang Lung

Ban Mae
La Na
Soppong
Wiang Ko Sai
■ National Park
2042m ▲
Pai
▲ 1962m
Pa-Pae
Hot Spring
■ Muang Paeng
Hot Spring
▲ 1731m
Nam Tok
Mae Surin
National Park
Ban Mae Surin
Waterfalls
▲ 1910m
Nam Mae Chaem
Ban Wat Chan
Ban Mae Sa
Doi Inthanon
2599m
Doi Inthanon
National Park
(1192)
(1009)
Mae
Chaem
Mae Klang
Waterfall
Chom Thong
Wat Phra That Sri Chom Thong ■
(1088)
▲ 1741m
Op Luang
Ban Op Luang
Ban Kiew Lom

■ Tham Lot
Ban Piang
Luang
Wiang
Haeng
▲ 1794m
Tham
Chiang
Dao
Hill Tribe
Centre
(107)
Mae Taeng
Mae Sa Valley
and Waterfalls
Elephants at Work ■
Samoeng
Phu Phing Palace
Wat Phra That
Doi Suthep
Ban
Mae Win
San Pa Tong
Doi Suthep
Mae Rim

Ban Tham
Tab Tao
Ban Ping Khong
Chiang Dao
Phrao
▲ 1718m
■ Elephant
Training
Centre
Doi Saket
San Sai
CHIANG MAI
San
Kamphaeng
Hang
Dong
Lamphun
Pa Sang
(11)
Mae Tha
(108)
Ban San
Hang Sua
Ban Hong
(106)
Ban Mae Lob

0   10   20   30   40 km
0   10   20 miles

154

Drive

A circular route starting at Chiang Mai

The wild northwest is an area of complex mountain ridges, thickly cloaked in forest and laced with waterfalls, caves and hot springs. Allow four to seven days for the circuit, with a few side trips. Take warm clothes in the cool season; unsurfaced side roads are prone to flooding in the rainy season, although the roads on this route are all surfaced.

Those not starting from Chiang Mai would do well to omit the city as, although there is much worth seeing in the centre, the busy roads leading from it are devoid of interest.

From Chiang Mai►►►, Highway 108 heads southwest through straggly villages. Just before Chom Thong►► turn off up Highway 1009 to see the natural wonders of Doi Inthanon National Park►►► (see pages 167–168). Either continue on Highway 1192 to Mae Chaem then take Highway 1088, or retrace your steps to Highway 108.
Just east of the junction of Highways 1088 and 108 **Op Luang National Park Office** is visible, with a pretty gorge► crossed by a wooden foot-

bridge just behind. In winter bright orange swaths of sunflowers make a fine show. In the section of road between Chom Thong and Mae Sariang the Chaem River is a prominent feature. **Mae Sariang** is of little interest but makes a pleasant enough stop-over.

Continue north on Highway 108. Northwards the scenery is unvaried; the hot sulphur spring of Nong Haeng (emphatically not for bathing) can be spotted near the 256km post. Slash-and-burn agriculture has denuded some hills, which are being reafforested with teak and pine. Dirt roads head off into the jungle to remote hill-tribe villages. Soon the road makes a dramatic plunge into **Mae Hong Son▶**, a noted centre for organised treks. The province of Mae Hong Son is peopled by an ethnic mix of Shan, Tha Yai, Karen, Hmong, Lisu, Lahu and others.

Continue along the main road to Soppong, forking left up a dirt track to visit Tham Lot▶▶▶, one of Thailand's finest caves. Back on the main road, carry on southeast to Pai, another good trekking centre. The road, proceeding now in roller-coaster fashion, is a scenic treat. Between Mae Hong Son and Pai, there are some magnificent views

to be seen.
Continue towards Chiang Mai. Highway 1096 bypasses the city to the west (see Mae Sa Valley▶▶, pages 164–165). Loop round from Mae Rim along Highway 1096 and turn south at Samoeng to rejoin Highway 108.

Recommended overnight stops: Doi Inthanon National Park is worth an extended stay and has bungalows available for stop-overs. **Mae Sariang** provides basic hotels and a few guest-houses. **Mae Hong Son** has a wide range of accommodation while **Soppong, Tham Lot** and **Pai** each have guesthouse accommodation. There are also resorts along Highway 1096.

Public transport *Buses from Chiang Mai to Mae Hong Son take about 9–10 hours, but the journey can be split up by overnighting at Mae Sariang, Soppong and Pai. There are no buses along Highway 1096, but songthaews leave from Chang Puak Gate in Chiang Mai, and travel to Samoeng via Mae Rim. Songthaews to Doi Inthanon leave only intermittently from Chom Thong on weekdays (the service is better at weekends) and it is necessary to return to Chom Thong for buses along Highway 108.*

Lisu hill-tribe girls at the rice harvest

155

The corner bastions of Chiang Mai's city walls are in excellent condition, though extensive restoration has taken place since the 13th century

►►► Chiang Mai 152B3

From Bangkok: by bus, journey time of 9 to 12 hours; by train, 12 to 14 hours; domestic flights, 1 hour

Chiang Mai is northern Thailand's largest city and often called the "Rose of the North". The city has a more agreeable climate than Bangkok and many visitors use Chiang Mai as their base. With a little observation you will spot distinct differences between the food, language and traditional culture of northern Thailand and other parts of the Kingdom. Chiang Mai has a fine legacy of temples and its popular Night Bazaar is one of Asia's greatest street markets.

History In 1296, the city superseded Chiang Rai as the capital of King Mengrai's Lanna kingdom, following the capture of the Mon city of Haripunchai (Lamphun) 15 years earlier. It prospered as a cultural and commercial centre, initially with its southern and eastern boundaries secure thanks to alliances with the kings of Sukhothai and Phayao. However it was to suffer centuries of hostilities with Ayutthaya.

In 1556 it became a vassal state after it was invaded by Burma (now Myanmar). Despite liberation by King Taksin in 1775, the centuries of warfare had sapped its spirit and its citizens deserted to Lampang. Twenty years later the population started to return to the abandoned city, which gradually became the major northern outpost of the newly formed kingdom of Siam.

The old city used to contain the palace and the nobles' quarters but now the most visible reminders of its past are the temples. There are dozens of them, many exhibiting signs of Burmese and Lanna influences. A particularly

distinct piece of evidence of the past is the neat square of the old moat which nicely frames the area of the old city. Five gateways exist on this fortification, but on closer inspection it can be seen that they are all reconstructions.

Times have changed The old-world Shangri-La found by visitors in the earlier part of this century has altered beyond recognition. Far from being fossilised in exotic charms, Chiang Mai is now developing faster than any other provincial centre. The first phase of egg-box architecture occurred in the 1950s and '60s, and high-rise condominiums are a 1990s addition to the increasingly prosperous-looking skyline. Residents complain that the traffic, worse every year, is developing at Bangkok-like intensity, and the city has a Los Angeles-style smog.

Chiang Mai's popularity with both visitors and Thais stems from its manageability and unsticky climate. The city is now sophisticated, commercially geared and visibly prosperous. A cultural mix is diluting the cultures of the hill-tribes – a feature which is probably accelerated by the numbers of tourists.

In the city, the number of *farangs* (Westerners) is immediately noticeable. The choice thrown up by this cultural mix is almost bewildering, particularly in the variety of its eating places.

There is an extraordinary choice of souvenir shopping, ready-made opportunities for hill-tribe treks (not the cheapest in the north), a vast amount of accommodation from top-class hotels to world-travellers' guesthouses and a bustling streetlife and nightlife.

Getting about Chiang Mai's simple geography, aided by the prominence of the river and moated area, make it an easy place in which to find your bearings. The huge form of Doi Suthep looms over the city, a reminder of its close proximity to the country's upland region.

It used to be a city to walk around, but the increasing traffic makes this difficult. Many visitors opt to hire small motorbikes, and for those with enough experience, courage and insurance, are probably the best way to get around, especially for trips further outside the city. Both motorcycles and bicycles can be rented cheaply from the Moon Muang Road area. Chiang Mai no longer has a public bus system, though *songthaews* offer a relatively safe and cheap means of getting around. Be prepared for long detours, depending on the destination of your fellow passengers. A smaller number of *tuk tuks* can still be found and bicycle *samlors* still ply the roads though these are finally giving way to the pressures of heavy traffic.

There are city tours organised by dozens of agencies and hotels as well as excursions to places outside Chiang Mai, such as the Golden Triangle.

The downtown area This stretches between Moon Muang Road by the eastern moat to the Mae Nam Ping River. Moon Muang Road itself is very tourist-orienated. There is a great concentration of trekking-tour operators, guesthouses, Western-food restaurants where travellers swap stories over beer, and ethnic fabric shops. The many bars add to its reputation as something of a red-light area.

SONGKRAN DAY
The Thai love of *sanuk* (fun) is much in evidence in the exuberant spirit in which festivals are celebrated here. During the three-day flower festival in early February and the boisterous festivities of Songkran Day on 13 April (Thai New Year) not many people escape a comprehensive dousing in water by hoses, water-pistols or even water-filled condoms; the elderly get a gentler treatment, with a sprinkling of jasmine-scented water – but be prepared – *farangs* are prime targets.

157

SAMPHET MARKET
A visit to Samphet market makes a good early-morning or early-evening stroll. A whole new world opens up here: there are exotic fruits and lady stallholders serenely skinning frogs or hacking up live fish. Further to the east there are several ugly and noisy main roads linked by quieter *sois*. This is the area of the Night Bazaar and Warorot Market.

Northern Thailand

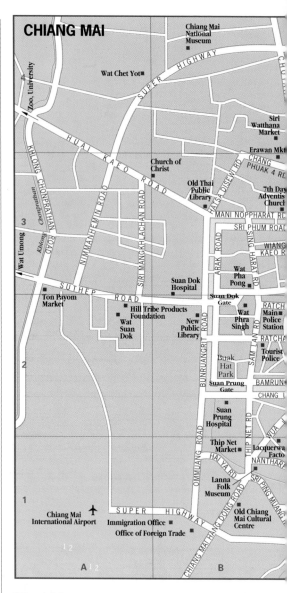

City sights

Chiang Mai National Museum ▶▶   *158B4*
*Super Highway (Highway 11, north of centre) tel: 053 408 568
Open: Wed–Sat, except national holidays, 9–4. Admission:
inexpensive*

A notable collection of religious art, dominated by an
enormous Lanna head. Upstairs there is an entertaining
miscellany, including hill-tribe gear, musical instruments,
domestic equipment, looms and some spectacular
elephant howdahs, as well as a mosquito-proof bed,
which was built for a 19th-century king of Chiang Mai.

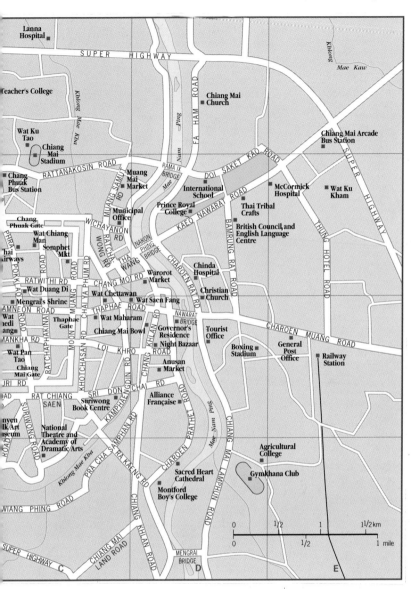

Chiang Mai Zoo▶

Off 158B4

Huai Kaeo Road, tel: 057 220 479

Open: daily 8–5. Admission: inexpensive

Thailand's best zoo has a semi-jungle setting and adjoins a large arboretum. Minibuses for Doi Suthep pass the door.

Lanna Folk Museum▶

158B1

185/3 Wualai Road

Open: daily 10–4 except Thu. Admission: inexpensive

Opened by the Siam Society, this modest display gives a rare glimpse of the interior of a traditional Lanna house built during the latter part of the 19th century. Note the

CHIANG MAI'S FLOWER FESTIVAL

The celebrated Chiang Mai flower festival takes place on the first weekend in February, with a parade of flower-laden floats and a host of beauty contests drawing big crowds to the city.

KING MENGRAI'S MEMORIAL

The city pillar close by Wat Chedi Luang commemorates the spot where King Mengrai was supposedly struck by lightning – his memorial is on the opposite corner of the Ratchadamnoen/Phra Pokklao intersection.

WAT PHRA SINGH'S BUDDHA

The Buddha Phra Singh in Wat Phra Singh is regarded as the original despite the fact that two identical ones exist at Nakhon Si Thammarat and Bangkok. The head of this one was stolen in 1922 and a replacement was made.

octagonal stilts on which it is built, and the walls sloping inwards as they rise – both typical features. The guide prepares crushed betel leaf in the time-honoured manner for visitors to try out.

Tribal Museum► *Off 158A4*

Rachamangkhla Park (5km north of the city)
Open: Mon–Fri 9–4. Admission: inexpensive

Built on a small peninsula jutting into a lake in Rachamangkhla Park on the road to Mae Rim, the Tribal Museum provides a wealthy insight into hill-tribe culture. It has three floors of well-presented exhibits including displays on the involvement and role of the Royal Family in the development and preservation of the hill-tribe people and culture.

Wat Chedi Luang► ► *159C2*

Phra Poklao Road

This is one of Chiang Mai's best-known temples. Its central *stupa* dates from 15th-century and was partly restored after an earthquake in the 16th century: however it remains incomplete. The *luk meuong* (city pillar) of Chiang Mai is here, guarded by two giant demons sent by the god Rama-Indra.

Wat Chet Yot► *158A4*

Off the super highway (Highway 11) just southwest of the National Museum; look for the sign for the Rajamangala Institute of Technology

Built in 1455 to house the relics of the monk Phra Mahathera Uttamapanya, the *chedi* retains outstanding stucco reliefs of cross-legged figures giving a *wai*. Wat Chet Yot is a copy of Buddha Gaya in India, where the Buddha attained enlightenment under a bodhi tree; the seven spires referred to in its name represent the seven weeks he spent there.

Wat Chiang Man► *159C3*

Ratchaphakinai Road

Built by King Mengrai in 1296, this is thought to be the city's oldest *wat*, known for two small but much venerated Buddha images: the 8th-century marble Phra Sila, thought to be from India or Sri Lanka, and the Crystal Buddha, supposedly presented to the Queen of Haripunchai in the 7th century.

Wat Pan Tao► *159C2*

Phra Pokklao Road (next to Wat Chedi Luang)

A fine, untampered example of a Lanna *wiharn*, retaining its original panelled walls.

Wat Phra Singh► ► *158B2*

Sing Harat Road

This absorbing temple in the old city was founded in 1345 to house the ashes of King Kham Fu. It has a new *wiharn* dating from 1925, a wooden *bot* behind and a late Lanna *wiharn* (ca1806–11) which contains the celebrated Buddha Phra Singh. The walls are decorated with murals depicting legends and scenes of old city life. Look for the textiles and tattoos popular at the time.

Wat Suan Dok▶
Suthep Road   *158A2*

Virtually next-door to the Hill Tribe Products Foundation, this contains the burial ground for many of the Chiang Mai royalty. The wedding-cake stucco on the *chedis* housing the remains presents a dazzling show. A central *chedi* contains a Buddha relic that was brought by a white elephant, so the story goes, hence the "White Elephant Gate"– Pratu Chang Puak – in the city wall. On offer here is herbal massage.

Wat Umong▶
Off Suthep Road (signposted)   *Off 158A3*

Located on an obscure *soi* (lane) in the extreme west of the city, this forest *wat* dates from 1296 and is perhaps the city's most quirky temple. A multitude of signs moralise from every tree: "Time unused is the longest time"; "Love is a flower garden to be watered by tears"; you can hardly see the woods for the wisdom.

Monks' bungalows are scattered around the forest, which gives on to a lake fringed with banana palms. At the top of the site, an emaciated Buddha image sits contemplatively close to a *chedi*, his ribcage sunken inwards as the result of fasting. Immediately below is a labyrinth of subterranean meditation chambers: sermons on meditation are given in English. They begin at 3 PM on Sundays and go on until about 6 PM.

Environs of Chiang Mai
Wat Phra That Doi Suthep▶▶▶
      152B3

This much-visited temple stands on the sacred mountain of Doi Suthep that towers over Chiang Mai. The white elephant that carried a Buddha relic to Wat Suan Dok (see above) is said to have fallen and died on this spot. From the road where jade and ivory factory showrooms do a roaring trade, a 300-step staircase flanked by a pair of huge *nagas* (dragon-headed serpents) leads to the top. Walking is not necessary, as s cable-car glides up in seconds very cheaply.

Wat Phra That Doi Suthep was founded by King Ku Na in 1383 and contains an exquisite courtyard with a gold *chedi* housing a Buddha relic, and intricate gold parasols. Frequent and inexpensive *songthaews* depart for Doi Suthep from the northwest side of Chang Puak Gate in Chiang Mai. You can travel on to the winter palace and Meo village.

continued on page 164

TREKKING COMPANIES
There are scores of trekking companies based in Chiang Mai and competition is fierce. Specific recommendations are hard to give because the situation is very fluid. The quality of a trek depends greatly on individual guides, who change companies frequently. Take up-to-date advice from the tourist office or tourist police before spending your money, as some companies are less reputable. The cheapest operators may not provide a safe or worthwhile tour.

TRADITIONAL THAI MASSAGE
(see page 47)
This is offered throughout the city. Ask for "ancient massage" to distinguish it from the sexual variety, and try to set aside three hours for a "full body" treatment. Many courses on Thai massage are available in Chiang Mai – highly recommended is the Institute of Thai Massage (ITM) just north of the moat (tel: 053 218 632, 224 197).

The spectacular temple of Wat Phra That Doi Suthep is a glittering assembly of intricately carved wood and filigree gold

There are dozens of shops between the Night Bazaar and Mun Muang Road selling ethnic clothes and crafts. Of the hill-tribe products, everyone has a personal favourite. The many designs are made into anything that will sell: oven mitts, jackets, cushion covers, rucksacks, bumbags and even baseball caps. Other ethnic goods include attractive Lanna-style cotton and silk fabrics, and Burmese-style souvenirs, many of which are actually made in Thailand.

162

UMBRELLAS
Umbrellas are a speciality product of the village of Bo Sang, 9km from Chiang Mai on the San Kamphaeng road, a popular venue for handicraft tours. Watching them being made is an entertainment, as cane stems are cut and trimmed for handles and bamboo strips are assembled into frames. Various materials are used for the canopy: fabric, paper or thin bark from the *sa* tree. The umbrellas are decorated with traditional designs of birds, flowers, butterflies and foliage.

Hill-tribe products Of the many different styles, Yao textiles are characterised by intricate cross-stitch embroidery, those of the Hmong by larger, coarser stitchwork, Akha fabrics by long stitches – bright diamonds and triangles on black with silver bangles and medallions, Lahu by bright colours and sequins, Lisu work by colourful bands and squares.

There is an assortment of highly idiosyncratic souvenirs including opium pipes, Karen *sung* banjos, Akha bamboo musical blow-pipes, double-sided drums, Yao dolls and lacquered buffalo horns.

Burmese-style souvenirs There are cushion-covers, typically with embroidered elephants, peacocks and scenes from Burma's (now Myanmar) folk tales sewn on to velvet. The better ones use silver for the sequins and quartz for the beads. The wall-hangings are spectacular.

Silk Thai silk is justly famous for its quality and is sold as plain coloured, check patterns or printed with designs. Beware of fake silk, often sold as the real thing.

Woodcarving An age-old tradition, as a glimpse at almost any temple in the city will tell. Ban Tawai, southwest of the city, is a major centre.

Basketry Straw, rattan and bamboo basket products of all kinds are made at Hang Dong, 13km southwest of Chiang Mai on Highway 108.

Umbrellas (see panel) These are made of cotton, rice-paper and bamboo, and hand-painted in bright colours.

Ceramics Celadon, a high-biscuit finish with a pale green glaze, is much prized by collectors and comes in plain light green or middle blue; beware of imitations. Benjarong, which means "five colours", is a low-biscuit finish which lends itself to richer decoration, including 12-carat gold.

Silverware This is hand-hammered before being given its final lustre by an application of tamarind. Beware of base-metal substitutes.

Lacquerware A three-month process of repeated coatings of clay and lacquer sap is the traditional method, this is followed by careful painting or the addition of a gold-leaf design. Burmese lacquer tends to be made on a bamboo base (as opposed to a teak one), which is less brittle.

Where to buy There are two excellent non-profit-making shops selling hill-tribe products, where all the money goes directly back to the craftspeople making the goods: the government-run Hill Tribe Products Foundation, 21/17 Suthep Road and Thai Tribal Crafts, 208 Bamrung Rat Road (not to be confused with Northern Tribal Crafts a few doors along).

The Night Bazaar▶▶▶ Situated in Chang Khlan Road, this is one of the great markets of Asia, both for its range and its atmosphere – indeed, part of the attraction is the people-watching. Virtually nothing carries a price tag and haggling is the order of the day.

Fake designer-label clothes, pirated cassette tapes, while-you-wait artist portraits, wooden toys, hill-tribe gear and inexpensive jewellery are good buys for those who bargain hard enough. Beware of fake silver, jade and gems, and don't expect those 800-baht "Rolex" watches to last more than a few months.

Home industries (factory tour)▶▶▶ Straggling along Highway 1006 on the eastern outskirts, the "villages" of Bo Sang and San Kamphaeng are really a huge industrial zone, where workshops produce handmade crafts in great quantity – most notably leather, umbrellas, lacquer, silver-ware, silk and ceramics. A tour can be taken by either bus, taxi or *tuk tuk* – the driver will pick up commissions regardless of whether you buy anything. It usually lasts three to four hours and you can stop off wherever that you choose.

Prices are often fixed and there is no hard sell beyond the occasional hovering attendant, and someone always greets you and explains the production process. Mailing services are provided for large items. Even if you don't buy a thing, it is great entertainment.

SHOPPING ADVICE
As with everything in Thailand, all that glisters…polyester may masquerade as silk, shaped resin looks very like carved teak, and those handmade hill-tribe products or precious antiques may prove to be mass-produced junk. Shop around, look closely at what you are buying and bargain hard. Except for gems or jade, the sums you are likely to spend are not large. Avoid buying "endangered species" products made of ivory, ebony or tortoiseshell. They will probably be fakes anyway.

163

It is hard to imagine how many teak trees have been sacrificed to fuel Chiang Mai's ancient wood-carving industry, now largely devoted to the production of tourist trinkets

continued from page 161

HMONG AND MEO
The hill-tribe which inhabits the village of Ban Doi Pui is variously known as Meo (the Thai name which means "barbarian") and Hmong (which means "free"). Understandably, the tribespeople prefer the name Hmong, but the term Meo is still some-times used. There are two main groups: the Blue Hmong who live west of Chiang Mai, and the White Hmong who live to the east. Some are refugees from Laos who fled during the Vietnam War.

Phu Phing Palace▶ (*Open* – grounds only – weekends 8–4. *Admission free when the King is not in residence*). King Bhumiphol's northern winter palace, 4km further along the road from Doi Suthep, can be viewed from outside. Although it is nothing remarkable architecturally, its temperate rose garden and neat lawns seem evocatively English (unfortuately so too does the winter air – bring a sweater). The gardens are open to the public on weekends and holidays.

Look out for the roadside verges hereabouts as they are full of wild sunflowers.

Ban Doi Pui Four kilometres past Phu Phing Palace is this spectacular example of a tourist trap (see panels), with stalls stacked up with imported souvenirs and villagers dressed in Hmong tribal costume posing for cameras for a few baht.

If this is regarded merely as a sociological insight into the decline of the hill-tribe culture, or as a shopping trip, then the village might be worth a visit. At least the wood-smoke smell, free-running chickens and dirt roads are authentic. There is a pleasant view from the waterfall (*Admission: inexpensive*), further enhanced by flowers planted on the banks.

164

BAN DOI PUI
The downside of tourism is seen in the effect it has had on the people of Ban Doi Pui. Their lives today are geared to the tourist industry and this has given them a keen eye for profit. Their knowledge of English extends to phrases such as "you buy" and "no profit". These once nomadic peo-ple used to depend on opium as a cash crop until the government tried to steer them to less harmful ways of subsistence.

Mae Sa Valley▶▶
Take Highway 107 north from the city, turn west at Mae Rim (16km) on to Highway 1096. Refer to page 154 for map.
Highway 1096 has been developed for tourist industry and this region is a popular half-day visit from Chiang Mai. The road is quite scenic and there are a number of attractive bungalow resorts, such as Mae Sa and Erawan resorts, with beautifully maintained gardens and views of the hills. However, accommodation tends to get booked up at weekends.

Mae Sa Snake Farm▶ About 25 types of snake native to Thailand are kept here; dare-devil antics with them are performed daily. The performance lasts about 30 minutes. (*Admission: moderate*).

Mae Sa Waterfall▶▶ *6km along Highway 1096; 300m access road. (Admission: inexpensive)* A mountain stream tumbles down a ravine over a series of ten waterfalls which pro-vide delightful shady pools for swimming. The trail along then gets rockier and noticeably quieter on the 1km trek to the top.

Butterfly and orchid farms▶▶ (*Open* daily 8:30–5. *Admission: moderate*) Thailand's most famous flower is the orchid. Examples can been seen at the **Sai Nam Phung Orchid and Butterfly Farm** (one of several similar attrac-tions to be found) which has a fine selection of both commercial cultivated hybrids and native species. Adding further ambience are the butterflies, which flit around the indoor tropical gardens. They do, however, end up as framed souvenirs which are sold at the entrance shops and in Chiang Mai's bazaar.

Elephant Shows▶▶ (*Open* shows daily in the morning. *Admission: moderate*) There are several elephant shows on offer around Chiang Mai. One of the most popular is **Elephants at Work**, at Chiang Dao on the road from Chiang Mai to Fang (a bus route). Elephants bathe, perform logging skills and obey commands. Shows take place in the morning, but in order to see the elephants' bath time, get there as early as possible. Although contrived and commercialised, it is an impressive spectacle, full of photo opportunities.

WOODEN ELEPHANTS
Most of the handicraft shops in Chiang Mai sell wooden elephants (many made of teak), ranging from half-life-size to those that could fit into a matchbox.

Working elephants having their daily bath: get there early to see this part of their routine in the shows near Chiang Mai

165

Tham Chiang Dao▶ (*songthaew* from Chiang Dao) is a cave system containing much Shan statuary; at the entrance to the main cave, *chedis* and an ornamental royal barge in a pool serve to enhance the mystical atmosphere.

Lamphun▶▶ *Frequent buses from Chang Puak bus station in Chiang Mai.*
Located 26km south of Chiang Mai, the area around Lamphun is famed for the beauty of its women, for its *lamyai* (longan) orchards and for its silk products.
   The main road from Chiang Mai passes along a fine avenue of *yang* (rubber) trees; pegs are placed on the trunks to facilitate regular pruning.
   Lamphun was founded in AD 660 as the capital of the great kingdom of Haripunchai, the centre of Mon culture. It was ruled by the Mons until the 13th century when infiltration by King Mengrai, monarch of the Lanna dynasty, led to its downfall: the King sent Ai Fa, an officer, to undermine the enemy's defence minister and viceroy, deliberately wasting the city's resources and whittling its defences, thus paving the way for rebellion and takeover by Mengrai's forces.

TEAK LOGGING
After five years of training, elephants work for 50 years; reaching peak efficiency around their 40s. Thai law dictates a retirement age of 61, after which they typically live another 20 years. Elephants make excellent loggers because of their night vision, their near-perfect memory of jungle trails and their ability to carry loads of up to 300kg. Teak logging now faces a government ban and it seems likely that the elephants' future role will be as tourist attractions.

Wat Phra That Haripunchai▶▶ No visitor to Lamphun should miss Wat Phra That Haripunchai. Located in the town centre, this is one of the most interesting temples in the region, and dates from the early 12th century. It is dominated by a 60m-high dazzling gold *chedi* (the model for the infinitely more visited Doi Suthep), and surmounted by a nine-tiered umbrella made of 6.5kg of solid gold. The library that is housed here is a fetching example

PASANG
About 12km southwest of Lamphun is the village of Pasang, famed as a cotton-weaving centre. The high-quality product is on sale as lengths of cloth, or made up into garments. You will find the products on sale all over Chiang Mai, but at Pasang you can see the cloth actually being woven, and you may get a better deal at the local cloth market, which also sells batik, silks, and other typical handicrafts.

BE VIGILANT
One sure way to have a holiday ruined is to have something stolen. It goes without saying that constant vigilance is needed, but beware: even supposedly secure places are not always so. There have been reports of items going missing even from guesthouse and hotel safes, so obtain an itemised receipt whenever possible.

of early 19th-century Lanna style, and a *sala* shelters an elaborate Buddha footprint (four prints, one inside the other). Also to be seen here is northern Thailand's largest temple gong, cast in 1860.

National Museum► (*Open* Wed–Sun, except national holidays, 9–noon, 1–4. *Admission: inexpensive*) Just across the road from Wat Phra That Haripunchai is this briefly interesting museum in a building that looks as if it was designed for something more comprehensive. However, there are good specimens of Lanna art, figures and silverware, and inscribed stones mostly dating from the 15th and 16th centuries.

Wat Chama Thevi (Wat Ku Kut)► Follow the minor road to the left of the museum, cross the main road and continue for 1km until the *wat* is reached on the left. The walk itself is rather dull, so it might be a better idea to take a *samlor* to the *wat*.

It is known for its late Dvaravati-style *chedi*, which stands 21m high and rises five tiers with trios of Buddha images (not the originals) in niches on each level.

► Chiang Rai   *152B4*
Buses from neighbouring cities; domestic flights; boats from Tha Ton; a four-hour bus trip from Chiang Mai
Chiang Rai was founded in 1262 as the capital of the Lanna kingdom, but despite its history and the mushrooming growth of new hotels and guesthouses, there is in fact little to see. Much of the city's recent industrial boom is a result of the upgrading of the highway north of Mae Sai and through Myanmar which will form part of a major land route into China. As a popular base for exploring the surrounding countryside and for hill treks it serves well enough. If this is your wish, you need only walk down the main street to find something that will suit your requirements.

Hill Tribe Museum and Handicrafts Shop► *Population and Community Development Association, 620/25 Thanalai Road.* (*Open* Mon–Fri 9–6) The association gives practical aid to local people in matters as diverse as water supply and family planning. The Chiang Rai branch helps tribespeople in particular, and has set up a small museum of tribal artefacts and a craft shop, the proceeds of which go directly to fund its projects. It holds an English-language slide show; an excellent introduction to hill-tribe culture.

Boat trip from Tha Ton to Chiang Rai► ► ► Rafts to Chiang Rai make a five-hour journey along the Mae Kok River, which is so shallow that they often run aground and the passengers have to get out and push them free. As a result of this, and the element of risk, interest has been fuelled in the journey as an adventure outing.

The trip winds its way past hill-tribe villages set beneath angular mountains. Possible stop-overs points include a Lahu village, a hot spring and a cave; but accommodation is best organised through a trek offered at one of several guesthouses at Tha Ton village.

Tha Ton itself is a peaceful little village sited on the river bank. Steps to the left of the bridge lead up to a hilltop *wat*, which gives fine views of the river.

Fang *Bus from Chiang Mai, minibus to Tha Ton.* Fang was founded by King Mengrai in the 13th century, but for most visitors this is just a bus change *en route* for the boat trip to Chiang Rai. At Ban Muang, 10km northwest, a hot sulphur spring gushes out of the ground at temperatures close to boiling point.

▶▶▶ Doi Inthanon National Park   *152A3*

Head southwest on Highway 108; turn off north near the 57km post. Buses from Chiang Mai and Mae Sariang to Chom Thong. A songthaew *service makes a tour of the main attractions. The service is sporadic in the week but frequent at weekends*

The park takes its name from the highest peak in Thailand. This statistic is just one of many exceptional features about this park. Attractions are signed in English and listed in the order they are passed. Another significant feature are the some 30 Hmong and Karen villages dotted around the area. The scenery, arguably the most beautiful and dramatic in the whole of the country, varies from unspoilt lowlands to rugged, partly wooded highlands which are being afforested by the government, and a number of fine waterfalls.

Mae Ya Falls▶▶ This is signposted on the left almost immediately after leaving Highway 108. The 15-minute drive affords magnificent views over rice fields set beneath the backdrop of the mountain range. The falls, a short walk from the car park, plummet dramatically for a full 250m.

Mae Klang Falls▶ Close to the road, easy access has been made to these, the most visited feature in the park, especially spectacular during the rainy months from August to November. A battery of souvenir and food stalls has inevitably grown up as a result. Close by, the Visitor Centre sells a useful map of the park and a booklet detailing the bird species found here.

Varchiratharn Falls▶ Signed by the road, this majestically graceful single fall involves a steep 10-minute walk down to its base. The effort is amply rewarded.

Just before the Park headquarters, a right turn (signposted Tribal Silverware) leads via a left turn to the 1km path to the double cascades of **Siriphum Falls▶**. On the way the route leads through Hmong village. It is highly commericalised to the extent that American Express is accepted at the silverware stalls and the women hard-sell everlasting flowers and chrysanthemums. The latter are grown in greenhouses visible below. This is part of the government scheme to introduce cash-crop farming among the tribes in an attempt to safeguard conservation interests.

Bungalows are available in the Park, and there is also a campsite at the 31km mark. Reservations are suggested and to do so, telephone 02 579 0529.

RAFTING
Rafting can be arranged at Tha Ton village and ten-seater boats can be chartered from Chiang Rai pier for exploring the river.

FANG
Fang's strategic location has made it an important trading base for centuries. In recent years it has functioned as a conduit and warehouse for Golden Triangle opium which, refined into less bulky heroin, finds its way to many parts of the world. Government attempts to persuade the local hill-tribes to concentrate their attentions on the fertile agricultural land near Fang have had partial success. But cabbages have their limitations...

MAE KOK ELEPHANT CAMP
Reached by boat or bus from Chiang Rai, the camp operates elephant treks; for details contact the office near the Wangcome Hotel in Chiang Rai (tel: 053 711800).

BIRDLIFE

Doi Inthanon is an outstanding area for birds. A species list of 380 has been recorded for the park, including the ashy-throated warbler and the green-tailed sunbird.

INTHAWICHAYANON SHRINE

Marking the summit of Doi Inthanon is a shrine to Inthawichayanon, after whom the mountain was renamed in a shortened form. In the 19th century he prophesied the dangers of loss of tree cover in this great watershed area and requested that his remains to be placed here.

SIVA

A prize exhibit in Kamphaeng Phet's museum is a fine bronze statue of the Hindu god Siva, cast in 1510 in Khmer style. In 1886, a deranged German decapitated the image and removed its hands, saying he wanted it for the Berlin Museum. An awkward diplomatic incident was averted by the astute King Chulalongkorn, who arranged for an exact copy of the statue to be sent to Germany. The original has since been restored to its former glory.

The summit of Doi Inthanon offers magnificent views of the surrounding hilly countryside and the national park, especially at sunrise and sunset

Drive to the summit of Doi Inthanon►►► A good road winds up to the very top of Thailand's highest mountain (2,595m). As the road ascends, views open out over distant ridges extending far to the southwest and east.

A modern octagonal pagoda erected in honour of the king, Napamaytanidol Chedi enjoys the most enthralling panorama of all, best on a clear winter's day, but is unfortunately all too often obscured by mist.

The summit itself, chilly in the extreme in winter, is something of an anticlimax, with trees almost completely obscuring the view and a huge Air Force radar installation dominating the scene. A sign gives the mountain's height to the nearest millimetre!

Walk back down the road a few paces and turn right on a path signed in Thai leading to the only site in Thailand of *Rhododendron delavayi*. This flower thrives in the temperate climate and produces red blooms from November to February.

Environs

Chom Thong *Chiang Mai–Mae Sariang bus passes by.* This is a small town on Highway 108, 58km southwest of Chiang Mai. On Saturday mornings, the cattle market presents an animated scene.

On the left side of the main street approaching from Chiang Mai, **Wat Phra That Sri Chom Thong►►** dates from 1451 and displays Thai and Burmese (now Myanmar) features. The *wiharn* dates from 1817 and has wood-carvings characteristic of the period. Carved tusks surround the central reliquary, which contains a Buddha relic. The *bot*, built in 1516, is a charming example of the old Burmese style.

► Kamphaeng Phet   152B1

Junctions of Highways 1, 115 and 111
Built by King Ki Thai in the 14th century, Kamphaeng Phet city was a replacement for Chakangrao, the garrison town for Sukhothai, sited on the west bank of the nearby Ping River.

Signposts from the city centre point to the museum and Historical Park, which covers a large area, both inside and outside the ancient moated fortification.

Buses from Sukhothai and Phitsanulok pass the Historical Park, sited 1km to the northeast of the modern city. Ask to be dropped off at the *muang kao* (old city) at Lak Muang Shrine. Cars can go into the Historical Park.

National Museum▶ (*Open:* Wed–Sun, except public holidays, 9–12, 1–4. *Admission: inexpensive*) This features art styles from the Dvaravati period onwards and also numerous terracotta fragments found in the old city.

Wat Phra Khaew▶ *Opposite the museum. Entry fee covers all sites and there is a free map from the entry booth.* The old royal temple for the (largely vanished) palace retains its elephant-buttressed base and three Buddha images.

Wat Phra Si Iriyabot▶ *From the modern Lak Muang Shrine, follow the main road east through the ramparts and branch off left as signposted.* The signs explain the sites hereabouts; few are more than piles of laterite rubble. This one has four much-weathered Buddha images in different postures.

Wat Chang Rob▶▶ *Further along the same road.* This is flanked at its base by 68 stone elephants dressed in ceremonial robes; steep steps give access to a fine viewing platform over the surrounding countryside.

▶▶ Lampang   152B3

Junction of Highways 1 & 11. Reached by domestic flights, bus, and train

Lampang, an old timber-cutting town, will never be a major tourist attraction, but it is of interest for its Lanna and old Burmese-style temples.

The north's second-largest city, it has a distinctly prosperous air. This is helped by the fact that rich Thais come here to retire. The river that forms the geographical middle is leafy and unspoilt, and the old part of town clustered on the south bank is characterised by wooden shophouses and well-kept teak residences set in lush gardens. All in all there is a relaxing and peaceful feel about this town.

LAMPANG'S HERITAGE
Despite its size, Lampang manages to retain its traditional atmosphere, largely because of its numerous teak buildings. At the turn of the century, a British-owned logging firm in Lampang arranged for Burmese supervisors to train its timber workers. Burma (now Myanmar) was then a British colony, and Lampang an important centre for the teak trade. The skill of these workers, and the money they made from this profitable enterprise, resulted in Lampang's magnificent collection of temples.

169

Only the square base survives of Kamphaeng Phet's Elephant Shrine, Wat Chang Rob. Carved from laterite and stucco, the sacred elephants are fittingly decked in ceremonial regalia

HORSE CARRIAGES

Unique to Lampang are the horse carriages that take visitors and residents for pleasure trips around town. These appeared in Lampang in 1915, having been in use as VIP transport in Bangkok until cars were imported from Europe for the purpose. The whole operation – carriages, drivers and horses – was transported by the newly opened railway. Many of the carriages are original, but the colours are not!

The ornate Burmese-style mondop *in the courtyard of Lampang's Wat Prakeo Don Tao is flanked by a bell-shaped golden* chedi, *reputed to contain one of the Buddha's hairs*

Ban Sao Nak *Radwattana Road.* (*Open* daily 10–5. *Admission: inexpensive*) Built on 116 pillars, this dark teak mansion is worth a short visit for those wanting to see inside a typical wealthy home built in the northern Thai/Burmese style. The two main rooms are filled with a briefly absorbing collection of antiques.

Wat Pongsanuk Tai▶ *Pongsanuk Road.* A modern *wat* encloses the raised platform which retains an excellent example of a *mondop* built in Lanna style; a tiered roof shelters four Buddha images gathered around the sacred bo tree.

Wat Prakeo Don Tao▶ *Prakeo Road.* The city's oldest major temple is known mostly for two Buddha images which are now elsewhere. The Emerald Buddha is now in Wat Phra Keo in Bangkok's Grand Palace (see page 79), and Don Tao is now at Wat Phra Luang. The temple possesses a square *mondop* of 1909 in Burmese style, with a typical multi-tiered roof. An adjacent museum displays mostly Lanna-style wood-carvings.

Wat Sri Chum▶ *Sri Chum Road.* Sadly, only the ornate porches remain of one of Lampang's loveliest temples after a disastrous fire in 1992. Another point of interest is that some of the monks here from Myanmar.

Environs

Wat Phra That Lampang Luang▶▶▶ *This is reached by* songthaew *as far as Kho Kha, followed by a 3km walk or a change to another* songthaew. *It is possible to charter one at a cost of about 300 baht for the round trip.* Situated 18km south of Lampang, this is the sole survivor of one of four fortified satellite settlements built in the Haripunchai period to serve Lampang. A triple rampart with moats encloses a farming village clustered round the *wat*, itself a supreme example of the Lanna style and in an excellent state of preservation. The main *wiharn* dates from 1496 and contains early 19th-century murals of nobles in Burmese costume. Another *wiharn* displays intricate mosaic-inlaid gables. An open-sided *wiharn* dating from the early 16th century is thought to be the oldest timber building in Thailand.

Young Elephant Training Centre▶▶▶ *36km west on Highway 11, on the Lampang–Chiang Mai bus route near Ban Thung Kwian.* (*Open* daily shows at 9 and 2. *Closed* on Buddhist holidays. *Admission: moderate*) This is one of the best and most genuine places to see elephants being trained for logging work. The performance is something like the Elephants at Work show near Chiang Mai (see page 165).

▶▶▶ Mae Hong Son   152A3

End of Highway 108. Buses from Bangkok, Chiang Mai, Mae Sariang, Soppong and Pai; domestic flights
Lying in a valley amid densely wooded mountains and tucked away in Thailand's northwest corner, Mae Hong Son has changed face from a remote small town to a booming resort full of guesthouses and trekking agencies.

A thick morning mist will often shroud Mae Hong Son, adding drama to the town's pretty **Chong Khum Lake**, which is fringed by neat lawns and shrubberies. Two adjacent Burmese-style temples make a splendid backdrop to the water; both of these look best from the outside, although **Wat Chong Klang** contains interesting wooden figurines and painted glass panels brought from Burma (now Myanmar) in 1857.

Perched on a steep hill, **Wat Doi Kong** presides over the town and is the place to make for at sunset with its pretty views. The 15-minute walk up can be started near the Mai Tee Hotel (take the road opposite Singhanat Bumrum Road, fork left and continue until the temple steps appear to your right). Back in town, there is a lively morning market (6–8); hill-tribe people come to buy and sell. Mae Hong Son has a fair range of Myanmar crafts, including lacquer, blankets and wall hangings.

The best guesthouse locations are by the lake or in Phachachon Uthit Road.

Environs

For journeys outside of Mae Hong Son, motorbikes, mountain bikes and jeeps can all be rented in town. Enquire locally before making independent trips – border fighting, treacherous roads and lack of signposting are major hazards.

Tour agencies offer trips to hot springs, caves, waterfalls and tribal villages. One excursion heads east to **Tham Plaa**► meaning "fish cave" and derives its name from the catfish that inhabit it. The excursion climbs the rough road to Mae Aw (a Kuomintang/Hmong village – see page 182 – now on the border with Myanmar) and passes the king's summer palace (Pang Tong). Trekking, elephant riding and rafting are also on offer. Trips to see the long-neck Padaung tribeswomen are much-touted and overpriced (see panel).

Tham Lot►►► *Reached by taking a bus to Soppong, where it is possible to get a* songthaew *or make the 1.5-hour walk. A fork at Soppong leads through the village and 9km*

continued on page 175

THE LONG-NECK WOMEN
Legend has it that the mother of the Padaung tribe was a long-neck dragon. Accordingly, the women of this now tiny tribe have traditionally worn metal rings around their necks, starting at the age of six and adding one or two each year until adulthood. The rings crush down the collar bones and ribs; removal of all the rings could cause the woman's neck to collapse. The long-necks' practice has been kept alive by the curiosity of tourists, but is in decline.

171

The entrance to Tham Lot, where swifts and bats enter and exit respectively at dusk

The forested limestone hills of northern Thailand are home to many races of hill-tribe people, all with distinctly different cultures. These cultures are being remoulded by the advent of Thai and Western influences and the standards of health and education are improving dramatically, as are their rights as Thai citizens and protection against exploitation. The biggest challenge remains to find the right balance between preservation of traditional culture and modern development – a learning process for the hill-tribes and the authorities.

Roots The Lahu and Akha came via eastern Burma (now Myanmar) and northern Laos, beginning to cross over into Thailand in the early 20th century. The Lisu migrated from the headwaters of the Salween River in China via Kang Tung state in Myanmar. To this day only a minority of these peoples live in Thailand, with the majority remaining in Myanmar and China's Yunnan province. The Hmong (or Meo) and Mien came across the Mekong River from Laos after siding with the royalists in their vain attempt to prevent the Communist takeover of Laos in 1975. They were settled at first in refugee camps on the border, and have since moved into Thailand's northern forests.

The Karen are the biggest tribal grouping of them all, numbering by some counts over four million. Their precise origins are shrouded in mystery but their culture contains Myanmar, Mon and Thai elements.

Separate tribal identities Karen culture centres on a sophisticated fallow agricultural system, and its feasts and rituals celebrate harmony with the natural environment which is extended to human society with an unquestioning submission to acknowledged leaders.

The people of the Hmong (or Meo) hill-tribe are strongly independent

The Hmong are fiercely independent. In Laos they expressed this by fighting Communism which threatened to engulf their way of life. Mien culture stresses propriety, etiquette and avoidance of open conflict.

The Akhas' rituals are based on keeping alive links with ancestors, whom they revere as awesome guardian spirits protecting the continuity of tribal history.

The Lisu are the most competitive in seeking to provide the best singers, weavers – or opium growers.

A typical day in a hill-tribe village begins early as the roosters herald dawn. The women and girls rise first; they roll up their sleeping mats to begin pounding the rice to be eaten that day. Children usually

collect water, sometimes – if they are particularly lucky – from bamboo aqueducts which carry the water right into the village. Breakfast consists of rice and vegetables from the garden, cooked with roots and jungle spices.

The workers returning from the fields at sunset bring firewood and food for the pigs. Families living far from their fields often camp out in them for days on end. After the evening meal the women congregate in groups around smoky kerosene lamps or pitch pine torches to sew, while the men gather to smoke pipes, drink tea and discuss the day's happenings.

In the dry season the air is choked with dust and smoke from the burning fields. During the monsoon the dust turns to sticky mud. Women and children must trudge ever-increasing distances to find firewood.

Crafts Each tribe has its own craft tradition – weaving cloths, making jewellery, musical instruments, baskets, tools, utensils, weapons and traps (see page 162). Some villagers become artisans specialising in one particular craft. The highest status is given to the blacksmith, on whom the villagers depend for making and mending their tools and weapons. In recent years Thai crafts which were previously practised only for domestic use have become much in demand from tourists. That demand has bred a whole new breed of skilled entrepreneur tribesmen who purchase handicrafts from the villages and sell them at the night bazaars of Chiang Mai, Chiang Rai or Bangkok.

Society It is becoming more commom now for the younger generation of a family to migrate to larger towns or cities in order to further their education and seek work, though this is usually just temporarily and the extended family remains an important part of society.

Marriage has traditionally been within the tribe, though intertribal marriage, and even marriage with Thais, are becoming increasingly common.

Spirituality and religion Another essential aspect of hill-tribe life is a deep sense of spirituality. Traditionally the tribes lived by animist beliefs and idol worship, heavily

COMMUNICATION
The main tradition of tribe communication is an oral one. This is entering a new era with the introduction of radio. Radio stations broadcasting to the tribes now transmit from Chiang Mai and Mae Chan.

173

TRIBAL FASHION
The hill-tribes people wear beautiful and elaborate clothing. The showiest garments are worn by young people of marriage-able age. The styles worn by each tribe are not unchanging but rather a result of constant innova-tion. Teenage girls spend hours weaving, sewing and beading, in the effort to produce the prettiest costume in the village.

174

CONFLICT AND DILEMMA
A serious problem is the destruction of the environ-ment in the hill-tribe areas due to the tribal practice of slash-and-burn cultiva-tion, which is now illegal (see page 34). With increasing population, the pressure on the land has tightened, reducing the period of fallow from 10 to five and sometimes as lit-tle as two years. The resulting soil erosion causes bigger floods on lowland rivers. The long-term solution
is reafforestation of water-shed areas, but this has become a major source of conflict between uplanders and the govern-ment. Restrictions on forest clearing threaten the very livelihood of some hill-tribes people, even if they survive the exposure to tourists and city merchants. Their cul-ture is on the edge of extinction.

influenced by Chinese forms of ancestor worship which they had brought to Thailand from Yunnan. Later on, these beliefs blended with Buddhism. Most villages would appoint head shamans and priests to perform whatever would appease the guardian spirits of the village.

Over the last 50, years Christian missionaries have successfully convinced many of the tribes to give up wor-ship of lesser spirits and worship the highest God according to the Christian Gospels. Conversions have been most pronounced among the Karen, Hmong and Akha tribes where many villages now have a majority of Christian families – though still retaining their traditional culture as far as their beliefs and political and technological developments allow.

Making a living Opium growing has now been reduced dramatically and with new skills and encouragement by the Royal Project, the government and NGOs, the hill-tribes people have new hope. Many villages now have electricity, improved water supply, nearby health clinics and schools, and with increasingly improved roads the carriage of goods has become more efficient. Government pressure has also meant charges on environmentally unfriendly slash-and-burn techniques.

While this opening up to the outside seems to be having mostly positive effects on the standard of living, potential for negative influeneces such as financial stress and fam-ily breakup also exist. So far this has been avoided and for the time being most hill-tribe people are satisfied with current developments.

King Bhumiphol first became interested in the plight of the hill-tribes in the 1960s when he was hiking in the forests around his hill palace of Phu Phing. He came across a desperately poor Hmong village with pathetically scraggy pigs. He patiently demonstrated to them how to raise a better breed of pig – and then became drawn into combating their "bad habit" of growing opium poppies.

Realising that the successful eradication of opium could not just be imposed legalistically, King Bhumiphol initi-ated a programme of research into alternative crops which could be profitably grown to replace opium. He set up an experimental orchard at Kasetsart University, which showed that roses, lilies, chrysanthemums, apples, peaches, strawberries, mushrooms, Brussels sprouts, coffee, turnips and cabbages could be grown in these areas. For a time the tribes took to these new crops, but there has been a degree of reversion to opium.

The main crops are rice and maize, supplemented by melons, squash, cucumbers, tomatoes, onions, beans and cabbages. The most common livestock are chickens and pigs. Cattle and water buffalo are highly prized, partly as a status symbol and also as a real asset which can be sold in hard times. The buffalo are used by the farmers for ploughing and harrowing.

Bartering is still common. A blacksmith may often be paid in rice or maize and a family might provide labour in a neighbour's field in return for some pork. When the vil-lagers travel to the nearest market to stock up on supplies, they take handicrafts, vegetables, charcoal, broom grass and bamboo shoots to sell.

continued from page 171

up to a Shan village, where this superb cave is signposted. Guides (about 150 baht per party) and lanterns can be hired at the entrance. The limestone formations and sheer size are impressive, but insist on seeing the third chamber (this involves some wading) where at dusk there is the breathtaking spectacle of huge numbers of swifts and bats entering and leaving the cave mouth.

Near by, Cave Lodge offers simple accommodation and cave treks.

Pai *Buses run from Mae Hong Son, Soppong and Chiang Mai.* An aimiably dozy small town, with inexpensive trekking and guesthouses, it is good for gentle excursions. East, over the river bridge, a dirt track leads past a hilltop *wat* 15km to a signposted hot spring. Thick-skinned visitors claim the water is not too hot for swimming. There are pleasant places to stay by the river.

►► Mae Sai
(The "Golden Triangle") 152B4
Highway 110. Buses are from Bangkok, Chiang Mai and Chiang Rai

The town Thailand's northernmost point is a classic border post, where a bridge spans the Mae Kok River and leads into the adjacent town of Tha Khi Lek in Myanmar. A constant procession of people from Myanmar and Thailand cross over for the markets on either side. Other foreign nationals may enter Myanmar for up to four days to visit the town of Kengtung. This lies 163km from Mae Sai, a six-hour jeep journey. Several agencies in Mae Sai can arrange this tour, but a substantial fee is payable for the necessary permits.

Mae Sai excels as a place for people-watching; hill-tribe children, some of them just Thais dressed for the part, pose for tourists' cameras, a blind beggar holds out a metal tankard, while a wizened old woman puffs on a fat cheroot.

On Buddhist holidays a fascinating market takes place on the bridge itself. At other times crafts from Myanmar (string puppets, wall-hangings, wooden musician figures and lacquerware) and jade are on offer – much of it brought in from Chiang Mai.

Mae Sai's modern main street is wide and drab, but a string of bungalow-style guesthouses by the river entice a few days' stay.

Opposite and to the left from the Top North Hotel, 207 steps lead up to Wat Doi Wao, which faces into Myanmar. Mai Sai lies in a district known for its cultivated strawberries, sold from stalls along the main road in the winter months. Motorcycles can be hired from Mae Sai for exploring the area.

Environs
Sob Ruak (The "Golden Triangle")►► *Hourly minibuses from Mae Sai, morning only, and all day from Chiang Saen, from where boats can be chartered*
A huge modern luxury hotel and a plethora of souvenir stalls pander to the needs of the hordes of tourists who

CASINOS
An additional lure for Thais to the Golden Triangle is a casino in the border town of Tha Khi Lek, Myanmar. Casinos are illegal in Thailand, but many Thais are fanatical gamblers, betting on any contest at every opportunity. Despite protests by the Thai government, this controversial, privately funded enterprise, tacitly permitted by the government of Myanmar, has aroused great interest.

175

ENTERING MYANMAR
Foreign visitors are allowed to cross into Myanmar at Mae Sai on a day-trip. Check current regulations before you travel (embassy address in Bangkok: see page 247). You have to pay a fee (US$5) for a border pass, and surrender your passport. Take a photocopy of the photo and visa pages in advance (local photo shops can arrange this). Over the bridge you can visit the Tha Khi Lek market, the Chinese cemetery and a small *wat*. Many people in Myanmar speak excellent English.

LITTLE CHINA IN THAILAND

Formerly known as Mae Salong, Santi Kiri ("hill of peace") has existed since 1961 as a refugee village for Kuomintang soldiers and their families following the 1949 Chinese Cultural Revolution. After settling in Thailand they engaged themselves in smuggling and in the opium trade. The Thai government has launched a re-education programme and persuaded them to switch to growing tea, coffee, herbs, fruit and corn. Thai language classes are given and a loudspeaker broadcasts information on taxation matters and health education.

Fearsome temple dragons reveal the strong Chinese influences in this part of northern Thailand, seen most clearly in Santi Kiri

come here to be photographed in front of a hideous concrete sign announcing this to be the Golden Triangle. Except on postcard racks, there isn't an opium poppy in sight; the growers of the illicit plant discreetly carry on elsewhere and the altitude is too low anyway. But despite the tackiness of the place, this is a view to remember – the confluence of the Mekong and the Mae Ruak rivers at the meeting of Thailand, Myanmar and Laos, with mysterious mountain ranges stretching into the distance. **Wat Phra That Phu Khao**, perched on a hill, gives the best panorama, with excellent views over the area.

Unfortunately, a casino has recently been constructed in the middle of the river to lure Thais to gamble their baht and prop up an ailing economy in Myanmar (casinos are banned in Thailand).

Chiang Saen► ► *Buses from Chiang Rai.* Nicely situated on the Mekong River, this sleepy small town lies to the east of Sob Ruak. Around the neat grid-pattern of streets are dotted a number of ancient ruins from the old town, which was founded in the 13th century and retains its 14th-century fortifications. The Burmese (now Myanmar) briefly controlled it during the 16th century, and Rama I later destroyed the town, fearing a repeat capture. Chiang Saen remained in an unoccupied state until the time of King Rama V.

The National Museum► (*Open* Wed–Sun 9–noon, 1–4. *Admission: inexpensive*) is in the main street, which leads away from the river. This contains hill-tribe artefacts, inscribed stones, ceramics, Buddha images and Lanna objects.

Close by is the 58m-high octagonal *chedi* of Wat Chedi Luang, built in 1290.

Wat Pa Sak► Keep along the main street and turn right as you cross the town wall for a ruined forest *wat* among the trees that retains some of its fine stucco decoration. Wat Pa Sak (the "Teak Forest Temple"), with its magnificent stuccoed *chedi*, is the most impressive monument in Chiang Saen.

Continuing along the road for 1km, with the moat on the right, brings you to **Wat Chom Kitti►**, which is approached by a long staircase. It has been well restored and provides a good view across to Laos.

Chiang Khong *Buses from Chiang Rai;* songthaews *from Chiang Saen.* The village is also on the Mekong River, which is the sole feature of interest. Riverside guesthouses and bungalows make the most of the view (more than in Chiang Saen, where accommodation is not particularly good, so it might be worth stopping here).

Doi Mae Salong/Santi Kiri►► *Frequent buses run between Chiang Rai and Mae Sai; alight at Basang for a* songthaew *(sporadic service)* High up on the Mae Salong mountain, 36km from the main road, perches Santi Kiri. It is an extraordinary and unexpected place, inhabited by Yunnanese and completely Chinese in character. Yunnan is spoken; the shops sell strange herbal liquors, lychee and prune wines and locally grown tea. Stalls along the street sell noodles; at daybreak the Akha women conduct a lively produce market. A *wat*, a mosque and a Haw Chinese shrine serve the community.

Stay overnight and experience this early morning life to get a real feel for the place: above the village there is a range of accommodation.

Doi Tung▶▶ *Frequent buses from Chiang Rai to Mae Sai; alight at Highway 1149 for a* songthaew *for Doi Tung.* The paved road winds up past Shan, Akha and Lahu villages to the 1,700m summit of this mount, 24km from the main road, where Wat Phra That Doi Tung and its vast assemblage of bells of varying pitches look far into the surrounding hills.

The views and rural atmosphere can hardly be bettered and is reason enough to visit and simple bungalows for overnight stays are available on the way. However, as opium is grown within the Doi Tung countryside, it would be wise only to trek in this area if you are accompanied by a guide.

The hilltop setting of Wat Doi Wao in Mae Sai provides an excellent vantage point over the town and the hills of Laos across the Mekong River

177

▶ Mae Sot 152A1
Off Highway 105. Frequent buses from Tak
The westernmost town in Tak province lies close to the border with Myanmar and is a smuggling post for teak and jade. The streets throng with Chinese, hill-tribe people smoking cheroots, people from Myanmar in sarongs and dark-skinned Muslims in lace skullcaps. The town centre is punctuated with Burmese-style *wats* whose golden *chedis* glint in the hard sunlight.

Mae Sot is a good base for exploring hill-tribe villages and the mountainous border areas in the vicinity. Among several tour companies which organise trekking tours is the Mae Sot Travel Centre (tel: 055 531409).

Environs
Songthaews leave frequently from various locations around town to the destinations below.

Rim Moei Market▶▶ *Ten minutes' drive west on Highway 105.* This border market town is on the River Moei, now a major crossing point with the completion of the Thai–Burma Friendship Bridge in 1996.

The market is full of wares from Myanmar – lacquer products, jade, rubies, embroidered waistcoats, currency and even school slates.

"Death Highway" to Um Phang▶▶
Songthaews; journey time about five hours. Highway 1090, south from Mae Sot, earned its nickname in the 1960s and '70s when Communists held the area and were known to attack road builders.

Today it is safe (there is a police checkpoint, so bring your passport) and the magnificent road looks over huge areas of scarcely inhabited terrain, including Thailand's second highest mountain, Khao Kha Khaeng (2,400m).

Um Phang, 165km from Mae Sot, is one of Thailand's remotest villages within reach by good road. Several guesthouses offer simple accommodation and organise one-day raft trips and three-day treks (dry season only) to **Tee Lor Sue▶▶**, which is one of Thailand's largest and most dramatic waterfalls.

Closer to Um Phang, guides will take you to **Tham Mae Klong Cave▶**, a 5km-long cave with limestone formations, a bat colony and a hermit monk. Also visited is **Doi Hua Mod** ("bald mountain") which has a spectacular sunrise view.

Forty-one kilometres from Mae Sot on this road, a sign-posted track leads 700m to **Pha Charoen waterfall▶**, which tumbles down a 93-step natural staircase.

▶▶ Nan 152C3
End of Highway 101. Frequent buses from Bangkok, Chiang Mai, Lamphang and Phrae. Daily bus from Chiang Rai; domestic flights
The town Relatively remote and considered a dangerous area until recent years, Nan is far from being the most visited part of the north. However, many visitors stay on longer than they intended, captivated by the town's laid-back atmosphere. The most exciting bus-route approach

---

MYANMAR (BURMA)
This former British colony has suffered brutal repression from dictatorships since 1962 when General Ne Win wrested power in a coup. In 1988, student demonstrations against the government were met with atrocities and many fled to Thailand, settling around Mae Sot. Despite a crushing electoral defeat by the National League of Democracy in May 1990, General Sauw Maung refused to cede power. In recognition of Myanmar's struggle for democracy, Anng San Suu Kyi, the NLD leader, was awarded the Nobel Peace Prize while under house arrest.

SILVERWARE
Silverware bargains can be had in Nan. Prices are about 25 per cent cheaper than those in Chiang Mai, and 50 per cent less than those in many western countries. Look out also for superb local textiles.

is on Highway 1148 from Chiang Rai, along a tortuous single track for five and a half hours, past mountains, Hmong villages and opium fields.

The National Museum▶▶ *Pha Kong Road.* (*Open* Wed–Sun 9–12, 1–4. *Admission: inexpensive*) Erected in 1903 as a palace for the feudal rulers of Nan, this houses one of the most impressive provincial museums in Thailand. Many of the exhibit labels are in English, and there is also a small shop next door.

Wat Phumin▶▶ (see panel) Opposite the museum, this 16th-century *wat* is memorable for its Lanna-style wood-carvings and superb murals depicting scenes of old Nan.

Environs

Nan province is relatively undiscovered, with villages apparently caught in a timewarp, mountain scenery and good views. Guesthouses organise trekking and tours. Motorcycles and bicycles can be rented from shops near the Devaraj hotel.

Doi Phukha National Park▶▶ *Highway 1256 northeast of Phua (north of Nan), signposted in English.* The highest point in the province (1,980m), the park abounds with water-falls, views and caves. One of the world's extremely rare Chompu Phuka trees, which produces pink flowers, is to be found here. Non-Thai speakers, however, are likely to need a guide. If visiting here on a day trip the salt mines at Bor Klua and weaving and silver-working villages could also be included.

WAT PHUMIN
On the murals in Wat Phumin, note the women wearing the local costume and the men adorned with tattoos and period hairstyles.

SAO DIN CANYON
The weird landscape of wind-eroded earth pillars in the extraordinary valley of Sao Din, south of Nan in Na Noi district off Route 1026, has been used as a setting in a number of Thai films. To reach the canyon by public transport, take a bus to Na Noi, then charter a taxi or *songthaew*.

Wat Manee Pasi Son, in Mae Sot, has a most unusual construction. Dozens of small chedis rise in tiers around a central spire, each con-taining a Buddha statue

THE LANNA BOAT RACE AT NAN
Nan's major event of the year takes place in late October or early November, when gaily decorated boats made from hollowed-out trees are used for an exuberant rowing race, the scene accompanied by singing, drumming and the usual commotion associated with northern festivals. The race dates back over 100 years, when it was introduced as part of the competitive games played on Songkran Day, but is now associated with a robe-giving ceremony at Wat Phra That Chae Haeng.

KING NARESUAN
Phitsanulok is no more than a provincal capital these days, but like several other northern cities, it had its days of glory. In the late 15th century, it was the capital of Siam. A century later, it became the birthplace of one of Thailand's greatest kings, Naresuan, who reigned from 1590 to 1605. In his youth, Naresuan ruled the principality as a "training exercise" before ascending the throne of Ayutthaya on his father's death.

Pak Nai▶ *Bus from Nan, changing at Na Noi and Na Muan.* A few hours' drive south from Nan is this peaceful fishing village, built on stilts over Sirikit Reservoir, a huge water bounded by hills. Simple and inexpensive rafthouse accommodation and boat hire are available.

Some 10km south of Na Noi, a turn leads to Sao Din, a curious area of pinnacles and pillars which were formed by water erosion.

Wat Khao Noi▶ *Just south of Nan, signposted off Highway 101.* A minor road leads to the hilltop *wat*; the statuary is garish in the extreme but the view over the rice-paddies of the Nan valley and surrounding hills is satisfying enough.

▶▶ Phitsanulok   152B1
Junction of Highways 12 and 117. Buses from Chiang Mai, Bangkok and neighbouring towns, trains and domestic flights Most tourists visiting this friendly city are passing through *en route* for Sukhothai but there is enough here for a leisurely half-day exploration. The tourist office at Borom Trailokanat Road has helpful handouts, including maps of the area and a recommended town walk.

Phitsanulok looks at its best by night along the Nan River – venue for annual boat races in October or November. Houseboats with rusting tin roofs and tottering TV antennae line the banks; amid them are a number of floating restaurants, one of which even has a boat attached for evening dinner cruises. Many of its traditional wooden buildings were destroyed in a fire during the 1960s. The night bazaar brings after-dark animation, with cheap food and clothes stalls.

Wat Yai (Wat Mahathat)▶▶▶ *Phuttabucha Road.* This *wat* contains a revered and beautiful image, Phra Buddha Chinnarat, much copied (see panel on page 181).

Folk Museum▶▶ *Wisuthikasartri Road.* (*Open* daily 8:30–12, 1–4:30. *Admission: donation*) Unprominently signposted in a sleepy backstreet, this two-storey house is crammed with the personal collection of retired Sergeant Major Tawee Booranakate. All kinds of bygones are here, mementoes of a lifestyle that Thailand is fast shedding. Among them are utensils, ploughs, home-made toys and vicious-looking traps.

Buddha Foundry▶ Roughly opposite the folk museum and even less prominent (it's the door to the left of the Music School), this is run by the same person. Visitors are welcome to look around and watch the production process, where wax images are coated in clay and sand prior to casting, then the cast image is covered with gold leaf and lacquer.

Environs
Kaeng Sopa Waterfall▶ *Highway 12, 72km east of Phitsanulok (signposted in English); 3km access road from main road. The Phitsanulok to Lom Sak bus passes along the main road; Kaeng Sopa is about 3km from here*
A waterfall rushing down three steps strewn with massive boulders, Kaeng Sopa is the best-known feature

of **Thung Sa-Laeng Luang National Park**, a large area of forest and wilderness. (There are a number of other waterfalls to be seen.) Although supposedly a national park, and one of Thailand's largest protected areas, around five per cent of its land has been illegally depleted. The park itself is home to many species of animals, from elephants and wild boar to buffalo and the occasional tiger or panther. With its wide expanses, it is also a good place for bird-watching.

THE "FLYING VEGETABLE"
At the night bazaar in Phitsanulok you can see the city's most eccentric claim to fame, *pak boong loi fah* (the "flying vegetable"), where morning glory is tossed high from the wok to be caught across the street by the waiter.

PHRA BUDDHA CHINNARAT
Cast in bronze in 1357, Phra Buddha Chinnarat is a magnificent example of the late Sukhothai style. In 1631 King Ekathotsarot of Ayutthaya melted down some of his gold and personally coated the image. In 1756 King Boromkot donated the doors inlaid with mother of pearl. Murals of the Buddha's life and a Jataka tale were added at this time. The image is the most important in Thailand after the Emerald Buddha in Wat Phra Keo in the Grand Palace.

181

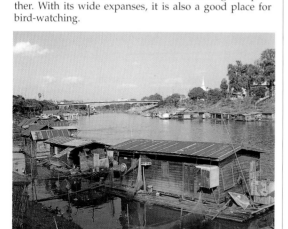

Houseboats make an atmospheric spectacle along the peaceful banks of the River Nan, in Phitsanulok

The opium poppy was introduced to the Orient by Arab traders during the Mongol invasions of the 13th century. Minority hill-tribes in southern China grew it as a cash crop to pay their taxes to the Chinese Emperor. They took it with them when they migrated south to Thailand and Myanmar.

OPIUM

The victims of opium include the hill-tribes who cultivate the poppies as well as Thailand's 500,000 heroin addicts. There are no millionaires living in the hills. The profits are all cornered by warlords, middlemen and international heroin syndicates.

182

The Golden Triangle The commericalisation of opium and its more lethal refined form, heroin, in Southeast Asia is a direct result of the tangled recent politics and warfare in the region. Its use by American GIs during the Vietnam War dramatically increased the demand for it, while also providing outlets to the world market. The illegal trade bolstered the power of the opium warlords. The whole inaccessible area between Thailand, Myanmar and Laos became known as the "Golden Triangle".

Drug barons and cash flows The "king" of the opium warlords is Khun Sa. In the 1950s, with US backing, he used opium to finance the futile rearguard battles of the Chinese Nationalists against Mao Zedong. By the late 1960s, however, he was in fierce competition with

his erstwhile comrades. The battle for the opium trade escalated into a full-scale war in 1967 during which one of his convoys of opium was napalmed. He survived this and a score of other violent clashes with the Thai and Burmese armies.

Counter-measures

Today the government prefers to wean hill-tribes away from opium to produce other cash crops. This is part of the broader hill-tribe development programme launched by King Bhumiphol. There has

The government is trying to steer the hill-tribes away from their reliance on opium

been some success; checks are made and large opium fields destroyed, although villagers still grow opium on a small scale for their own use, as many are addicts. However, Thailand now accounts for less than 2 per cent of world opium production.

Addicts are increasingly being sent to treatment centres rather than jailed. One such detoxification programme is in a Buddhist monastery run by Phra Chamroon Parnchand (see page 147), who administers an emetic to addicts which induces in them spectacular ritual vomiting.

Continual battling with neighbouring tribes and peoples has played a significant part in forming the identity of the Thai people. The Shans of northeastern Myanmar (Burma) and the Laotian people are ethnically related to the Thais while the Cambodians and Malays have both experienced some degree of Thai rule.

Border history Colonialism in the 19th century revealed the need for strictly defined geographical boundaries. Although Thailand was never colonised, its present boundaries reflect its role as a buffer state between the British in Burma (now Myanmar) and the French IndoChinese empire.

Myanmar The Golden Triangle, along the border with Myanmar, is notorious for its rebels, bandits and opium trade. Neither government has full control over this area.

Because of the practice of slash-and-burn cultivation many of the hill-tribes who live in Thailand frequently move over into Myanmar territory and vice versa.

Laos Problems along the Laotian border mounted when the Vietnamese-backed Pathet Lao came to power in the 1970s. Many anti-Communist royalist factions resisted from bases within Thailand, while refugees flooded across the border to be housed in camps (they are now being repatriated).

Much of the border is the Mekong River, which is also the main transport artery of Laos. Trade has increased since the recent building of a bridge across the Mekong.

Cambodia Thai fears over the border with Cambodia reached a high point after the Vietnamese invasion of Cambodia in the late 1970s.

Tensions eased following the 1991 peace settlement in Cambodia. But the potential for trouble remains. Thais have in the past claimed the Cambodian provinces of Battambang and Siem Reap.

Malaysia Relations with Malaysia appear to be stronger than with any other of the neighbouring countries and border crossing is a very relaxed affair – officials turn a blind eye to the boxes of household goods coming over the fence from the Malaysian side.

RADICAL SOLUTION
In 1989 the then Burmese government tried to cut off the finance to the Karen rebels by selling teak concessions to the Thai army. The *junta* were quite happy to see the rainforests destroyed if it reduced cover and hiding places for the rebels.

183

THE OPIUM TRADE
Khun Sa is one of the world's biggest drug-traffickers. Once he enjoyed US support for his anti-Communist activities, but now he has a hefty price on his head in Myanmar, Thailand and the United States. Financed by opium profits, he presides over the world's largest source of heroin.

Shoppers from Myanmar and Thailand meet at the border market at Rim Moei near Mae Sot. Handicrafts and jewellery are on sale, but not everything is a bargain

THE MRABRI

Seldom seen even by local people, Thailand's most primitive tribe, the Mrabri – known also as the Phithong Luan ("spirits of the yellow leaves") – pursue a nomadic lifestyle on the borders of Phrae and Nan provinces. These humble and gentle people wear loincloths and have no use for money, using instead a bartering system. Now numbering less than 100, they face extinction as deforestation continues apace. Their corpses are not buried, but placed on trees to be pecked to pieces by birds. They are excluded from the Thai social system but have become a tourist attraction in the worst zoo tradition.

Time-worn Buddha statues encrusted in patchy gold leaf contemplate enlightenment in the peaceful temple precincts of Phrae

▶ Phrae   *152B2*

Highway 101. Buses from surrounding cities, domestic flights
Phrae city has little to offer the tourist except as a base for exploring the surrounding uplands. The name of Phrae is associated with the indigo work-shirts *seua maw hawn*, much worn by farmers, *samlor* drivers and even the local schoolchildren and teachers – it becomes the Phrae school uniform on Fridays. Made at Ban Thung Ong, north of the city, these hard-wearing garments are on sale throughout town; a shirt will cost you over 100 baht, and you can get jackets and trousers made of the same material.

Downtown Phrae is blandly modern, but the adjoining old part of the city retains traces of its moated fortifications and has a maze of peaceful streets of traditional wooden houses.

Wat Chom Sawan, on the northeast side of the city, is an old Burmese-style temple, with multi-tiered tin roofs and a good deal of creaky, old-world charm.

Environs

Phae Muang Phi▶▶ *18km to the northeast; take Highway 101 towards Nan, branch off right as signposted in English after 12km. There are no buses.* The name of this town translates as "ghost land": soil erosion has left a surreal moonscape of earth pillars, which are best seen in the early morning when the shadows that fall create some strange effects.

Tham Pha Nanloi▶ *30km to the northeast, on Highway 101 towards Nan. On the Nan–Phrae bus route.* An electrically lit cave with limestone formations, this is used as a Buddhist shrine, extending 200m into the hillside. It is the setting for an ancient and famous legend regarding a king's daughter. It is said that she is saved by a soldier from drowning and that she elopes with her saviour and has his child. The king, furious at their behaviour, sends men after them to ambush the soldier as he leaves the cave. Unaware of his death, the princess waits eternally for his return; a rock in the cave is said to represent the princess and her child.

▶▶ Phu Hin Rong Kla National Park   *152C2*

Off Highway 12, east of Phitsanulok. Buses between Phitsanulok and Lom Sak; change at Ban Yang for bus to Nakhon Thai; change for songthaew *to the Park*

Approached by a road that rises through some rugged highlands and passes remote Hmong villages, Phu Hin Rong Kla has a magnificent setting – best appreciated from the knobbly rock pavement known as **Lan Hin Boom**, perched on a cliff above a hair-raising drop. Deep rock fissures harbour ferns, lichen speckles the boulders and orchids and white rhododendrons are to be found among the diverse flora.

Today the park is visited for its solitude and quiet beauty, yet from 1968 to 1982 it was the stronghold of the Communist Party of Thailand (CPT). In 1984 the national park was established, yet remnants of that era survive today (there are probably unexploded shells about, so keep to the trails), and are signposted in various places within the park.

Following the road west from the park headquarters (towards Nakhon Thai) for 300m, a left turn near the park sign leads on to a trail across the rock plateau. The memorial on the right near the road commemorates those who died in a major KMT (Kuomintang) conflict.

Eastwards from the park headquarters along the main road, a cluster of signs in English points to three KMT relics. The air-raid shelter is a deep natural rock crevice, explored by a short circular trail that leads up and down ladders. Close by, a waterwheel survives which is fed by a wooden chute. This was constructed for the purpose of grinding rice for CPT consumption. Further along from here, on the other side of the road, are the remaining huts of the **Political and Military School**, previously used as the camp training centre.

Adequate bungalow accommodation, starting from 100 baht per person (book in advance: 02 579 0529), and tents for one or two people, are provided.

The park headquarters gives away free but basic maps, and maintains a small KMT museum. See also the walk on page 186.

A COMMUNIST STRONGHOLD
Huts, air-raid shelters, bunkers, an abandoned digging machine, a flagpole, some rapidly overgrowing graves and a simple memorial are humble reminders of a period when the Communist Party of Thailand (CPT) fortified itself in one of the country's most impenetrable areas. From the 1940s, Hmong tribes settled in this virtually unpopulated region. They planted opium and many were arrested over the next decade. As their relationship with central government deteriorated, the CPT took up their cause. In 1982 the government weakened the grip of the CPT until they gave in.

185

For centuries, Phu Hin Rong Kla's rugged terrain offered a safe hiding place to bandits and insurgents. Now its more peaceful inhabitants include rare orchids, ferns and mosses

THE KILNS OF SAWANKHALOK

At the Sawankhalok Kilns, north of the Historical Park, you can visit some of the excavated kilns which produced world-famous ceramics in the 14th and 15th centuries. The typical grey-green glaze was often decorated with fish or chrysanthemums. Beware fake "antiques" – a local speciality!

▶▶ Si Satchanalai Historical Park   152B2

Junction of Highways 101 and 102, 2km to the south of the new town of Si Satchanalai and 1km off the Sukhothai to Phrae bus route
Open: daily 8:30–4:30. Admission: inexpensive

Cars are not allowed in the park itself, but elephant rides are available from the entrance and bicycles can be rented from the pink entrance gate to Wat Phra Si Rathana Mahathat, 2km from the park. Cycling is recommended, as it can be a quite far to walk.

The old city of Si Satchanalai coexisted with Sukhothai and was ruled by Sukhothai princes. It flourished as a centre for Sawankhalok celadon ware which was first produced by Chinese potters. Old kilns dot the area and

Walk

A walk in Phu Hin Rong Kla

Allow 1.5 to 2 hours for this 3.5km walk.

Start at the car park signed "Communist Headquarters" from the main road, 3km east of the national park headquarters. Take the path at the bottom of the car park. Fork left at the Thai signpost after 200m. Ignore a small path joining from the left and cross a rock pavement. Notice the pock-marks in the rock caused by shelling. (You will return to this point; to the right is your even- tual continuation.) Keep to the left of the abandoned gun and take the right-hand of two paths signposted in Thai. The left-hand path leads to the former huts of the Political and Military School, where it is a short walk left along the road for signed turnings to the waterwheel and air-raid shelter.

Immediately fork left again and reach a hut on your right, formerly used for pounding rice.
Just ahead lie the former CPT head- quarters and wooden-barred jail.

Take the path by the hut. It leads through another air-raid shelter (a natural rock crevice). Walk on and rejoin the main path, keeping left on

it to return to the rock pavement and the abandoned gun. Turn left.
The path soon leads to Pa Chu Thong, or Flagpole Cliff edge (passing to the right of the Flagpole Cliff itself) to the rock pavement of Lan Hin Boom. This is the most famous landform in the park.

Retrace steps to a fork; bear left. Later, Flagpole Cliff comes into view and you pass mushroom-shaped rock formations. At a wooden gateway on the left, a short path leads past the site of a CMT burial ground, where a few overgrown humps can be discerned.

Keep left on rejoining the main path and return to the car park.

The rock pavement of Lan Hin Boom leads to a spot for quiet reflection

this has lead to a revival of the industry, with stalls operating near the old city. Over 140 ruins cover an otherwise largely deserted 300-hectare area, the centre of which is enclosed by fortifications and contains the park. In its extent, it is almost as striking as Sukhothai itself. The sites are numbered to aide nagivation and a map is available at the entrance.

Wat Chang Lom (Site 1)▶
A Singhalese style *chedi* with 39 elephant buttresses; similar to its Sukhothai namesake but much better preserved.

Wat Chedi Jet Thaeo (Site 2)▶▶
Opposite Wat Chang Lom, this 14th-century temple has 30 monuments in various styles, including a Sukhothai-style lotus bud *chedi*, and it is thought to enshrine the three princes of Sukhothai.

Wat Nang Phya (Site 4)▶
Early Ayutthaya style; still embellished with intricate stucco on a column and on the *wiharn* wall.

PHAA HAAT SIAW
The village of Ban Hat Siaw, to the southeast of Si Satchanalai, is famous for its beautiful handwoven textiles, known as *phaa haat siaw*. These are made by a local ethnic group called the Thai Phuan, who fled here from northeastern Laos during the 19th century to escape a Chinese–Laotian conflict. The cloth produced is patterned in bold horizontal stripes edged with brocade. Weaving skills are passed on to the womenfolk of each generation.

Wat Chedi Jet Thaeo

Wat Khao Phanom Phloeng (Site 8)

Reached by a flight of laterite steps, the ruin is rather unremarkable but it commands a large view, partly obscured by the trees.

Wat Si Rathana Mahathat ▶ (2km southeast at Chalieng)

Approached from the main road by a rickety wooden suspension bridge, this working temple stands inside a loop in the Yom River and retains a Sukhothai-style seated Buddha image

▶▶▶ Sukhothai   152B2

Junction of Highways 12 and 101, west of Phitsanulok. Buses from Chiang Mai, Phitsanulok, Bangkok and neighbouring towns; domestic flights

Three examples of Sukhothai's many and varied temples include the 13th- to 14th-century Wat Chetupon, built partly of slate…

If you only have time to visit one ancient site in Thailand, it must be the old city of Sukhothai. New Sukhothai, 12km east, is a quite separate town, only of interest as a place to stay and eat. There are no inhabited buildings within the old city.

From the new city, cross the main road bridge over the Yom River, and take a minibus from just behind the police box on the right. Cars are not allowed in the old city ruins; buses tour the main sites from the museum and bicycles can be rented from the shop by the bus stop for a few baht. Distances are too great to cover on foot. There are admission charges for each of the city's five zones; the historic park is open daily until dusk.

History Established in 1238, when the central plains were inhabited by Mons and Khmers, Sukhothai was the capital of the first large Thai kingdom in Siam and became a vassal state of Ayutthaya in 1365. It was a cosmopolitan kingdom, host to a variety of cultures from Borneo, Ceylon and China, all of which contributed to the diversity of its monuments. King Ramkhamhaeng extended the kingdom with his warrior skills and was responsible for much of the flowering of Sukhothai culture. He brought in Chinese ceramic skills, introducing the Sawankhalok celadon industry to the region. Sukhothai-style Buddha images are unmistakable for their oval heads bearing crowns, their plain torsos and their serene, mystical smiles.

Of over 90 historic sites, about a third are within the walls, which are still visible and are pierced by four gateways.

The city is walled and threaded by beautiful canals and lakes carpeted with lotus flowers. These waters were supplied by a reservoir built to the southwest of the city and were both functional and ornamental.

The National Museum▶▶▶ (*Open* Wed–Sun, except national holidays, 9–12, 1–4. *Admission: inexpensive*) An excellent introduction to the historic city, including much in the Sukhothai style. Look, too, for the chart showing the evolution of the Thai alphabet, thought to have been invented by King Ramkhamhaeng; a set of photographs showing the overgrown ruins before restoration in 1953; and a copy of a Khmer stone which has told scholars much about the history of the site.

Royal Palace and Wat Mahathat▶▶▶ Only the base of the palace survives, but the royal temple ruins contain 200 structures.The main *chedi* bears a Sukhothai lotus-bud motif and its base bears a frieze of 111 Buddhas.

Wat Trapang Thong and Wat Trapang Ngoe▶▶▶ "The temples of the gold and silver ponds" adjoin the waterside, with a *bot* built on an island. This is the original site of the Loi Krathong festival (see page 228).

Wat Si Chum▶▶ The tallest and most famous Buddha image in the city stands 15m high and has eyes of inlaid mother of pearl. A passage on the left, bearing Jataka inscriptions, is blocked off because it would raise climbers above the Buddha's head.

Information Centre▶ (*Open* 9–4) A beautiful modern pavilion overlooking a lake; inside are a pleasant coffee shop and a fine scale model of the city.

Wat Phra Pai Luang▶ An atmospheric ruin, with partly restored Khmer *prangs*; rather overgrown. It is thought to be at the heart of the original city which was restricted from growth by the canals.

Wat Saphan Hin▶▶ Turn off just past the sign for a scout camp and you will reach this hilltop *wat*, from where the kings could survey their city and kingdom.

Rama Khamhaeng National Park▶ *Off Highway 101 towards Kamphaeng Phet at the 414km post.* A bumpy 15km access road finally leads to the National Park office and to bungalow accommodation. People come here to climb Khao Luang mountain (1,185m) and for the panoramas. Views from here are often misty but on a clear day can be huge. Tents for hire near the summit offer impressive sunset and sunrise vistas.

…Wat Mahathat, the city's most important site…

"SUKHOTHAI STYLE" 189
"Sukhothai style" describes the classic image of the enlightened Buddha. It is characterised by a precise list of physical features regarded as "marks of greatness", including: hands like lotus flowers, a chin like a mango stone, and skin so smooth that the dust would not stick to it.

…and Wat Sra Sri, whose bell-shaped chedi *makes a photogenic sight reflected in a mirror-like pond*

Northeast Thailand

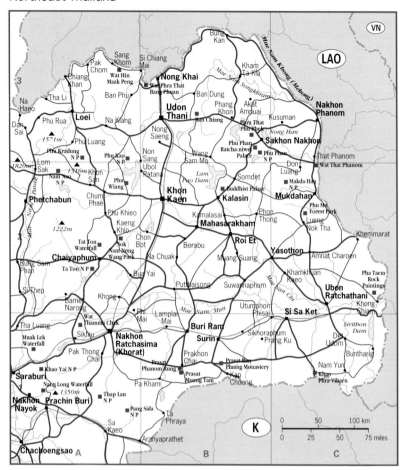

ECONOMIC MIGRATION
The infertile soils and sparse rainfall of the northeast combine to produce the poorest region in Thailand. Poverty and unemployment drive many Isan people to the status of economic refugees. Many migrate, at least seasonally, to large cities to look for work. Saddest of all are the young women (often barely more than children) who head for the bright lights of Bangkok or Pattaya and end up working as prostitutes to finance their families.

This region is known as "Isan" by the Thais, and many natives of Isan's 19 provinces are justly proud of their region's distinct identity. Khorat (Nakhon Ratchasima) and Khon Kaen have been earmarked for industrial development but agriculture is still the basic occupation of the majority of people. Nature here is a harsh master, with yearly droughts or flooding.

With the Mekong River and the Laotian Peoples' Democratic Republic to their north and east, many Isan folk identify themselves culturally as Laotian, rather than Thai, although their political allegiance to the Thai crown is still very strong.

Isan is famous for its food – the sticky rice staple, papaya salad and barbecued meat. Its folk music tradition, *mor lam*, is also special.

In a recent chapter of the region's history thousands of American troops fought in the Second IndoChinese war. Later upheavals have come in the wake of the Cambodian civil war.

Poverty here is still great to such an extent that many of the people who scratch a living from the soil supplement their diet with frogs and insects. The per capita income is also the lowest in the country, a paltry few thousand baht per year. Government attempts at development have been partially successful. The birth-rate is falling and increasing numbers of buffalo are replaced by the *E-taen*, a low-slung vehicle that can serve a multitude of purposes which include ploughing, pumping, threshing and ferrying people about.

For the visitor There are plenty of attractions in this region for the visitor. Be prepared for a trip through a land which, although barren at times, has much to amaze – both natural and cultural.

The northerly provinces of Loei and Nong Khai have stunning scenery along the Mekong River, Loei being particularly mountainous; southern Isan, with its strong Khmer (Cambodian) flavour, has a wealth of remains from the days of Angkor's glory; and Surin is famous for its elephants.

Warm welcome One thing that is immediately noticeable in the more obscure provinces of the country is the open curiosity and generosity of the local people. As you travel around the regions, you will find yourself constantly waving and smiling in response to roadside greetings. The famous Thai welcome to strangers is possibly warmer here, in the northeast, than anywhere else.

Northeast Thailand

*Temple ruins at
Suwannaphum*

The map shows the region of Northeast Thailand with locations including Ban Pak Mak, Pak Chom, Sang Khom, Wat Hin Maak Peng, Si Chiang Mai, Friendship Bridge, LAO, Nong Khai, Ban Po Noi, Kaeng Khut Khuu, Chiang Khan, Ban Chiang Klom, Nam Som, Tha Bo, Wat Phra That Bang Phuan, Ban Nong Song Hong, Phen, Sang Khom, Han Dung, Ban Tad Jomsee, Ban Krang, Ban Phu, Ban Khok Doo, Ban Baak Maak, Ban Fia, Suwankhuha, Ban Nong Hua Khu, Ban Nakhaa, Ban Dong Rai, Loei, Na Duang, Ban San Tom, Ban Kut Din Chi, Tham Erawan, Kut Chap, Udon Thani, Ban Chiang, Nong Han, Wang Saphung, Na Klang, Ban Kham Hai, Phu Luang 1571m, Phu Luang National Park, Phu Luang, Nong Bua Lamphu, Nong Wua So, Ban Puay Deng, Ban Loei Wang Sai. Highways 212, 211, 2, 2021, 22, 210, 201 are marked. Mae Nam Khong (Mekong), 853m, 997m peaks are shown. Scale: 0–40 km / 0–20 miles.

Drive

A tour around Udon Thani, Loei and Nong Khai

This tour is best spaced over five days.
Suggested schedule
(Book national park accommodation in advance.)
Day 1: Early morning, leave Udon Thani. Optional detour to Ban Phu. Arrive in Phu Luang National Park around twilight. Stay overnight in reserved accommodation.
Day 2: Leisurely drive to Chiang Khan. Stay in guesthouse.
Day 3: Leisurely drive to Sang Khom. Stay in guesthouse.
Day 4: Leisurely drive to Nong Khai. Stay in hotel or guesthouse.
Day 5: Short drive to Udon Thani. Day excursion to Ban Chiang.

Start in Udon Thani. To arrive in Loei before sunset take the main Highway 210 west. Alternatively, take Highway 2 (The Friendship Highway) north.
A diversion to **Ban Phu**▶▶ at the well-signposted Highway 2021 will mean arriving at dusk, especially if time is taken to explore the rock garden and cave systems of **Phra Putthabat Bua Bok**. This is not signposted in Ban Phu district.

On arrival at the crossroads go straight across by the market and look for Highway 2348.
The road down to Highway 210 and Loei from Ban Phu is not remarkable; there are a few interesting *wats* back from the road.
Mountains of awe-inspiring scale start at the border of Loei Province as the road climbs gently upwards.

Highway 210 swings a sharp 90 degrees right at Wang Saphung district to become Highway 201; keep an eye out for the turn-off to avoid plunging into the rice paddies.
Jeep drivers may have time for the very well-signposted 20km trip south from Wang Saphung to **Phu Luang National Park**▶, where there is accommodation. Phu Luang mountain can be seen from the road here, a grey stone leviathan dominating smaller neighbours.
The short approach to Loei in the other direction is no less scenic. Loei town may not amount to much but it has a ring of mountains and all the amenities of civilisation such as guesthouses and hotels.

Continue to Chiang Khan district 50km due north.
This is an excellent spot to rest before contemplating the 200km drive along Highway 211 into Nong Khai, where guesthouses taking advantage of the riverside ambience are plentiful.

Sang Khom is a modest target from Chiang Khan; Highway 211 sticks to the Mekong River for very long stretches. Khut Khuu Rapids is a short and reasonably signed left-hand detour just out of Chiang Khan. The scenery is formed by the meandering middle-aged river. The water level can go down so far in the dry season that it is unclear where the banks of the river actually lay. Shoals of rocks and extensive bogs dominate the view.

The 60km to Sang Khom are more of the same marvellous Mekong moonscape. The road scales a series of cliffs passing some viewpoints in order to cross the well-marked provincial boundary. Shortly afterwards **Than To waterfall▶** is prominently signposted with the blue tourist signs as seen earlier on the road to Phu Luang. **Sang Khom** provides a leisurely stopover to relax peaceably by the now broad and clearly defined river. There are budget guesthouses here. Near by is Wat Hin Maak Peng, an atmospheric spot enhanced by an interest in meditation.

Alternatively travellers may press on a further 40km into Si Chiang Mai. Shortly after Si Chiang Mai the road swings away from the river and you are back into dusty, featureless Isan. The road becomes wider as one approaches Tha Bo.

Highway 211 cuts across the flat fields past Wat Bang Phuan to link up with Highway 2, a full 10km short of Nong Khai. Note that following the white signs all the way will lead into Nong Khai.
A dirt track turning left about 5km out of Tha Bo returns to the river all the way into **Nong Khai** railway station, but the turning is difficult to locate. It will be easy to find a room in Nong Khai, although Highway 2 back into Udon is very fast. From Udon Thani it is a 50km drive (Highway 22) to **Ban Chiang▶▶▶**, where excavations have revealed bronze and clay artefacts thousands of years old (see page 194).

A Bronze Age skeleton from the Ban Chiang burial pits

STEPHEN YOUNG
When Stephen Young, an American anthropology student, came to Ban Chiang in 1966 he chanced upon one of the major archaeological sites of Southeast Asia. Dusting himself down after tripping over a tree root, he noticed pot rims protruding from the ground. He collected a sample and alerted the University of Pennsylvania, and the antiquity of his discovery was established.

Crude, mass-produced modern versions of the famous Ban Chiang pottery compete with convincingly antique-looking fakes. To see the real thing, head for the National Museum

▶▶▶ Ban Chiang   190B3
Off Highway 22. Buses from Udon Thani

The otherwise fairly nondescript province of Udon Thani made the headlines when pottery and bronze artefacts discovered in Ban Chiang were dated to the 3rd millennium BC, contemporary with Sumer, suggesting that metalworking was discovered independently in Southeast Asia.

Village crafts are largely reproductions of these ancient Ban Chiang ware in all shapes and sizes. The native Thai Lao weaves and embroideries are also to be found on display in the museum.

Archaeological finds Little is known of the early Ban Chiang people's language and their ethnic origins, but the large and beautiful pots which were found as well as the metal tools and weapons are a rich testament to their technical sophistication.

We also know that they farmed rice, domesticated animals, wove their own clothes and eventually progressed to working iron. The find stimulated research in geographical history, which showed a decrease in the region's water sources.

Pottery As further testament to their technical skills, the ancient pottery-making techniques of Ban Chiang are essentially the same as those used by modern villagers who sell cheap reproductions. The patterns show there is an evolution through the period of the culture (ca3600 BC–AD 300), the primeval inhabitants favouring the distinctive burnt-ochre whorl pattern. From about 2,000 years ago the potters incorporated figures of animals and people into their designs, and by the later period they had developed a process of printing patterns on to the pot with the aid of wooden discs.

Metalwork The metallurgy of the area, too, shows a progression through a long period of experimentation. The search for minerals, the control of temperature, the greater admixture of tin for a shinier finish and a "lost-wax" moulding process were all well-developed. It appears that bronze was first cast from around 2000 BC onwards. Axe-heads, spear tips and arrow tips bear this out. The people of Ban Chiang had discovered techniques of smelting iron by 800 BC and the stronger metal came to be used for heavier implements. Bronze came to be used for mainly decorative purposes, such as arm bangles and household objects like ladles.

Modern Ban Chiang The area was settled by an inward migration of the Thai Lao about 200 years ago. Like their forebears here, who were subsistence rice farmers, they are known to have built Wat Po Si Nai which is one of the excavation sites.

The National Museum (*Open* daily 8:30–5, except public holidays. *Admission: inexpensive*) Some of the choicest finds from the site are displayed in the modern National Museum. A *songthaew* drops passengers here from the main bus station in Udon for a few baht. Visitors are greeted on the stairs by a skeleton disinterred from a long sleep.

As with ancient cultures everywhere, burials supplied the greatest amount of cultural information about the past. Bones reveal that life expectancy was as low as the early 30s, while the relative scale of the burials indicates a social structure.

The main Princess Mother building is home to an exhibition which once toured the world. There are the fascinating details of the discovery, which was authenticated by a team from Pennsylvania University led by the late American archaeologist Chester F Gorman. One room has an absorbing display on the modern village's changing fortunes, leading to the revival through tourism of silk and cotton weaving.

The main characteristic of the Ban Chiang style of pottery is a swirling pattern in burnt ochre. Many of the pots were associated with burial rituals

BAN CHIANG FINDS
In any terms, the archaeological finds of Ban Chiang are remarkable, not least on aesthetic grounds. But the exact significance of the discovery has been hotly debated by experts. At first, Ban Chiang was dated at around 3000 BC, thus predating earlier evidence of the Bronze Age found in Mesopotamia. Later tests on the material revealed that it was not really so old. None the less, it seems that Thailand developed smelting techniques well before China.

195

BOOTY
Locals soon cashed in on the Ban Chiang booty, collecting the pots by the car load for worldwide distribution, and by 1973, when an organised archaeological dig at last got under way, the site had been sadly depleted of its treasures. But some artefacts were still to be found, most importantly the bronze which was to change archaeologists' understanding of the development of metal-making. Fortunately, the looting ceased, and much archaeological work on the site was carried out by Thai volunteers.

Rock painting of early Buddhists

▶▶ Ban Phu 190A3

Junction of Highways 2021 & 2098. Songthaew *from Udon Thani or Nong Khai*

This obscure corner of Udon Thani province is great for bushwalkers. Bring some water for the arduous hike. Getting there is relatively straightforward, and it is a feasible day-trip from Udon Thani, Nong Khai or Sang Khom. While the final part of the route is a bush-track, metalled roads and buses run into Ban Phu where there are motorbikes for hire, making it feasible to go another 10km to Nam Som.

The maze-like rock gardens to be found at Ban Phu have been designated as the Phu Phra Bat Historical Park. Within the caves in the park are paintings which date back approximately 4,000 years and it is fascinating to trace the rise and fall of civilisations and cultures through their sculpture.

Local legends grew around some of the stranger rock formations such as *Hor Nang Usa*, "Usa's bedchamber", Usa being a woman who followed her lover here.

Humans have arranged circles of stones, and there are curious formations caused by natural erosion. An imitation of That Phanom stands at the top of the hill. Wat Phra That Phra Putthabat Bua Bok, with relic and footprint, points the way along a path to the cave paintings and the mushroom-like sandstone "bedchamber".

The rocks of Ban Phu have provided local inhabitants with a blank canvas for thousands of years. These paintings reveal the artistry of early Buddhists

▶ Khon Kaen 190B2

Junction of Highways 2 & 12. Buses from Bangkok (north terminal), Phitsanulok and Khorat; trains from Bangkok and Khorat; domestic flights

Officially a "development centre", Khon Kaen is a large commercial and administrative city. Rapid industrial growth has been fostered by Khon Kaen University, the biggest in the region. The city's name came from Phra That Kham Kaen in Wat Jetiaphum, 30km north of town.

According to legend it was here that a tamarind log (*kham kaen*) began sprouting new shoots.

Particular attractions start with two large lakes, **Beung Kaen Nakhon**, and the larger **Beung Thung Sang**. The cool atmosphere makes these popular picnic spots, even if the views are nothing out of the ordinary. Stalls sell Isan food such as *som tam* salad and barbecued chicken.

The **Khon Kaen National Museum▶** (*Open Wed–Sun 9–12, 1–4. Admission: inexpensive*) has Dvaravati artefacts from Muang Fa Daet in Kalasin.

Environs

For those interested in palaeontology, **Phu Wiang** is a detour worth making off Highway 2038 to see the bones of a Cretaceous-period dinosaur.

Tham Pha Phu▶, Chum Phae district is a 4km turn-off some way along the road to Chum Phae. The huge cave is an indirect walk from the car park. There is a terrific view from the cave mouth, but it does not equal the scenery in Phu Kradung National Park (see page 198).

Pha Nok Khao ("Owl Cliff") on the border of Loei province is a name that refers to the strange shapes that can be seen on the Pong River. They can also be seen from Mount Phu Kradung, which is visible in the distance from here.

Pong Neep (Ubol Ratana Dam), 26km out of town, is the biggest multi-purpose dam in the northeast. Completed in 1966, it created a reservoir of 410sq km and provides electricity for eight provinces.

Chon Bot *Off Highway 2, 57km southwest of Khon Kaen.* This district of Khon Kaen is reached by a turn-off at 399km, Ban Phai, then follow the road for another 12km.

Chon Bot is famous for the locally tie-dyed *mut mee* silks (see panel). The silk is cheap and there is a good selection available. There are plenty of factories, which are busy serving markets in Chiang Mai and Bangkok. They are usually small, informally run and welcoming to visitors.

MUT MEE
Isan is famed for its textiles. One of the best-known types is *mut mee*, a tie-dyeing process, which produces a soft, subtle blend of colours and textures. *Mut mee* cloth is made from both silk and cotton yarns, the finer silk ones being more expensive. The geometric designs are based on natural patterns – flowers, snakes and so on. The revival of this traditional industry has been encouraged by Queen Sirikit, and by the growth of tourism.

197

The silk worms of Thailand expend their yellow labours for what is now a vast industry. Many Isan towns are important textile centres

PHU KRADUNG'S FLORA
Because of the cool temperatures, Phu Kradung has an unusual range of flora, including orchids and temperate species such as roses. Elephants frequent the pine forests. Pha Nok Aen is the place to go for sunrise views. There are numerous waterfalls.

COTTON BLOSSOM FESTIVAL
Loei province is an important cotton-growing region, and an excellent place to buy cotton goods, including sweaters and cushions. Heavy cotton quilts are another speciality, designed to ward off the chill of the cooler months in this mountainous area. A Cotton Blossom Festival celebrates the local product in February, with decorated floats and a Beauty Queen contest.

►► Loei Province   190A3

Highway 201; a border province with Laos. Regular buses from Udon; buses from Bangkok (northern terminal)

Temperatures in this mountainous province can plummet below zero, which is the coldest in the country: have warm clothing to hand.

Loei town is a cotton centre and goods are on sale in town at reasonable prices. There are many hotels here, of which King's Hotel is the most luxurious while still remaining in the moderate price range. Muang Loei guest house is typical of the budget accommodation on offer.

Northwest of Loei town an ancient city waits to be discovered at **Ban Khok Doo►**, while **Wang Saphung** district, a short way south out of town, has a few spots worthy of a visit amid a ring of mountains. On the Udon Thani road are the **Erawan Caves►**, where a long tunnel through a mountain is full of limestone formations.

National parks Loei's mountain national parks – Phu Kradung, Phu Luang and Phu Rua – are breathtaking in their scope and are centred around the mountains that lie to the town's south and west.

Heavily visited, **Phu Kradung►►** (sometimes closed during the rainy season) is best appreciated on weekdays. It is 84km south of Loei town on Highway 201. There are 50km of well-marked trails to explore across the forested plateau. The southern trail runs along a precipitous edge where gibbons can be heard calling from below. The park HQ is on the summit, a tiring 9km climb, but once there such civilised amenities as restaurants and bungalows are on hand to help you get your strength back. Stalls selling soft drinks are set up along the trail but are closed during weekdays in the off-season. The trail up the table mountain leads past fields of colourful wild flowers and carnivorous pitcher plants hidden in the grass (see panel). Wildlife includes wild boars, wild dogs, giant black squirrels, langurs, macaques and herds of elephants.

Phu Luang► lies southwest of Loei in Wang Sapung district, from where it is signposted. It is worth the trek up to the plateau for the sights of the waterfalls, stone gardens and forests of flowers.

Phu Rua lies 40km west of Loei, but drivers must skirt the thickly forested mountains after leaving Loei, turning right on Highway 203. *Phu Rua* means "boat mountain" and is so named because of its unusual prow-like summit.

There is a paved road up Phu Rua, but no regular public transport. The progression of vegetation from lush tropical to the more barren temperate varieties is as well defined as in a geography textbook. Early morning mist makes a breathtaking spectacle around the mountain. If you want to stay, the park bungalows are about halfway up the mountain.

Accommodation for any of the parks can be arranged through the national park central booking service in Bangkok, tel: 02 579 0529.

The border with Laos Driving west from Phu Rua, you reach Dan Sai district and Na Haeo near the Laotian border. Turn right off Highway 203 as it swings down towards Petchabun.

Passing Dan Sai, follow an unprepossessing sign right to **Ban Muang Phra▶**. This village is where it is possible, technically, to cross into Laos. There is a large sign bearing the inscription "The end of Siam", and a little wooden bridge with the legend, "Lao-Thai friendship will endure". See the Lao town hall and rickety little mudpile of a temple, dark inside with guttered wax. The area is still sensitive, although relations have improved of late, but always seek local advice.

The important *wat* in Dan Sai cemented a Thai–Lao pact in 1560, with *chedi* Phra That Sri Song Rak. Around May and June, there is dancing for the rain god in papier mâché masks that have a striking resemblance to African art, the dancers becoming fearsome *Phi Takone* ghosts.

Villages similar to Ban Muang Phra can be found all the way to Pak Chom, following the banks of the Heuang river which forms the border with Laos and flows into the Mekong near Chiang Khan. The Tha Li district is one of the most beautiful parts of Thailand, where western travellers are rarely seen.

Chiang Khan district, in the north, is an excellent starting point for a long scenic drive along the mighty Mekong River. The delightful small town of Chiang Khan is on the Laotian border, in a large valley surrounded by mountains, where Highway 201 becomes 2186. The road goes to the east past narrow rapids at Khut Khu and carries on to Pak Chom. There are a number of *wats* to be seen in Chiang Khan. The oldest is 17th-century Wat Mahathat, in the centre of town.

For accommodation, the **Nong Ball** has foreigner-friendly services and an English-speaking owner, its restaurant having a fine Mekong-side ambience.

The simple wooden huts of this Loei village indicate something of the standard of living in rural areas of the northeast. Many live below the poverty line

The Mekong, which forms the border between Thailand and Laos for more than 750km, is one of Asia's great rivers. It springs in the high Tibetan plateau, and then stretches more than 4,500km to the South China Sea to become the world's 12th longest river.

RIVER BOATS
On the Mekong River you will see the extremely simple Lao boat called "three planks", which translates into Lao as *sampan.*

Embarking to cross the Mekong

See how it runs The Mekong River (Mae Nam Khong to the Thais) first pursues a turbulent course through the high Chinese mountains of Tibet and Yunnan, then flows parallel to the Yangtze and the Salween through Yunnan province. The river forms the border between Myanmar and Laos, and then between Laos and Thailand. Even in some upper stretches it is more than 2km wide.

Along its way, it irrigates vast areas of land, supporting villages with rice, coconuts, sugar cane and fish, and provides miners with small finds of gold.

Passing Vientiane and Phnom Penh, an eventual 475 billion cubic metres of water per year burst into the sea in a Vietnamese delta. When it is in flood, the water can rise by 15m and yet in the dry season the flow is reduced to a trickle, and the people of northeastern Thailand can walk across the riverbed into Laos.

The river's banks are heavily forested except in the drier areas of northeastern Thailand. Thick bamboo grows, as well as kapok and banana trees. Crocodiles are rare these days, but monkeys, pythons and the ubiquitous mosquitoes abound.

Hydroelectric power Laos uses the Mekong for hydropower; a dam at Nam Ngum generates 150MW. Half of the electricity generated could be exported to Thailand, whose booming economy is hungry for power, but deforestation and resultant erosion is making the reservoirs silt up.

Several dams have been built across Mekong tributaries and others are under construction or being planned to supply the country with energy.

River language The people on both banks of the upper Mekong speak the same "northern language"; there are eight times as many Lao-speakers as there are in Laos itself.

For the people The river is a source of food – fish, shrimps, crabs and frogs – to supplement the staple diet of *kao niew* or sticky rice.

The Mekong has given its name to a fierce rice liquour, known as Mekhong whisky. When it is drunk on the river a measure is sometimes poured into the stream for the water spirits.

Prosperous Bangkok tells only one side of the story: poverty is still very much at large in dual-economy Thailand. The impoverished rural northeast and the squalor of much of the capital represent some of the worst of the nation's extremes.

Rich and poor Thailand's astonishing economic progress during the last three decades has placed it firmly among the success stories of the Pacific Rim, such as Singapore and Taiwan. Indeed, overall wealth just in Bangkok is close to the level of some of the poorer European countries such as Portugal. But in the kingdom as a whole there is an enormous gap between rich and poor, and poverty still exists. Things are improving: the proportion of the population earning below US$1 per day at 1985 rates fell from 10 per cent in 1985 to less than 1 per cent by 1995. But the gap between rich and poor continues to widen.

Isan in the northeast, where 40 per cent of the Thais live, is one of the most poverty-stricken regions of the country. Across the large, arid plateau stretching from Nakhon Ratchasima all the way to the Laotian border, millions scratch a living growing rice and tapioca.

Almost all but old people and children move away from home to search for work in the central plains region or in Bangkok itself. Some travel further afield to the rubber plantations of the south or to man Thailand's fishing fleet. They return to the villages only for the planting and harvesting seasons.

Solutions There are many schemes to help the very poor, from land-sharing to commercialised agroindustry, village adoption to co-operatives. In recent years hundreds of millions of baht have been poured into the region by the government and some improvement is noted. But the overall phenomenon of poverty remains.

ISAN
Isan still suffers from malnutrition, landlessness and poor infrastructure. Children are still forced to cut short education to go to work. Many of the poor and landless end up in one of Bangkok's numerous slums, where they lack the support of a village community.

201

Making a living from the sale of water melons in the poverty-stricken northeast Thailand

The weird, mushroom-shaped rocks of Phu Pha Thoep National Park in Mukdahan province make curious landmarks amid the surrounding dipterocarp forest

PHU PHA THOEP NATIONAL PARK
The small national park of Phu Pha Thoep lies south of Mukdahan, near the Laotian border. A remote, hilly area of dry forest and strange rock formations, it is renowned for its fossils and prehistoric finger-paintings. Near the park headquarters is a cave stacked with dozens of small Buddhas brought by local villagers. The park is an important habitat for wildlife, including barking deer, civets and monkeys. It can easily be visited on a day-trip from Mukdahan.

▶▶ **Mukdahan Province**   *190C2*
Highway 212, on the eastern border with Laos. Buses from Nakhon Phanom and Ubon Ratchathani
This province has one chief tourist attraction – views along the Mekong River. In Mukdahan town a laid-out riverside walkway extends from the customs checkpoint and car ferries work their way back and forth over the river. Across the river on the opposite side is the important Lao centre of **Savannaket**. A little further upriver is Kaeng Kabao, a dry-river islet.

The southern road is mountainous. Not far out of Mukdahan is **Phu Manorom**, a brisk climb up ending in a *chedi* and a pavilion. A good diversion off Highway 212 in this direction is **Phu Muu Forest Park**, near Nikhom Kham Soi. Rich in forestry, wildlife and water, the area has rest shelters on the mountain-top with good views of the plain below. Near town, on Jom Nang mountain, are "red-handprint" caves which are similar to those at Pha Taem (see page 206).

The area boasts a jumble of colourful Thai sub-tribes such as Phu Thai, Saek, So, Khaa, Yor, Kalerng and Kula. 9–15 January is when the local people stage The Thai Tribes of Mukdahan festival. The end of Buddhist Lent is marked by a boat race.

▶▶ **Nakhon Phanom Province**   *190C3*
Off Highway 22, near the Laos border. Buses from Nong Khai; possible to travel by bus from Udon (journey time is over seven hours)
Nakhon Phanom town▶ itself has a seductive charm with a fine legacy of dignified public buildings and old-fashioned houses. More memorable view of the Mekong River can be had from a number of restaurants and hotels. The main attraction within Nakhon Phanom province is

That Phanom►►, a striking *chedi* of great antiquity, located 50km to the south of town. On the site there is a museum containing relics, which includes one of Buddha, reputed to be a collar-bone, and a festival is held there in around January/February. **Renu Nakhon**, near the provincial capital, is a similar structure on a more modest scale.

► Nakhon Ratchasima (Khorat)   *190A1*
Highway 2, 250km northeast of Bangkok. Regular buses from Bangkok (northern terminal); trains from Bangkok; domestic flights available

Thailand's second largest city after Bangkok, Khorat (the more common name for Nakhon Ratchasima) is a day's drive by car from Bangkok and is an important railway junction for Nong Khai and Ubon Ratchathani.

The moated city has long been a Siamese redoubt against aggressive Lao and Khmer. It is often described as "the gateway to the northeast", and indeed, traffic to most Isan provinces must pass through Khorat. The **Silver Lake Park** is an artificial lake to be found just outside Khorat, off Mitraphap Road, with an aviary, flower garden and swimming pool.

The city owes its present plan to King Narai who hired a French architect in the 17th century. A worthwhile sight on the outskirts is **Wat Salaloi►**, representing a ship beating against the waves. Ceramic tiles used to roof this innovative modern *wat* were made in **Dan Kwian**, a stopover easy to spot on the southwestern road to Phanom Rung. Special black clay characteristic of Dan Kwian pottery is what gives the distinctive "latticework" patterns a bright metallic sheen.

No visitor to modern Khorat can fail to notice **Khunying Mo** (or **Thao Suranan**), one of Thailand's martial heroines. This scourge of the Lao, who rallied the women of the town during an invasion in 1826, is immortalised on a terrace in front of the city's main gates, and a parade in her honour is held every March. Near to her effigy is the **Maha Weerawong museum** containing a hotchpotch of exhibits.

Environs
Ban Prasat has been continuously inhabited for several thousand years. Skeletons have been found here of a Bronze Age culture which made patterned red pots. A museum, opened in 1991 on the road from Khorat, just before the turning to Phi Mai, contains finds believed to be second only in importance to those of Ban Chiang (see pages 194–195).

A southbound turning just before Ban Prasat leads to another important Khmer sanctuary, **Prasat Hin Phanom Wan**. There are a number of other Khmer sites in the area around Khorat.

Staying over Although not a major tourist spot, Khorat makes a useful base for exploring the ancient sites of Phi Mai and Prasat Phanom Rung (see pages 206–207). There is a plentiful supply of medium and expensive hotels in the city, though budget places tend to be poor quality and generally noisy.

Waterslides galore attract visitors to Silver Lake Park on the western outskirts of Khorat

WAT PHOCHAI
Wat Phochai, at Nong Khai town's eastern end, is the focus for festivals. The complex has a tall bell tower and the main image is solid gold.

SPANNING THE MEKONG
The Thai–Australian Friendship Bridge at Nong Khai is the first of several road bridges to span the Mekong, finally linking Thailand and Laos after decades of hostility delayed construction. Financed by US$30 million of aid from Australia, it opened in April 1994 with wide-reaching implications for the governments involved, for tourism, as well as for local people. Increased trade and travel have brought prosperity to the area.

A restaurant sign in English and souvenirs on sale indicate a strong farang *presence in the frontier town of Nong Khai, much visited since the construction of the Friendship Bridge into Laos*

▶ ▶ ▶ Nong Khai
190B3

Highway 2, near Vientiane on the Laotian border. Buses from Bangkok (northern terminal: journey time nine hours); trains from Bangkok

Like the province, the town of Nong Khai is long and thin, clinging to the Mekong River. The town preserves its old wooden houses by the river bank and along Meechai, the "main drag".

After an independent Vientiane had been crushed, King Rama I established controlling lordships, one of whom was based here in Nong Khai. The currents of history swept Marxism to power in Laos and until recently Nong Khai has been the most Communist-influenced of all the country's provinces, with many Russian goods available, such as watches, cameras and fur hats.

An enduring legacy of the earlier French presence in Laos is freshly baked baguettes. Once these were imported, but prohibitive taxes forced the Thais to bake them for themselves.

Orange robes are prominent in Nong Khai: there are many novices studying in colleges here. The classic spot for visitors, **Tha Sadet** (the jetty), is on Rim Khong Road. There are some quaint shops here selling filigree silver jewellery and Lao weaves. Locals are secretive about the market where Lao traders dispose of their goods.

Near here is a co-operative called the **Village Weavers**, a handicraft centre that weaves indigo-dyed *mut mee* cotton. The co-operative was set up in response to the lack of off-season opportunities causing many locals to go off to find new work in Bangkok.

Take a pleasant stroll among the *wats* and houses which look across at Laos and the river views. Here, more than anywhere, Laos seems poised to open up to the outside world. In 1994, the bridge linking Nong Khai and Vientiane (pronounced "Wiang Jan") was completed (see panel). Thai–Lao trade has boomed as a result of this, but the status of Western tourists is unsure. The Lao authorities are still very grudging with visas and group tours are favoured. The situation changes rapidly; check at the Lao embassy in Bangkok. The building of the bridge itself was funded by Australian government money.

Nong Khai is now rather overwhelmed by civil works. The rising water table led to the loss of a few houses, and a concrete bank was constructed. Just west of the jetty are some riverside restaurants with a very pleasant ambience. From here you can see a sunken *chedi* – under water for 150 years – but only in the dry season.

Nearer the town's centre of gravity, about halfway to the railway station, there is a monument to a failed rebellion of Haw Chinese outside the town hall.

In town and situated on the river bank, the spread-out and informal **Mut Mee** guesthouse is a suitable mine of local information. There are also many moderately priced hotels to be found.

Provincial Nong Khai is very pleasant, with the Mekong saving the province from the fate of its more barren southern neighbours.

Take Highway 211 west of Nong Khai to pass the *chedi* at **Wat Phra That Bang Phuan**, said to contain Buddha relics. The spectacular scenery starts around Sri Chiang Mai on the river, where Vietnamese make spring rolls; there are budget bungalows here.

Further on in Sangkhom district is Than Thong, a waterfall-cum-river feeder and popular stopping point. Among budget bungalows in Sang Khom town is the **TXK Guesthouse.** Its bamboo balcony is pure relaxed tranquillity and the atmosphere is engagingly informal, if the place is short on modern facilities.

Wat Hin Maak Pheng, near Sang Khom, specialises in *Thudong*, a voluntary ultra-asceticism. Its teachers and fine riverside setting attract visitors.

Along the border, nearly 200km to the east along Highway 212, **Wat Phu Tork** is reached by a spiral walkway around a strangely shaped mountain. The Hideaway Guesthouse in Ban Ahong, 100km east, makes a good touring base.

WAT KHAEK

No-one should miss Wat Khaek, just a short way out of Nong Khai town and a good stop for children. The eccentric Luang Puu in charge has built a garden of extraordinary statuary, loosely based on Buddhist and Hindu iconography. It often slides into the bizarre: dogs driving a car or a seven-headed snake. All the town *tuk tuks* will urge you there.

205

An old-fashioned tuk tuk *plies for hire in Nong Khai, still an engagingly traditional and relaxing town despite increasing numbers of tourists*

KALA
The lion-head of Kala adorns many Khmer sanctuaries in Isan. Kala was the god of Time and Death, the most feared of all the planetary gods, powerful enough to swallow the sun and the moon. Lunar and solar eclipses caused great terror among many Thais until comparatively recent times. King Mongkut did much to assuage this fear by his accurate scientific predictions of eclipses, showing they were entirely natural and explicable events.

Khmer ruins at Prasat Phanom Rung

KHMER ARCHITECTURE
As superb examples of Khmer architecture, the ruins at Phi Mai and Prasat Phanom Rung display the characteristics of the style that prevailed in the 9th to 13th centuries. At this time the Khmers ruled over much of present day Cambodia and northeast Thailand. Khmer sites have a central sanctuary featuring a tower or *prang* housing the most sacred image and abutted by four entrances or *gopura*, each with decorative lintels depicting Hindu or Buddhist figures. Staircases lined with stone serpents or *naga* lead to the *prang*.

▶▶ Pha Taem (rock paintings)   190C2

100km east of Ubon Ratchathani on the Laos border. Reach by private transport or tour

Take Highway 217 from Ubon east along the river (Mae Nam Mun), cross the rapids along Route 222 into Khong Chiam at the confluence of the Mun and the Mekong rivers. Turn right at Route 2112 through a strange rock garden to arrive at Pha Taem (see photograph, page 210).

This is a magical place. Layers of different civilisations are represented – Thai, Khmer, Mon, Ban Chiang – going back 4,000 years to when people first inhabited this lonely cliff overhanging Laos. Was it their art gallery, or temple? Pha Taem is the largest of many sites all over Isan where "hand" motifs appear on the cave wall, made by spraying paint over the hands from the mouth. There are also representations of fish, people pouring water into long-necked pots and elephants swimming.

▶▶▶ Phi Mai   190A2

60km from Nakhon Ratchasima province; off the Friendship Highway (route 2). Buses from Khorat
Open: daily 7:30–6. Admission: inexpensive

This sanctuary in the small district town of Phi Mai is set in a luscious garden of red sandstone with pools of water.

Evidence points to construction in the reign of King Jayavarman VI (1082–1107), and its dominant religion is presumed to have been Mahayana Buddhism. Four intricately carved porches surround a tall central *prang* (tower). Being so convenient to visit, the sanctuary is often used as a set for dancing troupes. Now restored, it is Thailand's best known Khmer shrine, and attracts a never-ending stream of visitors.

▶▶ Prasat Phanom Rung   190B1

Accessible in a day from Khorat, Buri Ram or Surin; turn off route 24 at Ban Tako to the west
Open: daily 6–6. Admission: inexpensive

Set a long way out in the dusty town of Buri Ram, this temple is dedicated to Siva and has a remarkable setting on an inactive volcano rearing up from bare, scrubby plain. Seven-headed serpents flank a long avenue which leads to the main *prangs*, in a series of terraces rising out of the crater.

The earliest inscriptions are 9th century; the story given in the stones tells of Hiranya, a religious leader who was ordained here and enlarged the sanctuary. One of the inscriptions in Sanskrit expounds the phallic dogmas of the Hindu Pasupat sect.

Aspects of Khmer belief can be seen in the cruciform main *prang* – such as the monstrous Kala head, representing Eclipse, the most fearsome planet god. A lintel of Vishnu, returned here from the US, attracts many Thais, who lobbied for its return.

Before leaving it is worth taking a look at the smaller **Prasat Muang Tam**, 8km south.

PHI MAI CARVINGS
The carvings at Phi Mai mingle Hindu and Buddhist mythology in a riot of energetic stonework. If you look closely over the entrance lintels you will see Krishna lifting Mount Goradhana and Siva dancing, and battle scenes from the Ramayana. Inside, the themes are mainly Buddhist, showing Buddha vanquishing Mara (the evil one), preaching, and sheltering from the floodwaters beneath a protective *naga* (dragon-headed snake).

The Khmer temple complex at Phi Mai was probably used as a model for the Cambodian temple of Angkor Wat

BANYAN TREE
Just outside the town of Phi Mai stands Thailand's largest banyan tree, a magnificent specimen of *ficus bengalensis*, covering an area half the size of a football pitch. It is known locally as Sai Ngam. Beautifully set on an island in a lake, it makes a delightful shady spot for a picnic or an evening stroll. Wooden walkways lead through the maze of branches. Food vendors, astrologers and merit-sellers ply their wares, and there are restaurants near by.

KAEN MUSIC

The *kaen* is one of the most recognisable sounds of Isan folk music. A reed instrument originating from Laos, it consists of a series of bamboo pipes arranged around a central sound box. Roi Et is one of the principle *kaen*-making towns of the northeast, where the instruments are widely on sale. It is a major component of the typical northeastern folk music, called *mor lam*, which is a fast-paced style featuring vocal and instrumental elements.

WAX CASTLE CEREMONY

The Wax Castle ceremony takes place each year in Sakhon Nakhon at *Ok Phansa*, the end of the Buddhist Lent (October). This custom is associated with a local ethnic group called the Phu Thai. Elaborately designed and intricately detailed models of *wats* are moulded from beeswax, filled with Buddha images and paraded through the streets of the town, accompanied by folk music and dancing and general *joie de vivre*.

An anti-AIDS sign on a Sakhon Nakhon hotel door

▶ Roi Et　　　　190B2

Highways 23, 214, 215, southeast of Khon Kaen. Buses from Ubon Ratchathani

Roi Et means "one hundred and one" in Thai. The town has modest ancient remains and a cool, refreshing lake full of fish. But the surrounding plain is not so blessed. The barren, salty region of Thung Kula Rong Hai ("where crops die and people cry"), ravaged by a harsh climate, is one of the poorest in Thailand. Huge amounts have been invested in land-improvement schemes, but rural depopulation is still a major problem as farmers commute to cities for work in the dry season.

At **Wat Burapha▶** there is a massive standing Buddha up on a hill; the view is panoramic. Climb up inside the statue and look over his right hand. At **Wat Neua**, in the northern part of town, there is an old *chedi*. The city shrine is unmistakably phallic.

The best place for souvenirs is the non-profit making Community Development Centre at the back of City Hall. Not least among local crafts is the *kaen*, a kind of bamboo mouth organ. All over Isan its reedy, jumping wail accompanies the *mor lam* singers. Also on sale are cushions, silks and basketry in the excellent market on Padung Panit road, near the *wat*.

Roi Et celebrates the **Bun Pha Water Festival** in March, including a parade with flags and 101 floats.

▶ Sakhon Nakhon　　　　190B3

Highways 22, 213, 223, east of Udon Thani. Buses from Udon, Nakhon Phanom, Khorat, and from Bangkok (northeast terminal)

This province in the northeast of the Isan region is home to Wat Phra That Choeng Chum, which is one of the most sacred in the country. The new 24m-tall, white *prang* was erected on the top of an earlier Khmer one, and the *wiharn* houses a statue of a seated Buddha. Two meditation masters, Ajaan Man and his disciple Ajaan Fan, lived in Sakhon Nakhon. Their remains are to be found at **Wat Pa Sutthavat** and **Wat Pa Udom Somphon** respectively.

Giant **Nong Han** lake, the largest inland lake in Thailand, has islands such as Don Sawan, reachable by boat. Swimming is not advisable.

West of the town near to the crossroads at Phang Khon district (the road to Mdon Thani) is **Nam Oon** dam and reservoir, where fish frolic in a whirlpool.

▶ Sikhoraphum 190B1

Highway 2080. Trains and buses from Surin

On the main road (and the main railway) from Surin to Si Sa Ket and Ubon, in the south of Isan, Sikhoraphum is a comfortable morning's tour from Surin.

The main sight, a five-pranged 12th-century Khmer ruin, is a 1km trek from the station. Standing on a 25m-long terrace, it creates an attractive picture set against a backdrop of trees. Inside are two fine Buddha statues. A ride on a *samlor* may save you from dehydration.

The craftsmanship of the carving here is delicate and entrancing. The Thais converted Sikhoraphum into a *wat* around the 16th century and an atmospheric gnarled old tree sits in the compound.

▶▶ Surin 190B1

Highway 214 in the south of the Isan region. Trains and buses (northeast terminal) from Bangkok

The villages of **Ban Ta Klang** and **Krapoe** provide all the elephants for the famous roundup during the third weekend of November (see panel), when the normally placid town comes to life. Throughout the year you can see some of the regalia and sacred elephant ropes used in the event in the one-room museum in Chitramboong Road (*Open Mon–Fri, 8:30-4:30. Admission free*). The Suay (called Kuy in Thai) tribe catch, rear and train the elephants with a special "spirit language". Accommodation is hard to come by at roundup time.

Surin province is famed for the variety of its silks and produces some 700 different patterns.

The southern border with Cambodia near Surin is still a remote zone and best explored with a guide. A cluster of Khmer temples lie near the frontier. Passing the eerily deserted refugee camp, ask for the *nam tok* (waterfall) and you can walk down the track to a tremendous panorama of Cambodia's flat, dense forest.

THE ELEPHANT ROUNDUP

In Surin's roundup, two teams of elephants, urged on in a tug-of-war by their drivers, take over the football field. The best time to visit Surin is in late afternoon when the elephants return to their stables. Do not approach an elephant without its *mahout* present. The Suay consider it sacrilege to kill an elephant for its ivory but a few chips off the end of tusks are often taken and then intricately carved.

209

Smartly turned-out elephants prepare for the Big Parade in Surin's annual roundup. Thousands of visitors converge for this colourful event

This strange cliff at Pha Taem on the Laotian border has witnessed aeons of Thai history. Many different peoples have left their mark on the rock-faces since prehistoric times

▶▶ Ubon Ratchathani 190C1

Highways 212, 23 & 24, bordering Laos and Cambodia. Buses from Nakhon Phanom and Bangkok (northern terminal); trains from Bangkok; domestic flights

The end of the road east and sited on the scenic Mun River, Ubon Ratchathani is a crossroads of Thai, Lao and Khmer influence and is one of the largest provinces in the northeast region.

Many old *wats* in town such as **Wat Thong Si Muang▶**, itself graced with a teak library built on stilts over a pond, become festive in late July. Locals parade giant carved beeswax candles symbolising the onset of *Phansa*, Buddhist Lent, and which burn for the duration. The **national museum▶▶** (*Open* Wed–Sun 9–4:30. *Admission: inexpensive*) is an entertaining Isan miscellany, with crafts, geology, musical instruments and other displays. Midstream in the Mun River is **Hat Wat Tai island** with a rickety wooden bridge and Isan food. For a night of traditional Isan music go to the **Pathumrat** hotel in town, which is both authentic and entertaining. Way out of town to the southwest is **Wat Pa Nanachat**, where most of the monks are from the West, and the abbot is a Canadian.

The incredible ruined temple of **Khao Phra Wiharn▶▶▶** (*Admission: moderate*) stands on the Thai–Cambodian border, accessed from the Thai side only, although it is actually in Cambodia. Because of unrest within Cambodia, the site is sometimes closed. It is also surrounded by land mine warnings and is guarded by Cambodian soldiers; your passport is retained whilst you are inside. Seek advice before travelling. Approximately 800 to 1,000 years old, and built on a limestone escarpment, it is approached by a straight pathway made of hand-hewn blocks, over 1km from bottom to top. There are three huge gatehouses on the way up. A special train service runs from Bangkok to Khao Phra Wiharn.

▶ **Utumphon Phisai**   *190C1*

Highway 2028. Trains from Surin

The district of Si Saket, on the highway and railway line to Surin, is the site of two Khmer ruins. **Prasat Hin Wat Sa Kamphaeng Yai** is on a high hill 2km from Utumphon Phisai; the entrance is well signposted. It was originally constructed by Suryavaraman I (ca AD 1042). Renovation by the Fine Arts Department is almost complete. Its younger sister, **Sa Kamphaeng Noi**, is less impressive but worth a stopover on the trip back into Si Saket town, 14km from Utumphon Phisai.

▶ **Yasothon**   *190C2*

Highway 23, east of Roi Et. Buses available from Ubon Ratchathani and Khorat

"Yaso" is famous for its rocket festival. The province is not one of Thailand's natural beauties, being mostly flat, its former forests decimated. **That Kong Khao Noi** stands out for its ancient *chedi*, the site of a matricide over a "little lump of rice" (*kong khao noi*). A Ban Chiang culture site, Tat Thong, is on Highway 23 to Ubon.

A rocket-float passes by at Yasothon's Bang Fai festival, a time when many locals let their hair down and have fun

211

Heading north on the main road to Mukdahan is **Phu Tham Phra▶**, a mountain cave system with weird rock formations, still difficult to reach. **Tham Kheng**, completely shut off from the elements, is favoured by wandering meditators. Yaso handicrafts are exemplified by the *morn khit*, or embroidered cushion, such as those made in the village of **Sri Than** in Patiw district (Highway 202 east). The triangular cushion has become a Thai symbol, the design passed on by an elderly nun.

The rocket festival When May comes, the northeast is scorchingly dry and the rains are eagerly anticipated. Around the 10th, Yaso folk try to tempt Phya Thaen, a rain deity, in the *Bang Fai* ceremony. The rockets are quite powerful; wealthy and corporate sponsors build decorated rocket floats which bear a local belle on top, dancers leading the way; and locals are liberally daubed with mud. The place is packed, and the two local budget hotels, **Yot Nakhon** and **Udomphon**, fill up. Phya Thaen public park was built with income from the festival. Out of season it is a pleasant green space.

HISTORICAL PARKS

The Fine Arts Department has developed a number of historical parks at major sights, many in the north or northeast. The aim is to defend the sights from theft and vandalism, and to protect visitors from the miscreants who once plagued remote places of interest. The more famous sites, such as Ayutthaya and Sukhothai, are well known, but other antiquities, such as the ruins of Utumphon Phisai, are also protected.

Map labels:

Prachuap Khiri Khan
Huai Yang Waterfall
BUR
Thap Sakae
Bang Saphan
Bang Saphan Noi
Tha Sae · Pathiu
Kra Buri · Ka Poh · Chumphon
Isthmus of Kra · Pak Nam Chumphon
La-un · Sawi · Mo Phon Herb Garden
Ranong · Thung Tako · Ko Tao
Ko Chang · Lang Suan
Ko Phayam · Suan Mok Buddhist Retreat · Ko Phangan
Ko Kam Yai · Kapoe · Ko Phaluai · Ko Samui
Ko Surin · Laem Son N P · Chaiya · Ao Ban Dan · Don Sak
Khuraburi · Chieo Lan Dam · Khanom
Ko Phra Thong · Phanom · Nong Thungthong Birds N P · Suratthani · Sichon
Takuapa · Khao Sok N P · Ban Na San · Ban Pak Long
Ko Similan · Phang Nga · Thap Put · Phra Saeng · Khao Luang N P 1835m · Tha Sala
Ko Payang · Ao Luk · Thung Yai · Nakhon Si Thammarat · Laem Talumpuk
Thai Muang · Thalang · Krabi · Thung Song · Chawang · Hua Sai
Ko Phuket · Wang Wiset · Thale Noi Bird Sanctuary
Phuket · Ko Yao Yai · Siban Phot · Ranot · Thale Luang
Ko Phi Phi · Ko Lanta · Khao Chong N P 1350m · Phatthalung · Boripath Waterfall · Thale Sap Songkhla
Sikao · Trang · Lamchan Waterbird Park · Khian · Kho Khut Waterbird Park
Ko Libong · Palian · Niang · Hat Yai · Songkhla
Pak Bara Harbour · Langu · Ton Nga Chang Waterfall · Pattani · Laem Tachi
Andaman Sea · Thale Ban N P · Khok Po · Panare
Ko Ta Ru Tao · Sa Dao · Wat Chiang Hai · Sai Buri
Ko Rawi · Satun · Yala · Narathiwat
Ko Adang · Raman · Tak Bai
Bannang Sata
Than To Waterfall
Banglang Dam · Chanae · Sungai Kolok
Hot Water Springs · Betong
MAL

Gulf of Thailand

Scale: 0   50   100 km
0   25   50   75 miles

Arguably the most popular of Thailand's four regions, the south gently woos its visitors with a predominantly seaboard atmosphere. Sun-worshippers, swimmers, divers and boat-lovers need look no further.

The coasts The Indian Andaman Sea washes the shores of the western provinces of Ranong, Phang Nga, Phuket, Krabi, Trang and Satun. Pacific provinces are Chumphon, Suratthani, Nakhon Si Thammarat, Songkhla, Pattani and Narathiwat.

Classic tropical islands float off both shores, and a few, such as Samui and Phi Phi, welcome the Western traveller with open arms.

This is a region inhabited since early times. The

Buddhist kingdom of Srivijaya blossomed here, while yet more ancient negrito tribes such as the Sakai still survive.

Inland there are many national parks – and some are real gems. The further away from civilisation you get, the wilder it becomes – mountains and waterfalls abound, along with whatever wildlife can stand up to the constant incursions of development.

The borderlands These are the provinces of Satun, Yala, Songkhla and Narathiwat. The Federation of Malaysia is Thailand's most friendly land neighbour and Westerners can come and go with little formality. However, smugglers, Muslim separatists and logging disputes keep security tight.

Islam has made some headway in the Malay-speaking extreme south, but it is not of the most fervent kind.

Economic activity Rubber is the south's number-one cash crop. Other popular crops are cashew nuts and durians. Offshore, Thai fishing fleets are rather too efficient for their own good, and are now being sent further into the seas of Myanmar and Vietnam as stocks diminish.

Meanwhile tin mining, once the mainstay of Phuket and Phang Nga, has declined somewhat mainly as a result of market forces. Tourism is the rising star. Everyone wants a piece of the action but official policy tends towards plush development.

Bungalows (simple thatched huts with not much more than a thin mattress and a mosquito net inside), which started Phuket on its road to world fame, are now a rare sight there. This stand-offish attitude to budget travellers is unfortunate for the small operators but the small-scale, laid-back ethos is still easy to find off the beaten track. Nowadays it just means having to look slightly harder!

Southern Thailand

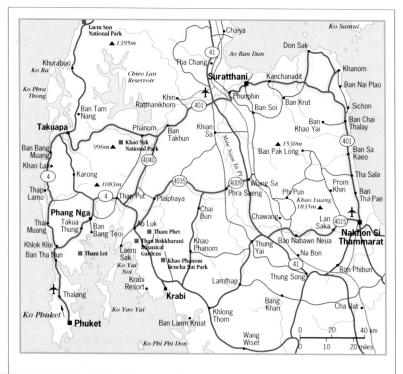

Drives

Two circular tours

A tour from Phuket

Allow four to five days for the round trip, which explores both west and east coasts as well as a majestic hinterland of limestone peaks and jungle. You can miss out Suratthani, but the back roads are treacherous and stopovers are a bit too far apart. Highway 4040 linking Phanom and Phang Nga town is only for vehicles that can cope with dust, mud and potholes. Highway 4118 is for dry weather only. In either case the tour can take a mere two days from Phuket, with an overnight stay in either Khao Lak or Khao Sok.

Start at Phuket▶▶▶. Phuket to Takuapa is an unhurried drive of 130km up Highway 4. The road is lined by beaches and waterfalls. Accommodation can be had on the first night at Khao Lak. (See Phang Nga, pages 238–239.) From Takuapa take Highway 401 towards Suratthani. An early start will make it possible to reach **Khao Sok National Park▶**, where there is a large cluster of simple jungle-style guesthouses.

The road here is spectacular as it climbs up into the watershed of the Tapi River. The fine scenery continues almost all the way into **Suratthani**, where the next night can be spent in a hotel. A trip to **Ko Samui▶▶▶** could be taken from Suratthani as there is a car ferry.

Carry on out of Suratthani, still on Highway 401.
The road goes past the attractive beaches of **Khanom** district down into **Nakhon Si Thammarat▶**, where the next night can be spent.

An early start is recommended for the next day; the destination can be Phang Nga or Phuket. Take Highway 4015 west on the main road out of Nakhon Si Thammarat.

The scenery around **Khao Luang National Park**►► is stupendous and there are many diversions.

The aim now is Highway 41, west at Jan Dee across the railway line. Travel north up the fast if rather bleak 41, looking out for a left at Wiang Sa, Highway 4009, becoming 4035. Wind through the rubber plantations to Ao Luk.

Accommodation can be found here. The smooth main Highway 4 goes through the lovely karst mountains to **Phang Nga**►►► and eventually crosses the Sarasin bridge to return to Phuket.

A day trip from Chumphon

This can be accomplished in a day, but a more relaxed pace can be maintained with a stop-over in Ranong, which has several modern hotels.

Start in Chumphon. The first half of the route runs west along Highway 4 via Kraburi and Ranong.

This part of the trip offers marvellous sea views as the mountain chain is crossed at **Kraburi**►. Waterfalls can be seen from the road, and the approach road to **Ranong**► is impressive. (This area is thinly populated, and it would be a good idea to get well equipped in Ranong for the journey.)

Signs for the Jansom Thara stand out well, but 30km out of town, the left turn at tiny Ratcha Krut is rather harder to spot.

Recross the mountains, avoiding the herds of cows on Highway 4006 (tarmac but substandard surface).

A left turn at the junction with Highway 41, near Lang Suan, is easy to spot, and from here it is a quick journey alongside paddy fields back into Chumphon.

Nai Harn Beach, at the tip of Phuket, was once a favourite haunt of hippies

216

▶ **Betong** 212C1

Highway 410. Buses from Yala town

This town on the Malaysian border, some 133km from Yala, has been developed on a par with the average provincial capital. The big market sells cheap Malaysian goods brought in on the major highway. There has been violence in this area – Muslim separatists are active here, and there has been border disturbance.

At the end of a 10km dirt road from Betong are hot springs, *bor nam rorn*, in a village of the same name. Betong is otherwise famous for the biggest pillar box in Thailand, nearly 4m tall, and the annual invasion of swallows from September to April. They darken the sky, crowd telephone wires and rain their droppings down, fortunately only at night!

▶▶ **Chaiya** 212B3

Off Highway 41. Trains and buses from Suratthani

Chaiya district of Suratthani province is famous for two temples: **Suan Mokapalaram**, or Suan Mok and **Wat Phra Boromthat**, one of the oldest in the south, a classic survival from the Indo-Javanese Srivijayan empire.

Suan Mok Buddhadasa Bhikkhu, the founder of Suan Mok (the Garden of Liberation), initiated a reform movement in the *sangha* (Buddhist order of monks) which is still working itself out. It is one of the several temples in Thailand which has attracted a significant number of Western devotees and accepts lay-people on ten-day retreats. Buddhadasa died in 1993.

Meditation through concentration on breathing and a vow of silence are on the programme which follows the strict regimen of the monks. Visitors of either sex are welcome to stay in dormitories and sample the simple life. Offerings of cash or food are readily accepted.

Wat Suan Mok is on the left off main Highway 41 going north from Suratthani – its imposing entrance arch cannot be missed. Buses run direct here from Suratthani.

Wat Phra Boromthat▶ This atmospheric temple lies on the western edge of town. It dates from the Dvaravati period (AD 500–700), and a life-sized Buddha image remains. The main *chedi*, in a pool surrounded by clusters of images, was erected by the Srivijayans (AD 700–1000), whose bronzes of the Bodhisattva Avalokitesvara are in evidence. The many red sandstone images are of Ayutthaya vintage. The Burmese overran the temple in the reign of Rama II, but it was fully restored in the reign of Rama V. There is a small museum opposite the entrance (*Open* Wed–Sun 9–4. *Donation requested*), where Srivijayan artefacts predominate.

▶ **Chumphon Province** 212B4

Highway 4. Buses from Suratthani and Bangkok (southern terminal); trains from Bangkok

Most travellers know Chumphon only as a midnight supper stopover on the way to or from Phuket. It came to the public eye when Typhoon Gay tore through it in 1989 (see panel). Almost completely recovered now, the province has quiet beaches and islands. Thai and Burmese fought here, and in World War II volunteers repelled a Japanese amphibious assault.

Sights

Pharadornphap Beach, near Pak Nam Chumphon, is some 13km southeast of Chumphon town. At adjacent **Sai Re** is a ship encased in concrete, a monument to Admiral Krom Luang Chumphon. Students of herbal medicine may be interested in the admiral's Thai herbal garden. He is most remembered though for re-creating the Royal Thai Navy as a modern fighting force.

Another such shrine graces the beach of **Arunothai** in Thung-Tako sub-district further south. Like Sai Re, it is a jumping-off point for long-tailed boat tours of the offshore islands.

Corals around here took a heavy beating from Typhoon Gay, such as those off the islands of Ko Raet (named for its rhinoceros-like form), Ko Lak Raet, Ko Thalu, Ko Jorakhe, Ko Mattra and Ko Lawa. The last three also have pleasant beaches. Pathiu district to the north has long beaches at **Phanung Tuk**, 8km out of town, **Ao Bor Mao** and nearby **Laem Thaen.** This last beach is ideal for camping. Best of all is Thung Wua Laen, 12km north. South of Chumphon there are famous caves in **Lang Suan. Khao Ngern** cave, near the town, is home to a group of monkeys. A further 18km to the south is **Khao Kriap,** with a large sunlit cavern.

SWALLOWS

Beware! Long, narrow Ko Maphrao, like the more famous island of Ko Phi Phi Le, has a swallow colony prized for its nests. Tourists are scared off the long white beach with a shotgun. Ko Ngaam Yai and Ko Ngaam Noi also have swallows' nests, and landing to sunbathe or snorkel could also be dangerous here.

Wat Phra Boromthat, in Chaiya, is a fine and rare example of the Srivijayan style, reminiscent of some of the temples of Java

217

Bird's nests have been eaten in China for at least 1,500 years, and their export by the collectors of the Malay peninsula and southern Thailand was well established by the early 18th century. Nowadays, the largest market is Hong Kong, which consumes 100 tons of them, worth at least US$40 million, every year. A perfect white nest can fetch well in excess of US$1,000.

GANG RIVALRY
Gangster-style killings have occurred as rival gangs fight over scraps of nests left behind after the season.

CONSERVATION
Nest collecting has unfortunately taken its toll on the numbers of swiftlets, whose nests are often over-harvested. Many fomer nest sites on open cliffs have been abandoned because they were too accessible to gatherers. Another even more serious threat to their survival is the destruction of the inland rainforests where the swiftlets feed.

What nest? The nest of the swiftlet *Collocalia esculenta* is edible, prized by the Chinese as a powerful pick-me-up tonic, and typically ingested at the banquets of the rich in the form of bird's nest soup. It is said to taste rather like noodles by those who have tried it. The nests themselves are tiny translucent cups about the size of a small egg. They are made by the male brown-rumped swift from glutinous threads of its own saliva, which it weaves into a cup that dries to become thin and translucent like fine porcelain.

Chinese people often feed bird's nest soup, cooked with chicken broth or coconut milk, to their children in the belief that it will improve their complexion, promote growth and generally act as a tonic.

Recent research has indeed shown that the nests do contain a water-soluble glyco-protein that may promote cell division in the immune system. Some have even speculated that it may help combat the immuno-deficiency in AIDS.

Collecting the nests Nests are collected in spring and September. This is skilled and dangerous work, high up on the ceilings of caves which abound on the Thai coast and its offshore islands. The intrepid collector shins barefoot up rickety trellises of bamboo scaffolding, ropes and bridges, tapping as he goes to make sure the bamboo is sound. He lights his way in the black caves with a torch of bark soaked in resin held between his teeth, and he uses a special three-pronged tool called a *rada* to harvest the nests.

To use bare hands to pick a nest would be considered stealing from the gods and would anger them. If a man happens to forget his *rada*, he will descend at once, taking it as a sign from the gods that it would be dangerous for him to climb that day.

The collectors work from sunrise without food or water until sunset, when the cave is filled with flocks of bats and roosting swiftlets. Sometimes nest-gatherers have to swim underwater to reach a submerged cavern, or squeeze through tiny blowhole passages to reach the cave ceiling.

The caves themselves are often spectacular, if messy, cathedrals of stalagmites and stalactites, covered with a thick carpet of guano, and seething with thousands of golden cockroaches.

Big business Collecting nests is a lucrative business and is tightly controlled. The Finance Ministry grants five-year concessions to competing private groups, the taxes from which can yield an appreciable sum. The nests are so precious that the islands are virtually off-limits, protected by armed guards during the season to deter robbers who might harm the baby swiftlets – which would affect the next year's supply of nests. They are also paid to protect the birds from natural predators such as snakes, cockroaches and eagles.

In spite of all this protection, attempts are made to bribe guards. In Thong Thum district in 1987, one gang of poachers began to encroach on other gang networks. The gang leader and his wife were sprayed with machine-gun fire at their home.

Ladders against the cliffside where swiftlets nest in Ko Phi Phi Le

▶ Hat Yai

212B1

Highway 4. Buses from Songkhla and Bangkok (southern terminal); trains from Suratthani and Bangkok; domestic flights

Hat Yai grew on border trade, rubber and, more recently, sex. Hat Yai's "night industry" generates a higher than average level of associated diseases. There are plenty of all-night cafés and lounges. The town itself is drab, a forced stopover for destinations further south. Hat Yai is an important railway junction, and trains were instrumental in the town's growth.

Sightseeing The Chinese presence here is evident in Channiwet Road, where **snake farms** make a strange concoction by slashing open a live snake and squeezing the blood out. It is often mixed with whisky and honey, which almost mask the taste.

Local farmers have established Hat Yai as a centre for Southern Thai **bullfighting**. Khlong Wa stadium by the bus station alternates with others in the area in staging the frenetic bull-against-bull contests. The moderate entrance fee includes three rounds of bulls, and the atmosphere is alive with manic betting and sizzling food.

Also on the edge of town but in a completely different direction is the **Thai Cultural Village▶** which stages dancing shows. The little theatre is set in rolling parkland which also has a small zoo.

People who are attracted to the bustle will enjoy Hat Yai's markets and nightlife which are both distinctive. It is here that all goods from Malaysia are unloaded. Smugglers once thought that if they made it to Hat Yai they were safe, but a recent police campaign has been giving them second thoughts.

A little way out of town, off Phetkasem Road, **Wat Hat Yai Nai** is remarkable for its very large reclining image of Buddha in white stucco. A curious contraption near by has ten plaster-cast monks bolted to a revolving platform, a novel way of making merit.

A scenic ride out of town is **Tone Nga Chang Falls▶**. The "elephant tusks" of its name are formed at one of the higher stages where the fall splits into two. The road does not go anwhere else but the waterfall is in a wildlife preservation area.

MALAYSIAN TRIPS
Trips to nearby Malaysia can easily be arranged from Hat Yai. The border lies just 50km away. The idyllic island of Penang is a popular destination, most conveniently reached by a shared taxi (these run regularly every morning from Hat Yai and are not expensive). Comfortable air-conditioned buses also provide a regular service. Make sure your papers are in order; you can renew your visa at the Thai consulate in Penang.

Hat Yai is a great shopping centre. On local market stalls Malaysian batik, electronic gadgetry and dried fruit are especially good buys

▶▶ Ko Lanta   *212A2*

Access by boat from Krabi town; or from Ban Hua Hin (a songthaew ride from Krabi)

The relatively little known Lanta islands, approximately 50km off the southwest coast of Krabi Province, have the status of a distinct district. The district takes in a total of 52 islands, of which only a handful are inhabited. The geography of the islands is mostly forested mountains (with a highest elevation of 492m), with not much in the way of flat land.

There are three main islands: Lanta Yai and Lanta Noi are almost one, being separated by a narrow 200m channel. Boats travel from Ban Hua Hin to Ban Khlong Mak on Lanta Noi; and from this island to Ban Sala Dan on Lanta Yai. Access to the western beaches for the tourist landlubber is best from Chao Fa pier in Krabi town, a few metres north of the Phi Phi pier. This regular supply boat takes 3 to 4 hours. Closer to Ko Lanta, a turning south from Highway 4 leads to Bo Muang, starting point for a much shorter ride.

Tourist development so far is fairly low-key but steadily increasing. The beaches are idyllic; the longer ones are on the west coast.

A favourite with yachties, the northern anchorage has bungalow accommodation. The locals mostly live from the sea and their villages dot the coast, most densely at this northern end.

NATIONAL MARINE PARK
Fifteen of Ko Lanta's southerly islands have recently been declared a National Marine Park, which may place a partial brake on the hasty and ill-conceived tourist development which has blighted some of Thailand's most beautiful islands. Despite the blandishments of tourism, there are indications that the local "sea gypsy" inhabitants wish to retain their traditional way of life. Land speculation, however, is hotting up on the inhabited parts of Ko Lanta.

221

In some parts of the south, the traditional ways of life on the water have not entirely been supplanted by tourism

PHUKET TO PHI PHI

A schedule that may appeal to the independent traveller involves a trip from Phuket to Phi Phi, at least a night or so in one of the island's many places to stay, followed by a boat ride into Krabi town. There are usually three services daily (fewer in the monsoon season), taking two or two and a half hours. Avoid the trip in rough weather.

Life on a tropical beach beneath coconut palms is the stuff of dreams for stressed-out Westerners. In southern Thailand, it is a reality

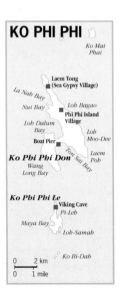

KO PHI PHI

▶▶▶ Ko Phi Phi 212A2
Boats from Phuket and Krabi town

This pair of islands, blessed with natural beauty, is now perhaps one of the absurdest examples anywhere of a Marine National Park. Some observers have already written it off, as thousands of tourists swarm all over it, the vast majority of them day-trippers from Phuket, threatening the fragile ecosystem. The main island, Phi Phi Don, is now quite built up, but strenuous efforts are being made to keep it clean.

Yet the attraction is easy to understand; nothing short of an earthquake would destroy the stunning natural formation of the back-to-back Loh Dalam and Ton Sai beaches, only 50m apart. Their clear waters are particularly inviting to swimmers, and are enhanced by the optical effect of the shallow sea floor, which gives a beautiful turquoise colour.

Getting there The island communities' needs are served with a regular boat service from Krabi, which takes two hours. The islands are almost equidistant from Phuket, and many companies based there offer day tours, the price of which depends on the luxury of the boat used. Top-of-the-line cruisers with every amenity you could desire ply the route daily. All the tours include lunch in one of the resort restaurants located by Ton Sai Bay on Phi Phi Don.

Phi Phi Don Accommodation on Phi Phi Don is now very comfortable as there is a large number of well-equipped bungalows to be found almost everywhere.

A general view of the island can be had from several mountain viewpoints to the east of Ton Sai. One path leads down to the beach of Loh Bagao, now site of the expensive **Phi Phi Island Village.**

Laem Tong, where Phi Phi Don's last remaining "Sea Gypsies" (see page 243) rub shoulders with wealthy guests of an exclusive resort, lies on the extreme northern tip of the island, accessible only by boat. A worthwhile glass-bottomed boat tour leaves from here, as at Ton Sai – an opportunity not to be missed, especially by non-swimmers.

Phi Phi Le Neighbouring Phi Phi Le has many fine corals such as those at beautiful Maya Bay and Pi-Leh. Spectacular turquoise inlets offer wonderful swimming. Boat tours invariably stop at Phi Phi Le's "Viking Cave", where mysterious unexplained paintings of boats (believed to be Chinese junks) adorn the walls near the entrance. The cave is also home to a swallow colony whose nests are harvested for the famous bird's nest soup (see pages 218–219). The smell of swallow droppings is quite overpowering! Because of the bird's nests, no one may stay overnight on the islands.

Fishermen are well served around Phi Phi Le. All types of fish await the intrepid angler. A group can charter a long-tailed boat for this purpose, either for a full day (six to eight hours) or for a half-day trip.

Boat paintings in the "Viking Cave" at Phi Phi Le

Lush vegetation clings to the rocky cliffs of Phi Phi Le, rising sheer from the waterline. The limestone formations of Thailand's Andaman Islands are unforgettable

DRUG OMELETTES
Ko Samui used to be famous for mind-expanding drug omelettes but after several notorious incidents that were too much even for the liberal and tolerant Thais, the local police were forced to clamp down on the activity.

KO SAMUI

Map labels: Laem Na Phra Lan, Ko Som, Ao Bang Po, Choeng Mon Beach, Mae Nam Beach, Bo Phut Beach, Laem Yai, Ban Bang Po, Ko Faan, Ban Mae Nam, Ban Bo Phut, Na Thon, Ban Chaweng, Ko Mat Lang, Hin Lat Waterfall, Samui Highlands, Ao Chon Kram, 635m, Chaweng Beach, Don Sak Car Ferry, Coral Cove, Thong Yang, Ban Saket, Lamai Cultural Hall, Na Muang Waterfall, Ban Lamai, Ban Thaling Ngam, Ban Suan Thurian, Ban Hua Thanon, Ao Phangka, Wat Sumret, Ban Bang Kao, Laem Set, Ao Thong Krut, Ko Tan

0 — 5 km
0 — 3 miles

Boats, beaches and turquoise sea create endlessly photogenic subjects on Ko Samui. Despite increasing tourism, there are still plenty of places to photograph scenes like these

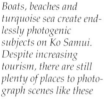

▶▶▶ **Ko Samui archipelago**   *212B3*

Off the east coast. Buses from Suratthani connect with ferries to Ko Samui; domestic flights; tour buses from Bangkok

A first stop for many visitors, Ko Samui has a laid-back atmosphere even for Thailand. As with most other currently booming destinations it was the much maligned backpackers who discovered it first. This is a luscious tropical island with coconut palms, beautiful sands and idyllic villages; it almost looks too good to be real. There's a vibrant party scene, but it is also possible to find peace and quiet.

Express boats to and from Suratthani moor up at the Na Thon jetty in the northwest.

Although the airport is now busy with regular daily flights, Ko Samui is still a paradise for young people who

A fishing boat tilts on the beach as the sun sets over Ko Samui, reflected in mirror-like water. In the monsoon season, the sea can look very different

want to enjoy themselves relatively cheaply. Rents have been creeping up, but bargains are still there to be had away from the popular Chaweng and Lamai beaches. Expect to pay anything from 250 baht upwards for a room.

The island's natural beauty remains much as it was and is not unduly spoiled by the development here, which has been low-rise, though not on a modest scale. Beach frolics by day are combined with Thailand's trendiest nightlife consisting of discos and bars. It proves that a *farang* tourist area need not be crawling with prostitution, although Ko Samui has inevitably attracted its fair share.

Around the island The concrete road circling the island is only 50km long and you can travel around the whole island in a day. As in Phuket, scooters are ideal, being slow and safe. Newer models have power to take on the bigger hills. Rent a scooter at Chaweng and follow the road south to Lamai, taking in the tremendous panorama as the road twists round past Coral Cove.

In **Lamai** you might check out the bizarrely designed **Mix club.** Lamai's landmark is the clearly phallic **Hin Ta** or Grandfather Rock and its female companion **Hin Yai** or Grandmother Rock. The long beach is fairly clean, given the number of visitors, although it certainly isn't as clean as it used to be.

Out of Lamai to the south the road forks. To the left it cuts across the island's south, past **Na Muang▶**, a spectacular waterfall. The right fork veers around the tidal coast of **Ao Thong Krut**. Boats here service the small **Ko Tan**. Further on is a long dirt road turn-off for the small, sweet and quiet **Phangka Bay**. There are modest facilities here on locally owned land.

KO SAMUI'S COCONUTS
Ko Samui has more to it than beaches; before the tourist boom, islanders' income came exclusively from coconuts, and the tall palms are still the dominant vegetation.

TOURS
The archipelago that makes up Ang Thong Marine National Park can be toured from Ko Samui, but it is impossible to stay without official permission. Most tours take in the fascinating Ko Mae Ko with its "crater lake".

North out of Phangka the road takes in wonderful views of distant shimmering sea before you get to the Don Sak car ferry terminal turn-off. Inland from here are two of Ko Samui's other waterfalls, **Hu Nam** and **Wae Khwai Tok**. The track up to them is quite difficult.

Na Thon is the district seat and as such has a market, post office, banks and other essential services. The road out north yields a fantastic view (if you can ignore the municipal tip in the foreground).

Ko Phangan, the other main island in the archipelago, is visible from all along Ko Samui's northern shore. Of the three main beaches along this shore, it is **Bo Phut** that has become the most popular. On the others, Mae Nam and Bang Rak, tourist facilities are still in the process of hasty construction.

Very prominent is the long causeway linking Bang Rak and Ko Fan where, in the temple of Hin Ngu, the so-called Big Buddha looks out over the sweeping bay.

Next on the circuit are roads leading to the airport at Ko Samui; flights from here to Bangkok take less than an hour and a half.

Turning south the route reaches the top end of **Chaweng**. At 7km it is the longest beach on the island and developers have made the larger projects a feast of traditional teak architecture. Because of its sheer size Chaweng has been able to absorb the feverish rush for the tourist dollar so far – as is usually the case, a balance must be struck between creature comforts and an unspoiled atmosphere.

Inviting Chaweng Beach is long enough to absorb the influx of tourists – the central section is the most beautiful

Ko Phangan Boats from Ko Samui and Suratthani land at Thong Sala on the island's southern coast. Phangan is now taking Ko Samui's overspill and although the beaches are just as good, the level of infrastructure here makes Ko Samui seem urban. Roads are unmetalled but a dirt bike is still useful.

Bungalows line the beaches, being concentrated on the double-backed Hat Rin, home to a lively travellers' society. Hat Rin is notorious for its all-night parties, which in December and January are hosted by top British DJs. Boats ply the beaches.

Waterfall fans may take in **Than Sadet▶**, where kingly visitors, including Chulalongkorn and Bhumiphol, have carved their initials in the stones. The journey upstream is still as hard as it was in their day.

Ko Tao ("Turtle Island") is only 8km long and the nearest land is well over the horizon. It can be reached from either Chumphon or Phangan. The former is a gruelling five-hour sea trip, which is available only in the high season.

The latter trip, from Thong Sala pier, takes three hours. As always when exploring Thailand, remember that remoteness and inaccessibility are usually related to a degree of unspoilt beauty. **Sai Ri** and **Mae Hat** are the main beaches lining the west coast. Rough jungle trails beckon for those keen to explore the interior.

A short boat ride from Mae Hat leads to the natural marvel of **Ko Nang Yuan,** where three islands are linked by sandbanks. It is possible to stay overnight here. As on Ko Tao, little bungalows are available, and are still very reasonably priced.

Life goes on at a relaxed pace on Ko Samui

ROAD SAFETY
Extreme caution is advised if you hire a car or scooter on any of the southern islands. Both roads and vehicles may be in poor condition, and the standard of driving is appalling. Many horrifying accidents are caused by foreign tourists driving under the influence of alcohol or drugs. Phuket and Ko Samui have the highest road fatality rates in Thailand – an unenviable record. Bear in mind local insurance cover is minimal or non-existent.

Sometimes life in Thailand seems like one festival or traditional ceremony after another. Some are rites of passage for the events in the lives of individuals, such as birth, puberty, ordination, marriage and death. Those linked with traditional farming rituals are concerned with the annual cycle of seasons and there are others that commemorate historical anniversaries.

228

THE SKY ROCKET FESTIVAL

Bun bang fai usually takes place in mid-May in Yasothon (see page 211). With its crude sexual pantomimes, it is performed to celebrate the generative forces of nature and the coming of the rains.

SONGKRAN

Songkran begins sedately with Buddhist merit-making ceremonies and offerings to elders and monks. Then it explodes into water-splashing, beauty contests and tippling of Mekhong rice whisky. Everyone gets splashed, even foreigners – all in good fun.

LOI KRATHONG

Loi means "to float", and *krathong* means "leaf cup". The use of polystyrene for floats was recently banned because of the river pollution it caused. The festival takes place throughout Thailand, but is celebrated with particular verve at Sukhothai (see pages 188–189).

Most festivals are fixed by the lunar calendar, so the dates vary yearly. The Buddhist holiday of **Maga Puja** is celebrated in February, and the **Chinese New Year** usually falls within this month too. Festivities for the latter often last three days. Gifts are exchanged, food is offered to ancestors via the ancestral tablets. Altars are set with the tablets and images of benevolent deities, and candles and joss sticks are lit. Chinese shops close for several days. See pages 94 and 268.

Songkran This is one of the great festivals – the old Thai New Year which falls in mid-April. It is a time when everyone goes in for water splashing, April being the hottest month of the year. The *Songkran* water-splashing festival was originally an occasion to pay homage to one's elders by pouring scented water over their hands and making offerings to the ashes of ancestors.

Loi Krathong This most unforgettable celebration is in November, after rice planting has been completed. To honour the water spirits toy boats made of moulded leaves, and carrying a lighted candle and incense stick, are floated along rivers and canals, swollen with rain and sometimes flooded at this time of year. Everyone goes to the river bank in the evening to see the flickering lights on the water, and fireworks are let off.

Rites of passage One recurring feature of personal Thai ceremonies is the tying of white thread around the wrists. It has been described as a kind of "spiritual telegraph" between the participants. At weddings the thread joins the heads of the marrying couple, while at funerals the thread is carried round the crematorium three times.

In their early 20s many Thai men spend a short period as Buddhist monks, which is regarded as a rite of passage into adulthood. Before the formal ordination there is a lay ceremony called *sukhwan nak*. The man's head and eyebrows are shaved (to show freedom from vanity and sexuality) and the ordination candidate or *nak* (meaning "dragon") is dressed in white robes, garlanded with flowers and banknotes. The friends and relatives of the *nak* gather in a circle around him, holding a ring of white thread, while a song recalling the pain and suffering of his mother in giving birth and stressing his

filial obligations is sung – sometimes for up to four hours. Additionally, they pass three sets of lighted candles around in a clockwise direction to protect him while he is in the vulnerable position of being neither a layman nor a monk.

The following day the ordination ceremony takes place. Inside the *wat* the new monk kneels before his father, who presents him with the saffron robe of the monkhood before approaching a quorum of monks and asking to be admitted to the *sangha*.

Songkran *water-splashing festival starts at a sedate pace and then takes off into mayhem…*

DIVING

The Similan Islands are rated one of the best sites for diving in the world, with clear, unpolluted waters and a wealth of sea life. Each island has a different ecosystem. Many companies organise diving trips, mostly from Phuket. If you are not an experienced diver, you can learn locally. Check your instructor's qualifications. Harpoon-fishing is carried out by some unscrupulous operators, but it causes immense damage to the reefs and is offically banned.

STRANGE FISH

Deep-sea divers can see such strange creatures as the star feather and the gross puffer fish off the Similans.

TURTLES

The turtle population of Thailand is rapidly diminishing, and all the four native marine species are now officially classified as endangered. The loggerhead turtle is already locally extinct.
Deliberately persecuted for their shells, meat and eggs, turtles are also incidental victims of trawler nets, pollution and the disturbance caused by tourism and development. Belatedly, several of Thailand's principle turtle habitats have been declared marine parks, and serious efforts are at last being made to protect them.

The densely wooded islands of the Ko Ta Ru Tao archipelago contain a great variety of wildlife habitats, from mangrove swamps and limestone caves to coral reefs

▶ Ko Similan   212A2

Access by boat from Takuapa or by tour from Phuket

This archipelago, far over the horizon to the west, forms a national park famous for its underwater diving opportunities. There are pleasant beaches which are used by snorkellers, swimmers and picnickers. Spear-fishing is officially prohibited by the national park authorities.

The Similans are a chain of nine islands (Malay *sembilan*, nine) of which number 8, Ko Similan, is the largest. They are low-lying and forested, uninhabited before the park wardens brought in regular supplies of fresh water. The park station is on Ko Miang, where there is a campsite with bungalows and a restaurant.
Islanders have come here to fish for a long time. Recent times saw the appalling practice of dynamite fishing when a whole coral reef would be blasted, dead and stunned fish then rising to the surface. Tourists, both daytrippers and yacht sailors, have scared off the dynamite fishermen, but have brought in their turn litter, which they leave on the beaches.
There are tour boats from Phuket. Alternatively, a boat can be chartered from Tap Lamu in Takuapa. The Similans are being increasingly used as stepping stones to other remote islands. Dive boats run regularly to Ko Surin, Ko Bon (an honorary "tenth" Similan further north) and Ko Tachai.

Ko Miang, island number 4, is a tiny island which has dramatic scenery. There is contrast between huge granite boulders and coral reefs, and is typical of the Similans as a whole. There is accommodation available in beautifully set bungalows run by the Royal Forestry Department. **Ko Ba Ngu**, island number 9, has tents for hire at normal park rates.

▶ Ko Surin   212A3

Ban Hin Lat in Khuraburi district, almost on the border with Ranong Province, is the jumping-off point for a five-hour voyage to Surin Marine National Park. (The five islands are actually part of Ranong Province.) Again, most people go to dive. The main islands have places to stay and great lobster fishing.

Ko Adang, one of the larger islands of the Ta Ru Tao group, consists almost entirely of wild rain forest and coconut palms, but there are a few places to stay

▶▶ Ko Ta Ru Tao

212B1

Off Satun Province. Boats from Pak Bara

The Ta Ru Tao archipelago is made up of 50-odd islands, from the largest, Ko Ta Ru Tao, down through Ko Rawi, Ko Adang and the smaller islands of Ko Lipe, Ko Hin Ngam, Ko Khai and Ko Rang Nok. Ko Ta Ru Tao is only about 5km from the Malaysian island of Pulau Langkawi. These islands are not geared to tourists; facilities are basic and transport is unpredictable.

Thickly forested with a peak of 704m, Ko Ta Ru Tao must count as one of the most unspoiled of the country's marine national parks; this one was the first, created in 1974. For overnight stays or camping it is possible to reserve a park space through the Forestry Department in Bangkok (tel: 02 579 0529).

Ta Ru Tao, a penal colony for political prisoners during World War II (see panel), now has an exhibition centre and aquarium. The region's famous powdery white sand can be found at Ao Son (Ta Lo Lii Ngai) on the western coast, a beautifully curving bay with clear and shallow waters, which has been established as a sea turtle conservation centre. Walkers can get a good view by climbing to the top of Khao Topu.

Ko Khai is a small island with white beaches and a rich community of coral and fish. Turtles come ashore to lay their eggs. **Ko Hin Ngam**, off Ko Adang, has lines of smooth, even, sleek rocks rounded by the sea, whereas next-door **Ko Rawi** has beaches. The area is populated by "Sea Gypsies", who build their houses on stilts; tiny **Ko Lipe** hosts a community of 600. Unfortunately, a great many trees have been felled here.

Diving is a popular activity among visitors to the archipelago. On the bigger islands there are interesting caves and waterfalls to visit. Long-tail boats service the park office from Pak Bara harbour, Langu district, a long day's drive from Hat Yai or Trang (Pak Bara is 98km south of Trang). The flimsy long-tail boats do get tossed about on the open sea, so the time to go is during the more clement months from January to April.

231

TRIPS TO MALAYSIA
Long-tail boats from Tam Ma Rang service Pulau Langkawi, a larger Malaysian island to Ta Ru Tao's south. The service runs Satun–Langkawi–Kuala Perlis, a small town connected by bus to the rest of Malaysia. You must make sure that papers are in order – Thai immigration will stamp them as you go out in Satun town; a Malaysian official will stamp them in Kuala Perlis.

PIRATES
The penal colony established on the tropical paradise of Ko Ta Ru Tao in 1939 may have seemed no bad place to spend a world war, but as hostilities increased in Southeast Asia, food supplies to the prison became more and more erratic. Eventually the starving prisoners and their equally desperate guards teamed up for survival, and formed a very successful band of pirates. After the war the British navy was sent in to sort them out.

The karst (limestone) scenery of Krabi province produces strange and memorable views. This overhanging cliff is dripping with vegetation and riddled with caves

232

▶▶▶ Krabi Province 212A2

Highway 4, south of Suratthani. Buses from Phuket and Phang Nga

Krabi town is a fishing harbour, giving access to over 100 offshore islands. Ferries arrive here from Ko Phi Phi, entering a mangrove-lined bay before mooring at the centrally located jetty on the broad Krabi River. A gaggle of touts is always on hand to greet passengers as they disembark from the boat.

Krabi town It is a mere minute's walk to the picturesque Uttarakit Road, parallel to the river and the town's main street. Guesthouses and hotels of all standards have sprung up here. Krabi ("Fighting Sword") town has not much going for it besides its views and bike rental shops. The night market which opens after sundown looks over the river.

Krabi Province▶▶▶ is quite another thing. Besides the famous **Ko Lanta▶▶** and **Ko Phi Phi▶▶▶** (see pages 221–223), other interesting islands among Krabi's total of 130 include the pretty **Ko Mai Phai▶**, "Bamboo Island", accessible from Ko Phi Phi Don. Many local squid fishermen are greatly bemused by the increasing numbers of day trippers from the larger island.

The **Por-Da archipelago** (Ko Dam Hok and Ko Dam Khwaan) is very well worth visiting. It is only 8km off Ao Nang, south of Krabi town, from where boats to the islands can be chartered.

Mainland beaches in Krabi are quite fascinating. **Laem Phra Nang▶▶** is cut off by mountains, so the strange arrangement here of three beaches and cliffs can only be reached by boat – 45 minutes from Krabi town or a mere 10 minutes from neighbouring Ao Nang.

Nopparat Thora Beach lies 22km west of Krabi town. Its beautiful setting (part of the Phi Phi National Marine Park) makes it popular with Thai picnickers

LOCAL LEGEND
According to a legend which is still told by locals, food used to appear by magic at the mouth of Phra Nang Cave, which looks out on to a gently curving lagoon.

Sights

Sa Phra Nang (Princess Pool) is a geological oddity – a saltwater lake high among the cliffs. The strenuous walk up to it leads through a series of roofless caves. **Ao Nang▶▶**, a magnificently sited but rapidly developing beach, is only a short *songthaew* ride out of town.

The inland karst (natural underground cavities) along the road makes bizarre scenery. **Nopparat Thora** beach, just west of Ao Nang, has little Ko An straddling a river mouth. Dense casuarinas and coconut trees provide shade on this beach, which is also the headquarters of the marine national park that includes Ko Phi Phi.

Palaeontologists may wish to stop off at the *Susan Hoi* or **"Shell Cemetery"▶**, one of only two or three such sites in the world. Here, tertiary-period fossilised shells which have been compressed into slabs jut into the sea like a causeway. Many *songthaews* going to Ao Nang pass by.

Other points of interest within easy reach of Krabi town include **Huay To waterfall▶** in Phanom Benja, a mere 20km due north. The falls are in ten stages, each stage with a large natural pond. Another road leading north off the main highway leads to **Wat Tham Seua** ("Tiger Cave Temple"), a meditation monastery with grim paintings as reminders of mortality.

Ao Luk is a small town on the road to Phang Nga, also with the strange inland karst. Regular buses to Phang Nga and Phuket stop there.

The nearby port of Laem Sak connects to **Ko Mak Noi** (which is actually in Phang Nga province), an island surrounded by beach. Only five minutes from Laem Sak is the **Chong Talat archipelago▶**, Ko Pai and Ko Klui, graced with the usual – but still beautiful – corals, beaches, caves and mountains.

CAVES

Ao Luk, in the north of Krabi province, has many caves. Tham Lot and Tham Hua Kalok (Skull Cave) are two neighbouring caves, which you can reach by chartering a boat from Bo Tho. Hua Kalok is well lit by the sun and features paintings 2,000 to 3,000 years old.

233

Krabi's traditional fishing fleet keeps local restaurants well stocked with fresh seafood, despite the increasing importance of tourism in the area

► Kra Buri · 212A4

Highway 4, north of Ranong

The last district before Chumphon in the north of the southern region is Kra Buri, head of the Isthmus of Kra, which at its narrowest is only about 25km wide at 545km on Highway 4.

Unsurprisingly in this mountainous territory there are plenty of waterfalls; **Punyaban►, Bokkrai►** and **Chum Saeng►** are three which you can visit as you travel northwards from Ranong town. Punyaban, as the most accessible, has the most visitors. **Tham Phra Khayang►**, a cave in Kra Buri district, 12km north of Kra Buri town, is sacred to locals who believe that "iron flows" here, taking the form of stalactites and stalagmites.

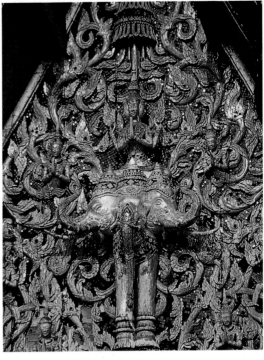

WET WEATHER
A warning: the rainy season in the provinces of Nakhon Si Thammarat and Ranong lasts longer than elsewhere and can be ferocious.

Gold leaf donated by centuries of devout pilgrims decorates Wat Mahathat, in Nakhon Si Thammarat, the most revered shrine in southern Thailand

►► Nakhon Si Thammarat · 212B2

Highway 401, east coast. Buses from Krabi, Suratthani and Bangkok (southern terminal); trains from Bangkok

"Nakhon Si", as the province is known to those who live in the south, is a paradox: it is the biggest and most populated southern province, while at the same time it remains relatively unexplored.

Communications are excellent: the town of Nakhon Si Thammarat (once called Ligor) is a rail terminus and has air and bus connections. A thriving Srivijaya centre back in the 13th century, it spread its Buddhist teaching to Sukhothai, seat of the first Thai kingdom. More recently, in World War II, local young men repulsed an amphibious Japanese assault; they are commemorated in bronze.

LOCAL CRAFTS
Crafts local to Nakhon Si Thammarat include nielloware *(kruang tom)*, the delicate Yan Lipao basketry and shadow puppets. At "Suchat's House" the puppets are cut from buffalo hide.

Inside the side chapels of the great Wat Mahathat in Nakhon Si Thammarat, colourful friezes illustrate the life of Buddha

The town's religious focus is the ancient temple **Wat Mahathat▶▶**. The tip of its large *chedi* is topped with several hundred pounds of pure gold and contains relics, venerated in the third lunar month. A **museum▶** in the complex houses an eclectic collection of bits and pieces donated by worshippers. The city wall dates from the Ayutthaya period. There is also a large National Museum▶ (*Open* daily 9–4. *Admission: inexpensive*). Shadow plays are performed here during temple festivals.

Highway 401 connects Nakhon Si with Surat, and near the border with Suratthani province (a right turn along Highway 4014; the Khanom bus) are attractive beaches, popular with locals and becoming increasingly discovered by foreigners.

The beaches of **Khanom**, **Nai Phlao** and **Nai Dan** sport many moderate to expensive places to stay, with the budget **Watanyoo Villa** on Nai Dan. Nearer town is Hat Sa Bua, and halfway up is the boulder-strewn Hat Hin Ngam. Inland nature lovers will not be disappointed by the scenery around **Khao Luang National Park▶▶**, skirted by Highways 4015 and 4016. There are many stunning waterfalls in the lush green wilderness, best appreciated on a car tour. The district is famous for durians and prawns.

FESTIVAL TIME
As the south's religious capital, the town has many festivals. One of them is Tamboon Deuan Sip, taking place over 15 days in Sep or Oct, which honours the dead. During this time people condemned to hell are believed to return to this world, and relatives present offerings at temples to help right the wrong-doings of their ancestors.

235

The exterior of Wat Mahathat reveals its distinctive Ceylonese style. The massive chedi *has undergone much costly restoration to save it from collapse*

NARATHIWAT BEACH
Reached by a *samlor* or taxi from the market, this beach nestles in the shade of casuarinas, with food stalls dotted about. It is an ideal camping spot; 5km of broad white sands end in a bar at the mouth of Klong Bang Nara, which is the site of a fishing village.

The Thai-Muslim fishing village in Narathiwat, at the mouth of the Bang Nara River, is lined with special fishing craft called reua kor-lae

▶▶ **Narathiwat Province**   *212C1*
Highway 42; a border province with Malaysia. Buses from Yala, Sungai Kolok and Bangkok (southern terminal)
This border province has a wealth of natural resources with forest and beaches at the end of a marathon journey of 1,149km from Bangkok. Gold is mined on a small scale. As Malaysia approaches, different customs become evident and concentrations of Muslims become denser, but this is Islam with a Thai flavour.

Narathiwat town is not of great interest, but it has some traditional character. Atmospheric wooden houses abound and the place has a village-like calm. **Khao Tan Yong Mas**, on the opposite bank of the river from town, has beautiful views and is a popular picnic spot for locals. As a point of interest, near by is the inaccessible Taksin Rachaniwet Palace.

Ba Joh waterfall▶▶ is on the Pattani–Narathiwat Road. A left turn out of town on Pattani Highway 42 becomes a dusty (or muddy) laterite road eventually reaching the fall, which flows off a very high cliff with force. One of the biggest waterfalls in the south, it comes within the Budo mountains and Budo National Park. The park office is in Ba Joh district near the waterfall. Budo National Park is a shelter for endangered rhinos, gibbons and tapirs, but there is no news yet of accommodation schemes. Other waterfalls in the region are **Ya Mu Raeney** and **Wang Thong**.

Further south of town is the medium-sized **Chatwarin waterfall**▶, reached by turning left at Sungai Padi district hospital. A dry season track winds through thick forest to the fall, passing To Deng village. A distance of 44km makes it a full day trip.

Phra Puttha Taksin Ming Mongkhol▶ is a huge image on Khao Kong mountain in the town district, 6km along Highway 42 to Ba Joh. The 24m figure is decorated with golden mosaic. The same "Buddhist park" contains a hollow bell-*chedi*, the top of which contains a "relic".

Two *wats* deserve a mention. In **Wat Chern Khao** (Ba Joh district) the body of a monk, Luang Phor Daeng, lies miraculously undecayed in a glass coffin – the object of great local veneration. **Wat Chol Thara Sing Hey**, near the border, has murals, eclectic southern Thai-Chinese architecture, Hindu statuary, Song dynasty ceramics and a reclining Buddha. However, it is not these features that distinguish it, but its history: this ancient foundation was invoked as the last Siamese territorial stand, when Narathiwat stood out against the British who threatened to incorporate the region in their Malayan possessions.

Tak Bai district▶ This border location can be of interest as a visit in itself. Ban Taba, at the end of the road, has reasonable views over the large mouth of the Golok River, which forms the national boundary. Fishing boats come and go and it is an easy matter to get the necessary papers stamped and nip out of Thailand and into Malaysia on one of these.

The atmosphere is frenetic, the market prominent. Vehicles must go through a modern passport check and cross over on a car ferry; Malaysian passport officials wait on the other side.

▶ Pattani   212C1

Highway 42, east coast, south of Songkhla. Buses from Narathiwat, boats from Songkhla

This old province of the south has a tradition of rebellion against Siamese authority, and today it is the focus for Muslim separatist politics. The **central mosque▶** just outside town on the road to Yala is the second-largest in Thailand and of great importance to the south's many Muslims. It is a recent construction, opened in 1963. Visitors are welcome from 9–3:30.

Seven kilometres out on the road to Narathiwat is the old **Kreua Se** mosque, dating from the reign of Naresuan in the 16th century. The Chinese shrine of Mother Lim Kor Nio near by is said to have put a curse on the mosque to prevent it being completed. There is a major festival in her honour during the third lunar month when her effigy is paraded and devotees walk on hot coals, as in Phuket.

Wat Chang Hai▶ is to be found 36km from town on the Khok Po–Yala road (Highway 409). At 300 years old, it is distinguished for its huge golden *chedi* visible from far away. Despite being so near Malaysia, the *wat* is wholly Thai in style.

North of Pattani town is **Bang Nara**, a picturesque village containing the campus of the Prince of Songkhla University. The **Princess Mother Gardens▶**, a newly laid out public park which connects with the campus grounds, is formed from a mangrove swamp tastefully planted with flowers.

Beaches Khae Khae and Panare, 43km out of town, are Pattani's most famous beaches. In Khae Khae valley, they follow the mountain's curve. Boulders and rock formations alternate with wide bays, and the water is clear for swimming. The laterite road winds for 8km; a limited food service serves a beach otherwise unspoiled.

About 53km from Pattani towards Sai Buri is Patatimoh beach and the village of Paseyawor, a large fishing community that builds decorative *kor-lae* boats.

Sai Khao National Park▶, a Royal Forest Department park, with its waterfall, is to be found off the Khok Po–Yala road. At the highest stage the fall drops 8m down a cliff on the side of Nang Jan mountain. This is a popular local spot.

SEPARATISM
The Libyan-funded separatist movement seeks to obtain independence for the Muslim, Malay-speaking provinces of Pattani, Yala and Narathiwat, which were formerly a semi-autonomous sultanate.

237

BATIK
A major Malay craft product on sale in the modern-looking town of Pattani is bright and busy batik.

The people of Pattani are racially and culturally more closely related to the Malays than to the Thais. Pattani was, until recently, part of an independent principality

Southern Thailand

KHAO SOK
Situated north of Phang Nga in Suratthani province, Khao Sok National Park heads the list of sites recently chosen for "ecotourism promotion", an attempt by environmentalists to steer Thailand's tourist industry towards conservation rather than destructive development. Khao Sok is one of only two habitats in Thailand for the world's largest flower, the spectacular *rafflesia*, measuring 80cm across. It blooms in January or February for just three or four days.

The bizarre limestone islands off Phang Nga loom sheer from the water, reaching heights of up to 300m

The chisel-shaped profile of Nail Rock (Ko Tapu) became familiar to all James Bond fans in The Man with the Golden Gun

▶▶▶ Phang Nga Province   *212A2*
Highway 4, west coast, north of Phuket. Buses from Phuket and Krabi

Phang Nga province consists of two very distinct coastlines: the mangrove-fringed bay formed by **Ko Phuket**

(see pages 240–243), and the long, straight, beach-lined Andaman coast, north of Phuket. Limestone rock formations rise out of the sea at **Ao Phang Nga▶▶** to dramatic effect. Inflatable-canoe tours are popular, and rubber dinghies can also be used to enter the island caves which are like weird "rooms" of water, but canoes are better for silently approaching any wildlife. The discriminating diver has long known about Ko Similan (see page 230) some 40km to the west, part of Phang Nga province.

Boat tours▶▶▶ from Phuket are something of a hackneyed tourist trip but one of the cheapest. Coaches whisk you to a long-tail boat jetty from where you snake out of mangrove channels to the open sea. **Khao Phing Kan▶**, not very far out, is a leaning megalith which with its nail-like companion **Ko Tapu▶▶** ("James Bond Island") was used as a setting in the James Bond film, *The Man with the Golden Gun*. The boats then head back to the unusual village of **Ko Panyi▶▶**, a Muslim settlement built entirely on stilts attached to a tall rock. It is as well to be aware of local customs and sensitivities; the Muslim village does not tolerate alcohol. Photograph the attractive little white and green mosque but show due respect. After a meal the tour re-embarks for the return to base. The coach may take a route round shops and temples in Phuket on the way back.

Phang Nga town, like Phuket, grew up around the tin-mining industry. The small town, set in a spectacular backdrop of mountains containing an assortment of caves, has little nightlife.

Suwan Khuha cave, to the west of town, contains images of Buddha and is important to the Thais.

Phang Nga port, 8km to the south, serves the important islands – the largest, **Ko Yao Yai** and **Ko Yao Noi**, are two hours away. There are beaches and even a pearl farm on Ko Yao Yai, but little in the way of accommodation.

The western coast of Phang Nga Province could not be more topologically different from the indentations of Phang Nga Bay. Starting at Khao Pilai off Phuket, the long, straight sands run for a score of kilometres into Thai Muang district. This is the territory where the endangered sea turtle lays its eggs from November to February; the eggs are eaten by some people.

There are plenty of stopovers as you carry on up through **Khao Lampi-Hat Thai Muang National Park**. **Khao Lampi▶**, opposite the beach side of the road, is a pretty waterfall where a swim in the pool below is possible. **Bang Sak** is a typically inviting large beach, not quite empty, and there are drinks for sale. There is also Tap Tawan beach and Coral Cape; signposted waterfalls are a way off the road.

North of here is **Khao Lak National Park▶**. There are many bungalows and resorts, and a few families of tin divers, in this park about 35km short of bus-stopover Takuapa. The **Nang Thong Bay Resort** is a typical example, with budget to moderate tariffs. Clean rooms overlook the ocean with fantastic sunsets, and there is yet another quiet and swimmable beach. Khao Lak is the closest departure point for Ko Similan (see page 230). Tours of the area can be arranged at several of the local bungalow complexes.

Other western Phang Nga attractions include Ban Bangklang Spa on Highway 401, and Lam Ru Fall, Laeng Hin Fall and Ban Plai Phu Spa on Highway 4032.

The stilt village of Ko Panyi is a regular lunch stop for boat tours from Phuket, whose Muslim inhabitants tolerate the regular invasions with remarkable forbearance

239

THALE LUANG AND THALE NOI

A huge brackish lagoon known as Thale Luang gives Phatthalung a "seaside", although it lies some 35km inland. A peaceful, picturesque scene, with beach resorts and islands, this landlocked water is now quite polluted and swimming is not advised. Many fish have died because of effluent-dumping. However, birdlife still flourishes. The reserves at Thale Noi and Khu Kut (see page 249) attract thousands of migants, which flock here between January and April.

PHUKET

To avoid embarrassment, note that "Phuket" is pronounced *poo-ke(t)*, with an almost silent "t".

The temple cave of Khuha Sawan contains dozens of Buddha images. Steps lead from the cave to a fine vantage point of the surrounding rice fields

▶ Phatthalung Province   212B3

Highway 4, east of Trang on the east coast. Buses from Nakhon Si Thammarat, Hat Yai, Songkhla, Trang and Phuket; trains from Bangkok

On the route of the main Trang–Songkhla artery, this inland province has its own peculiar attractions, such as a beach on the huge lake of Thale Luang, not far out of Phatthalung town. Dense casuarinas give welcome shade at Hat Saen Sukhrim (Lam Pa), which has a charming view of little islands in the lake.

Also near town are **Khuha Sawan caverns▶**, where light floods in through the spacious northern entrance, and huge Buddha images can be seen inside. **Thale Noi Waterbird Sanctuary**, 32km northeast of Phatthalung town, is a large watery swamp that connects with the lake through a canal. It is an ideal waterfowl habitat, and large birds such as cranes and storks can be spotted.

The nine-stage **Khao Khram Falls▶**, halfway to Trang, have pools large enough for swimming, and **Khao Pu Khao Ya National Park** spreads over a wild landscape to the northwest. Near the park office in Sri Banphot district are **Matja Pla Won caves▶**, with stalactites hanging like a delicate curtain near a large fish pool. Another famous waterfall among the many in the park is **Rien Thong▶**, otherwise known as "Roi Chan" or "Hundred Stages". Stage 13 is the most beautiful, with views over Thale Noi and the mountains, Pu and Ta.

▶▶▶ Phuket   212A2

South of Phang Nga on the west coast. Buses from Bangkok (southern terminal; journey time 13 hours) and neighbouring towns; domestic flights

Thailand's largest island is crammed with things to see. It is a major package holiday destination, much developed in places but with some lovely beaches and fine scenery. Boat trips to **Ko Phi Phi▶▶▶** (see pages 222–223) and **Phang Nga▶▶▶** (see pages 238–239) are popular, and there are day trips for deep-sea fishing and scuba diving. There is good snorkelling in the bays, and while at Patong you can hire a dinghy or go waterskiing. Windsurfing (with tuition) is available at the major beaches.

PHUKET

0 — 5 km
0 — 3 miles

Ban Tha Chat Chai · *Sarasin Bridge*

402

Mai Khao Beach

Ban Ao Tu Khun

Ban Mai Khao · Phuket Airport

Haad Nai Yang National Marine Park

Ban Som Poi

Ban Bang Rak Mai

Nai Yang Beach

Ban Sakhu

Ban Thum Phlo

▲ 450m

Ban Chang Taeng

Ban Bang Rong

Ko Nakha Yai

Khao Phra Taew National Park ■

Ao Po

Bang Pae Waterfall ■

Pearl Farm

Thalang

Wat Phra Thong ■

Tone Sai Waterfall

Ban Pa Khlok

Ban Khuan

Ban Phak Chit

Ko Nakha Noi

Bang Tao Beach

Heroines Monument

Laem Yabu

Golf Course

Surin Beach

Ban Lum Fuang

▲ 503m

Ban Tha Rua

Ao Sapam

Ko Rang Yai

Kamala Beach

Ban Kamala

Khao Phanthurat 325m ▲

Ko Mapbrao

Kathu Waterfall ■

Golf and Country Club

Kathu

Orchid Garden and Thai Village ■

402

Ban Kutu

Laem Nga

Patong Beach

Patong

285m ▲

Ban Thalat Nua

PHUKET

Gypsy Village ■

Ban Karon

Ban Suan

Karon Beach

Wat Chalong ■

Ko Pu

Ban Kata

Ban Khok

Ko Topao Noi

Kata Beach

Ao Chalong

Ko Topao Yai

Shooting Range ■

Ban Saiyuan

Kata Noi Beach

Marine Biological Research Centre and Aquarium ■

Nai Harn Beach

Ban Rawai

Ko Lon

Ko Mai Thon

Rawai Beach

Laem Prom Thep

Ko Kaeo Yai

Ko Hi

Andaman Sea

TIN-MINING

Phuket's former wealth was founded on tin-mining. The first deposits were discovered around 1640, whereupon Phuket was swiftly annexed by Siam. Chinese traders developed the mines. An English entrepreneur, Edward Miles, improved extraction methods. In the early 20th century, Phuket was the world's fifth largest producer of tin ore, but prices fell sharply after World War II when plastics developed.

Paragliding is popular at many of Thailand's coastal resorts, nowhere more than at Phuket's Patong Beach

TURTLES

Marine turtles always return to the beach where they were born to lay their eggs, which is why the destruction of any habitat is so disastrous. Choosing a cloudy night, they clamber above the high-water mark and dig a nest in the sand, laying up to a hundred eggs in a batch. Once hatched, the babies scuttle for the waves as fast as they can. Very few baby turtles survive their perilous early years into adulthood.

The upper west coast has some beautiful beaches. **Nai Thon Beach** is usually missed by the hordes – probably because it has awkward access. From here north up to Sarasin Bridge, which connects Phuket with the mainland, is all Nai Yang National Park. With its beautiful casuarina trees, **Nai Yang Beach** has managed to acquire limited (if exclusive) development. At the long and straight **Mai Khao** (White Trees) **Beach**, conservationists have made real efforts to save diminishing turtle populations whose females come to lay their eggs from November to February. Past the exclusive resort of Pansea is long **Bang Tao Beach.**

Going south from Bang Tao, access to the privately owned **Laem Sing Beach** is down a path off the road from

Surin Beach to Kamala Beach. For such perfection however, there is a charge in the high season.

Most package tours are catered for on the complexes of Kata and Karon Beaches, and Patong Beach. Diving and game-fishing are popular here. **Patong Beach**, big, loud and international, is where the trend towards mass tourism has gone the furthest, with the proliferation of high-rise hotels and blocks of flats, but it may yet be some time before even Patong is as crowded as Nice (with which Phuket has been twinned). Also here is a Pattaya-style transvestite show.

Kamala Beach, 3km to the north, gives an idea of what Patong must have been like before the feverish speculation started. **Surin Beach** to the north has a "front" of bars, restaurants and souvenir shops. **Karon** and **Kata**, to the south of Patong, have both witnessed rapid large-scale development – in the case of the smaller Kata, with rather claustrophobic results.

Phuket is a mecca for watersport lovers. Facilities at Patong Beach are especially good, but don't expect to enjoy the place by yourself in high season

HEROINES OF THALANG
In 1785, the widow of Phuket's governor and her sister fended off a Burmese attack by dressing all the local women in men's clothing, cutting their hair short and rolling up banana leaves to resemble musket barrels. The invaders were thus convinced that a vast army awaited them. Rama I honoured the brave sisters for their actions, and their monument stands at a crossroads on the Phuket–Thalang road.

The small **Kata Noi** and **Nai Harn Beaches** to the south each have one lavish resort which tend to dominate otherwise peaceful beaches.

Few visitors leave without a view of Prom Thep Cape, the island's southernmost extremity. Between it and Nai Harn is the diminutive and charming **Ya Nui Beach**, popular with the locals. Snorkelling is a pleasure and although corals on the coast have been degraded there are still some dazzling fish.

Many Thai tourists prefer **Rawai Beach** on the eastern side of the cape, with its restaurants overlooking the water. Boats go from here to nearby islands.

The main road north from Rawai into Phuket town passes **Chalong Bay**, a fine yacht anchorage, and thereby a firm base on the international yachting circuit: The King's Cup Regatta in November is becoming ever more popular.

Phuket Town The town takes its name from the Malay *bukit* meaning "hill". It became the capital of the province relatively recently.

The island has rich agricultural land and deposits of tin ore. Mining and smelting have been continuously carried out by Europeans and Chinese, and much of the town's architecture dates from the last century. The terraces of Krabi and Thalang Roads in particular are very quaint.

The modern town is centred on the market roundabout where blue buses leave for the beaches. The grassy hill called Khao Rang dominates the town; a metalled road goes to the summit where the view takes in offshore islands and much of the flat eastern plain. Another good trip is to the **Marine Biological Research Centre**, at the end of Laem Phanwa (Phanwa Cape), 9km south of town, where you can see a whale's skeleton and many varieties of the colourful reef fish.

Other sights The island's central landmark is the unmistakable **Heroines Monument►**, at the road junction for the upper west coast beaches. The two militant ladies are Thao Thep Krasatri and Thao Sri Sunthorn, who saved Thalang from the Burmese in 1785. Next door, and well worth a visit, is the **National Museum of Thalang►** (*Open Wed–Sat 9:30–4. Admission: inexpensive*). The displays are skilfully thought out and visually appealing.

The route north to Thalang passes the rather gaudy **Wat Phra Nang Sang** with its massive image of Guan Im, the female Bodhisattva. Near by is the buried Buddha image of **Wat Phra Thong** which not even a Burmese army could dig up. It was discovered by a buffalo boy who tethered his buffalo to the image's head. The gables and windows of the temples exhibit rich carving.

Back at the museum the road east leads to **Khao Pra Taew National Park►** with Phuket's two waterfalls, Tone Sai and Bang Pae. The park is a habitat for a variety of wildlife, including bears, porcupines, macaques, gibbons, lizards and more than a hundred bird species. Even further on is Ao Por, the port for trips to the pearl-farming island of Ko Naga Noi.

The village of **Ko Ban Yee** near Phuket Town is one of many built on stilts in and around the mangrove swamps. The once-nomadic Chao Le, or Sea Gypsies, who inhabit these villages, have their own Malay-related language, Moken, and still practise an animistic religion.

PRAWN FARMING
The mangrove swamps of southern Thailand have suffered serious degradation in recent times because of a sudden boom in prawn farming. Many coastal rice-paddies were converted into prawn ponds during the 1970s. The resulting salination and pollution from pesticides and prawn feed has made fertile land useless and damaged the fragile ecology of the mangroves, a habitat for many unusual species.
Local lakes and water systems have also been contaminated.

243

The mangrove swamps of Phuket island's eastern shores are a fascinating habitat for many kinds of wildlife, including the strange, amphibious mudskipper

The quality of Thai rice has been recognised world-wide since the 1930s. Apart from rice, the other traditional exports for which Thailand is famous are rubber, tin, teak and gems. Each of these has traditional export markets to different parts of the world.

Rice The distinctive quality of Thai rice is still recognised across the world. People will buy cheaper rice, from other countries, but would prefer the more expensive Thai rice if they could afford it.

The first Rice Experimental Station was set up, with the encouragement of the King, in 1916. Over 4,000 domestic varieties of rice were studied, of which the *Pin Kaew* variety won first prize at the World Grain Exhibition in Canada in 1933.

Rubber The southern provinces were traditionally dominated by the production of rubber and tin. Rubber trees are cultivated principally by Thai, Thai-Malay and Chinese smallholders, and the industry was mainly developed after World War I. Production is for export, primarily, and has boomed since World War II, especially in sales to the US market. Annual production has reached over 1.7 million metric tonnes a year.

A tree planted today can begin to be tapped for rubber within about six years. The raw sheets can then be sold, or smoked in a smoke house which costs the buyer more; the buyer is invariably a Chinese merchant.

Today, the development of synthetic rubber has challenged the production of natural rubber, and the planters face problems, although new, higher-yielding methods of cultivation since the 1960s have helped rubber to be more profitable.

Tin Tin-mining goes back to ancient times. By the post-war period, most mines had come into the hands of British, Australian and local Chinese mine-owners. The tin used to be exported, but now the canning industry for tuna and other food products has created a domestic demand. Entitlement to all mineral rights is vested in the King, allowing the government to control tin-mining.

Teak This is also an important export product, shared with neighbouring countries, particularly Myanmar. Teak from Thailand and Myanmar is considered to be of the highest quality in the world.

Tapping for rubber

Teak plantations were first set up in Thailand in the middle of the 19th century, and there has been an annual planting programme since 1942. Teak trees intended for timber export are usually replanted every 70 years, so this is a long-term business.

A new method of vegetative propagation of teak trees using tissue culture techniques has been tried. This means that one single bud from a mature élite teak tree can be mass-propagated to produce millions of plantlets of the same genetic make-up.

Teak is a quality hardwood used for speciality carving and a durable finish wherever wood is used as a material. The demand is such that the recent logging ban, imposed for ecological reasons, has sent Thai exporters into neighbouring countries for concessions. Thai teak is particularly valued for shipbuilding purposes.

The trees grow in the northern part of Thailand, and the timber is brought down by waterways. The teak forests belong to the state, and short-term leases are given. Some European companies have concessions.

Two years before a teak tree needs to be felled, its trunk is girdled by a ring cut through to the heartwood. This kills and seasons the wood slowly and makes it sufficiently dry to float. Felling takes place during the rainy season, and elephants drag the logs down to the nearest stream.

Gems In Bangkok you will see hundreds of shops selling gems and ornaments, another Thai speciality. Both unset gems and finished jewellery are popular buys in the Bangkok markets.

Jade, rubies and sapphires are the most popular stones, traditionally produced in Thailand but also found in neighbouring countries. Thailand is very much a centre of the gem trade in Asia.

The mines for these gems are often small, employing fewer than 40 people, sometimes only five. In some areas they have to be dug out from more than 15m below the ground. The gemstones can then be heated to a high temperature to improve their brilliancy and colouring for market purposes.

Nowadays locally produced gems are supplemented by imports from Laos, Sri Lanka and Australia. There are distinct districts in both Bangkok and Chantha Buri specialising in the gem trade. The trading tables, where the gem dealers sit *tête-à-tête* with their customers can be seen directly inside the shop windows – sunlight being essential in order to examine the stones' cut brilliance and blemishes.

245

EXPORT COMMODITIES
Rubber, tin and gems remain important export commodities for Thailand. Almost half of the rubber goes nowadays to meet the materials needs of Japan's industries, with Singapore, China and the USA providing other important rubber markets. Japan is the biggest customer for tin, and Holland is also a major buyer. Japan, Hong Kong and the United States are the principal markets for Thai gems.

BORDER CAMPS
The influx of refugees from Myanmar since the mid 1980s has led to the setting up of camps in Thailand. However, recent insurgencies and rebel activities involving Thai hostages have seen a crackdown, and people from Myanmar not in refugee camps are now considered illegal immigrants. In 1992 the Thai National Security Council announced plans to repatriate all refugees by 2002, but for this to happen safe areas must be created within Myanmar.

GEOTHERMAL PLEASURES
For a great jacuzzi, head for the Jansom Thara Hotel, 1km southeast of Ranong town, Here non-residents can bathe in hot jacuzzis fed by the adjacent geothermal springs.

A local lad points proudly to a fine display of drying fish at Ranong. The port is an important base for both Thailand and Myanmar

ILLEGAL IMMIGRANTS
Migrant workers from Myanmar fill many of the less attractive jobs around Ranong, for lower wages than the Thais. Many do not have work permits, but none the less find life in Thailand more appealing than the restrictions and low standards of living they face at home. Sadly, many are exploited by unscrupulous employers. Many workers have been sent back in recent crackdowns.

▶ Ranong Province   212A3

Highway 4 east of Chumphon, on the Burmese border. Buses from Chumphon, Suratthani and Phuket

Highway 4 is the main road running through the narrow province of Ranong. This is Thailand's wettest province, as indicated by its huge areas of lush rainforest. Thousands of tourists pass through but most only admire its scenery from a coach window on the journey southwards to Phuket, Phang Nga and Krabi. They can also catch glimpses of neighbouring Myanmar and its offshore islands.

The general public can "take the waters" in **Raksa Warin Forest Garden**, 2km to the east of Ranong town. This is actually in the compound of a temple, Wat Tapotharam, and the municipality has provided all the requisite amenities.

The three hot springs: Phor, Mae and Luk (Father, Mother and Child) are rich in dissolved mineral salts as they bubble up through the local limestone. A road leads away from here to Som Paen beach some 7km distant.

For nature-lovers Coming up by Highway 4 from Phang Nga the first main attraction reached is **Khlong Nakha Wildlife Sanctuary▶**. In order to make the most of your visit, dressing for forest walking is essential – stout shoes and covered shins may save you from pain. In recompense are the wonders of a real rainforest which is unlike anything that Europe has to offer. There is a fine waterfall here waiting to be discovered by intrepid walkers: the lovely **Khao Phra Narai** falls near Kapoe district.

Further north towards Ranong town is the huge (over 300sq km) **Laem Son ("Pine Cape") National Park.** The road leading to it at the Km 657 stone crosses a vast expanse of mangrove swamps to reach the national park headquarters at Bang Ben. This beautiful and little-visited beach gives access to a number of islands: Ko Kang Khao ("Bat Island"); Ko Kam Noi, known for its aquamarine waters and snorkelling; and Ko Kam Yai, with its fantastic coral, among others. The area around Ko Chang is also excellent for corals.

There are bungalows on Bang Ben and they must be booked in advance; contact the Forestry Department in Bangkok (tel: 02 579 0529).

Coastal trips

Ngao waterfall is 12km south of Ranong town and can be seen from a long way off, lying inside a bend of the road. The *tha reua* or port at Ranong is actually a few kilometres out of town. There is a great fishery here, accompanied by the unmistakable aroma of raw fish. A popular island to visit from here is **Ko Phayam▶** with its beaches, cashew nut plantations, pearl farm and *Chao Le* (Sea Gypsy) village. The trip takes two hours.

Another boat from Ranong crosses over to the coast of Myanmar; you must pay a day visa fee on landing. For border information contact the embassy for Myanmar, 132 Sathorn Nua Road, Bangkok 10500, tel: 02 233 7250, fax: 02 236 6898. Tours organised by the Jansom Thara Hotel offer the chance of a brief glimpse of Victoria Point, enabling you to visit a temple and the market. However, it is possible just to take a look without actually landing; the trip takes about half an hour via the Thai island of Ko Phi. Men wearing Myanmar dress can be seen around the port area; signs and notices in the town are written in Burmese script.

Victoria Point (Ko Sawng) is Myanmar's most southern extremity and Thais cross over to shop for ivory and gems. Near the village of Pak Nam, opposite Victoria Point and to the northwest of Ranong town, is Charndamri Beach, where it is possible to watch the sunset over the point.

North of Ranong, heading towards Chumphon, the road becomes increasingly idiosyncratic twisting up and down improbable hills. It passes the district of La-un where the hulk of a Japanese warship can be seen in the river at low tide.

KO CHANG
In contrast with its much larger namesake in Trat Province (see page 151), Ko Chang is a tiny island reached by long-tailed boat leaving early morning from Rayong town. It will appeal to those who like the simple life: facilities are basic, and accommodation is limited to simple bungalows (*Open* Nov–Apr).

247

The mineral springs at Wat Tapotharam are hot enough to cook an egg. Thermal water is piped through the Jansom Thara Hotel for hot baths and a huge jacuzzi

SONGKHLA
Songkhla has a large expatriate community, employed by the oil industry which exploits the southern gulf.

One of Songkhla's most recognisable monuments, a bronze copy of the little mermaid, suns herself on the beach

▶▶ Songkhla 212B2

Highway 408 south of Phatthalung on the east coast. Buses from Hat Yai and Bangkok (southern terminal)

A town of ancient heritage, much of which is still largely visible, Songkhla occupies the tip of a peninsula guarding the entrance to the vast **Thale Sap Songkhla (Songkhla Lake)**. The lakeside is busy with the town's port, where huge catches of fish are iced and packed. On the eastern side of the town is open sea with a couple of fine beaches. **Hat Samila** lines the wide part of the peninsula. **Son Orn** ("casuarina point") is a sliver of land further north which offers only sea, trees, beach and breeze. There are strategically placed restaurants along the road on the port side. The road from the town centre passes the stone mermaid, inspired by the one at Copenhagen, who sits with her back to the offshore Cat and Mouse islands, a favourite spot for anglers.

You can get a hilltop vantage point from either Khao Noi or Khao Tang Kuan; Khao Noi is easier as it is possible to drive up.

The beaches are fine for swimming but this area has a decorous Thai atmosphere, and many locals are reluctant to take the plunge.

The most relaxed beach lies towards Kao Seng, well away from the port, with strange rock formations such as "Mr Raeng's Head", and a Muslim fishing village which

decorates its boats in the colourful *kor lae* style. Hotels are plentiful. The budget **Saen Samran** by the clock tower is clean and comfortable enough.

The **Sunday market** gathers near here around Songkhla railway station, where groups of old men wait for a train that will never come: the branch was closed in 1972.

Other sights in town include the **National Museum** (*Open Wed–Sun 9 4. Admission: inexpensive*), housed in a Chinese mansion that has its own charm, especially the side away from the entrance where there are huge gnarled old trees. It houses a good collection of Srivijayan art. The 19th-century **Laem Sai Fort** stands to the north of the fishing port.

An extraordinarily cheap ferry connects Son Orn with the lake's top lip, a deep-sea port where the Khao Daeng is a sister fort to Te Noi on the Songkhla side.

Environs

For getting about, renting a motorcycle is easy in Songkhla town. To appreciate the lake properly, rent a vehicle and head west towards Hat Yai. About halfway there, take a prominent turning right which leads past a rather barren public park to the first of the **Tinsulanonda bridges**, linking the island of **Ko Yor**, straddling the mouth of the lake at this point to the mainland. There is a fine view from the bridge. Thale Sap Songkhla is not a true lake but a long lagoon which links with Thale Luang (see page 240). On the northern end of Ko Yor, the absorbing **Southern Folklore Museum**▶▶ (*Open* daily, 8–6. *Admission: moderate*) has more fine views.

The view over Thale Sap Songkhla from Ko Yor is spectacular, looking out over the second Tinsulanonda bridge which links the long thin land separating Songkhla Lake from the sea, with fish corrals – bamboo and net structures erected around houses in the ocean – to the leeward side.

The coastal Highway 408 leading north from Ko Yor to Ranot is a typical Thai country road with villages and *wats* every few kilometres. **Hat Sai Keo** is an isolated meditation island just north of Songkhla.

The town of Ranot and the ancient temple Wat Pa Kho lie about 60km north, served by a regular bus from Songkhla. Halfway there, and the reasonable aim of a day trip from Songkhla, are Wat Jathing Phra, with a 10th-century *chedi*, and **Khu Khut Waterbird Park**, a conservation area for many species of migratory birds.

A few kilometres inland, the lake and swampland are very popular with winter visitors, during which time there are many birds on the wing. Dedicated ornithologists can hire a boat quite cheaply at the sanctuary office, where there is also a small amount of English information available.

These colourful fishing boats, known as kor lae, *can be seen in the Muslim fishing village of Kao Seng. Sadly, this traditional craft is dying out*

249

The warm, tropical waters surrounding Thailand's islands are a relatively unspoiled paradise of multicoloured fishes, underwater marine life and intricate coral reefs.

ENDANGERED CORAL
Coral has a special meaning for many people, summoning up images of clear tropical water, white sand and the idyllic island life. But its allure is part of its undoing: it is collected to be used as a decorative item, it is damaged by the keels and anchors of tourist boats, and it is all too easily broken by careless handling or flailing flippers. A particularly destructive way of fishing – dynamiting – is also hastening this destruction. Coral grows slowly and it cannot possibly replace itself more quickly than it is being destroyed, so its future looks bleak.

Underwater swimming is obviously the best way to experience what the sea has to offer; for scuba diving it is essential to take a course with a qualified instructor; however, snorkelling or just using a mask in shallow water can also be very rewarding.

Exotic species can be seen surprisingly easily: parrot fish, with their wing-like blue fins, and dish-bodied butterfly fish built for manoeuvring in tight corners rather than for speed, can both be seen only a little way from the shore.

Coral is fascinating and precious. Like an underwater forest, it harbours many sorts of creatures; like a forest it is a living thing, gradually growing and evolving over the centuries. This treasure can be destroyed very easily by clumsy handling, and in any case a coral splinter is excruciatingly painful – so don't touch. Also beware the waving tentacles of sea anemones which are beautiful but which pack a painful sting. The boldly striped clownfish has developed an immunity to the anemone's poison and so can lurk in the protective tentacles, safe from attack, but ready itself to seek out its prey.

Other creatures have developed close relationships with one another: for example, moray eels (large, predatory, not friendly) have a following of cleaner shrimps, which feed on their skin parasites. Both species benefit.

Seahorses are among the most endearing of fishes, and are well worth seeking out. They are much easier to find than the aptly-named needlefish, which resembles nothing so much as a stick floating upright. At the other end of the size scale is the plankton-feeding

Beautiful but deadly sea anemones occur among the coral reefs in many astonishing shapes and colours, using their poisonous tentacles to trap their prey

whale shark, the world's largest fish, which is an occasional visitor to these waters. Marlin are much more frequently seen. These elegant beauties are one of the species most sought after by game-fishermen. Dolphins are often seen, and will sometimes frolic round boats such as the ones which go to Ko Si Chang on the east coast. This is also a good vantage point from which to look out for the flying fish, which sometimes glide up to a metre above the surface on their elongated fins.

On coastal beaches, you might still see sea turtles, although these huge creatures, which come ashore to lay their eggs, are now at great risk, their nesting areas disturbed and destroyed by tourist facilities. The nests themselves are often plundered for food. Here, pressure from concerned visitors might help to ensure a future for these gentle giants.

The quaint clownfish looks temptingly conspicuous to predators, but shields itself from harm amid the sea anemone's tentacles

251

SURATTHANI'S MONKEYS

A great tourist attraction in Suratthani is the Monkey Training College, where pig-tailed macaques (a particularly agile and intelligent species) are taught to pick coconuts. The tall, branchless coconut palm has always presented a challenge to human harvesters, but these simian helpers can fetch down up to a thousand nuts a day after an intensive training course lasting up to six months. Generally, male monkeys are used (the females are not strong enough to break the tough stems). Coconuts are Suratthani's most important cash crop, and the monkeys' wages are low (it costs about 10 baht a day to feed them).

▶ Sungai Kolok   212C1

Highway 4056; border town with Malaysia. Buses from Narathiwat and Hat Yai

This important border crossing with Malaysia is 60km from Narathiwat.

Sungai Kolok is a newish town and not really very remarkable within itself. The market is opposite the railway terminus, and inside the station compound are racks of goods from Malaysia.

There are modern duty-free shops on the Malay side. Pay in the shop and collect the goods from Malay guards on the bridge. If crossing by foot over the old bridge into Thailand, a *tuk tuk* is recommended for the 3–4km journey into town.

▶ Suratthani Province   212B3

Highway 401. Buses from Bangkok (southern terminal), Phuket and Nakhon Si Thammarat; trains from Bangkok

The "land of the good people" is a huge sprawling province whose major attraction is **Khao Sok National Park** along Highway 401 (see page 214). Dam politics have bedevilled the fate of the forests, one scheme inundated millions of acres. Another, however, was thwarted.

In Surrathani town, the ferry port serving Ko Samui, the Chak Phra festival (Sept or Oct), features a raft bearing a Buddha image through the water, plus processions through the streets. East of Suratthani town on Highway 401 at Kanchanadit is the "college" where monkeys are trained to pick coconuts (see panel).

▶ Trang   212B2

Highway 404, on the southwest coast. Buses from Hat Yai, Phatthalung and Bangkok (southern terminal); trains from Bangkok. Communications with Trang are excellent, with access by air, rail and road

Trang's Palian district is home to some of the Sakai tribe, a negrito people believed to be the aboriginal inhabitants of Indochina.

Out of town past the airport is **Thung Khai Forest Garden** and further along Highway 4 is **Lamchan Waterbird Park**, which is richly endowed with waterfalls.

Offshore islands A train journey to the end of the Trang branch line at Kantang is met by buses to the sea port with its fine views. **Ko Kradan▶** is considered the most beautiful of Trang province's many islands and Ko Hai, (which is actually part of Krabi province) has some accommodation. The boat from Hin Pak Meng takes 40 minutes. Ko Libong to the southeast of Ko Kradan is Trang's biggest island. Royal Forest Department accommodation (capacity of 10 people) is free.

The mainland has many fine beaches. Hat Yao (Long Beach), Yong Ling and Hat San (Short Beach) are all in Kantang district. Behind them is a hot spring. The southerly Palian district has some fine beaches in Samran and Hat Ta Se off Koh Sukorn.

The road up to Sikao district leads to Hat Chang Lang and Hat Pak Meng, with a waterfall; camping is permitted. Inland waterfalls, Tone Khlan in Huay Yot and Roi Chan near the Phatthalung border, are fairly remote.

RUBBER TREE

Thailand's first Yang Para or rubber tree was planted in Kantang district, Trang province by Phraya Ratsadanupradit, making him a local hero.

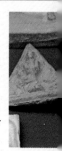

Superstition has woven itself into the fabric of Thai Buddhism, especially in rural areas. For example, Thais take astrology very seriously and Brahmin astrologers are still consulted at the royal court. The Buddhist church in Thailand is divided on these matters although Buddha himself was only concerned with the compatability of a belief with the quest for enlightenment.

Astrology and lucky charms The last prime minister, Chatichai Choonhavan, was led by an astrologer to announce the members of his new cabinet before his coalition partners had decided their nominations for cabinet posts.

Many Chinese and Thais are especially fond of lotteries, and tickets are sold on every street corner. In one village

an ant hill was worshipped because it was said to house a ghost who could foretell the numbers which were about to win prizes on the lottery.

Some monasteries earn an important part of their income by blessing lucky Buddha amulets. Amulets were issued by the army to officers fighting in the border areas, and even some science graduates are known to wear them as protection from unknown dangers.

Spirits In the animist tradition Thais believe that *khwan*, a spirit or genius which resides in the physical body, reflects a person's essential characteristics and is indispensible to a person's wellbeing. If the spirit is scared into leaving that person, misfortune or illness will ensue. The very first post raised in a traditional Thai house is known as the *khwan* post. Most woods used for building are said to possess female spirits.

There is a more nebulous realm of spirits or *phi*. A newborn baby is said to have a spirit mother. Three days after birth a child is initiated into the human world in a ceremony which involves buying it with a coin from its spirit mother.

Thais also believe in a spirit companion, called *chetabhut*, which leaves a person during dreams and times of worry. A man who walks alone in the forest, hears footsteps following and turns to find no one there, has heard his *chetabhut*.

SPIRIT HOUSES
Many houses have an elaborately decorated spirit house, which to foreigners may resemble a cross between a bird table and a doll's house. Offerings are placed on it every day and joss sticks burn there continuously.

253

Left: offerings to the spirits

A Bangkok spirit house

MOOBAN SAKAI
Yala's foremost ethnic minority, the negrito Sakai, are assumed to be the peninsula's oldest inhabitants. Formerly scattered around Betong and Bannang Sata districts, the government rounded them up into one village in 1973. Known simply as Mooban Sakai, the village is 80km from Yala town on the road to Betong. The 90 or so inhabitants were given a few hundred acres of rubber to tend, and all took the surname "Sri Than To", in honour of HRH the Princess Mother.

Wat Khuha-phimuk on the outskirts of Yala is one of the most important Buddhist temples in southern Thailand

▶ Yala   212C1

Highway 410, southernmost border province with Malaysia. Buses from Narathiwat, Pattani, Sungai Kolok and Bangkok (southern terminal); trains from Hat Yai, Sungai Kolok and Bangkok

Yala town itself is grand and spacious, the result of careful planning. There are several public parks. One is around **Sa. Jao Phor Lak Muang**, the city pillar, which was donated by the present king. Rites in respect of the town's tutelary deity occur here at the end of May. Near by is **Suan Khwan Muang**, more of a sports ground.

It is difficult to fathom the significance of singing doves among southerners, and Yala folk in particular, but entrants in the annual **ASEAN Barred Ground Dove Festival**, held here on the first weekend of March, come from as far afield as Indonesia and Brunei.

Environs

About 8km north of town by Highway 409 to Hat Yai is **Wat Khuha-phimuk▶**, also known as Wat Na Tham. Turn left down Highway 4065 to Yala district. The reclining image in a cave which is part of the temple is presumed to date from AD 757, and is of classic Srivijayan style. Fish fanciers might stop off at **Beung Nam Sai** in Raman district, famous for its decorative "dragon fish". Widely bred in Southeast Asia, these fish are supposed to bring their owner luck. The village is a further 8km from Raman on the road to Ruso district.

Than To waterfall▶, a seven-tiered fall in a forest garden surrounded by mountains, is one of Yala's chief attractions. It is to be found in Mae Wat sub-district, Bannang Sata district, 57km down Highway 410 to Betong. Visitors can bathe and there is easy access for cars. In the immediate vicinity is the Banglang dam over the River Pattani, which generates electricity. Although there are places provided to admire the view, the way up is steep and only recommended for four-wheel drive vehicles.

Ginseng is grown at the Than To self-built community near the waterfall.

Travel Facts

Arriving and departing

Visas Nationals of Australia, Canada, Ireland, the United Kingdom and the United States can stay in Thailand for 30 days without a visa; extensions are obtainable, but if you plan to stay only a few days longer, you could just pay the daily fine (see box). A confirmed onward travel ticket must be produced. Those who wish to stay longer must apply before travelling to Thailand for a 60-day tourist visa, valid for 90 days from the date of issue. New Zealanders can stay for 90 days without a visa.

Applicants must hold a passport valid for at least six months longer than their intended stay. Completed forms must be accompanied by two passport photographs; postal applications do take up to 10 working days, but personal applications are much quicker.

Non-immigrant visas, valid for 90 days, are issued to those who can show they are travelling for business purposes. These can be extended provided evidence of business or education in Thailand can be shown.

> ❏ Visa expiry: there may be a charge of 200 baht per day for every day exceeded, and overstays are recorded on your passport. ❏

Visa extensions Thirty-day extensions of tourist visas (500 baht) can be obtained at the discretion of the Immigration Division, Soi Suan Phlu, Sathon Tai Road, Bangkok (tel: 02 287 3101), or any provincial immigration office. Tax clearance certificates are no longer required.

If you leave Thailand, for example to visit Malaysia for a few days, you are given a new 30-day visa on re-entering the country.

Arriving by air Bangkok International Airport (also known by its former name Don Muang International Airport) is one of the major air destinations in Southeast Asia, with over 40 international airlines and a number of charter companies operating flights to the city. A second airport is planned. Remember to book flights well in advance.

Money exchange desks (offering slightly worse rates than downtown), a hotel reservation desk, a limousine service desk and cafeteria are open 24-hours; shops and restaurants open from 6 or 7 to midnight.

The hotel desk does not make a charge for reservations (the deposit is deducted from the bill) but only more up-market hotels are offered.

Travel into Bangkok Allow at least 60 minutes for possibly the ugliest road journey in Thailand. The painless way to do it is to go straight to the limousine counter and pay about 500 baht for the **limousine service** to any city hotel.

Across the road from the airport, infrequent **trains** leave for Hualamphong Station on Rama IV Road in central Bangkok, taking about 40 minutes.

The **public bus** option is of interest only to confirmed tight budgeters and masochists; the costs are negligible but first experiences of Thailand will probably be of standing for over an hour with people clambering over your luggage. There are bus stops under the right-hand footbridge over Vipavadi-Rangsit Road as you leave the airport; and down the slip-road to the right on the way out of the

airport. Buses 4, 10, 13, 29 and 59 run to the centre

An **airport bus service** is available to take you to either Sukhumvit,

> ❏ Travel to Pattaya: the limousine desk offers a bus service to the seaside resort (leaving at 9 AM, noon and 7 PM). There is also a more expensive sedan service. ❏

Silom or Banglamphu (major main hotel districts) for 70 baht. Another option is to take a registered taxi which is organised by the official booth at the main airport entrance; beware of touts.

Avoiding Bangkok Two long-distance trains per day stop at Don Muang Station across the road, offering immediate escape from the capital for those arriving before 9 AM. Ayutthaya and Lop Buri make interesting first-night stops; trains to Chiang Mai do not stop here. Bangkok's Northern Bus Terminal is easily reached by taxi or limousine minibus from which buses run to several northern destinations.

Arriving by rail Travellers from Singapore and Malaysia can enter Thailand by taking the train which runs the length of the Malaysian peninsula (1,927km) and takes over 34 hours, passing through Kuala Lumpur, Butterworth (for Penang) and Suratthani; second-class sleeping berths are comfortable and must be reserved in advance.

> ❏ Malaysia is ahead of Thailand by one hour, so the border closes at 5 PM on the Thai side. ❏

Arriving by road Possible from Malaysia via cheap taxis and minibuses. Malaysia closes the border each day at 6 PM. It is also possible to enter Thailand from Laos, at Nong Khai.

Departing by air Airport flight enquiries tel: 02 535 1111 (international and domestic).

Remember to keep 250 baht for airport tax which is payable for all international flights on departure.

Allow plenty of time to get to the airport – two hours should be safe. Tour agencies and guesthouses in Khao San Road provide cheap, hourly **minibuses**; book in advance. Even if you have a departure date on your ticket, it is essential to re-confirm 48 hours before travel.

Bookshops
Generally prices for English-language books in Thailand are high. This shortlist is a selection of shops which have English-language and foreign titles.

Bangkok Asia Books, 221 Sukhumvit Road; DK (Duang Kamol) Books, 180 Sukhumvit Road and Siam Square (both new books). Used books are sold from stalls in Khao San Road. Neilson Hays, 195 Suriwong Road, is a superb library for residents; 95 per cent of the books are in English and stock is constantly updated. The fascinating building, dating from 1922, is worth a visit.

Chiang Mai DK Book Store, 234 Tha Phae Road, (new books; hill-tribe trekking and contoured military survey maps, useful for hiking); Book Exchange, 21/1 Rathchamankha Soi 2 (used English-language paperbacks); Suriwong Book Centre, 54/1–5 Si Donchai Road (good range of new books on Asia).

Hat Yai DK Books, Thamnoon Wilkai Road outside Hat Yai station.

Pattaya DK Books, Pattaya Beach Road, Soi Post Office.

Phuket Seng Ho, Montree Road, (English newspapers and best sellers).

Camping
Beach camping shouldn't be a problem if you can ask permission politely: *Kor thort – rao garng dten tee nee dai mai?* However, rough camping is not advised, the risk of robbery – or worse – is too high. It always helps to establish a rapport with the locals.

Nearly all of Thailand's national parks have campsites. Ready-erected two- or three-person tents vary in price but are mostly around 40–80 baht per night; a minimal charge is made if you bring your own. Tents are provided in some up-market bungalow resorts (such as near Chiang Mai).

Be warned that camping is a chilly experience in the hilly regions. In some areas an additional hazard is the wildlife – a wandering elephant has been responsible for trampling a tent and destroying expensive camera equipment (fortunately the occupants were not inside).

Children

Many Thais love children and many visitors bringing young offspring report how easy it is to meet local people as a result. Climate and health hazards are obvious drawbacks, and sandals are advisable on major beaches, where broken glass may be lying around. Some children enjoy the breakfast fish soup if they dislike chillies (ask for *mai sai prik* – without chilli). For babies, western-style baby food and nappies are available in Bangkok and other major centres. Many people enjoy looking after babies and most luxury hotels provide a baby-sitting service. Hotel discounts are given for small children.

Climate

Most of the year is hot and humid, with daytime temperatures in the 30–34°C (86–93°F) range, falling to 24°C (75°F) at night. March to May or June is the hottest and stickiest period, as the thermometers rise to 38°C (100°F) and the humidity is uncomfortably high – at least 80 per cent most of the time.

The rainy season lasts from June or July to October, when most of the rain falls around dusk and there is widespread flooding. However, most of the day is fine and generally this is quite a pleasant time to travel, particularly as there are fewer tourists. Prices are cut and there are more hotel rooms available, but rule out about three days from a fortnight's holiday for adverse weather.

By far the most popular time to visit is the so-called cool season from November to February when rainfall is low and daytime temperatures are very warm – typically 28–32°C (84–90°F) – but rather less oppressive than at other times of the year. Accordingly this period is the main tourist season, when prices are at their highest.

❏ Leeches are a problem in forest areas in the rainy season. Do not pull them off but make them let go with salt or a lighted cigarette. ❏

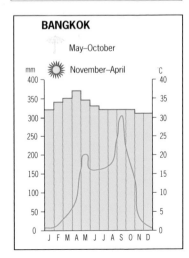

BANGKOK

May–October

November–April

mm   °C
400   40
350   35
300   30
250   25
200   20
150   15
100   10
50   5
0   0
J F M A M J J A S O N D

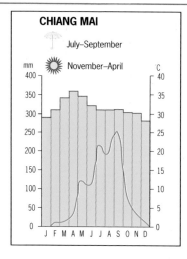

CHIANG MAI

July–September

November–April

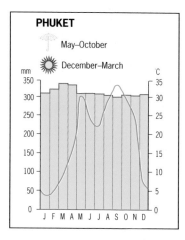

PHUKET

May–October

December–March

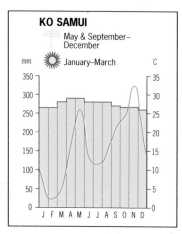

KO SAMUI

May & September–December

January–March

Regional factors If visiting the hills in the cool season, be prepared for some sharp drops in evening temperature to about 13°C (52°F); wind chill can make it seem a lot cooler, so take a sweater, and maybe a padded sleeping bag too.

Avoid the plains of the northeast region in the hot season, when temperatures are frequently over 38°C (100°F). Flooding can extend beyond the rainy season, as the subsoil is saturated for some time.

Monsoon winds can make the Ko Samui archipelago and the southeastern coast unpleasantly wet and windy in November and December when much of the rest of the country (even the nearby southwest coast) is at its best. Conversely, this coast is dry in Thailand's usual rainy season.

Crime
(See also **Emergency Telephone Numbers** – page 262; and **Money Matters** – page 267.)

Theft The friendliness of the Thai people is one of the country's great assets, but it pays to be streetwise, especially in Bangkok. Take special care of your baggage, particularly in crowded buses where the razor-blade thieves are at work and can remove the contents of a bag or cut through a camera strap without the owner realising it.

Never leave valuables unattended in hotel rooms. Most hotel and guesthouses have safe deposits; be sure to obtain an itemised receipt for all items left. If trekking for a few days, take credit cards with you as stories abound of visitors receiving their next credit-card bill back at home and finding that someone has gone on a spending spree in their absence.

At airports keep an eye on your luggage and never carry parcels for strangers; you might be unwittingly carrying hard drugs.

Gross overcharging for services such as taxi fares can be avoided by insisting on the use of the meter, or in the case of *tuk tuks* agreeing on the price beforehand.

Beware especially of seemingly friendly strangers offering to take you on a boat trip in Bangkok; this

259

can lead to a huge bill at the end, or even robbery in the middle of the river. The offer of a free can of drink or a bar of chocolate may be harmless enough, but some people have been drugged in this way and wake hours later to find all their belongings have disappeared.

Fakes Thailand is famous for fake goods – designer clothes which are obviously not the real Benetton or Lacoste represent the more innocent end of the scale. So-called Rolex watches look remarkably like the real thing at a fraction of the price.

Those trying to crack down on copyright pirating on behalf of American film and record companies often meet with bribery. More serious are fake gems. As it is possible to go *very* wrong buying gems, it is best not to buy unless you really know what you are looking for. Get a receipt and a certificate of quality in case of problems; disregard offers of helpful advice from strangers or promises of refunds at embassies.

Customs regulations
Items to be declared Video players, televisions, cassette recorders, radios, gold and currency (but not travellers' cheques) over US$10,000/£5,400.

Prohibited imports It is forbidden to bring in firearms, narcotics and pornography. It is advisable to fully label all tablets and first aid, and to carry proof of purchase with you. You may face a tax bill if several new-looking electronic goods of the same type are brought in. There is no limit on the amount of foreign currency brought into Thailand, but large amounts must be declared.

Prohibited exports An unlimited amount of baht may be taken to a neighbouring country (that is, Myanmar, Laos and Vietnam, under the ASEAN pact), but no more than 50,000 baht can be taken further abroad. An unlimited amount of foreign currency can be taken out of the country.

Permission to export Buddha and other deity images (even reproduction ones, but not small figurines worn as part of a necklace) should be

obtained from the Fine Arts Department at the Bangkok National Museum (tel: 02 226 1661); this is seldom granted even for reproduction images, unless it can be shown they are required for worship by practising Buddhists.

The export of other antiques also requires a permit from the Department of Fine Arts. To get this, you have to submit two photographs of the object (maximum five objects per photograph) and a copy of your passport to the National Museum in Bangkok, Chiang Mai or Songkhla; it then takes about three to five days for the application to be processed.

Rare species Taking home wildlife souvenirs from rare or endangered species may be either illegal or require a special permit, so it is a good idea to check your home country's customs regulations before purchase.

Duty-free allowances 200 cigarettes or 250g of cigars or pipe tobacco and one litre of wine or spirits can be brought in. Theoretically only one still camera and five rolls of film can be brought in duty free, but this regulation is seldom enforced.

Driving
Bangkok Nerves of steel are needed to drive in Bangkok, where factors to contend with include signs written solely in the Thai language, a complex and congested one-way system and poor lane discipline. Taxis or public transport in the capital are a better option.

In the country In country areas, public transport is so cheap and plentiful and driving standards so hair-raising that it is probably wise to forget about driving altogether. However, the Chiang Mai, Phuket and Pattaya areas are not too daunting to explore by car.

❏ Avoid travelling alone in the more remote areas of the country, particularly after dusk; travellers are sometimes attacked and robbed. ❏

Long-distance country roads are of quite a good standard, but surfaces are patchy on even major highways. Some minor country roads are still unsurfaced, making them a sticky experience in the rainy season; potholes and ruts are common.

Accident rates are high and adequate insurance is essential; most Thais do not carry even third-party insurance. In the event of an accident, foreigners seldom have the benefit of any doubt.

> ❏ Speed limits are 80kph on highways, 60kph in cities and 100kph on expressways. ❏

Usually the police will settle disputes about liability with the witnesses. Both parties will accompany the police to the nearest station or make an appointment to settle the dispute about damages.

In Bangkok, traffic violations are punished with a fine, instantly payable, of varying amounts.

Driving regulations Traffic drives on the left. Visitors driving cars must hold an International Driving Licence. It is possible to get a Thai licence with a letter from your country's embassy.

Fuel Both leaded and unleaded fuel are available; filling stations are Western style and often give a free windscreen cleaning service. Other filling stations take the form of red drums with glass meters above them.

A car must have at least "soo-per" whereas two-stroke motorcycles are fine on *thammadaa* (ordinary). Specify the amount needed and the petrol runs out of a hose by gravity.

Garages These are well distributed and spares and labour are very cheap; standard Japanese vehicles are easier to repair. Insist on spares *khorng tair,* made in Japan. *Khorng tiam* from a Thai workshop are cheaper but may be substandard.

Highway police (emergency number 191) can provide much assistance,

both in the case of accidents and breakdowns.

Motorcycle hire Widely available (deposit of passport normally required) and inexpensive by Western standards. It can be a fun way to explore country areas for those brave enough. A driving licence is not required.

Motorcyclists are very vulnerable to erratic Thai driving standards; take care and have adequate insurance. Insist on a crash helmet and protect the skin.

Check the vehicle (brakes, tyre wear and lights are among the easiest faults to identify) and clarify who is liable for repairs if it breaks down.

The biggest danger is undoubtedly from the *sip lors, or* 10-wheeled trucks. Drivers have punishing schedules to keep to, and the use of stimulant drugs is a known problem.

Buses make up for frequent stops with wild bursts of speed and reckless overtaking. The roads are full of ancient machines, push carts and herds of cows.

On main roads, signs are in English. Once on to minor roads Thai script has to be contended with so it is useful to have destinations written down in both alphabets.

Electricity

The standard electric current is 220 volts, 50-cycle AC. For those carrying 110-volt appliances, some hotels supply transformers, but if up-country travel is planned, bring your own

or else forget about hairdryers and shavers; towels and disposable razors are adequate substitutes.

Embassies and consulates

Loss of passport or tickets should in the first instance be reported to the Tourist Police (tel: 1155). Obtain a statement to present to your national embassy or consulate who will be able to assist.

Nearly all countries are represented in Bangkok, making it a good place to obtain visas for onward travel elsewhere.

Australia 37 Sathon Tai Road (tel: 02 287 2680).
Canada Abdulvahim Building, 15th Floor, 990 Rama IV Road, Bangkok (tel: 02 636 0540).
Ireland United Flourmill Building, 205, Ratchawongse Road (tel: 02 223 0876).
New Zealand 93 Witthayu Road (tel: 02 254 2530).
United Kingdom 1031 Witthaya Road (tel: 02 253 0191).
United States 120–122 Witthaya Road, Bangkok (tel: 02 205 4000).

Emergency telephone numbers
Fire 199.
Police 191.
Emergency dentist (Bangkok) Dental Hospital, 88 Sukhumvit Road (tel: 02 260 5000).
Hospitals (Bangkok) Bangkok Christian Hospital (tel: 02 233 6981); Bangkok Adventist Hospital (tel: 02 281 1422). (Chiang Mai) McCormick Hospital (tel: 053 262200); Maharaj Hospital (tel: 053 221122); Lanna Hospital (tel: 053 256234). (Phuket) Wachira Hospital (tel: 076 211114); Mission Hospital (private), Thepkasattree Road (tel: 076 212386). (Pattaya) Pattaya Memorial Hospital, Pattaya Road (tel: 038 429422).

Etiquette
See also pages 26–27.
Avoid shows of anger or irritation or even raised voices. Most Thais respect a *jai yen*, or cool heart. Criticism or blunt confrontation can cause loss of face. Politeness and respect are the rule. Because the head is considered the most honoured part of the body and the feet the most

❏ If a banknote blows away in the wind never trap it with your foot; this is the ultimate *faux pas* – touching a portrait of the King's head with the lowliest part of your body. ❏

base and despised, it is best to be aware of offending, even unwittingly. For instance, sitting with crossed legs might mean pointing at someone with a foot. Kissing and hugging in public is not generally acceptable.

On visiting a temple, the shoulders should be covered. Do not wear shorts or revealing dresses. Remove shoes when entering the main shrine and when visiting a private house. Nudity and topless sunbathing among tourists is common on many beaches but it is offensive to many Thais. First names are used universally. Thais also have nicknames, which tend to be shorter and easier to remember.

Never criticise the Thai royal family in front of another Thai. Each day at 8 AM and 6 PM, the royal anthem is broadcast over railway station loudspeakers, during which time you should stand and remain silent.

Smoking is banned in theatres, in railway carriages and in all buses. Never smoke in a *wat*.

Women travellers should try to avoid touching a monk. If this happens he will have to go through a complicated and lengthy penance.

Never climb on to Buddha images or show any signs of disrespect to Buddha.

Health
First aid Although virtually all medical supplies are on sale in pharmacies, it is advisable to have a first-aid box with you equipped with a few basic things:
- sticking plasters
- antiseptic cream
- elasticated bandages
- aspirins or paracetamol
- ointment to soothe insect stings and bites
- rub-in cream for muscular sprains
- talcum powder to ease prickly heat
- cigarette lighter or matches for lighting mosquito coils (the coils

themselves are too fragile to carry about)

• mosquito repellent
• tablets for diarrhoea and upset stomachs.

Travellers concerned about infected hospital needles can bring with them a specially sealed pack of needles marked as being a health and safety measure.

Heat Thailand's persistent heat can be quite debilitating; avoid over-exertion on the first few days. Drink plenty of fluids to avoid dehydration, but avoid alcohol in the daytime as it is dehydrating. Thirst is not always an accurate guide to the body's needs; do not let urine get too dark. Showering two or three times a day is refreshing.

A sun hat or umbrella will make the midday sun more bearable. Use a high protection sunscreen to avoid sunburn; remember it is possible to get badly burned in the sea too.

The heat often depresses the appetite, so make sure protein intake is adequate; rice is one of the commonest sources.

Malaria This is a serious problem in forest areas and certain islands, particularly in the hilly borderlands and on Ko Samet. There is no risk in cities or in the central plains.

Malaria is transmitted by malarial mosquitoes; if visiting a risky area be sure to wear clothes to cover arms and legs. Cover exposed skin with mosquito repellent and sleep under a mosquito net. The main danger time is between 6 PM and dawn. Malarial symptoms are a headache and fever; if you experience these, contact any malarial control centre (found throughout the country) for a 10-minute blood test.

Many visitors take malaria prophylactics. However, these are ineffective against most Thai mosquitoes and the **Malaria Control Centre** (18 Boonrhagjit Road, Chiang Mai, tel: 053 222 275) and the Tourism Authority of Thailand do not recommend them. Also, certain tablets often have side-effects, including skin problems, corneal damage and temporary hair loss. Ask your GP for the latest advice.

Stomach problems To minimise the risk of stomach upset, avoid unpeeled fruit, unwashed raw vegetables and tap water. Bottled water is on sale everywhere and is quite safe; many hotels, guesthouses and restaurants buy this in bulk, so water set down in front of you to drink is usually fine.

Similarly, cylindrical-shaped ice cubes are bought in and should be safe. Ice-cream bought from street vendors may have melted and been refrozen, which could cause problems.

Vaccinations The only mandatory vaccination is yellow fever if you are coming from an infected area, but it is strongly recommended to inoculate against cholera, hepatitis A, polio, tetanus and typhoid; check with your GP before leaving.

VD and AIDS Sexually transmitted diseases, particularly AIDS, syphilis and gonorrhoea are common.

Insurance
Don't leave home without it and shop around for the best price and most extensive cover. Annual travel insurance may be the best value if you take more than one trip abroad within 12 months. Take a photocopy of the insurance document with you and leave the original at home with a list of the items taken. Obtain the cover as soon as the flight is reserved to insure against cancellation.

The policy should cover:
• delayed departure and delayed baggage
• all reasonable medical, hospital and emergency dental treatment expenses, and flight home by air ambulance
• personal liability
• cancelling or curtailment in the event of the illness or death of yourself, your travelling companion or a close relative; or in the event of redundancy; or in the event of being called as a witness; or in the event of your home being damaged by fire, flood or storm or being burgled; the policy should compensate the cost of the holiday
• belongings and money, including sufficient cover for your camera

263

- items left in a car in daytime or overnight
- any special needs such as motor-cycling, water-skiing and rock climbing
- 24-hour emergency telephone number.

Points to note Delays below 12 hours are not normally covered; after a 24-hour delay you may be entitled to a refund for the full cost of your holiday if you cancel.

There may be a ceiling for the amount you can claim for the loss of any one item.

There is usually a small excess whereby you pay the first x amount of the claim.

Cover is not provided for pre-existing illnesses.

Contact lenses and dentures may need special insurance.

When things go wrong Get written evidence and receipts wherever applicable. Delayed departure of 12 hours or more usually qualifies for compensation, provided you have the length and cause of the delay confirmed in writing by the airline.

If luggage is damaged in transit, get two repair estimates; if it is lost by the airline get a report form from the airline before leaving the airport, notify the police (if the policy requires it) and keep relevant receipts.

Theft of personal belongings while in Thailand must be reported to the local police within 24 hours; ask for a **certificate of notification** from them.

Keep copies of any bills or receipts for any additional costs if medical treatment is required; many insurance companies give an emergency telephone number.

Language
The Thai language is extremely difficult to master, and even armed with a phrase book and dictionary intonation is likely to be a problem for westerners. Fortunately, the Thais are usually helpful in overcoming the language barrier.

Accordingly, it is well worth the effort of learning a few basic words and phrases; a little will go a long way. English is widely used in tourist areas, including the guesthouses, hotels and some restaurants, and many Thais have a smattering.

Basic phrases

hello	(man) sawat dee krup (woman) sawat dee ka
goodbye	laa gorn/bai-bai
thank you	(man) korb khun krub (woman) korb khun ka
sorry/excuse me	kor tort
how much?	tao rai?
too expensive	phaeng pai/pang pai
where is...?	...yu thii nai?
we want to go to...	...rao yahk bpai
how do I get to?	bpai...yung ngai?
how long does it take?	chai way-lah tao-rai?
that doesn't matter	mai pen rai
what is this called?	nee ree-uk wah a-rai?
yes	chai!
no	mai! chai!
turn right	lee-o kwah
turn left	lee-o sai
straight on	dtrong dtrong
I'm not feeling well	pom (woman: chun) roo-seuk mai koy sa-bai
I understand	pom (chun) kao jai
I don't understand	pom (chun) mai kao jai
do you understand?	kao jai mai?
see you later	pop gan mai

Numbers

1	neung
2	sorng
3	sahm
4	see
5	hah
6	hok
7	jet
8	bpairt
9	gao
10	sip
11	sip-et
12	sip sorng
20	yee-sip
21	yee-sip-et
30	sahm-sip
100	neung roy

200	sorng roy
1,000	neung pun
10,000	neung meuun

Glossary Common geographical elements of Thai place names often have optional letters: double aa, double ii and h, such as in thani/thaani (city), ko/koh (island).

baht	unit of Thai currency (100 satang = 1 baht)
ban	house, village
bang	waterside village
bot	the main chapel of a *wat*
chedi	a pagoda, topped by a spire, where holy relics are kept
farang	foreigner
hat, hatsai	beach
hoop kow	valley
khok, don noen	hill
nam tok	waterfall
ko/koh	island
laem	peninsula, cape, promontory
mae, mae nam	river
muang	city
pa	jungle
paknam	river mouth
pha	cliff
pu kow/phanom	hill
prang	Khmer-style *chedi*
nong	swamp
samlor	bicycle rickshaw taxi
songthaew	pickup van which is used as a minibus
tham	cave
tha	port, harbour
thale sap	lake
thanon	road
tuk tuk	motorised pedicab taxi
wai	Thai greeting (hands placed together as if in prayer)
wang	palace
wat	temple/monastery
wiharn	hall where religious duties are carried out

Pronunciation Thai has five tones: mid; high; low; rising, and falling. The differences seem small to the untrained *farang* ear but it is a crucial part of speech. Mispronounce the Thai for "snow" and you may find yourself talking about a delicate part of a dog's anatomy!

To make matters harder still, consonant sounds are slightly different: "k", "p" and "t" for instance, are mouthed rather than sounded at the end of a word. For example, the city of Phitsanulok is actually pronounced "Piss-anu-loh". "Th" and "ph" are pronounced like simple "t" and "p" – so Phuket is actually "Poo-ke(t)" – and there is even talk of getting the official spelling changed to make this obvious.

Other groups of letters to note:

kh	k
k	hard g
p	plosive "bp"
r	often silent (eg Krathong = "Katong")
th	t
t	plosive "dt"

265

Lost property
Contact the Tourist Police (tel: 1155).

Maps
The map enclosed with this book covers the entire country at a scale of 1:2,000,000, and will be adequate for much back-country touring; be aware that there are numerous additional unmapped dirt (unsurfaced) roads. Another useful publication is the 1:1,000,000 **Thailand Highway Map**, published by the Roads Association of Thailand. This shows all highways and many dirt tracks, with place names in Thai and major place names also in English; there are town plans at the back.

Two companies producing maps of high quality and that are easy to read are Berndtson and Berndtson and Collins, covering all areas of Thailand – by region as well as the whole country. Prannok Wittaya also produces maps which are of slightly inferior quality but are about a third the price and have all place names in Thai as well as English (the others have only English).

For bus travel in Bangkok the **Bangkok Thailand** map published by S.K. Thaveepholchareon is an essential aid; for Skytrains and tourist spots Nancy Chandler's idiosyncratic hand-drawn map is very informative and generally favoured. Chiang Mai has a similar version called the **DIC's Tourist Map**. All tourist spots in Thailand have locally published tourist magazines distributed free to hotels, with maps and additional local information.

Measurements and sizes

Although the metric system is widely used, certain Thai measurements are sometimes given, especially when referring to land.
1 *niu*: 2cm; 1 sq *wa*: 4sq m; 1 *rai*: 1,600sq m.

Media

Newspapers The *Bangkok Post* and *Nation* are English-language newspapers published in Bangkok but on sale throughout Thailand. Both have foreign coverage although the *Nation* is more parochial whereas the *Post* has many features taken from such publications as the *Independent, The Economist, Rolling Stone* and other international papers.

The most readily available foreign English-language paper is the Singapore edition of the *International Herald Tribune. Where?* magazine, free from hotel desks and tourist offices in Bangkok, Chiang Mai, Pattaya and Phuket, lists events and restaurant promotions, and is filled with advertisements for shops and nightspots. Bangkok Metro is another useful listings magazine serving the capital.

> ❏ The Thai year dating system is 543 years "ahead" of ours; for example, AD 2000 becomes in Thailand 2543. ❏

Radio There are a few radio stations which devote time to English language programmes throughout the day, though these are mostly in Bangkok. Try 95.5Gold FMX, Smooth 105FM or Easy FM105.5 – BBC and Voice of America also have

266

CONVERSION CHARTS

FROM	TO	MULTIPLY BY
Inches	Centimetres	2.54
Centimetres	Inches	0.3937
Feet	Metres	0.3048
Metres	Feet	3.2810
Yards	Metres	0.9144
Metres	Yards	1.0940
Miles	Kilometres	1.6090
Kilometres	Miles	0.6214
Acres	Hectares	0.4047
Hectares	Acres	2.4710
Gallons	Litres	4.5460
Litres	Gallons	0.2200
Ounces	Grams	28.35
Grams	Ounces	0.0353
Pounds	Grams	453.6
Grams	Pounds	0.0022
Pounds	Kilograms	0.4536
Kilograms	Pounds	2.205
Tons	Tonnes	1.0160
Tonnes	Tons	0.9842

MEN'S SUITS

UK	36	38	40	42	44	46	48
Rest of Europe	46	48	50	52	54	56	58
US	36	38	40	42	44	46	48

DRESS SIZES

UK	8	10	12	14	16	18
France	36	38	40	42	44	46
Italy	38	40	42	44	46	48
Rest of Europe	34	36	38	40	42	44
US	6	8	10	12	14	16

MEN'S SHIRTS

UK	14	14.5	15	15.5	16	16.5	17
Rest of Europe	36	37	38	39/40	41	42	43
US	14	14.5	15	15.5	16	16.5	17

MEN'S SHOES

UK	7	7.5	8.5	9.5	10.5	11
Rest of Europe	41	42	43	44	45	46
US	8	8.5	9.5	10.5	11.5	12

WOMEN'S SHOES

UK	4.5	5	5.5	6	6.5	7
Rest of Europe	38	38	39	39	40	41
US	6	6.5	7	7.5	8	8.5

programmes; for current details of frequencies and programming times check the *Bangkok Post* or *Nation* newspapers.

Television Cable TV with a range of international channels is available in top-class hotels; it is also possible to get TV news on 105.5FM for Channel 3, 103.5FM for Channel 7, 107FM for Channel 9 and 88FM for Channel 11 (which mostly broadcasts educational programmes and documentaries; news is at 10 PM).

Money matters
Currency The unit of currency is the baht (often abbreviated to B) and this is divided into 100 satang.

Coins are 25 satang, 50 satang (both copper), 1 baht (currently three sizes, the older designs do not have Arabic numerals), 5 baht (with copper edge) and 10 baht. Notes have Arabic numerals and are issued in denominations of 10, 20, 50, 100, 500 and 1,000.

Foreign exchange It is not possible to obtain Thai currency outside of Thailand, so on arrival at the airport a visit to the money change desk is necessary. This is open 24 hours and the rates on offer are reasonable.

Most banks will exchange foreign money and travellers' cheques; exchange dealers in tourist areas offer competitive rates and are open 7 AM–8 PM or 9 PM. The Bangkok Bank is open daily, even on national holidays, 7 AM–8 PM. Exchange rates do not vary much but are generally better for travellers' cheques than for cash.

Big hotels have exchange desks, but rates here are poor. The best bet is to take cheques in major foreign currency, in reasonably large denominations as commission is charged on each cheque cashed.

Additionally you can change money using a credit card (Access/MasterCard, American Express, Diners Club and Visa are the most commonly used). Be sure to to keep a record of the emergency telephone numbers in case you need to report lost or stolen cards.

For security reasons banks advise that you keep travellers' cheque counterfoils separate from the cheques themselves. Make a record of which cheques have been cashed, so if some are lost you know which ones to claim for. Collection of new cheques can be arranged through any bank.

Most exchange centres do not accept old-style (small-headed) US$100 notes.

Haggling *Tuk tuk* drivers and vendors of clothes and souvenirs will expect you to bargain over the price. While there are no hard and fast rules, offering half of what is asked seems to be common practice, then settling for about two thirds. Bangkok taxis are a slightly different matter, as most have meters.

Sometimes the first price offered may be ten times over the odds so ask other people – Thais and seasoned travellers – what they would expect to pay. Don't worry about not getting haggling down to a fine art immediately; the sums involved are often paltry anyway. Above all, keep cool and smile.

It is also sometimes possible to negotiate cheap rates for hotel rooms, particularly outside the main tourist season. However, as expected, restaurants and street-stall food and items in department stores (except for expensive goods such as jewellery) nearly always have fixed prices.

National holidays

As in some other Asian countries, certain public holidays are calculated according to the lunar calendar and vary from year to year.

Accommodation can be hard to find, especially during the New Year, *Songkran* in Chiang Mai, and when a holiday forms part of a long week-end. Tourist offices, some banks and all government offices close during these periods; the Bangkok Bank (branches nationwide) and hotel money desks are open, as are most shops.

31 Dec and 1 Jan	New Year
Early to mid-Feb	Chinese New Year
Mid-Feb	*Maga Puja*
6 April	Chakri Day
12 to 14 April	Thai New Year (*Songkran*)
Early May	Royal Ploughing Ceremony
1 May	Labour Day
5 May	Coronation Day
May/June	*Visaka Puja*
July/August	*Asalha Puja*
12 August	Queen Sirikit's Birthday
Mid to late Oct	*Ok Pansa*
23 Oct	Chulalongkorn Day
5 Dec	King Bhumiphol's Birthday
10 Dec	Constitution Day

Festival days The biggest festivals, with their locations, are given below

to provide an idea of where and when accommodation may be hard to find.

7–9 Feb	Flower Festival (Chiang Mai)
April	Pattaya Festival (Pattaya)
21–22 Nov	Elephant Round-up (Surin)
Nov full moon	*Loi Krathong* (nationwide, especially Sukhothai and Ayutthaya)
Nov–Dec	River Kwae Bridge Week (Kanchana Buri)

National parks

Thailand's 80-plus national parks are dotted nationwide, and include mountainous, forest and coastal regions, individual waterfalls and archipelagos.

Many offer accommodation in the form of tents (about 40–80 baht per night for a ready-erected one sleeping two or three) and typically ten-person bungalows at around 400–1000 baht per night. Prices depend on the season. Additionally some offer basic dormitory accom-modation at a very low price (barely a step up from camping; bring your own sleeping bag).

Reservations are advisable for weekends and public holidays, through the Forestry Department, Phahon Yothin Road, Bangkok (tel: 02 579 0529).

Warm clothing is needed for the mountainous areas, where temperatures can drop to 5°C, and it is advisable to bring a torch. Mapped information for walking is generally poor and it is imperative to keep to the marked paths.

Opening times

Banks Monday to Friday, 8:30–3:30; **Bangkok Bank** (branches nationwide) and foreign exchange counters (in tourist areas) 7 AM–8 PM daily.
Government offices Monday to Friday, 8:30–12, 1–4:30.
National Museum branches Mostly Wednesday to Sunday, 8.30–noon, 1–4:30; closed Monday, Tuesday and public holidays.
Tourist offices Daily, 8:30–4:30; closed on public holidays.
Small stores Daily, 12 hours a day.
Large stores Daily, mostly 10–6:30 or 7.
During Chinese New Year in February, many small shops are closed. Large stores stay open but take a holiday afterwards.

Pharmacies

Thai pharmacies are extremely well-stocked for the most part; in fact it is possible to buy over the counter many products, such as antibiotics, for which a doctor's prescription would be needed in other countries. Pharmacies are open daily from 8–5 or 6 in smaller places, or until 9 in large cities.

There is no all-night emergency service; in case of difficulty, contact a hospital.

Photography

Daylight is very bright so use a 50 or 100 speed film for best results outside.

> ❏ Pack silica gel with cameras or another drying agent in order to counter the effects of humidity. ❏

Thais are very tolerant of having their picture taken, but it is common-sense manners to point to your camera first (smiling as you do so) to make your intention clear; some hill-tribe folk are more shy, and some may demand a few baht.

Many temples display signs in English prohibiting photography inside the main *wiharn*, and some museums request that exhibits are not photographed. Video cameras are banned entirely from the grounds of the Grand Palace in Bangkok. Print and slide film is widely available and reasonably priced and films can often be developed inexpensively within a few hours.

Places of worship

For non-Buddhists these are fairly thin on the ground, with the notable exception of the significant Muslim community in Southern Thailand (with the largest mosques in Pattani and Yala).

Roman Catholicism is followed in some towns that have a substantial Vietnamese or Laotian population, particularly in Si Chiangmai in northeastern Thailand (not to be confused with the city of Chiang Mai in the northwest). There is a Roman Catholic cathedral in Chantha Buri.

In Bangkok, the following welcome non-believers:
Hindu Thamsapu Association, 50 Soi Wat Prok New Road (tel: 02 211 3840).
Jewish Jewish Association of Thailand, 121/3 Soi 22, Sukhumvit Road (tel: 258 2195).
Muslim Darool Aman Mosque, Phetchaburi Road (near Rajtewi Intersection); Haroon Mosque, Charoen Krung (New) Road (near post office); Al-Aia-Tisom, Sukhumvit Soi 77 (tel: 02 321 3487).
Protestant Calvary Baptist Church, 88 Soi 2, Sukhumvit Road, (tel: 02 251 8278); Christ Church (Anglican/Episcopal), Convent Road, (tel: 02 234 3634); International Church, 328 Phyathai Road (tel: 02 258 5821).
Roman Catholic Assumption Cathedral, 23 Oriental Lane, Charoen Krung (New) Road (tel: 234 8556); Holy Redeemer Church, 123/19 Soi Ruam Rudee (tel: 02 256 6757).
Seventh Day Adventist Bangkok Ekamai Church, 57 Soi Charoenchai, Ekamai Road (tel: 391 3593).

Police

The brown-uniformed policeman is a common enough sight; many speak a little English and they often approach lost-looking *farang* (maybe just to practise their English). Police boxes (small police stations) are placed at frequent intervals along main roads. For Bangkok, Chiang Mai, Pattaya and Phuket a special Tourist Police service assists visitors (see **Emergency telephone numbers** page 262).

Contact the police in the event of road accidents, theft, lost property, disputes or car breakdowns; they will also help with giving guidance (occasionally as escort) in remote or dangerous areas.

Post offices, fax and email

Postal services in Thailand are efficient and domestic rates are cheap. Approximate times for airmail to arrive are 5–7 days for Europe, and 7–10 days for Australia, Canada, New Zealand and the US. Large parcels (maximum weight 15kg) should be sent surface mail; this takes 10–12 weeks. Main post offices sell boxes in different sizes, and bubble-wrap; some of the largest offices (including Bangkok and Chiang Mai) offer a parcel-wrapping service.

Bangkok Central Post Office is at Charoen Krung (New) Road. It is open Monday to Friday 8–4:30; weekends and holidays, 9–1. Telephone and telegram services are open 24 hours.

Post offices outside Bangkok are open Monday to Friday, 8:30–4:30, major ones are open 9–1 on Saturdays.

Nearly all post offices offer a *poste restante* service (1 baht per item), by which mail can be sent to a given post office until the addressee claims it; such mail should be labelled "Poste Restante" and the surname of the addressee should be underlined.

Additionally, many hotels and guesthouses are happy to keep mail for guests; in Bangkok particularly many guesthouses have screens with letters for guests attached to them (often with six-month old postmarks).

Main post offices, large hotels and some street bureaux have fax facilities. Stamps are sold at some hotels and at many newsagents. Aerogrammes (fixed price anywhere in the world) and postcards are a bit cheaper to send than airmail letters.

Internet cafés are found in many cities, making email an inexpensive and efficient way of staying in touch with friends and family.

Public transport

See also pages 48–49, 114–115. Thailand is well-served with a dense network of inexpensive public and semi-public transport. Some is quite luxurious, much is crowded and uncomfortable; some forms of travel will leave you aching, hot or cold, while others will entertain with scenery, *en route* snacks and sheer downright eccentricity; all of it is part of the experience.

The language barrier can be frustrating (attempts at pronouncing place names often encounter blank looks), but generally bus and *songthaew* drivers and conductors are helpful about making sure that foreigners alight at their intended destinations.

Embarrassingly, in crowded buses Thais (and sometimes elderly Thais) may give up their seat for you.

Internal flights If time is short, consider these as a method of seeing more; it only takes an hour from Bangkok to Phuket or Chiang Mai (against a full day or night by bus or train).

Thai Airways flies to Chiang Mai, Chiang Rai, Lampang, Mae Hong Son, Mae Sot, Nan, Phitsanulok, Phrae and Tak in the north; Khon Kaen, Loei, Nakhon Ratchasima, Sakon Nakon, Ubon Ratchathani and Udon Thani in the northeast, and Hat Yai, Ko Samui, Nakhon Si Thammarat, Narathiwat, Pattani, Phuket, Suratthani and Trang in the south.

Reserve seats well in advance if flying from Bangkok, through Thai Airways (tel: 02 513 0121).

Each of these towns has a Thai Airways office, where advance bookings can be made.

Rail While the rail network does not serve every corner of Thailand and

270

services are less frequent than buses, for views from the window and for general comfort, the train wins easily over the bus as a means of travel.

There are three classes, covering the range from first-class air-conditioned two-berth compartments, to second-class air-conditioned reclining seats, to third-class padded bench seats (wooden slat variety on ordinary trains may need improvised padding).

Generally, unbooked third class is adequate for short journeys, while the other two classes may give a bit more room; first class is about twice as expensive as second, and four and a half times more than third.

Sleeping berths on overnight journeys must be reserved in advance (even the berthless carriages get packed on the Bangkok–Chiang Mai and Bangkok–Singapore lines).

The sleeping berths on second class are excellent (berths are arranged so that you sleep in the same direction as the rails, and not across them). On longer journeys, there is a restaurant service, with the menu and food brought to your seat.

For long journeys out of Bangkok it is usually necessary to book several days in advance as trains are often very full, especially on the Bangkok–Chiang Mai and Malaysia routes. Reservations can be made through travel agents or booking counters at most major stations. For Bangkok (Hualamphong) station, tel: 02 223 0341-8.

Passport holders can purchase 20-day passes giving freedom of second and third-class rail travel throughout Thailand. The cost is 1,100 baht for adults (550 baht for children); passes including supplementary charges, based on the type of train taken, are 2,000 baht for adults (1,000 baht for children).

Buses Thailand's excellent bus network fans out from Bangkok (see page 115), connecting with virtually every town. Services are cheap and frequent; air-conditioned buses are more expensive but less crowded. Tickets are on sale at bus stations or on the bus and can be bought just before travelling, or sometimes in advance. On long routes the bus

stops for toilets and refreshments, and vendors often come on board offering snacks and drinks.

Few buses show where they are going in Roman script, but foreign visitors always get plenty of assistance. The major **bus stations** for Bangkok are Taladmochit, Paholyothin Road (for journeys north and northeast), Ekamai, Sukhumvit Road (east) and Sai tai, Nakhon Chaisri Road (straight on from the Pin Klao bridge) (south).

Private bus operators abound and are a popular budget method of long-distance travel; numerous agencies, particularly in Khao San Road in Bangkok, advertise these.

Driving standards on buses are not that good and the fact that private companies often race against each other doesn't help. One lasting memory of Thailand will be looking in the driver's mirror and spotting his reflected glance – five seconds on the road alternating with five looking at the video suspended above the garland of everlasting flowers that decorates the window.

Private overnight buses organised for foreign visitors can be a grim experience as the driver turns out the reading lights just as the journey begins ("power failure") and a Thai voice blares out for most of the night, entertaining the driver but no one

else. There have been hair-raising tales of thefts on one or two of these buses where the passengers were given doped colas as they boarded and woke to find everything gone.

Government-operated buses on shorter inter-city routes generally run 6–6 daily. Long-distance VIP and 999 buses are pricier than ordinary ones but are quite comfortable, with reclining seats and leg-room.

Minibuses Known as *songthaews*, (literally "two rows"), these are covered trucks or vans with two long, hard benches at the back. They fill up to capacity with passengers squashed together, hanging on to the back and standing on the footplate. You seldom see anything apart from other passengers' limbs and shopping baskets but the *songthaew* is often the only way of reaching your destination.

Fares are fixed, strictly no haggling, and very cheap. The destination is not advertised, but usually the driver and conductor are shouting it out and will usher you aboard.

Taxis Plentiful in supply, and most now have meters (look for the "taxi-meter" sign on the roof). Drivers seldom speak much English and may not understand your attempts at Thai (or at English) pronunciation. It is useful to have your destination written down in Thai. All taxis are air-conditioned, and the minimum fare for a metered journey is 35 baht.

Tuk tuks The less luxurious version of the taxi; also known as pedicabs or motorised *samlors*, these are covered, open-sided two-passenger chariots

> ❏ As taxi drivers seldom speak fluent English, ask your hotel to write your destination in Thai and suggest the fare. ❏

built around a scooter and unmistakable for their *"tuk tuk"* noise. They are not particularly safe, but cheaper than taxis for short distances and you have to try a ride as part of the Thailand experience. Bargain hard before travelling; short trips are

generally in the 30–50 baht range, although there is talk of making fares standardised.

Bicycle *samlors* The trishaw, an unmotorised version of the *tuk tuk*, is seen in many provincial towns. Again, agree the fare in advance; 30 baht is the rule.

Long-tailed boats Beside the service along the Bangkok canals west of Thonburi there has recently started a service from Wat Saket to Bangkapi along Klong Saen Saep. Be prepared for a ride in an open sewer, although the trip takes just half an hour as against two hours by road.

Get off at Ekamai and get a 72 bus down Soi Ekamai for the Eastern Bus Station. Reach the Southern Bus Station by long-tail from Tha Chang.

Sport
See also pages 110–113.
Scuba diving and swimming
With so many idyllic beaches to choose from it is no surprise that Thailand has come to the fore as a major destination for sand and sea holidays. Scuba-diving boat trips are widely available in places such as Ko Samui, Chumphon Province, Pattaya, Krabi Province and Phuket. The spectacular array of marine life makes the experience unforgettable.

> ❏ Corals grow in profusion but are endangered because of the numbers of tourists who break off souvenir chunks. Do not follow suit; apart from the ecological damage caused, the coral never looks as pretty back home after it has dried out. ❏

Numerous places hire out snorkels, masks (often not large enough for the largest *farang* heads) and flippers, but you can save yourself quite a few baht by bringing your own equipment.
Golf Green fees vary widely from a few hundred baht to around 4,500 baht. Caddy fees are around 150 to 220 baht, and club rental anything from 300 to 1,800 for a round. There are several courses in and around

Bangkok, including the popular **Navatanee Golf Course** (tel: 02 376 1034), designed for the 1975 World Cup Tournament. Courses are also found at Hua Hin, Lanna near Chiang Mai, Phuket, Sattahip near Pattaya and Tong Yai in Songkhla.

❏ A booklet free from the Tourist Authority of Thailand gives details of over 20 golf courses, with reservation information. ❏

Spectator sport Thailand's national sport is *Muay Thai* (Thai Boxing). Also popular are kite fighting, sword fighting and *tagraw* (see pages 110–113).

Less exotic but also popular are soccer and horse-racing. Racing takes place every Sunday from 12:15 PM and alternates between a number of places: the Royal Bangkok Sports Club, Henri Dunant Road, and the Royal Bangkok Turf Club, Phitsanulok Road.

Telephones

Local calls can be made from any telephone and cost 1 baht minimum. The Telephone Authority Thailand phones (blue or silver phones) accept 1, 5 and 10 baht coins and calls can be made to anywhere in Thailand including mobile numbers.

It can often be a frustrating exercise trying to find one of these phones in working order. However, deregulation of the phone industry is seeing an increasing number of credit and card phones springing up in more developed areas – many of which can be used to make international as well as national calls.

While it is generally straight-forward to make long-distance calls from Bangkok, smaller places up-country may require a visit to the local post office, where you may have to queue.

International calls can be made from some hotels (often with substantial surcharges) and guesthouses, from major post offices and from private telephone offices.

Hotels with International Direct Dialling telephones often charge 20 per cent or more for the service. The international dialling code is 001, followed by the number of the country. Country codes are:

Australia	61
Canada	1
Ireland	353
New Zealand	64
United Kingdom	44
United States	1

Omit the 0 prefix for the city code after dialling the country code. Alternatively go via the operator (dial 13 in order to get an English-speaking operator service).

Local codes Bangkok 02, Chiang Mai 053, Pattaya 038, Phuket 076. For directory assistance, dial 13.

Time

At noon in Thailand it is 3 PM in Sydney, Australia; 5 pm in New Zealand; 5 AM in the UK and Ireland (6 PM, BST); 9 PM the previous day in Los Angeles and midnight in New York.

Tipping

Tips are not generally expected in Thailand, but you could leave a tip for good service – up to 30 baht for taxi drivers and 10 per cent of the bill in restaurants. For porters a tip of 10 baht is adequate.

Toilets

The more expensive hotels have Western-style WCs, but if you are intending to stay in guesthouses you will doubtless encounter Thai-style toilets, which involve squatting over a floor-level basin. Initially it seems a feat of both careful balancing and aiming, but as no part of the body is in contact with the basin (in theory) it is quite hygienic.

A hose with spray attachment may be provided for cleaning your nether portions afterwards; the water pressure can be ferocious and mildly alarming first time around. For those who prefer to use toilet paper (which is commonly available) bins are usually provided as the discarded pieces often block the pipes.

Public toilets are rare but most restaurants do not object to non-customers using this facility. Simply ask for the *horng nahm*.

Tourist offices

The Tourism Authority of Thailand (TAT) has offices across Thailand but do not provide a booking service.

TATs in Thailand

Bangkok	(Head Office) 4–372 Bamrung Muang Road, Bangkok 10100 (tel: 02 694 1222).
Cha-am	500/51 Phetkasem Road, Amphoe Cha-am, Phetcha Buri 76120 (tel: 032 471005).
Chiang Mai	105/1 Chiang Mai–Lamphun Road, Chiang Mai 50000 (tel: 053 248604).
Chiang Rai	448/16 Singklai Road, Chiang Rai 57000 (tel: 053 717433).
Hat Yai	1/1 Soi 2 Niphat Uthit 3 Road, Hat Yai, Songkhla 90110 (tel: 074 243747).
Kanchana Buri	Saeng Chuto Road, Kanchana Buri 71000 (tel: 034 511200).
Khon Kaen	15/5 Prachasamosorn Road, Khon Kaen 40000 (tel: 043 244498).
Nakhon Phanom	184 Soontomvijit Road, Nakhon Phanom 48000 (tel: 042 513490).
Nakhon Ratchasima	2102–2104 Mittraphap Road, Nakhon Ratchasima 30000 (tel: 044 213666).
Nakhon Si Thammarat	Sanam Na Muang, Ratchadamnoen Road, Nakhon Si Thammarat 80000 (tel: 075 346515).
Pattaya	382/1 Mu 10 Chaihat Road, Pattaya City, Chon Buri 20260 (tel: 038 427667).
Phitsanulok	209/7–8 Surasi Trade Center, Boromtrailokanat Road, Phitsanulok 65000 (tel: 055 252743).
Phuket	73–5 Phuket Road, Phuket 83000 (tel: 076 212213).
Rayong	153/4 Sukhumvit Road, Amphoe Muang, Rayong 21000, (tel: 038 655420).
Suratthani	5 Talat Mai Road, Ban Don, Suratthani 84000 (tel: 077 288818).
Ubon Ratchathani	264/1 Khuan Thani Road, Ubon Ratchathani 34000 (tel: 045 243770).

TATs Overseas

The TAT website (www.tat.or.th) is worth a look and easy to use. It allows you to download information on many tourist areas such as Bangkok, Sukhothai and Phuket.

Australia	2nd Floor, 75 Pitt Street, Sydney 2000, (tel: 9247 7549, fax: 9251 2465).

UK   49 Albemarle Street, London W1X 3FE, (tel: 020-7499 7679, fax: 020-7629 5519).

US   1 World Trade Centre, Suite No. 3729 New York, N.Y. 10048 (tel: 1-800-THAILAND, fax: 212 912-0920). 611 North Larchmont Boulevard, 1st Floor, Los Angeles, CA 90004, (tel: 1-800-THAILAND, fax: 323 461-9834).

There are also offices in France, Germany, Hong Kong, Italy, Japan, Malaysia, South Korea, Singapore and Taiwan, but not in Canada, Ireland or New Zealand.

Walking and hiking

If you want to see Thailand on foot, the obvious way is to take an organised trek. There are trails in national parks, two described in this book, but

the nationwide spread of purpose-made walks is rather thin and the central plain is too monotonous for worthwhile hiking anyway. The dangers of getting lost in remote areas are very real, and foreign visitors have been attacked in borderlands. Those who plan to do some hiking should take some light boots with ankle support, plenty of water and spare food; be prepared for mosquitoes, leeches and heat exhaustion.

Treks to hill-tribe villages Treks are big business in the north; street bureaux, hotels and guesthouses offer packages lasting between two and seven days, where you stay in tribal village homes, and trek in the hills on foot, by elephant and by bamboo raft. At best this can offer exhilarating views and a fascinating insight into subsistence cultures. However, a poorly run trek, passing zoo-like commercialised villages and going through unvarying scenery can be an expensive disappointment.

275

Hints

- Recommendations from other travellers is the best way to choose a trek. Check exactly what is included (food, first-aid, transport, itinerary) and what the trek is like.
- Don't necessarily restrict yourself to treks from Chiang Mai; less frequented places (Mae Hong Son, Chiang Rai, Pai, Mae Sot and Nan among them) may be better.
- Try to meet the other members of your party before you go. Four to eight is a good group size.
- Leave valuables behind (except your credit cards); take only a little cash (but itemise anything you leave in a guesthouse).
- Walking can be tough going in the hills, elephant rides are uncomfortable and rafts often capsize.
- Travel light; take a backpack, sleeping bag, sweater, washkit, towel and swimsuit, and rainwear between June and October.
- Ask before taking photos of tribespeople.
- Carry mosquito repellent and take clothes to cover your arms and legs; tobacco and water combined makes a good leech repellent.

HOTELS

Thailand offers a vast range of accommodation, varying hugely in price. The smartest international hotels in Bangkok or Phuket charge as much as anywhere in the West, whereas at the cheaper end of the market, you can find simple double rooms for very little money.

Prices are extremely seasonal in Thailand, and rates vary according to supply and demand. It is possible to negotiate generous discounts on higher-priced accommodation during the low season, or at any time when rooms are empty. But local festivals and conferences may cause a sudden unexpected dearth of bedspace and sharp tariff increases. Within any one hotel, room rates may vary widely according to the standard of facilities available. Air-conditioning, or a private bathroom with hot water, will inevitably add to the bill.

Luxury
Nearly every major city and tourist stopover will have at least one hotel which could be classified as luxurious by Western standards – wall to wall carpet, chrome and marbled bathrooms, satellite television and first-class round-the-clock service. The tariffs for these places can get surprisingly cheap especially in the off peak tourist seasons where discounts are offered. Most major international chains operate in Thailand: Amari, Hyatt, Novotel, Regent and Sheraton all have more than one hotel in Bangkok; Chiang Mai, Pattaya, Ko Samui and Phuket also have a large number of international chain hotels operating alongside Thai and Asian-based counterparts.

Business centres have also become an attractive proposition for the business traveller, as they provide email and fax services, and in some cases, a consultant will help you to arrange contacts and provide updates on local affairs.

The restaurants in top hotels will provide dining quality comparable to their Western counterparts and most menus will have a wide range of Thai, Asian and Western cuisine. All top-class hotels provide an email booking service which invariably offers cheaper prices than those offered by an agent or walk-in rates. Government tax and service charges usually add 17–20 per cent to the room rates quoted, unless it is already included.

Moderate
The minimum standard facilities for a moderately priced hotel are private bathroom, air-conditioning and a TV with up to half a dozen channels of Thai television. Depending on what end of the price scale your budget is you may also get satellite channels, a fridge, telephone and carpeted rooms. The standard of service tends to drop from the expensive hotels category, especially during the night-time.

Most hotels in this range will have at least one restaurant or café, a small swimming pool and some form of a landscaped garden.

Budget
The budget category can be divided into two main areas: cheap hotels and guesthouses. Cheap hotels, often run under Chinese management, tend to be impersonal run-down affairs which offer little more than a bed (usually with clean bedding) and a private bathroom with cold water. Prices usually start at 200 baht per night though always ask to check the room first and avoid hotels where they refuse permission to do so before booking: most of these places double as brothels (especially in southern Thailand in towns like Hat Yai).

Guesthouses tend to be more hospitable; many are private Thai homes adapted for the purpose, while some in country areas are thatched bamboo bungalows. Nearly all offer meals, with an English menu. Beds are hard; you may even sleep on a thin mattress on the floor. Guesthouses are excellent for meeting other travellers (Thais rarely stay in such establishments), and often have local tourist information; many offer tours and treks (in Chiang Mai trekking is a hard-sell business; guests who don't want to go on a trek are often told to leave).

There is rarely a problem with finding accommodation except during certain holiday periods. *Tuk tuk* and *samlor* drivers get commissions from guesthouses when they bring you to them and will ask virtually any luggage-bearing *farang* if they need somewhere to stay. Even in non-tourist towns there is usually a cheap hotel (not necessarily with an English sign).

Eating out
This is an essential part of the national lifestyle. Accordingly, food is served on virtually every street corner and prices are very low. However avoid the streetside stalls where there is no running water and select only cleaner looking places – if the restaurant looks clean then the food should be and you will not have to be concerned about your stomach.

Run-of-the-mill restaurants tend not to dress themselves up; plastic tables are usual and you will often find yourself sitting outside. Look for the restaurants frequented by locals; some will have an English menu, but it is wise to carry a phrasebook. If you get stuck, simply point to a dish someone else is eating if you think it looks appetising.

Menus are often very long, typically based on stirfry rice concoctions, seafood, soups and noodles. Sometimes you pay a little more for the surroundings; floating restaurants are popular in many waterside towns. Western food is offered in many tourist areas; prices are substantially higher than Thai food and often poor quality. But there are numerous places where you can eat as well as back home; many of these are included in these listings.

The smarter eating establishments are plentiful in the main tourist centres; in smaller, less frequented towns the best are often to be found in the top hotels. Except in big centres, try to eat reasonably early; many places will close by 9 PM.

276

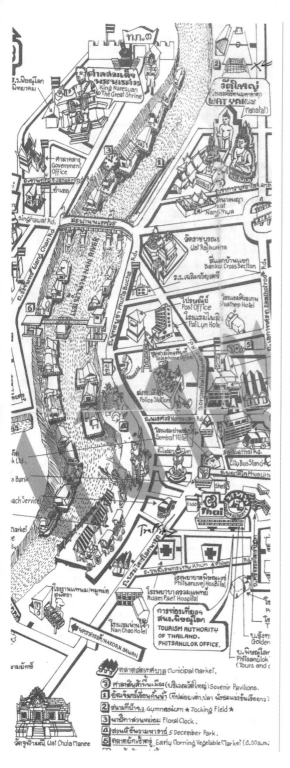

Hotels

The hotels listed below are divided into three price categories:

Inexpensive (£) up to 500 baht
Moderate (££) 500–1500 baht
Expensive (£££) over 1500 baht

The price bands indicated are given as guidance only. Always check room rates when you book.

BANGKOK

Amari Airport (£££)
333 Choet Wuttakhat Road tel: 02 566 1020
This four-star hotel is connected by air-conditioned walkway to Bangkok's international airport. It has a good range of restaurants and business facilities.

The Asia Hotel (£££)
296 Phayathai Road tel: 02 215 0808
The Asia offers full amenities for both business and leisure travellers including a business centre, two outdoor swimming pools, a health club, four restaurants and two bars offering live music.

Atlanta Hotel (££)
78 Soi 2, Sukhumvit Road tel: 02 252 1650
This historic hotel offers good facilities and services (including a swimming pool) at moderate rates and is a welcome stop for travelling families. There is a wide range of tariffs and benefits from its proximity to the Skytrain.

The Baiyoke Sky Hotel (£££)
222 Rajprarop Road, Rajthevee, Bangkok 10400 tel: 02 656 3000, 02 656 3456
Thailand's tallest hotel, rising to 94 storeys (accommodation to the 74th floor) above the city skyline. It is within easy walking distance to the major shopping centres of the World Trade Centre, Siam Square and the MBK Centre.

Evergreen Laurel Hotel (£££)
88 North Sathorn Road tel: 02 266 7223
A small, stylish "boutique"-type hotel, adapting oriental artistry to convenience and comfort, emphasised by high standards of service and attention to detail.

Grand Hyatt Erawan (£££)
494 Rachadamri Road tel: 02 254 1234
Resort-style facilities, a fine collection of Thai art and polished wooden floors covered in oriental carpets ensure an atmosphere of comfort with an Eastern ambience. Close to Siam Square and the World Trade Centre.

Khaosan Palace Hotel (£)
139 Tanon Khosan tel: 02 282 0578
There are plenty of fan- and air-conditioned rooms to choose from here, and expect smart service. It is an ideal base for those seeking the excitement and fun of the Bangkok travellers' scene.

Little Home Guest House (£)
Behind the National Library, Sri Ayuttaya, Tawet tel: 02 282 1574
The Little Home is a short hop away from the noise of Khao San Road. This ultra budget, well-established guest-house has been providing a home for short and long-term visitors alike for some time with its relaxed and friendly atmosphere.

Merry V (£)
33–35 Phra Athit Road tel: 02 282 9267
A popular budget hotel with clean, but small, rooms and friendly service. There is a choice of fan and air-conditioned rooms available.

The Narai Hotel (£££)
222 Silom Road tel: 02 237 0100
At the heart of Bangkok's commercial and entertainment districts, The Narai has traditional Thai décor and elegantly furnished suites, with all the facilities that a five-star hotel can offer.

Novotel Bangna (£££)
114/49 Srinakarin Road, Nongbon, Bangna tel: 02 255 6888
Located close to the International Trade & Exhibition Centre, recreational malls and a huge array of championship golf courses. Facilities include six distinctive restaurants and bars, a spacious pool deck and a business centre.

Racha House (£)
Soi Wat Racha, Samsen Road tel: 02 241 5137
This used to be a favourite stop-over with peace corps volunteers when they still had much involvement in Thailand. A quiet hideaway, brimming with art and artifacts from around Asia.

River View Guest House (££)
768 Soi Phanurungsri Sangwat Road (no telephone)
With tidy and spacious rooms with a view of the river, the River View Guest House is handy for the Silom district, the river ferries and Chinatown.

Royal Orchid Sheraton (£££)
2 Captain Bush Lane, Si Phaya Road tel: 02 266 0123
All rooms are fully equipped and serviced in usual Sheraton style. The riverbank location ensures great views and riverboat convenience, essential for sightseeing in Bangkok.

Sathorn Villa (£££)
481 South Sathorn Road tel: 02 212 7090
Small enough to provide a relaxing and private atmosphere, yet has good facilities with fully serviced suites of one or two bedrooms.

Shangri-La Hotel (£££)
89 Soi Wat Suan Plu, Charoen Krung Road tel: 02 236 7777
Consistently voted one of the best hotels in the world, the Shangri-La offers exclusive riverside accommodation as well as complete business and leisure facilities.

The Somerset (£££)
10 Soi 15, Sukhumvit Road tel: 02 254 8500
Elegant and cosy, The Somerset has just 76 comfortable rooms and suites. Facilities include an indoor pool, sauna and fitness equipment.

Thai Hotel (££)
78 Prajatipatai Road Pranakorn tel: 02 629 2100
A moderately priced, family-run hotel with a friendly atmosphere. Its central location makes it convenient for both business and leisure travellers.

Woodlands Inn (££)
1158/5-7 Charoen Krung 32 Road tel: 02 2353 894
Established in 1995, the Woodland Inn is a high-standard, moderately priced hotel, which consists of 75 well-kept guestrooms. There is friendly service from the south Indian management team.

CENTRAL THAILAND

Ayutthaya
U-Thong Inn (£)
210 Mu 5, Rochana Road tel: 035 242236
Situated next to the river, the U-Thong Inn provides comfortable and traditional accommodation with good service. Facilities include a pool and sauna.

Hua Hin
Ban Somboon (£)
13/4 Damneon Kasem Road tel: 032 511538
"The Complete Home" has well-equipped rooms including TV, hot showers and the choice of air-conditioning, and is close to the beach.
Sofitel Central (£££)
*Hua Hin I Damneon Kasem Road
tel: 032 512021*
Originally built as a holiday residence for members of the royal family before becoming a railway hotel, the Sofitel Central has an atmosphere as rich as its history. Superbly refurbished to its former glory.
Thipurai Hotel (££)
*13/27 Phetkasem Road, Hua Hin
Prachuabkhirikhan 77110 tel: 032 532096-7*
Totally renovated in 1998, the hotel is just 150m from the beach and convenient for the city. Facilities include a swimming pool, bar and restaurant with Thai seafood, Chinese, European and Scandinavian food.

Kanchana Buri
Felix River Kwai (£££)
Kanchanaburi 9/1 Moo 3, Thamakham, Muang Kanchanaburi tel: 034 515061
Low-rise houses picturesquely set in natural gardens and landscaped grounds on the banks of the Kwai Yai River. The famous bridge and numerous attractions are nearby. Fully serviced and offering all facilities.
Jolly Frog (£)
28 Soi China Mae Nam Road tel: 034 625103
Good value single and double rooms with private or shared facilities and a friendly environment despite its large size.
River Kwae Hotel (££)
*284/3-6 Chooto Road, Muang District
tel: 034 511269*
River Kwae offers a warm welcome with friendly service. Deluxe single bedrooms or double bed suites are available, along with seminar rooms, a banqueting room and a pool.
The River Kwai Jungle Rafts (££)
(no address or telephone)
In the heart of the jungle and moored along the historical river, getting to this magical place is half the fun. It is an exhilarating forty-minute boat trip from Pakseng through spectacular gorges. Reservations can be made via the Internet Reservation Office in Bangkok (tel: 02 677 6240).

Khao Yai
Juldis Khao Yai Resort (££–£££)
*45 Mu 4, Thanarat Road, Pakchong
tel: 02 255 1712*
A huge resort providing a wide range of accommodation in suites, rooms and bungalows right on nature's doorstep.

Ko Samet
Ao Prao Resort (££–£££)
Ao Prao Bay tel: 02 438 9771
Just 2.5 hours' drive from Bangkok, on the western side of the island, this modern resort has a range of secluded bungalows, beach cottages and suites.

Lop Buri
Asia (£)
1/7–8 Sorasuk Road tel: 036 411892
The Asia provides standard clean rooms close to the old palace grounds. Air-conditioned rooms are available and there are two restaurants to dine in.

Pattaya/Jomtien
Ambassador City (£££)
Jomtien 21/10 Mu 2 Sukhumvit Road, Jomtien Beach tel: 038 255501
Relax in comfort in any of the five wings, including the superb Ocean Wing, with its lofty atrium and well-appointed rooms and suites. A resort within itself with 40 acres of prime beachfront property.
Asia Pattaya Beach Hotel (£££)
Cliff Road, Pattaya tel: 038 250491
Luxurious air-conditioned rooms and suites are equipped with private marble bathrooms and good views. Expect all the usual facilities of a top hotel.
Sawatdee Sea View (£)
Soi 10 Tanon Pattaya tel 038 428229
This hotel offers tidy and comfortable rooms with air-conditioning, TV and hot water at good rates and is close to the beach.
Seaview Resort Hotel (££)
Soi 18 Pattaya-Naklua Road tel: 038 429317
Comfortable air-conditioned rooms with easy beach access and well located for trips into either Pattaya or Jomtien.

Petcha Buri
Khao Wang (£)
174/1–3 Ratwhiti Road tel: 032 425167
The Khao Wang provides fairly basic yet clean air-conditioned rooms with television.

Si Racha
Thiw Phai Guesthouse (£)
Tha Therawong tel: 038 216084
A variety of rooms to choose from here, with a friendly atmosphere, added to by the late night café.

Trat
Banpu Koh Chang Hotel (££)
199 Moo 1, Nongkansong tel: 039 542355
A private resort with uniquely crafted bungalows made of wood, ceramics and stone. It is set on a white sandy beach, with great views of Ko Chang. All rooms have a seaside view and are surrounded by lush tropical garden.

NORTHERN THAILAND

Chiang Mai
Amari Rincome Hotel (£££)
1 Nimmenhaemin Road tel: 053 221130
Just west of the old city is The Amari, with its comfortable rooms, and a range of facilities. Features include the trademark La Gritta Italian restaurant, a swimming pool and tennis courts.

Hotels and Restaurants

Chiang Mai Orchid (£££)
23 Huay Gaew Road tel: 053 222091
Luxuriously appointed, The Orchid is adjacent to
Chiang Mai's biggest shopping plaza (Huay Gaew).
From here it is easy to catch a *songthaew* to the zoo
and then change over for a trip up to Doi Suthep.

Empress Hotel (£££)
199/142 Changklan Road tel: 053 270240
Within easy walking distance of the Night Bazaar,
the Empress has pleasing rooms with good amenities. There is a choice of four restaurants with
excellent buffet dinners, which attract many locals
as well as guests from other hotels.

Galare (££)
*7/1 soi 2 Charoenprathet Road
tel: 053 273885*
The Galare has spacious rooms, and is made
popular due to its riverside location and easy
access to the Night Bazaar.

Holiday Resort (££)
39/3 soi 6 Rat Uthit Road tel: 053 277104
Cosy and peaceful rooms in a traditional
Lanna–Thai style, set amongst lush gardens and
tropical fruit orchids add up to a relaxing stay.

Lai Thai (£)
11/4-5 Kotchasara Road tel: 053 271725
This hotel has Northern-Thai style rooms. Varied
amenities include Khantoke dinners, a swimming
pool, traditional massage and the facility to rent
motorbikes.

Porn Ping Tower (££)
46–48 Charoenprathet Road tel: 053 270099
Modern luxurious rooms, close to the Night
Bazaar, with many features including a French and
Chinese restaurant and one of the area's most
popular discotheques "Space Bubble".

Star Hotel (££)
*36 soi 4 Loi Kroh Road, Changklan
tel: 053 270360*
This is a "boutique" style hotel near to the Night
Bazaar, with hospitable staff, a classy reception
area and pleasing décor throughout. A feature here
is the Korean Restaurant.

Top North Guest House (£)
15 soi 2, Moon Muang Road tel: 053 278900
Situated in the old city, close to Chiang Mai's
nightlife, there is a range of rooms to choose from.
Facilities include a swimming pool and a travel
agency on the premises.

The Westin (£££)
*318/1 Chiang Mai – Lamphun Road
tel: 053 275300*
One of Chiang Mai's premier hotels, with a riverside
location. It provides deluxe accommodation in
spacious rooms, and facilities include a great
restaurant, fitness centre and swimming pool.

Chiang Rai
Chian House (£)
172 Si Bun Ruang Road tel: 053 713388
Chian House offers functional rooms and bungalows
with hot water showers and a small swimming pool.

Dusit Island Resort (£££)
Dusit Island tel: 053 715777
A huge hotel built on an island just away from the
main town, the Dusit offers the most exclusive
(and expensive) accommodation in Chiang Rai,
with pleasant views of the Mae Kok River.

Mae Kok Villa (£)
445 Singhakhai Road tel: 053 711 062
A friendly and helpful management team run this
collection of bungalows in a quiet park-type
atmosphere situated at the bottom of town.

Wang Come Hotel (£££)
869 Premawiphat Road tel: 053 711800
The Wang Come has very comfortable rooms and
all the facilities of a top class hotel, including a
recommended coffee shop and a nightclub.

The Wiang Inn (££)
893 Phanayothin Road tel: 053 711533
The Wiang Inn has well-appointed rooms at the
southern edge of town, and offers a swimming
pool and coffee shop.

Lampang
Asia Lampang (££)
229 Boonyawat Road tel: 054 227844
The firmly established, yet unspectacular, Asia
Lampang has comfortable air-conditioned rooms of
varying sizes. A café downstairs provides a good
place to relax.

Lampang River Lodge (££)
330 Mu 11, Tambon Chompu tel: 054 217054
The rooms here are quaint and private Thai-style
stilt bungalows which nest on the bank of the Wang
River, providing a relaxing atmosphere.

Mae Hong Son
Holiday House (£)
23 Pradit Jongkham Road (no telephone)
With lovely views of Jongkham lake, the Holiday
House offers fairly basic accommodation and
shared hot water showers.

The Panorama Hotel (££)
*51 Khunlum Praphat Road
tel: 053 611759*
The Panorama has a choice of air-conditioned and
fan rooms, and the hotel is convenient for the
town. Hot water showers and a certain number of
television channels are also available.

Rooks Holiday Inn (£££)
*114/5–7 Khunlumprapas Road
tel: 053 611390*
A comfortable yet imposing block, which is just
outside of town, The Holiday Inn has good facilities and a restaurant serving a wide range of
international cuisine.

Rooks Resort (£££)
*114 Khunlum Praphat Road
tel: 053 611390*
Comfortable and well-appointed rooms adjoining
the Rooks Holiday Inn, Rooks Resort represents
top class accommodation with a range of rooms
or bungalows to choose from.

Mae Sai
Ban Tammila (£)
Tambon Wiang Chiang Khong tel: 053 791234
Ban Tammila provides a quiet place to stay, with
thatched bungalows in a tiny garden by the
Mekong River.

Northern Guesthouse (£)
402 Tumphajom Road tel: 053 731537
This guesthouse has pleasant riverside bungalows
and air-conditioned rooms. The restaurant has a
fairly basic menu but the food is reasonable.

Mae Sot

No 4 Guest House (£)
736 Indharakiri Road (no telephone)
Set in a large teak house and away from the main road, the No 4 Guest House provides an adequate stopover for budget travellers.

Um Phang Hill Resort (£)
53 Mu 6 Amphur Umphang, Tak
tel: 055 561064
This resort provides attractive bungalows of various sizes in a picturesque waterside setting.

Nan

Therawat (££)
466 Sumon Therawat Road tel: 054 710078
The Therawat is a bit basic, but nevertheless has large clean rooms, is centrally located and is rated as the best in town.

Phitsanulok

Pailyn (££)
38 Baromatrailokanart Road
tel: 055 252412
Located just back from the river and close to the centre of town, the Pailyn has good rooms with basic, yet functional interior designs.

Sappraiwan Grand Hotel & Resort (£££)
79 Moo 2, Tambon Kaengsopha, Amphur Wangthong, Phitsanulok tel: 02 236 2711
An exclusive resort, set in 150ha of exotic landscaped grounds. It is surrounded by beautiful mountains and the river.

Phrae

Mae Yom Palace (£££)
181/6 Yantarakikoson Road tel: 054 522904
Pleasant six-storey block which is conveniently located near to the bus station.

Si Satchanalai

Wang Yom (££)
78/2 Mu 6, off route 101 to Sawankhalok
tel: 055 611179
The rustic bungalows are set in peaceful gardens by the old city. The facilities are quite basic but the restaurant serves good food in a lovely garden.

Sukhothai

Pailyn (££)
10 Mu 1 Jarodvithithong Road
tel: 055 613310
The Pailyn has a hexagonal courtyard set around a pool. Facilities include a nightclub and health centre. A bit out of the way, but handy for the old city.

Ratchathani (££)
229 Jarodviththong Road tel: 055 611031
Convenient for town, the Ratchathani has a dining room, a coffee shop and air-conditioned rooms.

NORTHEAST THAILAND

Khon Kaen

Sofitel Raja Orchid (£££)
9/9 Prachasaran Road tel: 043 322155
Arguably the best hotel in town, The Orchid is lavishly decorated. There are plenty of dining and entertainment options to choose from, including a German microbrewery.

Suksawasd Guesthouse (£)
2/2 Klang Muang Road tel: 043 236472
This guesthouse benefits from its central, yet quiet, location, offering clean rooms and shared facilities.

Loei

King Hotel (£)
11/9-12 Chumsai Road tel: 042 811701-83
This is a well-run hotel providing rooms with air-conditioning and hot water. The restaurant serves a good range of Asian and European food.

Muang Fai Hotel (££)
Charoenrat Road tel: 042 811302
Comfortable, well-equipped bungalows and rooms are available and there are nice views of the river.

Mukdahan

Hua Nam Guesthouse (£)
36 Samut Sakdarak Road tel: 042 611137
This guesthouse offers clean air-conditioned rooms with private bathrooms.

Ploy Palace Hotel (££-£££)
40 Pitakpanomkhet Road tel: 042 631111
A wide range of well-appointed rooms and suites are available, and facilities include a swimming pool, exercise room and sauna. There is also a top floor restaurant which provides pretty panoramic views.

281

Nakhon Ratchasima

Doctor's Guest House (£)
78 Soi 4, Sueb Siri tel: 044 255846
This small-scale operation offers a warm welcome thanks to the friendly owners, who also help out by providing good local information.

Pegasus Tower (££)
444/4 Mitraphap Nongkai Road
tel: 044 272841-6
This is a well managed high-rise hotel with comfortable rooms and tasteful décor. Entertainment facilities include a karaoke bar, nightclub and snooker room.

Nong Khai

Mekong Guesthouse (£)
Rimkhong Road, on the river tel: 042 412119
A fairly rickety old structure, but the rooms are comfortable enough. A great place for just hanging out by the river.

Phantavee Hotel (££)
1241 Hai Sok Road tel: 042 421106
The Phantavee has air-conditioned rooms with hot water, while fan rooms are also available. There is also a casual coffee shop downstairs, which provides a place to relax.

Surin

Phirom's Guesthouse (£)
242 Krung Sri Nai Road tel: 044 515140
Fairly basic rooms, though good service is provided by a friendly owner who also arranges tours around the district (see page 209).

Thong Tarin (£)
60 Sirirat Road tel: 044 514281
This is considered to be the best hotel in Surin. A buffet breakfast is available, and traditional massage is one of the amenities.

Hotels and Restaurants

Ubon Ratchathani
Ruanrangsi Mansion Park (££)
*Ruangrangsi Complex, Ratchathani Road
tel: 045 244744*
The Ruanrangsi is located behind the main town centre, and offers tidy and well-appointed apartments, which can be rented on a daily basis for comparatively good rates.

Udon Thani
Charoen (£££)
549 Phosri Road tel: 042 248155
A varied selection of both moderate and expensive rooms here, with facilities including a pool and a fairly average disco.

SOUTHERN THAILAND

Chumpon
Chumpon Cabana (££)
*Thung Wua Laen Beach, Saphil
tel: 077 560245*
The Cabana provides pleasant bungalows and modern hotel rooms on a deserted beach. Guests can enjoy various activities during their stay, such as scuba and skin diving, climbing and windsurfing.
Jansom Chumpon (££)
*188/65–66 Sala Daeng Road
tel: 077 502502*
Expect excellent service here, which complements the very comfortable rooms. Deluxe rooms are also available, where breakfast is provided.
Si Tai Fa Hotel (£)
73–4 Sala Daeng Road tel: 077 511063
An old Chinese-style hotel with basic yet clean rooms. Air-conditioned rooms are also offered and the veranda provides a comfortable place to view the green gardens and the city.

Hat Yai
Cathay (£)
*99/1 Niphat Uthit Road, near railway station
tel: 074 235044*
The Cathay is a favourite stopover for travellers to and from Malaysia, where backpackers like to get together to swap information.
J B Hotel (£££)
*99 Jootee Anusorn Road, Hatyai
tel: 074 234300*
Located in the middle of town, the J B Hotel has tastefully appointed rooms, good restaurants and a jazz bar.

Ko Phi Phi
Phi Phi (£££)
*Island Cabana 201/3–4 Uttrakit Road
tel: 075 612132*
The smartest place on the island, with a good (if pricey) restaurant.

Ko Samui
Central Samui Beach Resort (£££)
38/2 Moo 3, Borpud Chaweng Beach, Koh Samui Surat Thani tel: 077 230500
This exclusive resort is situated on the island's finest beach, Chaweng Beach, and only 15 minutes from Samui Airport. There are four restaurants and three bars to choose from.

Chaweng Blue Lagoon (£££)
Chaweng Beach tel: 077 422037
Classic Thai-style bungalows and hotel suites are available. A large swimming pool, restaurants, bars, plus 160 metres of beach frontage form part of the facilities. The hotel is set at the end of an access road for extra peace and quiet.
Moon Bungalow (£)
*Mu 2, Chaweng Beach
tel: 077 233169*
A friendly, laid-back and peaceful place.

Krabi
Dusit Rayavadee (£££)
*67 Mu 5, Susan Hai Road, Ao Phra nang
tel: 075 620740-3*
An exclusive luxury resort in the romantic surroundings of Phra Nang headland with good amenities and facilities.

Phang Nga
Phang Nga Valley Resort (££)
5/5 Phetkasem Road tel: 076 412201
This is an attractive bungalow complex in a nice relaxing environment, with helpful staff and a wide range of prices to suit your budget.

Phuket
Cape Panwa Hotel (£££)
*27 Mu 8 Tambon wichit, Amphur Muang
tel: 076 391123*
Situated on a hill top, every room has a spacious balcony and commands a view of the Andaman Sea and nearby islets. Bungalows are also available with two bedrooms, a living room, pantry and a large patio. The hotel's private yacht offers daily excursions to nearby coral islands.
Phuket Garden (££)
*40/12 Bangkok Road, Phuket Town
tel: 076 216900*
Reasonable rates are offered for comfortable rooms with all the usual luxuries, and is situated just on the edge of the inner commercial district.
Rawai Plaza and Bungalow (££)
64 Wiset Road, Rawai Beach tel: 076 381346
A smart and friendly complex on a fine beach, with facilities including air-conditioning, hot showers and TV.
Talang Guest House (£)
Talang Road, Phuket Town tel: 076 214225
A friendly husband and wife team manage this conveniently located guesthouse which provides large cool rooms with beautiful timber floors and furnishings; it's excellent value.

Songkhla
Lake Inn (££)
301–3 Nakhon Nok Road tel: 074 321044
The Lake Inn is well-appointed throughout and has been recently renovated. Lovely lake views add to its charm.

Suratthani
Muang Thai (£)
390 Talad Mai Road tel: 077 272367
Tidy but fairly basic double rooms with the option of air-conditioning and TV are offered. Travel operators and internet shops are close by.

RESTAURANTS

The restaurants listed below are divided into three categories (prices are based on a meal for two with no alcohol):

Inexpensive (£) up to 200 baht
Moderate (££) 200–500 baht
Expensive (£££) over 500 baht

BANGKOK

Ban Thai (££)
7 Sukhumvit Soi 32 tel: 02 258 5403
A set menu offering a wide range of Thai cuisine designed for newly arrived visitors (that is not too spicy!) and Thai dancing from 9 PM.
Bourban Street (£££)
29/4–6 Washington Square, Soi 22, Sukhumvit Road tel: 02 259 0328
A popular place for expatriates and visitors alike. Mexican food, jambalaya, crawfish pie and other Cajun and Creole specialties are available, as is live music some nights.
Cafè Siam (£££)
4 Soi Sriakson tel: 02 671 0031
Difficult to find but worth the effort to dine in this classy art deco restaurant that specialises in Thai and French cuisine (phone for directions). It is closed in the afternoon till 6 PM.
Himali Cha Cha (££)
1229/11 Charoen Krung Road tel: 02 235 8915
This is a firmly established Indian restaurant with a good reputation and an extensive menu.
Inter Restaurant (£)
432/1-2 Siam Square Soi 9 tel: 02 2551 4689
A good selection of Thai and Isan food is served in this busy restaurant. It is popular with local students and daytime shoppers, making Inter a good people-watching spot.
Lang Suan Balcony (£££)
2/f Soi Lang Suan tel: 02 251 7767
Thai and international cuisine is served here, and the restaurant has one of Bangkok's best selection of wines. Eat in the cosy dining room or on the balcony overlooking busy Soi Lang Suan.
Mah Boon Krong Food Centre (£)
Mah Boon Krong Shopping Centre, On the corner of Phaya Thai and Rama 1 Roads tel: 02 217 9199
A huge selection of Thai and international food is offered by 90 different stalls. Don't expect elegant dining, but do come for the experience.
Patpong Seafood (££)
Opposite Patpong Night Bazaar tel: 02 637 0508
A huge range of seafood dishes cooked just the way you like it. Fresh fish is delivered daily from Thailand's biggest fresh seafood market.
Vijit (£)
77/2 Ratchadamnoen Klang Road tel: 02 281 6472
Set in the Banglamphu area, Vijit offers excellent value for money and good food in air-conditioned comfort. Open till late.

CENTRAL THAILAND

Ayutthaya
Chainam (£)
U-Thong Kalahom Road tel: 035 252013
This is a good place for decent Thai and Western food, especially Western-style breakfasts, and is reasonably priced.
Phae Krung Koa (££)
Moo 2 U-Thong Road tel: 035 241555
This floating restaurant specialises in seafood and Thai chicken and pork dishes. Chinese delicacies are also served.

Kanchana Buri
Mae Nam (££)
On the river at the end of Lak Muang Road tel: 034 512811
The Mae Nam is an agreeable, floating seafood restaurant, but meat and vegetarian dishes are also available. There is live music at night.
Punnee Café and Bar (£)
Ban Neua Road tel: 034 513503
This café is popular with expatriates, and serves Western and Thai food.

Lop Buri
Anodard (££)
Sa Kaeo Circle tel: 035 411433
Anodard serves excellent quality Thai and Chinese cuisine, plus some good alternatives for those who do not like their food too spicy.

Pattaya/Jomtien
Lobster Pot (£££)
288 Beach Road tel: 038 426083
The Lobster Pot is known for its great seafood and extensive menu. There is a good atmosphere, which is helped by its location on the pier at Pattaya Bay.
Pan Pan San Domenico (£££)
Tappaya Road tel: 038 251874
This Italian restaurant is beautifully decorated, which complements the superb food that it serves. The veal is particularly recommended.

NORTHERN THAILAND

Chiang Mai
Aroon Rai Restaurant (£)
45 Kotchasarn Road tel: 053 276947
A good place to try out Northern Thai specialities, which are served here in the pleasant surroundings of a recently refurbished restaurant. It is popular with locals and visitors alike.
Chez John (£££)
18 Airport Road tel: 053 201550
Superb food prepared by a Swiss chef and his son. Pictures of the Queen dining in this restaurant, on more than one occasion, testify to Chez John's well-deserved reputation.
Le Coq d'Or (£££)
68/1 Koh Klang Road tel: 053 282024
The Le Coq d'Or draws large crowds of visitors, which is a result of its fine European cuisine and good selection of imported wine. The restaurant has been established in an English country house setting.

Hotels and Restaurants

The Gallery (£££)
25–29 Charoenrat Road tel: 053 248601-2
Set in an art gallery, with a fine Thai restaurant and bar. The Gallery itself has been built inside a 100 year old teakwood house on the banks of the River Ping. In the evenings guests are entertained by a dance troupe and a Thai classical string band.

J J Bakery and Restaurant (££)
Opposite Thapae Gate 2–6 Ratchadamnoen Road tel: 053 213088 and Chiang Inn Plaza Basement, Changklan Road tel: 053 281353
The two branches of this bakery have an extensive menu of both Western and Thai favourites. Freshly baked goods are served daily and all kinds of rolls and hamburgers can be custom made. A take-away service is also available.

Kalare Food Court (£)
*Night Bazaar, Changklan Road
tel: 053 272067/271496*
Set amidst the Night Bazaar, this wide range of food stalls caters for all tastes, and includes Thai, Asian, BBQ and vegetarian. This is also a great place to view classical Thai dancing, performed here every night free of charge to diners.

Whole Earth (££)
88 Sri Donchai Road tel: 053 282436
The Whole Earth is set in a lovely colonial-style house, convenient for the Night Bazaar. It specialises in Indian food, though a range of Thai style vegetarian dishes are also available.

Chiang Rai
Ga-re Ga-ron (£)
897 Jet Yod Road tel: 053 714779
A good selection of reasonably priced Thai and Western food is provided in a relaxing environment.

Mae Hong Son
Fern (££)
87 Khunlum Praphat Road tel: 053 611374
Fern is a well-established restaurant with a good reputation for authentic Thai cuisine. Pleasant surroundings add to a satisfying dining experience.

Golden Teak Restaurant (££)
149 Moo 8 Tambon Pang tel: 053 611021-5
The Golden Teak is part of the smart Imperial Tara complex, which serves good quality Western food.

Mae Sai
Rabieng Kaew (££)
256/1 Phahonyothin Road tel: 053 731172
Set in a Lanna-style wooden house, Rabieng Kaew ("Glass Balcony") specialises in serving excellent Northern Thai food.

Mae Sot
Pim Hut (£)
Tangkimchiang Road tel: 055 532818
In a outdoor setting, the menu here consists of a wide range of dishes, from fried frogs to chips.

Nan
Da Dario (£)
*37/4 Rajamnuay Road, Ban Prakerd
tel: 054 750258*
Good authentic Italian food is prepared here by an Italian chef. The restaurant is well laid out and a cheery atmosphere prevails when the crowds are in.

Phitsanulok
Rim Nan (££)
63/2 Wang Chan Road tel: 055 251446
Moored by the west bank of the Nan River, this floating Thai restaurant has a relaxing atmosphere, bathed in the cool breezes from the river.

Sukhothai
Dream Café (££)
86/1 Singhawat Road tel: 055 612081
With its antique-laden fantasy interior, The Dream Café offers a good mixture of Thai, Chinese and Western food.

NORTHEAST THAILAND

Nakhon Ratchasima
Veterans of Foreign Wars Café (VFW Café)
Pho Klang Road tel: 044 256522
Set up by expatriate Gls, this relaxing place offers travellers a venue to eat and meet.

Nong Khai
Thai Thai Phochana (£)
257/1 Bantherdgit Road tel: 042 420373
A popular restaurant providing a reasonable selection of authentic Thai and Chinese food.

SOUTHERN THAILAND

Ko Samui
Captains Choice (£££)
Choeng Mon Beach tel: 077425041
This is a top quality place to eat that serves seafood; the shark delicacies are recommended.

Happy Elephant (£)
19/1 Moo 1 Bophut tel: 077 245347
Good Thai food, with an emphasis on seafood, offered at reasonable prices.

Pakarang (££)
3 Moo 2 Tambon Bophut tel: 077 422223
For an atmospheric dining experience, sit outside under the flower-covered trellis, and sample the good (if strongly flavoured!) Thai food.

Krabi
Kotung (££)
36 Kongkaa Road tel: 075 611522
This is a welcoming place to find sensibly priced central and southern Thai seafood.

Phuket
Boathouse Wine and Grill (£££)
Kata Beach tel: 076 330015
A well-known restaurant in a "boutique" resort, serving Thai and European food of international repute. It also has a good wine cellar.

Kan Eang Seafood (££)
Chalong Bay tel: 076 381323
This good quality restaurant displays its seafood, allowing diners to make their own selection. There are lovely views over the Chalong Bay yacht harbour.

Regatta Bar and Grill (£££)
*Phuket Yacht Club, Nai Harn Beach
tel: 076 381156*
This is one of best places to eat in Phuket, which has views over Nai Harn Bay. Superb *nouvelle cuisine* prepared by a European chef.

285

Index

Index

Index/Acknowledgments

Publisher's Acknowledgments

The Automobile Association would like to thank the following photographers, libraries and associations for their assistance in the preparation of this book.

RICK STRANGE took all the photographs in this book (© AA Photolibrary) except those listed below: BANGKOK POST 60b, 62a, 62b, 63a, 65b, 66/7a, 67b, 68b, 69b, 70a, 70b, 71a. JIM HOLMES 8a, 14a, 15c, 256. TIM LOCKE 8b, 133b, 186, 253c, 271a, 275. NATURE PHOTOGRAPHERS 250e (S C Blisserot), 251 (S C Blisserot). PICTOR INTERNATIONAL F/Cover a, F/Cover c. PICTURES COLOUR LIBRARY Spine, 226. POWERSTOCK/ZEFA F/Cover b. REX FEATURES 51. SPECTRUM COLOUR LIBRARY 49, 104, 105. TOURISM AUTHORITY OF THAILAND 18, 50a, 51, 83, 93, 94a, 110a, 121a, 195a, 197a, 202a, 203a, 209a, 210a, 211a, 213a, 215a, 221, 224, 225a, 229, 230a, 231a/b, 248. WORLD PICTURES 17, 47a, 47b, 172b, 182b, 227.

Contributors
Original copy editor: Beth Ingpen
Revision verifier: Tim McLachlan